D1281265

MILESTONES 2:
THE MUSIC AND TIMES OF MILES DAVIS SINCE 1960

164805

JACK CHAMBERS

Milestones 2: The Music and Times of Miles Davis Since 1960

781.65
D263c
v. 2

BⱢB
BEECH TREE BOOKS
WILLIAM MORROW
New York

Alverno College
Library Media Center
Milwaukee. Wisconsin

Copyright © 1985 by University of Toronto Press

All rights reserved. No part of this book may be reproduced or
utilized in any form or by any means, electronic or mechanical,
including photocopying, recording or by any information storage
and retrieval system, without permission in writing from the
Publisher. Inquiries should be addressed to Permissions
Department, Beech Tree Books, William Morrow and Company,
Inc., 105 Madison Ave., New York, N.Y. 10016.

Library of Congress Catalog Card Number: 85-70574

ISBN: 0-688-04646-0

Printed in the United States of America

First U.S. Edition

1 2 3 4 5 6 7 8 9 10

The word "book" is said to derive from *boka*, or beech.
The beech tree has been the patron tree of writers since ancient times and
represents the flowering of literature and knowledge.

Contents

Acknowledgments

It is my pleasure to acknowledge again the help and encouragement of Colette Copeland, Dale Dickson, Bernard Lecerf, Jan Lohmann, Dan Morgenstern, and Chuck Netley, and to thank Harald Bohne, Chris Chambers, Lewis Porter, and Frank Tirro publicly for the first time. I am grateful again to Jack Maher and Deborah Kelly of *Down Beat* for their help with the photographs, and especially to those who took the photographs that appear in this book. My thanks also go to John Parry for copy-editing, Will Rueter for designing, and Ron Schoeffel for editing. The index is dedicated to The Dog at Peppard. The book is dedicated to Sue, for all the usual reasons and then some.

Concert, by Norman Humphreys, p. 177. Copyright © *Jazz Journal*, January 1970. All rights reserved. Used by permission of Jazz Journal Limited.

Your Mama Wants You Back and *He Was a Big Freak*, by Betty Davis, p. 228. Copyright © 31 January 1974 by Higher Music Publishing Inc. and Betty Mabry Music Co. Administered by Famous Music Corp. International rights secured. All rights reserved. Used by permission of Chappel Music Canada Limited.

Alone, by Michael S. Harper, p. 233. Copyright © by Michael S. Harper. All rights reserved. Used by permission of the author.

The Man with the Horn, by Randy Hall and Robert Irving, p. 300. Copyright © 1981 by Jazz Horn Music Corporation. All rights reserved. Reprinted by permission of Jazz Horn Music Corporation.

No financial assistance was sought or received for the research and writing of *Milestones* I and II.

ABBREVIATIONS

The following standard abbreviations have been used in the discographical entries:

arr   arranger
as   alto saxophone
b   bass
bs   baritone saxophone
clnt   clarinet
comp   composer
cond   conductor
dms   drums
flt   flute
frh   french horn

gtr   guitar
perc   percussion
pno   piano
ss   soprano saxophone
tba   tuba
tbn   trombone
tpt   trumpet
ts   tenor saxophone
vcl   vocal
vib   vibraphone

PART THREE
PRINCE OF DARKNESS

I wish I was blacker than you.   Bud Powell to Miles Davis

9

Pfrancing
1960–2

Everything doesn't make me mad, angry. It takes a lot to make me angry enough. It's not that I'm angry, it's the way I speak. I don't *lie*, so it comes off like that. Miles Davis

The promise of change was all around as the 1950s gave way to the 1960s, although it would have required a prophet to see the shape of things to come in the portents of the day. There was no such prophet, but many Americans in 1960 seemed willing to confer that title on their president-elect. His name was John F. Kennedy, at 44 the youngest man ever elected to the presidency, and he brought a new style into politics for these new times.

In his inaugural address on 20 January 1961, Kennedy proclaimed the new order in rhetoric that his immediate predecessors might have choked on. "Let the word go forth from this time and place, to friend and foe alike," he declared, "that the torch has been passed to a new generation of Americans, born in this century, tempered by war, disciplined by a hard and bitter peace, proud of our ancient heritage, and unwilling to permit the slow undoing of those human rights to which this nation has always been committed, and to which we are committed today at home and around the world." Kennedy's statement could almost stand as a clarion call to the political activists who would emerge not only in the United States but everywhere in the world by the middle years of the decade. It was closer to a prophecy than Kennedy himself would ever really know, because he was assassinated 34 months later, but it was also wrong in its details in a way that Kennedy could never possibly conceive.

The "new generation" was not the one "tempered by war" but the one conceived during and immediately after it, and "the torch" was not so much passed to it as seized by it. It was the generation of the 'baby boom,' the children born in the 1940s and early 1950s, who formed a new majority in all of the industrialized nations of the world and exercised their plebiscite with surprising power as they reached adolescence and early adulthood. By the time they reached the age of 30 – a birthday which, in their *Weltanschauung*, symbolized the age of hoary powerlessness – they revaluated virtually all their parents' values. Even as John F. Kennedy intoned the words of his inaugural address, they were pressing for more choice in education, which under the weight of their numbers became the fastest growing industry in the world. Still to come, though not far off, were confrontations on the folly of war for any putative principles, the incipient imperialism of foreign affairs, the covert elitism and racism of institutions, the sexism of traditional families, and much else besides. Their spokesmen were unelected and untitled, coming from the student ranks in the universities, the protest singers and poets in coffeehouses, the welfare workers in minority ghettos, and the international cadre of rock 'n' roll stars.

To anyone who could stir their imaginations, the new majority was willing to pay more than lip service. It was, above all, a generation of free spenders, raised in the relative peace and unbroken plenty of the post-war years. If the Great Depression still lurked neurotically in the minds of parents and caused them to extol the virtues of thrift and moderation, that only went to show how hopelessly antiquated the parents were. The new majority bought concert and movie tickets by the hundreds, books by the thousands, and records by the millions. It was a bonanza that promoters and publishers and record companies could not ignore, and their response soon made over large sectors of the economy until it seemed to serve under-30s only.

In the opening years of the new decade, Miles Davis seemed neither more aware of nor more responsive to the changes that were brewing than did any other jazzman his age. On 26 May 1959, he had turned 33. His altercation with the police outside Birdland that summer and its legal aftermath resulting in the dismissal of all charges on both sides merely hardened his veneer of cynicism about the world he never made. He was, for all that, riding a crest of popular and critical acclaim after the years of the first great quintet and the magnificent sextet. He seemed at first perfectly content to ride the crest. His supporting players from the great bands drifted away over the next few years, and replacing them with new sidemen who measured up to his exacting standards turned out to be a much harder task then it had ever been in the past. Because he was less than satisfied with the performances of many of his sidemen over the next four years, Davis spent even less time in the recording studios than he had in 1952, when his career was at its lowest ebb.

The first of the handful of studio recordings that he did make was with Gil Evans's orchestra, the *Sketches of Spain* sessions, and although it was a popular success it posed extraordinary technical problems, but a later one with Gil Evans from this same period, the *Quiet Nights* sessions, offered few technical challenges and turned out to be mediocre, an even more daunting result. Besides these, Davis made only two other LPs and a few isolated tracks in the studio, and Columbia Records was forced to record his live performances in order to keep its catalog up to date.

In his live performances, Davis often played less than he had a few years before, the result not only of his lack of interest in what his bands were doing but also of the acute pain he began suffering in his hip, a chronic ailment which in moments of crisis forced him to remove himself from the stand. His modal experiments with his sextet dimmed in their importance for his playing and for his band, and he seemed perfectly content to disengage himself from the formal innovations in jazz which John Coltrane and others took up in his stead. As for the other innovations coming into jazz at the time through the music of Ornette Coleman, Don Cherry, Cecil Taylor, and Eric Dolphy, Davis seemed positively hostile in his public pronouncements about them.

For Davis, these years were an interlude for discovering the resources that would lead him to his next great quintet, late in 1964. In the meantime, his music, when he chose to play it, perpetuated many of the strengths he had revealed so abundantly in the five years before. At its very best, whether with Gil Evans's orchestra or with his working quintet, it suffers hardly at all even in comparison to the music that went before it.

Davis made a last-ditch effort to dissuade Julian Adderley from leaving his band in September 1959 by offering him a guaranteed annual salary of $20,000, more money than Adderley could hope to make if he re-formed his own band. Adderley declined, choosing instead to resume his career as a leader alongside his brother Nat. He felt he had learned all he was going to with Davis, including some subtle lessons in leadership. "From a leader's viewpoint, I learned, by watching Miles, how to bring new material into a band without changing the style of the band," he said later. "And when it was necessary at times to change the style somewhat, Miles did it so subtly that no one knew about it." In fact, Adderley went on to become a popular leader without really changing his band's style from its basic blues-funk groove, although he started using an electric piano and bass in the late 1960s. He was confident that his band would succeed because of the exposure he had had with Davis. "I'd been getting inquiries from club owners about when I'd start my own band again because they kept noticing the response when my name was announced," he said. His band started off making $1,500 a week after he left Davis, compared to the $1,000 a week he had had difficulty commanding before he joined him.[1] Soon afterward, he had a string of successful records, first on the Riverside label and then on Capitol, depending largely on the pop-gospel compositions of Bobby Timmons, his first piano player, and Josef Zawinul, who replaced Timmons. His band became one of the biggest attractions in jazz for most of the decade.

With Adderley gone, Davis's band became a quintet again, with John Coltrane on tenor saxophone, Wynton Kelly on piano, Paul Chambers on bass, and Jimmy Cobb on drums. Coltrane could hardly muster more enthusiasm for playing Davis's music in their nightly routines than Davis himself could. He had declared his intention to become the leader of his own band repeatedly throughout 1959, and he would keep on doing so every time he spoke to the press or to other musicians. He stayed in Davis's band largely because he could not bring himself to set a date for his departure and stick to it, but his activities made it clear to everyone that he was more interested in his career outside the Davis Quintet, leading pickup groups on Atlantic recording sessions and in clubs on the quintet's night off. When the quintet made its tour of cities late in the year that would take it to Chicago for the usual Christmas engagement, Coltrane often stepped aside to let local saxophonists play in his place. At the Storyville Club in Boston, Rocky Boyd, one of Coltrane's admirers, often played as much as Coltrane did during the later sets of the night, and both of them played more than Davis did in those sets.[2] On returning in the new year to New York, where the quintet now worked regularly at the Village Vanguard instead of at Birdland, George Coleman played Coltrane's saxophone in some of the late sets.[3] Whether they knew it or not at the time, both Boyd and Coleman were auditioning for Coltrane's job.

Davis accidentally discovered that his career had reached a new plateau even if his music was, for the moment, standing still. In the marketing mentality of American culture, he had become the equivalent of a brand name. His name rather than his presence seemed to guarantee the success of the club engagements by his band, and he would sometimes play no more than eight bars of an opening melody before leaving the stand, or sit at the back of the club throughout an entire late-night set. Any carping about his absence was *lèse majesté*, and the complaints, for the time being, were few. Positive proof of Davis's stature surfaced in numerous glossy magazines in 1960, in the form of an advertisement for the Bell Telephone Company which showed a businessman in a hotel room talking on the phone, saying, "I was sitting here thinking of you while Miles played *My Funny Valentine* and I thought I'd call..." There was no need, of course, for further explanation.

Off the bandstand, Davis was less accessible than ever. Sy Johnson, who had moved to New York from Los Angeles, caught the quintet at the Village Vanguard and again photographed the group on the stand using available light. Where Davis had shown keen interest in Johnson's photographs of his band a few years earlier in Los Angeles, he now showed none at all. Instead, he approached Johnson and said, "I don't wancha takin' no more pitcha's, ya hear," and walked away. "He never said anything else," Johnson adds, "but he did frequently leave his trumpet on my table while he wandered around the club during solos by the rest of the band, and stub his cigarettes out in the ashtray."[4]

Max Gordon, the owner of the Vanguard, recalled another occasion when an avid fan of Davis was expected to feel privileged because Davis used his ashtray. "When Gary Giddins, the jazz critic, was fifteen, he used to spend the $2 allowance his father gave him to go to the Vanguard to hear Miles Davis on Sunday afternoon," Gordon wrote in *Live at the Village Vanguard*. "He'd come early, get a front seat. Miles was one of his jazz heroes. One Sunday, Miles, walking off the bandstand at the end of the first set, stopped to rub out his cigarette in the ashtray on Gary's table. 'Here, save it,' he said to Gary. 'Some day it's gonna be worth some money.'"[5]

If Davis approached his audiences, and his music, glibly when he played in jazz clubs, he certainly could not carry that over into the music he was recording in the Columbia studios. He was once again involved in a major project with Gil Evans, their third in three years, and even Davis feared that it was too ambitious. The music was later released, as *Sketches of Spain*, to the same popular acclaim as their earlier collaborations but a rather uneasy critical response, and it was recorded in two concentrated periods in the studios, the first in November 1959 and the second in March 1960.

The 1959 session provided most of the challenges for Davis and for the top studio men who comprised Evans's orchestra. The music they recorded, a single track lasting slightly more than sixteen minutes, was the adagio movement of Joaquin Rodrigo's *Concierto de Aranjuez for Guitar and Orchestra*, adapted for Davis's trumpet and flugelhorn. Davis first heard a recording of Rodrigo's *Concierto* earlier in the year in California. "After listening to it for a couple of weeks, I couldn't get it out of my mind," he says. When he played it for Evans in New York, they decided to adapt it for an album of Spanish themes. "As we usually do, we planned the program first by ourselves for about two months," Davis says. "I work out something, he takes it home and works on it some more; and then we figure out how we're going to do it. He can read my mind and I can read his."[6] Their score for the *Concierto* was so complex that the twenty-piece studio orchestra required eight sessions before producing the takes that were eventually released on the record.

Evans and Davis used the recording company's facilities, in effect, for protracted rehearsals, a practice that Davis would take up routinely by the end of the decade, when he began taking his working bands into the studio, recording several hours of music, and evaluating the results later. As a result, Columbia holds hundreds of hours of unissued material in its vaults that is unlikely to be issued as long as Davis is around to withhold his approval, and the first accumulation of rejected tape dates from the *Concierto* sessions. In 1959, it seemed a radical and probably expensive way of proceeding, and one that Teo Macero, Davis's producer, had to justify. "Who'd sit in a studio like I did for five sessions and hear a rehearsal?" he wondered, fifteen years later, and then he explained why he did it: "I knew there was something tangible there. Miles didn't show up for the first four sessions. He came and then he sat for the next two or three and I think most of the stuff came out of the last session. But you had to have some foresight. You had to have some understanding to say, 'Maybe it's tomorrow.' The experiment won't be completed until we finish. We don't really know, it's sort of a mixed-up jungle at the moment."[7]

Evans took charge of the sessions. Nat Hentoff attended one of them, on a Sunday probably just five days before the issued recording was made, and he noted that Evans "insists on hearing exactly what he has written," an observation that sharply contradicts those critics who claim that Evans is too easygoing when he conducts. Against pressures of time and grumblings of musicians, Evans persisted with the rehearsals until his score was finally mastered. "These look like flute parts we're playing," Ernie Royal, the lead trumpeter in the orchestra, complained. All the players found Evans's shifting, uneven tempos difficult. "To count at all," trombonist Frank Rehak said of one section, "you have to count four on every beat." Hall Overton, the classical composer who earlier in the year had scored some jazz arrangements of Thelonious Monk's music, was also in the studio on the Sunday that Hentoff was there. "This is the toughest notation I've ever seen in a jazz arrangement," Overton said. "It could have been written more easily for the players and the result would have been the same, but Gil has to have it exactly the way it happens in the piece." He added, "Fortunately, these guys are among the best readers in town." Later jazz adaptations of Rodrigo's first movement, notably by Laurindo Almeida with the Modern Jazz Quartet and by Jim Hall, have taken Overton's suggestion by simplifying the music, mainly using Rodrigo's melodies and tempos against a conventional jazz background, but they have missed entirely the rich textures that provide the substance of Evans's score. If Evans was undaunted by the difficulty of that score, Davis was not. "I always manage to put my foot in it," he said as he listened to yet another spoiled take at the Sunday session. "I always manage to try something I can't do. I'm going to call myself on the phone one day and tell myself to shut up."[8]

Then all the parts took shape, almost before anyone really expected them to. "All of a sudden," Macero said, "the last session comes and Miles plays and he plays straight through it and everything just sort of falls into place."[9] The details are as follows:

Miles Davis with Gil Evans and His Orchestra: Sketches of Spain
Miles Davis, tpt, flugelhorn; Ernie Royal, Bernie Glow, Taft Jordan, Louis Mucci, tpt; Dick Hixon, Frank Rehak, tbn; John Barrows, Jimmy Buffington, Earl Chapin, frh; James McAllister, tba; Albert Block, Eddie Caine, flt; Danny Bank, flt, bass clnt; Romeo Penque, oboe; Harold Feldman, oboe, bass clnt; Janet Putnam, harp; Paul Chambers, b; Jimmy Cobb, dms; Elvin Jones, perc; Gil Evans, arr, cond. New York, 20 November 1959
Concierto de Aranjuez
(Columbia CL 1480)

The complexity of Evans's score, from a listener's viewpoint, is reflected in the constant shift of textures throughout the sixteen minutes that the recording lasts. Its unity is a bit tentative, depending upon recurrences of Rodrigo's dominant melody, which is stated by Davis on flugelhorn right at the beginning (as it is stated by english horn in Rodrigo's original score), and then reinterpreted by him almost immediately (as by the guitar in the original). It is played by Davis as a highly personal lament, all of which occupies only the first quarter of the score; Rodrigo's melody returns to the foreground only in the last quarter, where it is played powerfully by the whole orchestra. In between, Davis plays in no less than four settings, all attractive in their own right but connected only by his unique sound, whether on open flugelhorn in the first half and coda, or on muted trumpet in the second half. Davis himself is the connecting thread, by design. "The thing I have to do now is make things connect, make them mean something in what I play around it," he said at the Sunday rehearsal.

It is a large responsibility, perhaps even too large. Davis and Evans's *Concierto* is likely to be heard by listeners who know it best as a medley of disparate pieces bounded by Rodrigo's melody. "That melody is so strong that the softer you play it, the stronger it gets, and the stronger you play it, the weaker it gets," Davis said at rehearsal, and Evans agreed, calling it a "distilled melody": "If you lay it on too hard, you don't have it."

That melody remains indelible because Davis states it and reinterprets it so strikingly at the start, separated by a beautiful interlude by a choir made up of trumpet, trombone, flute, and oboe. Much more than the melody echoes after a few listenings. In the middle of the score Davis plays a solo punctuated irregularly by trilled flutes and the harp. Immediately before and after, in two parts of Evans's score that are completely beyond Rodrigo, he plays the only segments that include anything resembling jazz rhythms. The second, with Davis playing muted, is underscored by a bass ostinato and carried along by the (sometimes slightly awkward) pulse of finger cymbals. The first has the syncopated rhythms of a walking bass and brushes on a snare drum.

The combined playing time of the two sections with quasi-jazz rhythms comes to less than four minutes, which may explain some of the coolness from the critics when the *Concierto* was released. Martin Williams said, "The recording is something of a curiosity and a failure, as I think a comparison with any good performance of the movement by a classical guitarist would confirm."[10] Max Harrison called it "a boring re-write" and "a strange miscalculation."[11] Even Rodrigo objected, according to Gil Evans. "There was only one version of it available then and now there's maybe fourteen," Evans pointed out in 1983. "The melody is so powerful. Rodrigo didn't like Miles' version of it but it brought him a lot of money in royalties. A *lot* of money."[12] Whether it is 'good' Rodrigo, or 'good' jazz, or even jazz at all can be debated endlessly. Most listeners seem to be as unconcerned about such matters as Davis and Evans apparently were, and they have kept the record in demand, and in print, ever since its release.

The remaining titles for Davis and Evans's collaboration on *Sketches of Spain* were more straightforward, but still very ambitious jazz orchestrations. They were recorded almost four months later in two sessions, after Davis returned from a tour of Boston, Chicago, and other cities with the quintet. Evans spent the interval listening to recordings of Spanish folk music and logged several hours in the library reading books on flamenco music, refining the bases of the other compositions and giving the next sessions a kind of scholarly diversity. The details are as follows:

Miles Davis with Gil Evans and His Orchestra: Sketches of Spain
Miles Davis, tpt, flugelhorn; Ernie Royal, Bernie Glow, Johnny Coles, tpt; Dick Hixon, Frank Rehak, tbn; Joe Singer, Tony Miranda, Jimmy Buffington, frh; Bill Barber, tba; Albert Block, Eddie Caine, Harold Feldman, flt; Romeo Penque, oboe; Danny Bank, bass clnt; Jack Knitzer, bassoon; Janet Putnam, harp; Paul Chambers, b; Jimmy Cobb, dms; Elvin Jones, perc; Gil Evans, arr, cond. New York, 10 March 1960
The Pan Piper; Song of Our Country
(*The Pan Piper* on Columbia CL 1480; *Song of Our Country* on Columbia KC2 36472 [1981])

Add Louis Mucci, tpt. Same place, 11 March 1960
Solea; Will o' the Wisp; Saeta
(all on Columbia CL 1480)
Song of Our Country was dated 11 March 1960 when it was issued in 1981, but the absence of Louis Mucci in the orchestra suggests that it was recorded the day before, as listed here.

The variety of orchestrations defies any concise description, and the success of the scores is mixed. *Song of Our Country*, which was not issued until 1981, stands apart from the rest musically. It opens with a full-bodied orchestral fanfare and closes with a suspended note by Davis, on flugelhorn, suggesting that it might have been written as a bridge between two of the other compositions in the original master plan, but, if so, that master plan is no longer reconstructable from the music available. The body of the piece is Davis's flugelhorn solo over orchestral figures, and it is much more in the spirit of Davis and Evans's *Miles Ahead* collaboration of 1957, and worthy of comparison with it in many ways.

Will o' the Wisp develops a theme from Manuel de Falla's ballet *El amor brujo*, thus resembling the *Concierto* in its provenance, but there is no resemblance in the result. However successful *Will o' the Wisp* may or may not be in adapting the original, on its own it fails rhythmically in its static seesaw of repeated orchestral figures, ending up as a kind of stiff-legged dance. *The Pan Piper* also includes a repetitive orchestral figure, representing the street cry of a vendor in the original folk recording which Evans adapted, but the repetition here is far from static, and over it Davis plays lyrically on muted trumpet; of Evans's orchestration, Davis said, "He made that orchestra sound like a big guitar."[13]

The remaining compositions, both credited to Evans but based on traditional Andalusian melodies, are masterful additions to the collaboration, notwithstanding Max Harrison's dismissal of them as "bogus flamenco."[14] *Solea* is indeed bogus flamenco, that is, flamenco adapted for a jazz soloist and orchestra, in which Davis plays an extended blues for twelve minutes over Evans's rich backgrounds. Davis's lament — *solea* is the generic term for a flamenco lament — sustains a single mood, in contrast to his caprices on *Concierto*, and the whole composition is powered by the two percussionists, used with a resourcefulness seldom given to percussion in Evans's arrangements. Throughout the entire composition, one of the drummers marks the flamenco rhythm on a snare drum and the other marks the 4/4 jazz rhythm on a ride cymbal. The two rhythmic pulses are felt alternately in a remarkably subtle exchange, the dominant flamenco rhythm subsiding imperceptibly until Davis and the orchestra are playing big band jazz in the middle section and then slipping as subtly back to flamenco by the end. The contending rhythms quite literally embody the musical forces at play throughout *Sketches of Spain* and counterbalance them brilliantly.

Saeta is no less successful, but on entirely different terms. It is essentially a three-minute exploration of a single scale by Davis, playing flugelhorn, supported all the while by nothing but a sustained chord from the woodwinds and the occasional march cadence of a snare drum. For Davis, it is an unflagging showcase of his taste and imagination, as he begins with a Spanish tinge in his phrases and a slight vibrato in his tone and builds an exotic blues solo in bent notes. His solo is framed by a march played as a crescendo at the opening and a diminuendo at the end, giving the aural effect of a parade approaching and stopping while Davis addresses it, and moving on when he is finished. The effect of the passing parade was used before this in Evans's *Here Come de Honey Man*, on *Porgy and Bess*, but without the emotive effect that it has here. The form is derived from an Andalusian procession through the streets on Good Friday which halts while a singer on a balcony directs her pain and remorse – *saeta* means 'arrow' – to the cross-bearing Christ. Davis's solo is raw in its emotion, and it seems all the more bitter and pained framed by the trite, business-like march cadence. Of the solo on *Saeta*, Martin Williams says, "Miles Davis plays with a stark, deeply felt communal anguish that jazz has not heard since King Oliver."[15]

In the previous collaborations of Davis and Evans, separating the parts from the whole proved almost impossible, and one could hardly avoid the conclusion that the whole was an unqualified success. In *Sketches of Spain*, the parts can be dealt with much more readily and almost require it. The success of the whole project is qualified, but among the parts *Solea* and *Saeta* are outstanding.

Later in the month, when Davis arrived in England on the first leg of a European tour, a reporter asked him if he enjoyed working with Evans's large orchestra. "I prefer to work with the quintet," he stated. "I like to hear the rhythm section."[16] His choice was clear no doubt because the arduous *Sketches of Spain* sessions remained so fresh in his mind. But some of his enthusiasm for the large-scale orchestral projects seemed to be gone for good.

So was some of Gil Evans's, although he did not realize it immediately. "You know, an arranger's job is kind of a loser's job, in a sense, because once you get paid for an arrangement, that's the end of it," he told Zan Stewart. "Like for the Miles Davis sides – *Miles Ahead*, *Porgy and Bess*, *Sketches of Spain* – I got paid and that's it. The people who wrote the original lines get the royalties. But at the time I never thought about it. I was having such a good time writing that music that it never dawned on me that years later I wouldn't be getting those checks in the mail."[17] Where Evans had composed only one title on each of the first two projects, on *Sketches of Spain* he is credited with three, *The Pan Piper*, *Saeta*, and *Solea* (as well as the belatedly released *Song of Our Country* from the same sessions). In 1983 he told Richard Cook, "I wised up when we did *Sketches of Spain* – those numbers credited to me are traditional tunes. You don't get royalties on public domain numbers."[18] Even so, he remained unlucky with royalties; he gave them to his first wife as alimony, and, according to Evans, by 1982 she had collected $240,000 on them.[19]

With *Sketches of Spain* finally completed, neither Davis nor Evans seemed anxious to return to the recording studio for a long time. For Davis, all recording, even with his quintet, was put off for a full year.

The studio sessions finished just in time for Davis to leave with his quintet for Europe. Coltrane presented a problem. He did not want to go on the tour, but instead of facing Davis with his decision he tried to recruit Wayne Shorter to take his place. "I had just gotten out of the army," Shorter says, "and one night Trane came over to Newark on his night off from Miles at Birdland. We had known each other, and Trane used to say to me, 'You're playing all that funny stuff like me ... all over the horn, funny.' Anyway, Trane then told me he wanted to leave Miles' group, and he told me, 'You can have the job if you want it.' He was giving me the gig for Miles! Anyway, he told me to call Miles, so I called him and said, 'Hello, I'm Wayne Shorter and I'm from Newark, New Jersey.' And you know Miles, he said in that voice, 'Who told you I needed a saxophone player?' And I said, 'Trane, John Coltrane,' Well, Miles says, 'If I need a saxophone player I'll get one.' Then we kind of measured each other to see who would hang up first."[20]

Norman Granz, who booked Davis's tour, advertised it as his "first extended European tour," with the emphasis, presumably, on "extended," since Davis had already played in and around Paris in 1949 and 1957 and in several European cities in 1956. As on all of Davis's European engagements, and indeed on those of all major American jazzmen, this one was well documented in unofficial tapings of the concerts, usually made informally by members of the audience but sometimes, judging by the quality of some of the tapes, taken directly from the sound system in the auditorium. For this tour, tapes of varying quality have turned up from the concerts in Paris (21 March), Stockholm (22), Copenhagen (24), and Scheveningen, a North Sea resort near The Hague (9 April). Two of the titles from the Stockholm concert were issued as recordings a few years later on a label called Bird Notes which has long since disappeared, and in 1979 a more generous sample of what the Davis Quintet played was issued on LP. The details are as follows:

Miles Davis Quintet in Stockholm and Scheveningen
Miles Davis, tpt; John Coltrane, ts; Wynton Kelly, pno; Paul Chambers, b; Jimmy Cobb, dms. Stockholm, 22 March 1960

Miles Davis (Columbia Records)

John Coltrane playing soprano saxophone (Lars Aastrom, courtesy of *Down Beat*)

Walkin'; All Blues
(both on Bird Notes; reissued in Europe on BYG 529608)
Both titles are incomplete; *All Blues* is mis-titled *Somethin' Else* on BYG.

Same personnel. Scheveningen, Holland, 9 April 1960
Green Dolphin Street; Walkin' / The Theme; So What; Round Midnight
(all on Unique Jazz UJ 19 [1979])
On aural evidence, *Round Midnight* is probably from a different concert from the other titles; the recording is shrill, and the piano is out of tune.

The next few years include several recordings of live performances by Davis's quintets made by Columbia with very good sound quality, but none of them is as valuable as this one, documenting the final days of Davis's veteran working band, even though its sound quality ranges from good (on *Green Dolphin Street*) to awful (on *Round Midnight*). The hours logged by the members of this band had not made them complacent, at least not in these performances. Wynton Kelly, the newest member, had joined the band in February 1959, more than a year earlier, and Jimmy Cobb had joined a year before that; both Coltrane and Paul Chambers had been with Davis since 1955, although Coltrane had been removed from the band for a few intervals in that period. They play together with an easy confidence that can bring out the best in each of them.

   Even *Round Midnight*, in the familiar 1956 quintet arrangement by Gil Evans, is enlivened by some new dissonances in the ensembles, although this recording is diminished not only by its low fidelity but also by an apparent splice after Coltrane's solo. *Walkin'*, even more shopworn in Davis's repertoire, is saved from another stale recitation by opening with Chambers's arco solo, which impels Davis into less familiar territory for his own solo; in his last chorus Davis toys with a childish jingle played in thirds for several bars, a surprising foreshadowing of his composition *Jean Pierre*, which became part of his repertoire only in 1981.

   The other two titles, *Green Dolphin Street* and *So What*, are stunning reworkings of two of Davis's most striking recordings with his sextet. Both are played as unfettered romps in contrast to the carefully controlled studio versions. On *Green Dolphin Street*, which lasts more than twelve minutes, Davis constructs a hot solo that pulls apart the familiar melody almost as thoroughly as do Coltrane's sheets of sound, but *So What*, extended to seventeen and a half minutes in this performance, goes even further. Kelly, who had been asked to sit out on the original recording in favor of Bill Evans, fashions an ingenious solo in the style of Ahmad Jamal by sustaining the bass motif of the ensemble and building spare melodic phrases around it. On both *Green Dolphin Street* and *So What*, Coltrane plays long, intense, almost frenetic solos with enormous impact. He was by this time well launched on his career away from Davis's bands, and he was no longer holding back on his harmonic experiments when he played with Davis, as he had complained he was a year earlier. The spirit that would very soon bring him recognition as the most influential soloist of the time suffuses these live performances as clearly as it would his own recordings of *My Favorite Things* and *Equinox* for Atlantic later in the year. His solo on *So What* lasts nearly nine minutes and builds from an almost casual half-time vamp to a busy, moaning exploration that ranks with his best work.

Coltrane's playing with the quintet in Europe makes no compromises. He was restless and uneasy throughout the entire tour, making it clear to all the members of the band that he would rather be elsewhere, working on his own music on his own terms. His feelings hardly disrupted the others. All of them had watched him separate himself from their company and occasionally listened to his mild grumblings about needing to get out on his own. By now, they all openly wondered if he would ever get around to making the break he kept talking about, but in Europe they realized that he could not stay much longer. "All he had with him were his horns, an airlines bag, and a toilet kit," Cobb remembers. "He didn't really want to make the gig, but Miles talked him into it. He sat next to me on the bus, looking like he was ready to split at any time. He spent most of the time looking out the window and playing oriental-sounding scales on soprano [saxophone]."[21]

Soon after the quintet returned to the United States, Coltrane gave Davis two weeks' notice. He had done that before, of course, and had ended up staying, but this time there was a note of finality because he was already booked into the Jazz Gallery with his own quartet for nine weeks, beginning in May. After almost five years, his tenure in Miles Davis's bands was finished.

The break, when it finally came, proved far more traumatic for Davis than for Coltrane. Davis seemed unprepared despite all the signs that Coltrane was serious this time. He spent the next four years trying to find a suitable replacement, until the passing parade of saxophonists added up to a long list: Jimmy Heath, Sonny Stitt, Hank Mobley, Rocky

Boyd, Wayne Shorter (on a 1962 recording date), Frank Strozier, George Coleman, and Sam Rivers. None of them stayed long. Sonny Rollins, whom Davis had originally preferred to Coltrane and had enlisted as his replacement a couple of times, was not available, having retired from music yet again; this time he remained inactive for almost two years, until the fall of 1961.

Coltrane, who had for so long feared leaving the security of Davis's band, moved straight ahead. At the Jazz Gallery he received the same salary he was getting from Davis. His quartet there had Steve Kuhn on piano, Steve Davis on bass, and Pete LaRoca on drums, but after two weeks he replaced Kuhn with McCoy Tyner, thus finding almost at the beginning the piano player who would form the cornerstone for his working bands.[22] He played and recorded the music on which his reputation largely rests between the fall of 1961 and the end of 1964, in a series of brilliant recordings under his own leadership on Atlantic and Impulse. After that, his health began to deteriorate, and his music, though undeniably powerful, became so freighted with excesses that it became hard to understand and even harder to appreciate, seemingly requiring listeners to refer back to his music of 1960–4 for clarification. The difficulties posed by his later music hardly seemed to impose any burden on listeners who were paying attention at the time it was being made, when his earlier music was still fresh, and he found a large, almost idolatrous following among both musicians and fans until his early death in 1967.

The character of Coltrane's music undeniably changed after he left Davis, by degrees in the first few years and then by leaps. Soon after leaving he said, "I think I'm going to try to write for the horn from now on, just play around the horn and see what I can learn. All the time I was with Miles I didn't have anything to think about except myself so I stayed at the piano and [played] chords, chords, chords. I ended up playing them on my horn." His music eventually became less dense, especially when he played the soprano saxophone, and more melodic, but he explored modal frameworks until the last few years of his life, when he often chose freer forms. In 1965, he looked back on his years with Davis and noticed the similarities in his music. "I don't think it has changed basically – though I suppose I've grown a little musically," he said. "But then in some respects I think I might have been a little more inventive in those days."[23] With Davis, he had been forced to discover and integrate his own individuality in contexts determined by Davis. No one, before or since, rose so forcefully to that challenge.

The timing of Coltrane's quitting was unlucky for Davis not only because of the problem of finding a replacement. Coltrane's presence gave Davis's music an aura of experimentation, of restless searching for formal and harmonic expansions, that even the most unschooled listener could hardly miss. No matter that Coltrane's experiments originated with Davis and were, at least in the beginning, impelled by him; on the surface it was Coltrane, not Davis, who was the experimenter. That fact counted heavily on the tote board that jazz critics began drawing up in 1960.

Critics and fans suddenly took a vital interest in the search for new directions in jazz. Whether it was cause or effect, the central event of the new interest was the arrival in New York of two Los Angeles musicians named Ornette Coleman and Don Cherry. The hullabaloo surrounding their engagement at the Five Spot placed alto saxophonist Coleman and trumpeter Cherry at the center of the noisiest controversy in jazz since the "war of the moldy figs" fought over bebop in the 1940s, but this time the controversy had a much larger and more conspicuous battlefield because in the interim the jazz audience had expanded socially, culturally, and geographically.

It began innocently. John Lewis, doyen of the Modern Jazz Quarter (MJQ) and one of the most respected figures in jazz, was quoted in the *Jazz Review* in 1959 extolling the virtues of the two unknowns: "They're almost like twins; they play together like I've never heard anybody play together," he said. "It's not like any ensemble that I have ever heard, and I can't figure out what it's all about yet." From that germ, Coleman and Cherry's meteoric careers took shape.

Through Lewis's good graces, they were signed to a recording contract by Nesuhi Ertegun of Atlantic Records, the MJQ's recording company, and sent to the summer session at the School of Jazz in Lenox, Massachusetts, where Lewis was the director. Curiosity about the pair was further fuelled by Martin Williams's column on the School of Jazz in October's *Jazz Review*, of which he was co-editor, in which he wrote, "I honestly believe (not that I am alone or particularly original in believing it) that what Ornette Coleman is doing on alto will affect the whole character of jazz music profoundly and pervasively."

By the time Coleman and Cherry opened in New York in November for what would become a six-month engagement at the Five Spot, the critical artillery was already in place and the battle could begin in earnest. The music that Coleman and Cherry played, usually called "avant-garde" or "the new thing" at the time but perhaps more

appropriately called "free form," inspired passionate paeans and deri-
sive denunciations in about equal proportions and drew dozens of
names into the fray. For a short time, one counted one's friends in terms
of whether or not they shared one's opinion of Ornette Coleman.

Davis and Coltrane, like nearly all other jazz musicians, were
profoundly curious about the music, and both were frequent visitors at
the Five Spot, which was packed for weeks after the opening. Coltrane,
typically, watched Coleman with a wide-eyed but noncommital look
and said nothing; Davis watched too and even ventured onto the
bandstand at the Five Spot with him, but when he was asked directly for
his opinion, he issued a typically blunt judgment: "Hell, just listen to
what he writes and how he plays it," he said. "If you're talking
psychologically, the man is all screwed up inside."[24] That statement
was more than enough to relegate Miles Davis into the reactionary
faction in the hypersensitive critical climate of the moment.

Davis was not the only critic of Coleman and Cherry: virtually every
established jazzman who said anything at all expressed doubts about
their music. But very few had the temerity to say anything at all, and the
main reason for the silence was the enormous weight of articulate
opinion promoting their music as the "new thing." When Coleman took
the stage with his tiny white plastic alto saxophone and Cherry joined
him with his tinier pocket trumpet to play the rapid, daring, original
ensembles of Coleman's tunes – ensembles that cohered magically, but
seemed to have such a magical musical basis that even as astute a
listener as John Lewis could not figure out their theoretical underpin-
nings – they were hailed by a small but influential group as the
harbingers of the next step in the evolution of jazz. Not only John Lewis
and Gunther Schuller of the Lenox School, and Martin Williams and
Nat Hentoff of the *Jazz Review* spoke out, but notable figures beyond
the jazz world were convinced too. The Five Spot counted dozens of
artists among its Greenwich Village clientele when Coleman and
Cherry were playing, including Jackson Pollock, the patriarch of
modern American painting, and writers as different as LeRoi Jones (now
Amiri Baraka) and James Baldwin, among the leading young writers in
America, and Dorothy Kilgallen, the social columnist and television
panelist. Leonard Bernstein, the most prominent figure in American
music, was not only conspicuous in the audience; he was demonstrative
too. He sat in with Coleman's quartet, an act of more symbolic
significance than musical; one of the sidemen quietly told A.B.
Spellman, "He didn't really know what was going on."[25] Bernstein also,

on one memorable evening, leaped to his feet at the end of one set and declared that "this is the greatest thing that has ever happened in jazz" and that "Bird was nothing."

The display only hardened the suspicions of players like Randy Weston, who was booked opposite Coleman and Cherry that night, that the extravagant praise was nothing more than an attempt by the white establishment to foist their sensibility onto the development of jazz. Davis thought so too. Of Don Cherry, he said, "Anyone can tell that guy's not a trumpet player – it's just notes that come out, and every note he plays, he looks serious about, and people will go for it – especially white people. They go for anything. They want to be hipper than any other race, and they go for anything like that."[26]

Of Davis's turn on the bandstand with Coleman, Cherry says, "He wanted to try the pocket trumpet and he played practically all night." Davis even tried altering his musical conception to conform to theirs. Cherry recalls, "After I played, Miles said, 'You're the only mother I know who stops his solo right at the bridge.' And then he tried it."[27] Davis remained unconvinced that Coleman and Cherry offered anything worthwhile for the progress of jazz. And he saw no reason to alter his opinion a few years later, when he let Cherry sit in with his quintet for an evening.

Davis's outspoken criticism caused a few critics to wonder if his own success had not spoiled him and to evaluate his reaction as that of an established figure threatened by innovation. Davis insisted that he was only being honest where others were not. "People are so gullible," he told Leonard Feather, one critic who remained cool to Coleman's music. "They go for that – they go for something they don't know about ... because they feel it's not hip *not* to go for it. But if something sounds terrible, man, a person should have enough respect for his own mind to say it doesn't sound good. It doesn't to me, and I'm not going to listen to it, it doesn't sound any good."[28] Some other musicians were also willing to take a stand. "They're afraid to say it is nothing," Milt Jackson, Lewis's cohort in the MJQ, said. "There's no such thing as free form."

Looking back on the controversy more than two decades later, it is possible to sort out some home truths on both sides. Ornette Coleman and Don Cherry made music together that was eccentric and off-the-wall, and at its best, on a track like *Ramblin'* (on Atlantic 1327), it is full of feeling. It does not sound "terrible" at all; most jazz listeners would agree, at this late date, that it sounds beautiful. However, their music has only a tenuous formal framework, and it was never substantial enough to supplant the chordal and modal forms dominating jazz, as several commentators obviously thought it would. Coleman and Cherry played "melodically," in their terms, which meant that they responded spontaneously to one another's mannerisms, relatively unconstrained by the conventional formal guidelines of bars, chord progressions, choruses, scales, and the other musical trappings that comprise the shared, communal basis of Western tonal music.

In numerous statements, Coleman implied that the rudiments of his playing which everyone found so elusive were not essentially *musical* at all. "It seems impossible for Ornette Coleman to talk about music without soon using the word 'love'," Martin Williams wrote in his column from Lenox, "and when he plays one knows that, undeluded, it is love of man his music is talking about." "I just play life," Coleman said, "things that I encounter and experience." "There's a law to what I'm playing, but that law is a law that when you get tired of it, you can change it," he said later, and among the changeable elements he included tempo: "My music doesn't have any real time, no metric time. It has time, but not in the sense that you can time it. It's more like breathing, a natural, freer time." On the same point he said, "When you speak, the meaning itself gives the speed to the word. The same thing happens in music."[29] Assembled side by side, these statements emphasize the extramusical basis for Coleman's music, and its essential paradox. None of the activities he compares to his music is communal at all. Speaking happens with people taking turns, one after the other, and when two people try to speak simultaneously communication breaks down; breathing is done individually, without regard for the inhalation pattern of anyone else; experiences of life and love are felt and interpreted differently by different people, or at least will not be articulated similarly by them. But music usually takes place in groups and is a common expression by several individuals. It requires a shared body of "laws," and those laws can change only for the group, not for the individual. The logical conclusion of Coleman's pronouncements, if taken literally, would be musical anarchy, with the individual defying the group and standing apart from its expression.

Coleman's early history personifies that. In Fort Worth, Texas, where he was born in 1930 and lived until 1952, and in Los Angeles after that, Coleman sometimes earned a little money playing his tenor saxophone in rhythm and blues bands, but he was repeatedly excluded by jazz players whenever he attempted to play his alto saxophone with them. His fortunes took a turn only in 1958, when Don Cherry and a few other young musicians in Los Angeles got involved in trying to figure out what it was that Coleman was pursuing in his music. After repeated exposure, Cherry and the others, notably pianist Paul Bley, bassist Charlie Haden, and drummer Billy Higgins, managed to intuit so many of Coleman's mannerisms that they could play compatibly alongside him in his solipsistic flights. Cherry was the key, and by the time John Lewis heard them playing in Los Angeles he and Coleman had developed a rapport that was telepathic. Their music was beyond category, and they were playing together with utter conviction.

Their collaboration lasted a little longer than the Five Spot engagement, but the pressure of the critical controversy swirling around them and of the bloated expectations of a jazz revolution brought disruption. Soon afterward, Cherry went his own way, leaving Coleman on his own, as he had been when Cherry joined him. In the years since, Coleman has played and recorded very little, and while the aura of critical enthusiasm that surrounded him when he first became an international figure in jazz still gives a sense of occasion to his infrequent performances, he has probably never played as well or as convincingly as he did at the moment of his initial triumphs.

For all that, his influence has been and still is keenly felt. The avant-garde in jazz plays free form music in the terms that Coleman originally defined for it, either in tightly knit groups such as the Art Ensemble of Chicago and the World Saxophone Quartet, in which the members can comprehend and play off individual idiosyncrasies and at the same time develop and exploit group idiosyncrasies, or increasingly in solo performances by the likes of reedman Anthony Braxton and pianist Anthony Davis, where individual virtuosity can reign supreme without the fetters of group play.

Coleman and Cherry were not the first of the jazz avant-garde to emerge at the end of the 1950s, although their critical reception made them the most prominent. Cecil Taylor, a pianist from Boston, began being heard in New York fairly regularly in 1959, just before they arrived there, and Eric Dolphy, a reed and flute player from Los Angeles, joined Charles Mingus's band in 1960. One of Coleman's edicts said: "You can play flat in tune and sharp in tune," and Dolphy convinced most jazz listeners of the truth of that statement even if Coleman had left them unconvinced. Dolphy arrived in the public consciousness with an extraordinary individual voice on his several instruments, including flute and bass clarinet, but he was at his best on the alto saxophone, the instrument that Coleman favored. Dolphy's distinctiveness lay mainly in his use of tonality, which he altered with such fine control that his solos sometimes took on an eerie vocal quality. It was easy to recognize that he was 'playing flat' or 'playing sharp' in his solos, and just as easy to recognize that he was doing it in the service of his art. Where even Coleman's champions suspected that he not only would not play in a more conventional jazz framework but that he *could* not – a suspicion that Coleman would neither lay to rest nor confirm because he always refused to make the attempt – Dolphy left no doubt whatever about his musicianship. He could, and did, play in all manner of contexts from orchestral to bebop to free form, and he played as effectively and as distinctively in all of them.

Cecil Taylor had begun to find a few opportunities to display his rapid-fire, percussive, volcanic piano style when the fuss erupted over Coleman and Cherry in New York. His presence along with theirs at that moment naturally added to the critical impression that jazz was about to undergo the throes of revolution, the more so because Taylor had arrived from the opposite corner of the country, had never had any contact with the men from Los Angeles, and played equally eccentric jazz. Taylor's unique style seems to derive technically from jazz drummers rather than from other pianists, featuring an incredible outpouring of notes that mixes in a powerful thrumming of overtones. It is hard to imagine a piano style more antithetical to the one favored by Miles Davis in his bands, based on the harmonic niceties of men like Ahmad Jamal and Bill Evans, and Davis wasted little time in letting his feelings be known about Taylor's music. Symphony Sid Torin had started playing selections from Taylor's LP, produced by Nat Hentoff for Contemporary Records in 1958, on his radio show, prefacing the tracks, according to Taylor's bassist Buell Neidlinger, with remarks like: "This is a record by some gentlemen we understand have just escaped from Creedmore," a hospital for the criminally insane.[30] The publicity, and Hentoff's advocacy, helped to get Taylor occasional Monday night engagements at Birdland. Davis attended one of them along with Dizzy Gillespie, Sarah Vaughan, and Errol Garner. As Niedlinger remembers it, "Miles just laughed and split," but Taylor was left with a residue of more bitter memories: "Miles just cursed and walked out. Dizzy wandered in and out and kept making all kinds of remarks to Sarah, who was in a pretty vicious mood."[31] It was a hard baptism for the young piano player, and while he, unlike Coleman, persisted in developing his music publicly until he found, or developed, his audience, he has had little positive to say about his early detractors. Of one of them, he once said, "Miles Davis plays pretty well for a millionaire."[32]

Davis's involvement with the musicians who were emerging at the start of the 1960s comes as no surprise; he had always been aware of young musicians and new currents in jazz. More surprising is the apparent firmness of his stand on the side of the old order. He had been a member of the bebop revolution, the leader of the cool reaction to bebop and also, paradoxically, of the neo-bop reaction to cool, and then the leader in the modal reorganization of jazz structure. No one was in a better position to appreciate the inevitability of change. Now, he seemed determined to stake a claim for the status quo. Not content to watch and wait until the critical dust settled, as John Coltrane and others did, he waded in oblivious to the hypersensitivity of the time. When a supporter of Ornette Coleman declared that Art Blakey was "old-fashioned," Davis snapped, "If Art Blakey is old-fashioned, then I'm white." Against the enthusiasm of John Lewis and other spokesmen, Davis claimed he could not see any value in it at all. "What's so avant-garde?" he asked. "Lennie Tristano and Lee Konitz were creating ideas fifteen years ago that were stranger than any of these new things. But when they did it, it made sense."[33]

Once committed, he refused to revaluate, and for the first and only time in his career Davis was willing to stand aside and allow the innovations to proceed without him. It was remarkably out of character for him, and it did not last long, only during the short period when his own music seemed to stand still. Apart from these few years, his credo is well expressed in what he told Sy Johnson in 1976: "I got into music because I *love* it. I *still* love it. All kinds."[34] For the time being, he seemed to despise the kind of music known as the "new thing," and three or four years would pass before his own band responded to the newer, freer currents in jazz.

Davis's first choices to replace John Coltrane reflected his conservative mood. As soon as Coltrane left, Jimmy Heath was brought in. A tenor saxophonist and composer whose style was largely formed by the bebop revolution, Heath had just finished serving a fifteen-month term in the Lewisberg Penitentiary on a narcotics conviction when he joined Davis's band in the summer of 1960. He stayed in the quintet for about two months, playing engagements with them in Toronto and at the French Lick Jazz Festival, but after that, according to Bill Cole, Heath's parole board refused to let him travel beyond a ninety-mile radius of Philadelphia, his home town, and Davis, with another European tour set for the fall, was forced to find a replacement.[35] He invited Wayne Shorter, Coltrane's personal choice as his replacement, but Shorter was just settling in with Art Blakey's Jazz Messengers. "Miles called one time and asked Art if he could speak to me," Shorter recalls. "Art was saying 'He's trying to take my saxophone player,' and I told Miles that I felt an obligation to stay with Art. I didn't want to be one of those guys who just went from one band to another band every few months. Anyway, I stayed with Art for five years."[36]

In the end Davis hired Sonny Stitt, an alto saxophonist who doubled on tenor, another bebopper who had been Davis's bandmate with Billy Eckstine in 1946. Heath and Stitt were both solid and competent players, about the same age as Coltrane and Davis, but neither of them had shown any inclination to update their styles since their formative years. The spirit that Coltrane had brought to Davis's bands simply vanished.

Davis arrived in London on Friday, 23 September, to begin a round of concerts that would take him to the Gaumont Cinema, Hammersmith, in London (24 September), Colston Hall in Bristol (1 October), and Manchester (6 October). The leisurely pace of the English leg of the tour allowed him to spend some time sight-seeing, and he arrived with a small entourage that included his wife, Frances, who made a striking impression on every Fleet Street newsman who caught a glimpse of her, and Harold Lovett, his lawyer-manager.

Davis seemed completely unprepared for the hail of bad publicity in the tough London dailies covering his arrival. They played up his aloof stage manner, reiterating the old accounts of his turning his back on the audience and leaving the stage when his sidemen were soloing. That kind of notoriety was old hat to Davis, but the London tabloids added a sensational twist by implying that the reason for his unconventional behavior was hostility for white audiences. They also claimed that his entourage included a bodyguard and made it clear that this was a slight on British civility. "What do they think I am? A monster or something?" Davis asked John Martin, the editor of London's *Jazz News*. His treatment in the tabloids was, of course, no different from that routinely given to other visiting celebrities, but it had never before been dished out to a jazz musician.

He fared little better when the reporters turned their attention to his music. *Sketches of Spain* had just been released, and one reporter asked him if he thought that it was "really jazz." "I think so," Davis replied, and then he asked, "What do you think?" The reporter, it turned out, had never heard the record.

Davis provided fodder for controversy with his off-hand remarks to the press. "Some guy even said I didn't want to come here because I don't like the way Britishers speak," he complained to Martin. "I don't know who he was. He just came up to the stand one night and asked me. I said I didn't like the accent."[37] The remark, needless to say, kept the pot boiling on Fleet Street.

The publicity probably did him no harm at the box office. The concert at the Gaumont Cinema drew more than 7,500 fans. One of its reviewers complained that Davis was visible for no more than fifteen minutes.[38] While this was almost certainly an exaggeration, similar complaints would become familiar in the next few years.

The quintet's music with Sonny Stitt on saxophones survives, as expected, in private tapings from the Manchester concert and also from two concerts the following week on the continent, in Paris (11 October) and Stockholm (13 October). So far, only one title, *Walkin'*, has been issued on record, from the performance in Stockholm, and even it exists only on an obscure European label. The details are as follows:

Miles Davis Quintet
Miles Davis, tpt; Sonny Stitt, as, ts; Wynton Kelly, pno; Paul Chambers, b;
Jimmy Cobb, dms. Konserthuset, Stockholm, 13 October 1960
If I Were a Bell; All of You; Walkin; All Blues; Theme
(*Walkin'* issued in Europe on Bird Notes; others unissued)
Stitt plays tenor saxophone on *If I Were a Bell* and *Walkin'. No Blues* and
Green Dolphin Street also exist on tape, in incomplete versions, apparently
from this concert.

Asked about sharing the front line with an alto saxophonist after so many years with a tenor man, Davis said, "I don't think about instruments. I pick a guy for what he can do. If I like the way he plays, then he's in."[39] When Stitt plays tenor, on *If I Were a Bell* and *Walkin'*, it is surprising to hear how much things stay the same. Stitt fills Coltrane's spaces in these familiar arrangements with fast, facile bebop solos, and everything else is unaltered. When he plays alto, the instrument on which he always seemed more comfortable, the spaces he fills are more lyrical than Coltrane's, with occasional runs and phrases invoking the ghost of Parker, and the whole band responds to the difference, most noticeably in the subdued, thoughtful reading of *All Blues* at this concert. There is an hour of interesting music in these extended concert performances and much more from the other sites in Europe; they will enhance the catalog when they are finally issued.

Soon after Davis and the quintet returned to the United States, they

Frances Taylor Davis and Miles Davis emplane for Europe, 1960
(KLM Royal Dutch Airlines photo)

Sonny Stitt and Miles Davis (Jim Marshall, courtesy of *Down Beat*)

began the round of club dates that would land them in Chicago for Christmas again. In Philadelphia, Davis became the go-between for a significant meeting between Elvin Jones and John Coltrane. Jones showed up at a club where the quintet were playing one night, and Davis passed along Coltrane's message that he wanted to hire him. Through exchanges of telephone numbers for which Davis served as the intermediary, Jones was able to join Coltrane in Denver a couple of weeks later, at first sharing drumming duties with Billy Higgins in Coltrane's quartet but soon taking over the drum chair.[40] Jones became a fixture in Coltrane's band, along with McCoy Tyner, staying with him from late 1960 until 1966 and providing the undercurrent for Coltrane's greatest work. The Coltrane Quartet, with Tyner, Jones, and initially Reggie Workman on bass but soon afterward, and for several years, Jimmy Garrison, moved almost immediately into the front rank of jazz. In *Down Beat*'s Critics Poll for 1961, Coltrane was named best tenor saxophonist and best "new star" on soprano saxophone, and his band were named best "new combo." Although Davis openly hoped that Coltrane would return to his band, he quashed any real chances of that when he brought him together with Jones, who proved to be the catalyst for Coltrane's success as a bandleader.

As generous as Davis could sometimes be with people, or at least with musicians, he seemed to spend much of his time practicing what Michael Zwerin once called "his famous salty-dog act." Anecdotes about Davis's mooning of the world circulated rapidly among his fans. When the advertising manager of *Down Beat* sent him the standard letter informing him that he had won a poll and suggesting that he take out a "thank you" ad in the magazine, Davis returned the letter with a circle around "thank you" and the words "fuck you" scrawled in the margin.[41] During his Christmas engagement at a Chicago club, Don DeMicheal, then newly appointed to *Down Beat*'s staff, suggested to Davis that he should present him with the 1960 Critics Poll plaque on the stage during a set, but Davis said, "You're not gonna plug that goddamned magazine on *my* bandstand. Give it to me at the bar."[42] Around this time Davis became a fearsome figure among the secretaries at Columbia, referring to them as "white bitches."[43] For a segment of his fans, each new anecdote added lustre to the mystique surrounding him.

So, of course, did his appearance on the list of best-dressed men in *Gentlemen's Quarterly* for 1961. Along with his Ferrari, his four-storey home near the Hudson, his beautiful wife, Frances, and the other women he sometimes escorted, the sartorial honor from *GQ*, which was followed two years later by a similar citation from *Playboy*, seemed to add a crowning touch, at least in the value system of most Americans raised in the 1950s.

All the accouterments of Davis's mystique were concentrated into an anecdote recounted by Joe Goldberg: "I chanced to be in Miles' white Ferrari when he was driving it up the West Side Highway at about 105 miles per hour. Frances got very frightened and asked him to slow down. Miles gave her the perfect Milesian reply, and I doubt that Brando, or Sinatra, or even Hemingway, could have said it better: 'I'm in here too.'"[44]

Max Gordon, who owned the Village Vanguard, felt the bite of his star attraction's lifestyle more keenly than most jazz club owners. Gordon also owned the fashionable Blue Angel in downtown Manhattan, and Davis became a regular customer. "Nights when Miles wasn't playing at the Vanguard he'd bring his current girl to The Blue Angel and order Piper Heidseick champagne," Gordon recalled. "One night I told the waiter to hand him the check. He tore it in two and sent the waiter back with this message: 'Tell your boss I'll never pay a check here. Tell him he's been underpaying me at the Vanguard for years. I gotta get even somehow.'"[45]

Any hard feelings that lingered among the critical fraternity as a result of Davis's position in the controversy over free jazz at the close of 1959 were pretty well dissipated by the start of 1961. For one thing, there was a critical reaction to free jazz, a kind of backlash, that left Ornette Coleman scuffling to find work soon after he closed at the Five Spot and led him to withdraw from active playing altogether during 1963–5, although several other players whose entries into the field were less meteoric than Coleman's continued to work fairly regularly and to show the way in freeing some of jazz's formal organization. For another thing, the jazz business was just beginning to feel the pinch of an economic recession. Unlike many other recessions that come and go in jazz history, the one just beginning in 1961 was destined to last for several years, until it touched almost everyone.

Jazz clubs closed frequently, as they always have and still do, but this time they were not replaced by new clubs a month or a year later. By 1965, when the recession bottomed out, it began to look like a permanent state of affairs. Looking back, it is easy to see that the recession involved a large swath of the entertainment industry, not just the jazz clubs. Many of the more fashionable supper clubs closed too (including Max Gordon's Blue Angel, in 1963), without replacements, as the whole concept of night-time entertainment underwent revision in America. But at the time, for those closest to the jazz business, its death looked real enough to cause some soul-searching.

The recession fed the backlash to free music, as more and more commentators looked around and noted that the empty clubs were featuring young players whose music seemed to be a lot more interesting to play than to hear. Stan Getz noticed that when he returned to the United States in 1961 after three years of living in Copenhagen and playing in Europe. "When we first got back, he was starry-eyed, happy, excited, and eager to hear what had been happening in the States during his absence," Getz's wife, Monica, told Don DeMicheal. "He eventually became disappointed at what he felt was a dead-end street of pretentious experimenting and repetitious self-indulging choruses – the more pretentious the music, the more ecstatic the hipsters. In fact, hipsters had seemed to become the larger part of the audience. Many true jazz aficionados had quit coming, being confused and bored. Only old friends like Miles and Diz gave him solace and hope and worried with him about the directions of jazz."[46] For Getz, as for Gillespie and Davis, the hard times to come were discomforting but not disastrous; many other musicians, including established players like Earl Hines, Gigi Gryce, Al Haig, and Tal Farlow, would be forced out of music altogether in the next few years.

Getz's quandary on first returning to the United States might have been resolved very simply if he had joined Miles Davis, who again found himself searching for a saxophonist for the quintet. Unfortunately, both men had worked too long as leaders for them to consider joining forces, even temporarily. Instead, Davis hired Hank Mobley, a solid journeyman whose best credentials stemmed from the neo-bop bands of the second half of the 1950s, when he played in the original Jazz Messengers of Art Blakey, moved out of that group with its pianist, Horace Silver, when he formed his own group, and ended the decade back with Blakey again.

Mobley's presence in Davis's quintet, while giving it a competent, experienced soloist, imported nothing new. In that sense, Mobley further diminished the probing, experimental cast of Davis's finest band only a few years earlier. While Julian Adderley remained unreplaced, Wynton Kelly had replaced Bill Evans and now Mobley was replacing Coltrane. The parallels in these two replacements were noted by Roger Cotterrell in the English magazine *Jazz Monthly*. "As Kelly is to Evans so, to some extent, Hank Mobley is to Coltrane," he wrote. "Mobley and

Kelly have certain points in common – primarily that they are both straightforward, fairly uncomplicated players who can usually be relied on to make a workmanlike job of a solo."[47]

Although Mobley lasted in the band for a year, Davis seems to have been less than enthusiastic about his playing the whole time. One night while Mobley soloed on the stand, Davis leaned over to Joe Goldberg and said, "Any night Sonny Rollins shows up with his horn, he's got a job."[48] When Goldberg told Coltrane about Davis's remark, Coltrane just smiled and gave it the most generous interpretation imaginable. "He'd hire Sonny, he'd hire me, he'd hire all of us, just to hear us play," Coltrane said. "He's got a lot of money, and he loves to listen to music."[49]

Davis did hire Coltrane, though only temporarily, when he finally got around to making a new studio recording in March 1961, his first in a year and the only one for another sixteen months. It was also his first with his working band for more than two years, since the final session of *Kind of Blue*, and it would be the only one with the working band for another two years. Nothing shows better Davis's disaffection for the work of his bands during this period, although he submitted the quintet to on-site recordings by Columbia at concerts and in clubs in the same period. It took three studio dates to complete the recording for the LP released as *Some Day My Prince Will Come*; only on the first does the working quintet appear on its own. On the next two, Davis brought Coltrane along with him, making the band a sextet for the album's title piece at the second session and replacing Mobley with Coltrane for one title at the third. The details are as follows:

Miles Davis Quintet: Some Day My Prince Will Come
Miles Davis, tpt; Hank Mobley, ts; Wynton Kelly, pno; Paul Chambers, b;
Jimmy Cobb, dms. New York, 7 March 1961
Drad-Dog; Pfrancing [No Blues]
(both on Columbia CL 1656)

Add John Coltrane, ts, on *Some Day My Prince Will Come*. 20 March 1961
Some Day My Prince Will Come; Old Folks
(on Columbia CL 1656)

John Coltrane replaces Mobley on *Teo*; Philly Joe Jones replaces Cobb on *Blues No. 2*. 21 March 1961

31 Pfrancing 1960–2

Teo [*Neo*]; *I Thought about You*; *Blues No. 2*
(first two titles on Columbia CL 1656; *Blues No. 2* on Columbia 36278 [released 1979])
Drad-Dog is mistitled *Drag-Dog* in most references, from Jepsen on, but appears as *Drad-Dog* on both the liner and label; *Pfrancing* was issued under the title *No Blues* in subsequent recordings of live performances; *Teo* was issued under the title *Neo* in a subsequent recording.

These recording sessions are a puzzling mixture of carefully controlled, rehearsed pieces (*Pfrancing, Some Day My Prince Will Come, Old Folks, I Thought about You*) and extemporaneous head arrangements (*Drad-Dog, Teo, Blues No. 2*). Some of the puzzles will probably disappear when the whole session is finally collated; there is certainly more music from it in the vaults, and some of the issued titles are merely excerpts.

Davis seems to have used his studio time partly to work out some new ideas, as he had done for *Concierto de Aranjuez* and would do routinely a few years later. *Drad-Dog* and *Teo*, in particular, seem to be the result of editing longer takes. *Teo* catches Davis playing with a Spanish tinge, very much in the style of *Sketches of Spain*, and Coltrane follows him with a tinge that drifts eastward toward, say, Lebanon as he goes, but the whole piece seems poorly defined and incomplete. *Drad-Dog* seems even more obviously a paste-and-scissors job. Notwithstanding its boppish (but so far unexplained) title, it is a quiet ballad, without an identifiable melody – an improvisation with a theme unstated or deleted – and it stops without really ending.

These tracks show the imprint of Teo Macero, Davis's producer at Columbia for the previous two years and for many years to come. They are not the first; *Porgy and Bess*, on which Macero worked in post-production, apparently includes some post-recorded solos by Davis, and *Concierto de Aranjuez* seems to be spliced together from two or three different takes, its continuous flow an aural illusion. Now, on *Drad-Dog* and perhaps on *Teo*, Macero seems to have taken a further step, not only pasting together disparate parts, but actually selecting a part of the whole to stand alone.

The first hint about the rest of the music made at these sessions came to light in 1979, with the release of *Blues No. 2*, an extemporaneous blues at a lively tempo that spotlights the muscular drumming of Philly Joe Jones, a guest in the studio that day who sat in behind Jimmy Cobb's drums. Jones trades four-bar breaks with Davis and later follows solo choruses by Davis and Mobley with a solo of his own, but he is hardly less conspicuous when he is supporting the other players, and this performance is a belated reminder of the strength he added to Davis's bands as a regular sideman from 1955 to 1958.

The real interest of these sessions, however, comes from the set pieces that Davis introduced into the band's repertoire. *Pfrancing*, a wonderfully evocative title capturing references to Frances Davis and to a whole semantic field taking in prancing, dancing, and frantic, all of which suit it nicely, quickly became a nightly fixture under the more prosaic title *No Blues*, with its call-and-answer theme abbreviated to only a couple of bars and its tempo almost doubled. Here, at its first airing, Davis's call is echoed by Mobley in alternating bars three times, and the ensemble is stretched out for another six bars holding the last note of the call. The twelve-bar ensemble thus forms a memorable little ditty to frame the round of solos, where in later versions it is never more than a few perfunctory bars before the solos.

Old Folks is a tightly muted standard ballad very much in the style of Davis's affecting ballads for Prestige a few years earlier, and worthy of comparison to them, while *Some Day My Prince Will Come*, a waltz sung by Snow White in Walt Disney's first animated feature in 1937 (re-released in movie theatres with great acclaim in 1958), is another masterly conversion of unlikely material by Davis along the lines of *Fran Dance/Put Your Little Foot Right out* and a worthy addition to the line of lilting ballads that includes not only *Fran Dance* but also *Round Midnight*, *All of You*, *Green Dolphin Street*, and *If I Were a Bell*. Those bright ballads, conceived by Davis out of elements he heard in the work of Ahmad Jamal, were — and still are — the basis for Davis's appeal to listeners whose tastes were formed by singers like Frank Sinatra, Peggy Lee, and Sarah Vaughan, and *Some Day My Prince Will Come*, true to form, found a wide audience. It did so, needless to say, without pandering in any way.

Davis plays the original melody with more than a little respect, but his tone is ambiguous and leaves no doubt that the coming of the prince might not be such a wonderful thing. Mobley and Kelly solo after Davis, and then Davis returns to play the melody again, just as he would at the finish of a regular quintet performance, only instead of closing he sets the stage for Coltrane's explosive solo, a brawny dismembering of the fragile melody that somehow manages to be lyrical. The performance evokes the powerful interplay that Davis and Coltrane worked on for so many years, and although it is something of a postscript to those brilliant years it maintains the same high style.

When the LP was released a few months later, more than a few heads turned at the sight of the portrait of a doe-eyed woman with a Mona Lisa smile that graced its front cover. The model, it turned out, was Frances Davis. "I just got to thinking that as many albums as Negroes buy, I hadn't ever seen a Negro girl on a major album cover unless she was the artist," Davis told Alex Hailey in an interview for *Playboy* magazine. "There wasn't any harm meant – they just automatically thought about a white model and ordered one. It was my album, and I'm Frances's prince, so I suggested they use her for a model, and they did it."[50] Davis himself appeared in a black-and-white photograph on the back cover, in place of the usual liner notes, which he had been trying to get rid of for some time. "I've been trying to get Irving [Townsend, Columbia's chief of production] for years to put out these albums with no notes," Davis told Ralph J. Gleason, in an oft-quoted statement. "There's nothing to say about the music. Don't write about the music. The music speaks for itself." The back cover of *Some Day My Prince Will Come* simply named the six musicians, listed the titles played and their playing times, but gave no clue to the deployment of the tenor saxophonists on the various tracks.

With or without liner notes, Davis's albums were automatic best sellers in the jazz field and had been for some time. Columbia's biggest problem in these years was to persuade him to record often enough to keep it supplied with new albums for the marketplace. Finally, Columbia decided that if Davis would not come to it, it would go to him, and it began recording him in live performances a month after the studio sessions for *Some Day My Prince Will Come* were completed.

The quintet were scheduled to make a tour of jazz clubs in several cities that would include two weeks at the Blackhawk in San Francisco, a well-known and long-lived club, as jazz clubs go, where the previous year Riverside Records had made a successful on-the-spot recording of Thelonious Monk. For Davis's engagement there, Columbia set up recording facilities in an adjoining bar and added hours of material from Davis to its stock. These live performances were the first Davis ever knowingly made for later release on record, the extensive collection of his earlier performances, including those from Newport and the Plaza Hotel in 1958 later issued on Columbia, having all been taped incidentally, sometimes surreptitiously. That circumstance made Davis's sidemen more than a little self-conscious, according to Ralph J.

Gleason, the jazz columnist for the *San Francisco Chronicle*, whom Davis told, "They're all worried about making records with me," and then he added: "And I'm just standing here, minding my own business, being my own sweet self." But Davis was not unaffected by it either, and he kept checking on the sound quality the engineers were getting next door, or he dispatched Wynton Kelly to check on it, on the nights when recordings were being made. One result is that Davis plays long, generous solos on all the titles recorded, something that he was not always inclined to do during a regular night's work at a jazz club in these years.

When the recording equipment was not in place, he ran true to form at the Blackhawk, seldom playing the last set of the evening and never playing the Sunday matinée set. The Blackhawk, as Gleason describes it, was obviously a club where Davis felt relaxed and where he apparently knew that his absences from the stand when his sidemen were working would not cause problems for him. The owner simply shrugged, "I should complain, as long as the people come."[51] When he was avoiding the bandstand, Davis was not avoiding the people; he signed autographs and answered questions, usually with a word or two, and wandered around the club freely. He did not join the other members of his band at Jimbo's Bop City, the after-hours club where they went almost nightly after their 2 a.m. closing at the Blackhawk.[52] Instead, he got some sleep and spent the daytime hours visiting friends in the area. Gleason, a nonsmoking, nondrinking diabetic whose voluminous jazz journalism was always infectiously enthusiastic, discovered that Davis's easy manner around the Blackhawk did not mean that he had mellowed in any way. "Once he told me he had been past my house that afternoon en route to Dave Brubeck's," Gleason said. "'Why didn't you stop in?' I asked in a stereotyped social response. 'What for?' he answered with shattering frankness."[53]

His easy manner did, however, mean that Columbia could capture some good playing from him at the Blackhawk, and the amount of music it added to its catalog was considerable, as it had hoped. So far the music from the Blackhawk recordings comes to almost 112 minutes, with, surely, much more to come. The details are as follows:

Miles Davis Quintet: At the Blackhawk
Miles Davis, tpt; Hank Mobley, ts; Wynton Kelly, pno; Paul Chambers, b; Jimmy Cobb, dms. The Blackhawk, San Francisco, 14 April 1961
Walkin'; *Bye Bye Blackbird*; *All of You*; *No Blues*; *Bye Bye* [*The Theme*]
(all on Columbia CL 1669)

Same personnel, same place, 15 April 1961
Well You Needn't; Fran Dance; So What; Oleo; If I Were a Bell; Neo [Teo]
(all on Columbia CL 1670)

Same personnel, same place, 21 April 1961
Green Dolphin Street
(on Columbia 13811 [1977])

Same personnel, same place, 22 April 1961
Round Midnight
(on Columbia KC2 36472 [1981])
Hank Mobley does not play on *All of You* and *If I Were a Bell*; Columbia CL
1669 also includes Wynton Kelly, unaccompanied, playing *Love I've Found
You*; both *Walkin'* and *Round Midnight* are followed by a few bars of *The
Theme* tagged on to the end, and *So What* is followed by a few bars of *No Blues*.

While Davis plays at great length on these performances, Mobley gets to
play much less. Not only does he sit out on *All of You* and *If I Were a
Bell*, where Davis had occasionally asked other tenor saxophonists to sit
out in the past, but he also does not solo on *No Blues*, *Bye Bye*, and *Well
You Needn't*, where the saxophonist, under ordinary circumstances,
would be expected to solo. Mobley's solos were apparently edited out,
but Wynton Kelly's solos are preserved on every track. On *Well You
Needn't*, Mobley's solo may be missing because he did not know this
Monk composition, as his ragged playing in the ensemble suggests.
    Generally, the performances are interesting verions of mainly famil-
iar fare in Davis's repertoire, noticeably freer and more expansive than
the original studio versions. Davis makes allusions to other pieces,
playing snatches of *Bye Bye Blackbird* in the first chorus of his
improvisation in *So What* and a few bars of *I Get a Kick out of You* in his
solo on *If I Were a Bell*, something he does very infrequently in his
studio solos. Two of the compositions recorded only a month earlier
have been added to the working repertoire, another relatively unusual
occurrence, and both are retitled – *Pfrancing* as *No Blues*, and *Teo* and
Neo – even though the originals were not yet available and Davis could
have easily standardized the titles on the two releases if he had wanted
to. The second of these new pieces, *Neo*, receives a performance far
superior to the one in the studio a month earlier, which was tentative
and ill-defined. Here, after a slightly awkward opening bar by Wynton
Kelly (who is obviously reading from the lead sheet), the rhythm section

finds its way much more confidently, and both Kelly and Davis end up taking two long solos.

When the two LPs of this material were released together in the fall, they were packaged identically except for the color of the print on the front covers, which was nearly illegible on the black background of the cover photo. The near-identity of the two packages caused no end of confusion among buyers, who had to discern the words *Friday Night* on one and *Saturday Night* on the other. The cover photo again featured Frances Davis, this time looking worried behind the shadowy figure of her husband, in what looks like a still from an old Hollywood melodrama.

A little less than a month after the Blackhawk engagement, Columbia recorded Davis again in a live performance, this time in New York, with his quintet and the Gil Evans Orchestra at Carnegie Hall. The concert was a benefit for the Africa Relief Foundation, and, true to the temper of the times, the sidewalks outside Carnegie Hall were picketed by protesters carrying placards declaring "AFRICA FOR THE AFRICANS" and "FREEDOM NOW." The Africa Relief Foundation, a nonprofit organization raising funds for goods to be sent to Tanganyika and Zanzibar (later united as Tanzania), was viewed by the picketers as a tool for perpetuating colonialism.

Davis and the other musicians began the concert unaware of the political controversy out on the streets, but they soon learned about it. As Davis finished stating the melody of *Some Day My Prince Will Come*, the third composition on the program, Max Roach and another protester walked to the stage carrying placards and sat on the edge holding them up to the audience. Davis faltered and then stopped playing and walked into the wings. Roach and the other man were finally persuaded to leave the hall. After a long interval, with the audience at first restless and then almost ready to give up hope, Davis returned and, without a word, kicked off the opening bars of *No Blues* with the quintet.

When a reporter for the *New York Post* asked Davis about the incident he snapped, "I don't know what Max was doing. Ask *him*." Roach offered this explanation: "I was told some things about the Foundation that I thought Miles should know. Some people tried to contact him but they couldn't get to him. I went on stage because I wanted Miles to be aware of these things."[54] Roach spent much of the rest of the decade as an activist in black nationalist and civil rights causes, playing jazz and recording infrequently. His most ambitious record was the *Freedom*

Now Suite (recorded in 1960 for Candid, reissued in 1980 as Columbia 36390), its title bearing a reminder of the placard he carried onto the Carnegie Hall stage at Davis's concert.

Musically, if not politically, Davis's Carnegie Hall concert was unblemished. It was an enormously ambitious undertaking, and the reviews were unanimously enthusiastic. The recording, released about a year later, somehow misses the impact that the concert, by all accounts, had. One cause of the discrepancy may be the imperfect balance of the sound recording, but another cause, perhaps more significant, is the heavy editing of the master tape. The recording recapitulates the concert only very indirectly, and the transformation from concert to record remains a second-rate document of one of Davis's greatest critical successes. The details are as follows:

Miles Davis at Carnegie Hall. New York, 19 May 1961
Miles Davis Quintet: Miles Davis, tpt; Hank Mobley, ts; Wynton Kelly, pno; Paul Chambers, b; Jimmy Cobb, dms
Gil Evans Orchestra: Ernie Royal, Bernie Glow, Johnny Coles, Louis Mucci, tpt; Jimmy Knepper, Dick Hixon, Frank Rehak, tbn; Julius Watkins, Paul Ingraham, Bob Swisshelm, frh; Bill Barber, tba; Romeo Penque, Jerome Richardson, Eddie Caine, Bob Tricarico, Danny Bank, woodwinds; Janet Putnam, harp; Paul Chambers, b; Jimmy Cobb, dms; Bob Rosengarden, perc; Gil Evans, arr, cond
Orchestral introduction (orch); *So What* (quintet and orch at beginning); *Spring Is Here* (Davis, Kelly, and orch); *No Blues* (quintet); *Oleo* (quintet); *Some Day My Prince Will Come* (Davis, Kelly, Chambers, Cobb); *The Meaning of the Blues* (orch); *Lament* (orch); *New Rhumba* (orch)
(all on Columbia CL 1812)
The version of *New Rhumba* on the record may have been recorded later and spliced in; some discographies list the re-recording date as 27 July 1962, but by then this record had been released (Priestley 1982).

The concert, insofar as it can be reconstructed, included several additional compositions and also presented them in a different order, with longer versions of *No Blues* and perhaps some of the other quintet performances. No tape of the concert has shown up in private collections, no program was distributed on the occasion, and, as usual, no announcements were made from the stage, so that the members of the audience, including the professional reviewers, were uncertain of some of the titles played, but the critics' descriptions were fuller than they might otherwise have been because of the significance of the event itself, and those descriptions along with what can be gleaned from the record allow a tentative reconstruction. The critics' accounts do not, of course, completely agree. Describing Davis's stage manner, John S. Wilson, writing in the *New York Times*, says, "Although he has often been charged with treating his audiences disdainfully, he not only smiled on a couple of occasions but acknowledged applause with a quick glance over the footlights and a slight nod of his head."[55] Whitney Balliett, however, reviewing the same concert in the *New Yorker*, says, "Davis never lets his audiences know that he knows that they're there; he neither speaks to them nor looks at them nor even plays to them."[56] Balliett's and Wilson's accounts of the music played, along with that of George T. Simon in the *Herald Tribune*,[57] suggest the following program, in this order:

Orchestral introduction (orch)
So What (quintet and orch at beginning)
Spring Is Here (Davis, Kelly, and orch)
Someday My Prince Will Come (quintet)
No Blues (quintet)
The Meaning of the Blues (orch)
Lament (orch)
New Rhumba (orch)

Oleo (quintet)
perhaps *All Blues* (quintet)
Saeta (Davis and orch)
Solea (Davis and orch)
Concierto de Aranjuez (Davis and orch)

The listing of *All Blues* is nothing more than a guess based on Simon's description of the piece as "a groovy, middle-tempoed blues." The other titles are quite firm, and the order shown cannot be far off, although there might have been an additional quintet title.

Some Day My Prince Will Come includes little more than a recitation of the melody by Davis, which may be all he played before he was distracted by Roach's protest, but the truncated version as it stands hardly fits Simon's description as "a passionately swinging waltz."

The issued version of *No Blues* lasts almost twelve minutes, but its climax has been deleted in spite of Simon's praise for it as "a fast blues climaxed by exciting two-bar challenges between Davis and drummer Jimmy Cobb," one of the highlights of the concert.

Some justifications for doctoring the original tape so heavily are not hard to guess. One was to improve the quality of the sound, which would also account for the post-concert re-recording of *New Rhumba*, spliced into the master tape in place of the version played at the concert. Some of the high frequencies of the orchestral playing are fuzzy in *The Meaning of the Blues* and *Lament*, played here as a continuous suite with *New Rhumba*, as they were in the original recording on *Miles Ahead* (1957), and on *New Rhumba* they might conceivably have been worse. Another reason was to fit the material onto a single LP. Not only were double-album sets rare at the time (although the Blackhawk sessions came out on two LPs), but *Saeta, Solea,* and the *Concierto* were probably felt to be too recently recorded, with *Sketches of Spain* only two years old. However, *Some Day My Prince Will Come* was only one year old and was released in the new, but brief, concert version. But however cogent Davis and Teo Macero's reasons might have seemed for altering the tape of the Carnegie Hall concert, one has to second-guess their validity. From the tape of a magnificent concert, Columbia managed to release a moderately interesting LP. The LP might have been commensurate with the concert if it had retained the integrity of the original program and allowed the immediacy of the playing to compensate for the extra length of some of the compositions and the imperfect sound.

The LP that resulted has its merits. Chief among them is a driving version of *So What*, the playing of the quintet clearly invigorated by the setting. Among its delights is the aggressive drumming of Jimmy Cobb, sounding less docile than he had become in recent outings and, in fact, more like Philly Joe Jones, whose style he favored when he first replaced Jones in Davis's bands. *So What* also includes Hank Mobley's best solo on any recording he made while he was in the Miles Davis Quintet, a confident, inventive solo that holds together from start to finish.

The only new writing in the concert, apart from the orchestral introduction which lasts just under a minute, is *Spring Is Here*, a beautiful voicing by Gil Evans for Davis's reading of the ballad. Although the entrance of Wynton Kelly (or perhaps Evans, on piano) as Davis's accompanist on the last chorus where the orchestra is expected suggests that the arrangement was not quite finished when the concert day arrived, the rest of the arrangement is a good example of Evans's ability to create motion with wind instruments, leaving the rhythm instruments in secondary roles. The harmonization of Evans's arrangement was shaped by Bill Evans's recording of *Spring Is Here* with his piano trio (on Riverside RLP 12-315),[58] and out of that sketch Gil Evans built an arrangement for a twenty-one-piece orchestra that sounds hardly less compact than the trio version. Gil Evans's *Spring Is Here* exists only in this concert version, and that alone almost vindicates the release of the LP in its received form, if justification is really needed.

After this spurt of well-documented activity in the spring of 1961 – in the studio making *Some Day My Prince Will Come* in March, at the Blackhawk in April, and at Carnegie Hall in May – Davis went through another long period, lasting more than a year, of relative inactivity, from which no permanent transcripts of his playing survive. He stayed close to New York, working sporadically with Gil Evans on a new project for Columbia, their fourth. He worked occasionally with the quintet, but the tenor saxophone chair remained unsettled. Hank Mobley stayed for a while, without getting much gratification from the job or giving much enthusiasm to it. Rocky Boyd replaced Mobley late in 1961, and soon after that he vanished.[59] One of the more mysterious figures in an art form peopled by them, Boyd had been on the fringes of the jazz world for a couple of years, occasionally seen in the company of John Coltrane, notably on a couple of Coltrane's visits to Boston, which may be Boyd's home city. In 1961, Boyd seemed prepared to make a breakthrough in New York. He led a quintet with Kinney Dorham at the Jazz Gallery in the spring and made a recording as a leader with a group that included Dorham, pianist Walter Bishop, who had recommended him for the record date, bassist Ron Carter, and drummer Pete LaRoca (reissued under Dorham's name in 1974 on Muse 5053). The record reveals Boyd as a competent, apparently confident, tenor player who has learned several lessons from Coltrane, and it gives a promising start for a relative newcomer, but there is nothing else. During his time with Miles Davis, no records were made and no tapes of their club dates have turned up. Early in 1962, Boyd left New York as a member of Philly Joe Jones's quintet, and he has seldom played publicly since.

Davis played frequently at the Village Vanguard, and at his request the performer who shared the bill with him was Shirley Horn, the singer-pianist from Washington, DC, whose first record impressed him immensely. But he had little enthusiasm for his night's work. Joe Goldberg described his laconic performance on a Sunday afternoon around this time. "From various parts of the room, the members of the group walked casually toward the bandstand," Goldberg wrote. "Davis materialized from a dark corner of the room where he had been talking to the small son of his bassist Paul Chambers. Resplendent in a tight white suit and green sportshirt, he strolled to the piano and, cigarette in mouth, played a few chords. A waiter handed him his trumpet. He stepped to the microphone, without any perceptible word to the other musicians, assumed the familiar introvert stance, horn pointed toward the floor, and began to play *Some Day My Prince Will Come*. The tight sound that prompted British theater critic Kenneth Tynan to refer to him as a musical lonely-hearts club was heard briefly ... and the audience applauded wildly. By the time the applause had subsided, Davis was off the stand."[60]

For many members of the audience, even a brief appearance was enough; it was hardly new to his more experienced fans, although Davis had usually played at least a full chorus before moving to the back corner of the room in years past. Some fans inevitably complained. Davis's absence had been easier to tolerate when Coltrane was left on the bandstand in his stead, but Hank Mobley or Rocky Boyd could scarcely make up the difference, as Davis himself knew too well.

As Davis's performances became more offhand, more people began resenting him. They could hardly be expected to know, because neither Davis nor anyone who knew him ever talked about it, that he was suffering physically most of the time now, from pains that shot through his joints and left him numb and aching, especially in his left leg. He refused to show it, neither wincing when the pain hit nor limping when his hip stiffened. Instead, he played a few notes and stood in the shadows behind the audience, leaving them to draw whatever conclusions they pleased.

The pains were nothing new to Davis – only their severity was. For several years an arthritic knuckle had been visible on his right hand, the hand used to manipulate the valves of the trumpet; that knuckle was the most obvious sign of his affliction and would remain the only one until about 1981, when, returning to performing after a long layoff, every part of him, from his sunken cheeks to his shuffling gait, showed his pain. But that was almost two decades away, and in the meantime he kept up a stoic facade, as he had, in fact, from his adolescence on. For his disease was not recent. It is called "sickle-cell anemia," a congenital disease that afflicts members of the black race only, and he was born with it. When Davis first felt its effects in his joints, mildly, as a youngster, he started the lifelong pattern of working out in a gymnasium. "The reason I started doing it was to make my legs stronger," he said,[61] and his legs, at the hip joints, were most seriously affected. Exercise of the kind Davis has always done – skipping rope, punching bags, shadow boxing – speeds the circulation of the blood and thus may postpone the severity of the sickle-cell symptoms.

Davis's case is described medically as "mild," but he has felt pain for years. He is not alone. In the United States, one black baby in 400 suffers from it, and for many of those, the disease is acute, not mild, causing destruction of red blood cells, jaundice, and critical pains in the abdomen, back, and bones and leading to stunted or slow growth and usually early death. One American black in 10 carries the recessive gene for the disease.[62] In equatorial Africa, where it originated, the figures are probably much higher.

The disfiguring symptoms are caused by a physical mutation visible only under a microscope. Some red blood cells, normally saucer-shaped, are crescent-shaped, like "sickles" in the description of the rural Illinois doctor who identified the disease in 1904 and gave it the name that has stuck to it ever since. The sickling effect, in turn, results from defective hemoglobin, the protein in red blood cells responsible for carrying oxygen to all parts of the body, which lacks one of the hundreds of amino acids that do the work. The disease affects black people exclusively because the missing amino acid proved in some undetermined way to be a defense against malaria. After hundreds of generations in equatorial Africa, carriers of the sickle-shaped cell increased because they survived malaria epidemics, but away from malaria-infested environments, the defective cell becomes not only dysfunctional but also a crippler and a killer in its own right.

The elongated blood cells tend to become trapped in the small blood vessels of the body, blocking the flow of blood and causing local death due to oxygen deficiencies. In acutely affected children, the high concentration of defective cells affects both vital organs and joints, but in mild cases the cells affect joints mainly, especially the upper arm and hip, causing arthritis.[63] By 1962, when Miles Davis turned 36, the deterioration of his hip joints and other parts of his body was so advanced that he felt some pain all the time.

His music inevitably began to show the effects. He finally returned to the Columbia studios in late July 1962, more than sixteen months after his last studio date. Instead of returning with his quintet, which still did not include a regular saxophonist, he was back with Gil Evans and a large orchestra, but this time the result, perhaps predictably given the highly commercial impetus that lay behind the music, was something of a shambles. The recording that finally resulted was called *Quiet Nights*, and it attempted to cover the current craze for a Brazilian samba form called the bossa nova. Stan Getz started the trend with an album called *Jazz Samba* (on Verve) recorded in February, in which he and acoustic guitarist Charlie Byrd introduced some beautiful melodies by a Brazilian songwriter named Antonio Carlos Jobim. The album became an instant success, and in a branch of the music industry where successes of any kind were suddenly few and far between the race was on in several quarters to cover the same territory. Dozens of jazz-samba LPS were produced in the next months, none of them more successful than Getz's own; Getz even scored popular hits with an instrumental version of Jobim's *Desafinado* from the first album and a vocal version of *The Girl from Ipanema*, sung by Astrud Gilberto and including Jobim on piano, from *Getz/Gilberto* (Verve v-8545), his fourth bossa nova LP in a little more than a year and perhaps the best of them all. *Time* magazine reported at the beginning of 1963 that there were at least forty bossa nova albums on the market.[64]

Miles Davis and Gil Evans's entry into bossa nova began soon after Getz's first album was released, but they never completed the LP, and it was released, incomplete, only after another year had passed. It amounted to less than twenty-one minutes of almost motionless music filled out with another six minutes by Davis and rhythm trio. Compounding the half-hearted music of *Quiet Nights* were anonymous liner notes apologizing gratuitously for "Miles the man and Miles the dedicated and instinctive musician" – apologizing for his stage manner and the infrequency of his recordings – and claiming, with bald chicanery, that *Quiet Nights* "has been three years in the making, and is most likely the first 'Bossa Nova' music recorded in the country." It was not the first by several months; it was not the best by an even wider margin. The details are as follows:

Miles Davis with the Gil Evans Orchestra: Quiet Nights
Miles Davis, tpt; Steve Lacy, ss; other members of the orchestra unidentified; Gil Evans, arr, cond. New York, 27 July 1962
Corcovado [*Quiet Nights/Slow Samba*]; *Aos pes da Cruz* [*Slow Samba*]
(both on Columbia CL 2106)

Similar personnel, same place, 13 August 1962
Song #1; *Wait till You See Her*
(both on Columbia CL 2106)

Some discographies list *New Rhumba* on the July session and give its issue details as *Miles Davis at Carnegie Hall* (Columbia CL 1812), but Brian Priestley (1982) notes that this LP was issued before the July recording date.

The music lacks the bright lyricism that gave bossa nova its charm and made it interesting in other hands, especially Stan Getz's. The arrangements seem to be little more than sketches, and they are played without any real conviction. *Song #1* builds a dramatic setting quite effectively, but its foreground remains empty. *Aos pes da Cruz* finds Davis noodling over an indiscriminate hum from the orchestra. Even *Corcovado*, one of Jobim's most striking melodies, falls flat in the brief, dirge-like treatment it gets here. On the issued take, *Corcovado*'s length is doubled by splicing onto it an alternate take of *Aos pes da Cruz*, and while the splicing is done so cleverly as to seem almost seamless the expedient adds nothing. The LP is mood music with no discernible mood, and neither Davis nor Evans was satisfied.

Before they could return to the studio for the remaining session, which would be no more successful, Davis and Evans collaborated on another, even stranger, recording project for Columbia. The managers, searching for a gimmick to bolster sales in their jazz department, came up with the idea of putting together a Christmas jazz album and commissioned their leading jazz artists to contribute one track each. Davis, understandably nonplussed, finally found a solution of sorts. He and Evans had spent some hours listening to an LP of winsome, jazzy vocals by a man named Bob Dorough. The LP, entitled *Devil May Care* (reissued in 1976 as *Yardbird Suite*, Bethlehem BCP-6023), had been around since 1957. It attracted a small but enthusiastic coterie of listeners at the time, and Davis first heard it by chance while visiting a friend. He liked it well enough to borrow it and play it for Evans. Its showiest tune is *Charles Yardbird Parker Was His Name*, Dorough's vocalization of *Yardbird Suite*, but it also includes a clever original called *Devil May Care* and several offbeat ballads, notably Hoagy Carmichael's *Baltimore Oriole* and Duke Ellington's *I Don't Mind*. The whole thing is sung and played with the kind of whimsical originality that, then as now, either wins over its listeners immediately or leaves them cold.

Davis was won over, and when he was faced with the necessity of coming up with a Christmas song he tracked down Dorough, then living in California, and called him up. Dorough, who had spent years on the fringe of the jazz and entertainment worlds in New York, Paris, and now Los Angeles, supporting himself by doing musical odd jobs in the long wait between club dates, could hardly believe – or readily understand – the gravelly voice at the other end of the line talking about Christmas carols in July. He remembers Davis exasperatedly asking, "What the fuck am I supposed to play for them? *White Christmas?*"[65]

He enjoined Dorough to write a song for him called *Blue Xmas*, and Dorough arrived in New York in August with an outline for that song and a couple of others under his arm for a date with Davis at the Columbia studio. The details are as follows:

Miles Davis with Bob Dorough
Miles Davis, tpt; Frank Rehak, tbn; Wayne Shorter, ts; Paul Chambers, b; Jimmy Cobb, dms; William Correa (Willie Bobo), bongos; Bob Dorough, vcl; Gil Evans, arr. New York, 21 August 1962.
Blue Xmas (To Whom It May Concern); *Nothing Like You*
(*Blue Xmas* on Columbia CL 1893, reissued on CBS [Fr] 62637; *Nothing Like You* on Columbia CL 2732 [1967])

Omit Dorough. Same place, 23 August 1962
Devil May Care
(on CBS [Fr] 62637 and Columbia C 32035 [1973])
A few notes on piano, by either Dorough or Evans, are heard at the beginning of *Blue Xmas*.

The small band assembled to play Evans's arrangements of Dorough's tunes includes Frank Rehak, a solid studio musician and capable jazz player who often played in Evans's studio orchestras; William Correa, known a little better by his stage name, Willie Bobo, who was probably the percussionist in the *Quiet Nights* band; and Wayne Shorter, still committed to Blakey's Jazz Messengers, who filled in because Davis's working band lacked a saxophonist. (Wynton Kelly's absence is not unusual, because Evans's arrangements for Davis had never included a piano.)

Blue Xmas is handsomely arranged, with effective ensemble voicings for the three horns and the bongos, obbligatos by Davis around Dorough's vocal, and a full solo chorus for Shorter that is worthy of, and indeed all but indistinguishable from, Coltrane. All of this can hardly hide the fact that *Blue Xmas* is an almost unsingable muddle of sophomoric cynicism. Dorough, an effective, quirky singer well versed in handling unusual lyrics, is stymied by couplets like these:

It's a time when the greedy
Give a dime to the needy ...
Lots of hungry, homeless children in your own backyards
While you're very, very, very busy addressing twenty
    zillion Christmas cards ...

(Dorough does not have to bear full blame for the lyric; Davis is listed as the co-composer.) Most seriously, the dark sentiments of the song simply ring false when intoned in Dorough's huckleberry talking-singing style.

Nothing Like You, the other new song he brought with him, is more in his line. Subtitled *An Extravagant Love Song* when Dorough finally got a chance to record it on his own in 1976 (on his own label, Laissez-Faire 2), the lyric, by Dorough's occasional collaborator Fran Landesman, piles up praise for the lover ("Nothing like you has ever been seen before / Nothing like you existed in days of yore...") until it amasses a heap of euphoria. In Evans's arrangement, Dorough sings from start to finish over chords held by the three horns, with no instrumental breaks at all. The brief recording made an unexpected, and unexplained, appearance as a filler at the end of an LP by Davis's 1967 quintet (*Sorcerer*), a context so alien to its high spirits that it has furrowed listeners' brows ever since.

The most successful use of Dorough's music by Davis and Evans came on *Devil May Care*, the bright song from Dorough's Bethlehem LP which, unluckily for Dorough, dispenses with his lyric altogether and is played as a straight, uptempo instrumental. Dorough's original arrangement had featured a trumpeter prominently, and Evans's arrangement capitalizes on that by turning it into a real romp for Davis, who plays variations on the melody, and also for Shorter, who sounds completely confident on his chorus as Davis's saxophonists seldom had since Coltrane.

More than two months passed before Davis and Evans returned to the studios to continue their work on *Quiet Nights*, but in the interim, almost incredibly, they had done nothing at all to strengthen the concept they were working on, and the results were, if anything, even more insipid. The details are as follows:

Miles Davis with the Gil Evans Orchestra: Quiet Nights
Miles Davis, tpt; orchestra unidentified except for Ernie Royal, tpt; Frank
Rehak, tbn; Jimmy Buffington, John Barrows, frh; Janet Putnam, harp; Jimmy
Cobb, dms. New York, 6 November 1962
Once Upon a Summertime; Song #2
(both on Columbia CL 2106)
Most discographies list Elvin Jones, perc, but similarities between the bongo
playing on *Nothing Like You* (recorded August 1962) and on *Once Upon a
Summertime* suggest that the player could be William Correa.

Song #2 consists of a twelve-bar phrase, which is repeated by the
orchestra several times, and Davis, sounding small on muted trumpet,
playing the same phrase once; the whole performance lasts about one
and a half minutes. *Once Upon a Summertime* somehow fails to
become bossa nova at all in Evans's arrangement, and the bongo player
heard patting away behind the orchestra seems to be playing a different
arrangement from the others. (Two years later Evans tried again with
Once Upon a Summertime, including it among his arrangements for
vocalist Astrud Gilberto on a Verve pop album [v-8643]; Gilberto, who
scored some bossa nova hits with Stan Getz by projecting innocence in a
frail, off-key voice, projects little more than sour notes on Evans's
arrangement.)

Quiet Nights was far from finished in any real sense, but Davis and
Evans gave up on it. They did not return to the studios either to revise or
extend or augment what they had already recorded. They would
probably have forgotten it completely if Columbia had not released it
the following year.

The critical response was predictable. Leonard Feather placed the
blame for its release squarely on the company; "Columbia, despairing of
ever luring Davis and Evans back into a studio together," he wrote,
"scraped the bottom of its corporate barrel and came up with an LP called
Quiet Nights."[66] Others saw in it all the worst tendencies of their work
together. It "exposed the partnership's weaknesses," Max Harrison
said,[67] and Martin Williams made the same point less tersely: "Evans
has frequently provided a fascinating and effective setting for Davis's
improvisations. On the other hand, it seems to me that Evans does not
utilize the rhythmic idiom of modern jazz. And in his approach there is
the implicit danger that one may end up providing only a succession of
beefed-up, quasi-impressionist color-harmonies and background for

Davis's horn, a danger which is fully encountered in some selections of the languid Davis-Evans LP called *Quiet Nights*."[68] Williams's criticism seems to lay the blame unfairly on Evans, and both he and Harrison imply that the very existence of *Quiet Nights* somehow tarnishes the previous collaborations, but regardless of the details their overall impression was unanimously seconded.

"They should have never released it. It was just half an album," Evans said, and then, typically, he qualified even that mild complaint: "But I guess they had to."[69] Davis was not so mild. He refused to talk to Teo Macero for two and a half years. When Gregg Hall asked him why, he said: "'Cause he fucked up *Quiet Nights* ... In the studio he was busy looking at the score, saying, 'Jesus, you use these chords.' I said, 'Man, just record it and don't worry about no chords.' You know what I mean, instead of looking at the score, he should have just brought out the sound. He fucked it up." Davis complained to Goddard Lieberson, Columbia's president, but he backed off when Lieberson asked him if he wanted Macero fired.[70]

Macero continued producing for Columbia, including some of Davis's records. "I was working on his projects as if he were walking in the door every day," Macero says. "Records just kept coming out. I was sending him the records, but if I got a response or not was immaterial. I didn't care because I knew they were right and I knew he would like them."[71] But for the time being, Macero had little contact with Davis's projects. From the time of the second session for *Quiet Nights*, in November 1962, until late in October 1966, a period only two weeks less than four years, Davis recorded only three titles – one afternoon's work – in Columbia's New York studios, where Macero was stationed. In the same period, Columbia released five LPs by Miles Davis's bands, and CBS affiliates in Germany and Japan released two more, but apart from those three tracks – about half an LP – all the music was recorded either at live performances or in Columbia's Los Angeles studios. Macero is credited as producer on three of the seven LPs.

Davis's inability to turn out recordings that came close to the level he had maintained since he first signed with Columbia in 1955 was now obvious. Since the pair of LPs that had been put together from the Blackhawk engagement, Columbia had offered Davis's fans only the disappointing edition of the Carnegie Hall concert, one track of Christmas humbug, and some motionless bossa nova. Stretched out over a period of two years, those releases provided little sustenance for Davis's following. His personal appearances, which continued to be lethargic and became even more infrequent, gave them even less. Inured by success and bothered by pain, Davis seemed indifferent to fans and foes alike. At the beginning of 1963, the year in which Davis would turn 37, he appeared to be ready to assume the mantle of elder statesman, along with Dizzy Gillespie, Thelonious Monk, and his other mentors from the bebop revolution, or perhaps even to join Sonny Rollins in premature semi-retirement.

As it turned out, he did neither. His resolve to keep on playing at the head of his own working band beat back his indifference when he faced what might have been the final crisis. His rhythm section, the only stable element in his band for the past two years, quit the quintet together at the close of 1962. By then, their departure seemed little more than a formality. Because of the sporadic bookings with Davis, they had already set themselves up as the Wynton Kelly Trio for some club dates and record sessions. They simply decided to stop being a splinter group and work full-time as the Wynton Kelly Trio, sometimes collaborating with guitarist Wes Montgomery in bookings where they received equal billing. As a trio, they were well known, well established, and very good – much better, in fact, than they appeared to be in most of their recent work with Davis, which had been suffused by stale familiarity.

For Davis, their departure compounded his immediate problems. Now he needed to recruit not merely a saxophonist, as he had almost semi-annually since Coltrane's departure in 1961, but a whole band. More than that, their resignations finally severed the links with the bands with which he had made his finest music. All three men had been associated with him for so long that their presence was taken for granted, not only by the fans but by Davis. Faced with deteriorating health and, at least as crucial, with the kind of complacency born of commercial success – which seemed to cling to him even when he was giving less than his best efforts – he might easily have coasted, headlining concert packages with other 'all stars' when he chose to and devising recording projects with Gil Evans and others.

Instead, he set about rebuilding his band. It would not be easy, starting from scratch, and it would not be fast, but in less than two years he would be leading a new band in a new style that many observers would laud as a rival for his quintet and sextet of the 1950s. Certainly it would be the best small band in the land. In the interim, he had to shake off his complacency and go through a period unlike any he had been through since 1954–5, a period of actively scouting young musicians, aggressively recruiting them for his band, even when it caused some friction with his old colleagues such as Jackie McLean and Art Blakey, and firing men who did not have the mettle he was looking for. It proved an effective antidote for everything that ailed him, as piece by piece, musician by musician, he inched toward the new order, in his band and in his music.

10

So Near, So Far
1963–4

Art forms require [father figures] just as much as people do, usually opting for innovators who are also guardians of tradition, creative yet holding a watching brief for the past. Louis Armstrong was the first, then Duke Ellington ... To suggest that Miles Davis has now taken over – from Ellington more than anybody else – will stir up protest, but only from jazz fans who are blind to both his innate conservatism and his revolutionary fervour.   Charles Fox

The defection of the rhythm trio at the end of 1962 seemed to catch Davis by surprise. They had given their notice – had in fact indicated that they were planning to leave together months before – and he had ignored it, assuming they would show up to work with him now just as they had so many times before. Partly to give them more work, he had accepted several bookings in eastern cities for January and in California for February, March, and April, starting at the Blackhawk in San Francisco.

When the commitments had to be fulfilled he found himself without a band. He failed to appear for the first engagement, a weekend booking in Philadelphia, and the promoter sued him for expenses, eventually winning a settlement of $8,000. He canceled the next engagement in Detroit at the last minute, and the promoter there also launched a suit for expenses. He tried to persuade the rhythm section to return for a concert in St. Louis, and he showed up for it himself, claiming that it was the absence of Wynton Kelly and Paul Chambers that forced him to cancel, but the promoters there launched a suit against him too.

As the opening date for his engagement at the Blackhawk neared, he faced the fact that he would never be able to coax the rhythm trio to rejoin him, and he telephoned the owner just a few days before the date to postpone the opening by a week. Davis then got down to the real business of trying to assemble a new band.

Ironically, the saxophone chair was the only one more or less settled. For a club date in New York at the end of the year, Davis had used a young alto player named Frank Strozier, a brilliant technician whose style derived from Charlie Parker's, although Strozier was conversant with everything after Parker as well. He invited him to join the band for the California tour, making a start on the recruiting job.

Davis soon discovered that in hiring Strozier he had tapped a small network of able, young musicians who hailed from Memphis, Tennessee. Strozier eagerly recommended a piano player, Harold Mabern, a high-school friend who had left Memphis with him for Chicago in 1954, when Strozier was 17 and Mabern 18, played beside him there in a band called MJT+3, organized by Walter Perkins, a Chicago drummer, and moved to New York with him in 1959.

The new bassist came highly recommended by everyone Davis asked. He was Ron Carter, a Detroiter like Paul Chambers. Carter had earned a bachelor's degree from the Eastman School of Music in Rochester, New York, and arrived in New York to take his master's degree from the Manhattan School of Music in 1960–1. He kept busy working as a freelancer in pit bands and orchestras as well as jazz groups. He had toured Europe for three weeks with Julian Adderley's band, primarily as the accompanist for Adderley's regular bassist, Sam Jones, when he played a cello feature. After graduating in June 1961, he gained attention playing with Randy Weston, Herbie Mann, Bobby Timmons, and Thelonious Monk.

Carter was working regularly at the Half Note in a quartet led by Art Farmer and Jim Hall, with Ben Riley on drums, when Davis approached him. Carter turned him down because he felt committed to Farmer and Hall, but Davis went to Farmer and persuaded him to let Carter join his band that night at the New York try-out. "It was the most important turning-point of my career," Carter told Louis-Victor Mialy, "and maybe of my life." Like Strozier, he was 25 when he joined Davis's band in the first months of 1963.

Davis surrounded himself not only with a complement of new men, but with men who were more than a decade younger than he was. It was a striking change of direction for him. For the New York try-out of the new band before heading west, Davis borrowed Jackie McLean's drummer, a 17-year-old whiz kid from Boston named Tony Williams. Williams could not join Davis for the West Coast tour because of his commitments with McLean, but Davis knew that Williams was the drummer he wanted for his band.

During the try-out, Davis expanded the band to a sextet, adding tenor saxophonist George Coleman, who had been playing regularly with organist Wild Bill Davis in one of the many organ-tenor duos that had found favor in bars at the time. Coleman, who had played John Coltrane's tenor in some late-night sets by Davis's bands a few years before, was less polished than Strozier and Carter, and more emotive, playing ebullient jazz with a heavy tone that could hold its own night after night alongside a Hammond organ. He also was part of the Memphis connection, having attended high school with Strozier and Mabern, who probably recommended him to Davis. He eventually found favor with Davis as they never did, outlasting both of them in Davis's band. (Two other members of the Memphis group were trumpeter Booker Little, one year younger than Strozier, and pianist Phineas Newborn, five years older; their continuing presence in jazz might have elevated Memphis as a modern jazz breeding ground comparable to Detroit a decade earlier, but Little died of uremia in 1961 when he was 23 and Newborn was hampered by psychiatric problems that prevented him from working regularly and fulfilling his enormous potential.)

When Davis reached California, he recruited Frank Butler, a Los Angeles freelancer, as his drummer. With so many changes after such a lengthy period of relative stability, Davis found the adjustments hard to take. He felt uncomfortable soloing over Mabern's accompaniment. He also felt uneasy about extending the solo space to accommodate the extra horn. "I think what he really wanted was a quintet," Coleman told Andrew Sussman, "'cause he used to always complain about the lengthy solos. And what he would do, he'd say (in a whisper), 'Hey, Frank, go tell George he's playin' too long'; and then he'd come to me and say the same thing – 'Tell Frank he's playin' too long.'"[1] Under these circumstances, the sextet could not last very long.

Near the end of the Los Angeles engagement, Davis was scheduled to record in the Columbia studios, but he used only Ron Carter and Frank Butler at the recording session. George Coleman turned up on a title issued several years later and probably played on the other titles which are so far unissued and unidentified. (At the end of *Summer Night*, Davis is heard saying, "I'm gonna play another one, Teo, but I want to hear that one first"; the session almost certainly included versions of *Seven Steps to Heaven* and *Joshua*.)

Mabern was replaced at the recording session and the final Los Angeles club date by Victor Feldman, an English pianist who also plays vibraphone and drums. Feldman had first earned a reputation with a few American jazz fans during the war, when he was not yet a teenager, as the drummer in a band led by his older brothers at his father's London pub. The band attracted all kinds of servicemen posted in England, including alto saxophonist Art Pepper, who sat in with it every time he could get leave. Feldman moved to the United States in 1955, when he was 21, and made a strong impression on several people, including Davis, as a piano player and vibist. "Why does everyone here apologize for British musicians?" Davis asked John Martin in 1960. "You can play jazz in Britain. You've got some good men here ... Victor Feldman, he's good. I told Cannonball [Adderley] to get him. He's playing with Cannonball right now."[2] Feldman played in Adderley's band until 1961, including the European tour with Ron Carter in the band, and then moved to Los Angeles where he has worked ever since on film scoring and studio work with only occasional forays into jazz.

One of these forays, perhaps the most auspicious of Feldman's career, was in Columbia's Hollywood studios with Miles Davis. Davis not only used him as his piano player at the Los Angeles sessions, but also solicited two compositions from him, *Seven Steps to Heaven* and *Joshua*, which he added immediately to the working repertoire. If he was hoping to lure Feldman away from Hollywood and back into the jazz life, he was disappointed, but in Feldman's playing for the recording session and in his contributions to the repertoire Davis proved his point about Feldman's ability. The details are as follows:

Miles Davis with Victor Feldman: Seven Steps to Heaven
Miles Davis, tpt; George Coleman, ts (on *So Near So Far*); Victor Feldman, pno; Ron Carter, b; Frank Butler, dms. Los Angeles, 16 April 1963
I Fall in Love Too Easily; *Baby Won't You Please Come Home*; *So Near So Far*; *Basin Street Blues*
(*So Near So Far* is on Columbia KC2 36472 [1981]; the other three titles are on Columbia CL 2051.)

Same personnel, without Coleman. Same place, 17 April 1963
Summer Night
(on *Quiet Nights*, Columbia CL 2106)
The second session probably includes unissued versions of *Joshua* and *Seven Steps to Heaven* as well.

While Davis's band has the appearance of an all-star group, he obviously recognized its limitations when the results were in. Only the slow ballads were released at the time. Anything played faster than a medium tempo was re-recorded a month later in New York with a different piano player and drummer, and the New York versions of *So Near So Far*, *Joshua*, and *Seven Steps to Heaven* were coupled with the Hollywood ballads *I Fall in Love Too Easily*, *Baby Won't You Please Come Home*, and *Basin Street Blues* to make up the LP *Seven Steps to Heaven* (Columbia CL 2051).

Another of the Hollywood ballads, *Summer Night*, filled out the second side of *Quiet Nights*; it is a haunting ballad and a superb example of Davis's ability to evoke a quiet mood, but its inclusion on *Quiet Nights* could not rescue that LP from the critical blast. *I Fall in Love Too Easily* seeks the same quiet mood less successfully, with Davis's pauses in the melody line interrupting the flow of melody and leaving the impression of formlessness.

Baby Won't You Please Come Home and *Basin Street Blues* are much more successful. Davis reached back into the history of American song for these titles, both composed by black songwriters in the early decades of the century. *Baby Won't You Please Come Home*, credited to Clarence Williams, a controversial figure in early jazz who allegedly took advantage of Bessie Smith and other black performers by shaving their royalties and laying claim to their songs, is played as a languid ballad that shifts into a lilting blues after Davis's introduction of the melody. *Basin Street Blues*, written by Spencer Williams (no relation to Clarence), was part of the standard repertoire of New Orleans bands in the earliest days of jazz history and subsequently passed into the repertoires of revival bands. Traditionally, it was played as a medium-tempo paean to the city that the musicians had left behind them when they moved north along the Mississippi:

Basin Street is the street
Where the élite always meet
In New Orleans
My land of dreams ...

Davis plays it as a kind of requiem, slow and mournful, emphasizing the element of nostalgia which in traditional versions exists only as an undertone. His deliberate, wispy tone makes a striking reinterpretation of the content of the original song.

Of the remaining titles recorded in Hollywood only *So Near So Far* has been released, belatedly. Compared to the version re-recorded in New York and released with these ballads, the Hollywood version is much more straightforward but by no means inferior.

Davis's working sextet on his California tour, with Strozier on alto and Mabern on piano, was destined to go unrecorded. As soon as he returned to New York, Davis quickly set about assembling yet another new band. Only George Coleman and Ron Carter kept their places.

Young Tony Williams came in as the drummer. "When Miles asked me to play with him, it felt like the most natural thing in the world for me," Williams said. "I was prepared. I knew all of his music. I had studied everything he had done up to that point. I felt deep down that I was without question the best drummer for the job."[3] Davis agreed, and from the very beginning of their association he worked with Williams closely, as he had with Philly Joe Jones at the beginning of their association almost ten years earlier. "I made Tony play his bass drum, because he didn't play it at all," he told Arthur Taylor, another former drummer in Davis's band who published a volume of "musician-to-musician" interviews years later. "And he didn't play his sock cymbals, so I started him on the sock cymbals. I made him play the bass drum even, and all the rest he had."[4]

Besides his remarkable technique, Williams brought into the band an infectious enthusiasm for life in general and for Davis's music in particular. It shone through in his playing and seemed to move everyone on both sides of the bandstand. He made his tastes known to everyone, and they included a boundless affection for the music on *Milestones*, the first LP Davis made with his great sextet of 1958. "That's a smoking record," Williams said. "That's the definitive jazz album. If you want to know what jazz is, listen to that album. That has all you'd ever want to hear. It embodies the spirit of everyone who plays jazz."[5] The music on the *Milestones* LP had been set aside by Davis by the time Williams joined his band, and Davis's composition *Milestones* had never been included in his working repertoire, even though it is among his most interesting and memorable compositions. Now, with Williams's enthusiasm urging him on, Davis finally began playing *Milestones* in public. Its resuscitation would be only one of the first, and the most obvious, signs of Williams's influence. There would soon be more, and in all of them Williams would serve his new bandleader superbly. "The first music I fell in love with was the music that Miles Davis wrote," he told Julie Coryell. "I just heard other things in that music and liked it." Some

Victor Feldman (Bernie Senensky)

Miles Davis with Ron Carter and Tony Williams (Don Schlitten, courtesy of *Down Beat*)

Tony Williams with Miles Davis (Heye Wessenbergh, courtesy of *Down Beat*)

of those "other things" had been hidden in Davis's music for the past few years, but they would not stay hidden for long with Williams around.

Davis in turn became an indefatigable champion of his new, young drummer. "Tony Williams can swing and play his ass off," Davis told Don DeMicheal. "Tony Williams is a motherfucker ... I don't think there's a drummer alive can do what Tony Williams can do ... Tony plays to the sound, and what he plays to the sound is real slick shit. He might play a different tempo for each sound."[6]

Williams was only a few years older than Miles Davis's sons. He was born in Boston in 1945, and his father was Tillmon Williams, a jazz saxophonist who stayed close to Boston throughout his career. When Tony was only 10, his father set up a drum set for him in the attic, showed him a few rudiments, and watched as the boy outgrew his home-made lessons almost immediately. Luckily, a superb jazz drummer, Alan Dawson, lived just a couple of blocks away, and Tillmon Williams often played with Dawson in bands around the city. The elder Williams dropped around and asked Dawson to start teaching his son, but Dawson had never done any teaching or even thought about doing any and appeared reluctant. Williams asked him to listen to the boy. "He took me up to the attic where Tony, who was eleven but looked about nine, was seated behind this set of drums," Dawson remembers. "Tillmon picked up his horn to blow, and this baby started to cook, playing beautiful time and fills. Believe it or not, this youngster had good time, good taste, and good feeling – everything but chops."[7]

Dawson became his teacher and, incidentally, launched himself on a new career, eventually joining the faculty of Boston's prestigious Berklee School of Music. Under Dawson's tutelage, his first student's natural gifts flourished. Williams began playing publicly in Boston a few years later, and in 1962, when he was 17, he moved to New York as the drummer in Jackie McLean's band. From the beginning, Williams showed little patience with the traditional timekeeping aspect of the drummer's role, preferring instead to let his feeling for the mood or melody of the piece guide the tempo. That approach would have been highly unconventional, an abberation even, just a few years earlier, but Williams's tastes were partly shaped during the first burst of free form playing, and in Boston, the home of Cecil Taylor, Sam Rivers, and other early free form players as well as the seat of the progressive New England Conservatory, Williams felt the effects of the freeing of form and incorporated it into his style almost subconsciously.

For a lot of older musicians, Williams's style caused havoc, but for Davis, himself an amateur drummer, it was a perfect challenge. "A lot of musicians can't play with him," Davis told Arthur Taylor, "because they're used to playing on the first beat and he accents on the second and third beats if you're in 4/4 time. Sometimes he might accent on any beat. And he might play 5/4 time for a while, and you've ... got to know about rhythms and the feel of different rhythms in order to play with him, because he might haul off and do anything rhythmically. If you don't have any knowledge of time and different time changes, he'll lose you."[8]

Williams's ability and his unquenchable enthusiasm pervaded Davis's performances from the beginning, and Davis's admiration for what he was doing sometimes made it hard to tell who was leading whom in the band. Summing up Williams's contribution years later, Barry McRae wrote: "Never before had a percussionist exerted so much personal influence on the overall sound of a Davis group. Philly Joe Jones had never been a boring back-room boy but his role had been to provide colouration in the ensemble and rhythmic impetus to the solo voices. This he had done brilliantly without ever moving out of the rhythm section ... In musical terms [Williams] had become a powerful voice on equal footing with the horns but more significantly he had introduced an intensity that spoke of the avant garde movement in a way that Davis and his sidemen had previously avoided almost consciously."[9] He was only the first of Davis's young sidemen who would import the influence of the new wave, sometimes subtly and sometimes not so subtly, into his band.

Davis's new piano player was Herbie Hancock, a Chicagoan who had just turned 23 when he was hired. Davis had met him a year earlier, not long before Wynton Kelly announced that he was quitting his band, but if Davis was impressed by Hancock's playing at that first meeting he did not show it by renewing his acquaintance when Kelly left. The meeting had taken place at Davis's house when trumpeter Donald Byrd arrived one evening with Hancock in tow and introduced him as his new piano player. Hancock had come to New York as a member of Byrd's band early in 1961 and had played regularly with him ever since without attracting much attention from reviewers. At their first meeting, Davis asked him to play something and Hancock sat down and played a ballad. Afterwards, Davis said to Byrd, "He's got a nice touch."

More than a year later, in May 1963, Hancock was surprised by a telephone call from Davis asking him to come over to his house.

Hancock later described the events of the next three days to Leonard Feather in *From Satchmo to Miles*. He spent them rehearsing Davis's repertoire with George Coleman, Ron Carter, and Tony Williams, while Davis apparently listened to them on the house intercom. Only on the third day did Davis join the group and then only briefly, but at the end of the day he reappeared to tell them to go the Columbia studios the next day. Hancock told Feather: "I said, 'Wait a minute – what? I thought you were auditioning ... Does that mean I'm in the group or what?' He said, "You're making the record, ain't you?'"[10] Hancock became a mainstay of Davis's working band for the next five years.

The new Miles Davis Quintet assembled at the Columbia studios to complete the recordings begun in California. The details are as follows:

Miles Davis Quintet: Seven Steps to Heaven
Miles Davis, tpt; George Coleman, ts; Herbie Hancock, pno; Ron Carter, b; Tony Williams, dms. New York, 14 May 1963
Seven Steps to Heaven; So Near So Far; Joshua
(all on Columbia CL 2051)

The recording session is marked by brisk, confident playing for the most part, making a good debut for the new band and a strong portent of even better playing to come. The one noticeable lapse comes on *So Near So Far*, which has been almost completely reworked from the arrangement recorded in Hollywood. The original version was played in 4/4 time with the song-like melody played by the trumpet and tenor in unison, where this version is played in 6/8 time with Davis's statement of the melody accompanied by Coleman's arpeggios. In the opening ensemble, Coleman sounds ill at ease, and his arpeggios come out like awkward practice scales; the closing ensemble, following solos by Davis, Coleman, and Hancock, corrects the problem, suggesting that another take might have been all that was needed to bring this title up to the standard of the rest of the session. However, this take preserves Hancock's most effective solo of the day, an easy recitation in block chords which Davis had long favored in his pianists.

Joshua, Victor Feldman's composition, and *Seven Steps to Heaven*, by Feldman and Davis, introduce two new modal pieces into Davis's book, and both also entered the working repertoire immediately. *Joshua* sounds vaguely like a reorganization of the vamp from *So What*, and *Seven Steps to Heaven* recalls the declamatory opening of *Milestones*, but both are distinctive in their details and make welcome additions to the repertoire. The arrangements make good use of the new talent surrounding Davis. Both are introduced by a line from Carter, and on *Joshua* Hancock's piano cues the repetitive theme, while on *Seven Steps to Heaven* Williams's drums play fills around the simple, seven-note theme stated by trumpet, tenor, and bass. Davis leaves no doubt about his feelings for his young sidemen, alloting Hancock a solo on all titles, and giving Williams a prominence that he had not allowed his drummer in studio recordings since the days of Philly Joe Jones. Williams even gets a solo chorus on *Seven Steps to Heaven*, and although he is less adventurous on both his solo and his accompaniment than he would be when he settled into the band, this playing is solid enough to serve notice that an important new drummer was emerging.

Davis knew the potential of his new band and filled his calendar with concert and club engagements. During one of the band's first stints, at the Showboat in Philadelphia, while New York suffered the first of a series of 'brown-outs,' a widespread electrical failure that dimmed the lights, stopped elevators, and made walking in the city more perilous than it was in ordinary night-time circumstances, Teo Macero escaped the city by organizing an impromptu excursion to Philadelphia with some friends to give them a preview of the new band.[11] For the young sidemen, Macero's cheering from a stage-side table in a distant club bolstered confidence, and perhaps even Davis took some heart from it.

Soon afterward, Columbia released *Quiet Nights*, and Davis blamed Macero. He refused to enter Columbia's studios at all for the rest of 1963 and all of 1964, a period of twenty-two months. Columbia was forced, as it had been in 1961, to set up its recording equipment at Davis's performances in order to keep its catalog current. As a result, there is no lack of material by the new band on record, but there is a lack of the kind of careful material, including new compositions and new arrangements, that Davis reserved for his studio sessions. The full schedule of playing dates did nothing to help Davis's health, which continued to deteriorate alarmingly, to the point where at times he could not bend his joints or walk at all immediately after rising from sleep. The few people who were close enough to know about his health problems – his wife, his manager, and his sidemen – knew that some attempt would soon have to be made to correct his condition.

The quintet's major projects for the summer involved jazz festivals, which were springing up all over the world as the flagship festival at Newport moved into its ninth successful year. Davis had the quintet booked to play both the festival at Antibes, France, in July and the one at

Monterey, California, in August, and the round of engagements on the club circuit helped the band pull together. One stop was Davis's home territory, St. Louis, and a part of a set played there was later released on record. The details are as follows:

Miles Davis Quintet: In St. Louis
Miles Davis, tpt; George Coleman, ts (except *I Thought about You*); Herbie Hancock, pno; Ron Carter, b; Tony Williams, dms. Jazz Villa, St. Louis, June 1963
I Thought about You; All Blues / The Theme; Seven Steps to Heaven
(all on VGM 0003 [1981])
I Thought about You is apparently missing the first eight bars of the melody; *Seven Steps to Heaven* is missing the opening theme.

This unexpected half-hour of music preserved from the first days of the new quintet is interesting mainly for the obvious enjoyment the sidemen were finding in playing together. On *I Thought about You*, the slow ballad recorded by Davis in 1961 and now brought into the working repertoire, Hancock and Carter are featured in consecutive solos that sound at times like a duo instead, so rich is the comping of one for the other. On *All Blues*, Williams obviously relishes playing the 6/8 meter, especially behind Coleman's long and lively solo, which Williams propels uninhibitedly. On *Seven Steps to Heaven*, both Coleman and Hancock fool with the tempo, which has accelerated considerably from the recorded version of a month before, as is usual in Davis's club performances; Coleman and Hancock both halve the tempo at unexpected moments, and Carter and Williams scramble behind them to keep pace.

The next month the quintet were in France, where they played a concert in Paris on 25 July and starred in the Jazz Festival at Antibes from 26 to 31 July. They were recorded in action at the festival, this time officially rather than informally as in St. Louis.

The Antibes recording was produced by the French corporate arm of Columbia's mother company, CBS, from the transcription of the French national radio-televsion network. Since the mid-1950s, industries had been expanding internationally at an alarming rate, creating multinational giants beyond the purview of governments and far removed from individual consumers. CBS, long a dominant corporation in the American entertainment industry, with branches in motion pictures, radio, and television as well as records, was expanding by the mid-1960s not only into publishing and other areas in the United States, but also into the global entertainment industry, in France, Germany, and Japan, where it eventually linked up with Sony, itself a multinational corporation.

For Columbia in New York, French CBS's record of Davis at Antibes represented one of the first realizations that its recording artists had become multinational properties too. For Davis, recording in France maintained his resolution to stay out of the New York studios. While the record produced by French CBS was released almost simultaneously by Columbia, later recordings of Davis by CBS branches in Germany and Japan would be completely independent, even when the recordings were mastered from tapes produced in the United States. Davis's shift from Columbia's roll of exclusive recording artists to a multinational property was an insignificant ripple in the global shift of economic power.

For jazz fans, the much more important fact was that French CBS caught Davis and his quintet in a brilliant performance at Antibes, a sparkling Mediterranean resort town in the region of the Riviera. The details are as follows:

Miles Davis Quintet: At Antibes
Miles Davis, tpt; George Coleman, ts; Herbie Hancock, pno; Ron Carter, b; Tony Williams, dms. Festival du Jazz, Antibes, 26–31 July 1963
Autumn Leaves; Milestones; Joshua; All of You; Walkin'
(all on CBS [Fr] 62390 and on Columbia CL 2183)
The CBS release was titled *Miles à Antibes*, the Columbia release *Miles Davis in Europe*. Transcriptions of ten more titles by the Davis Quintet at Antibes exist but have not yet been issued.

In every respect, this release seemed newsworthy for jazz fans. French CBS managed to pack a little more than an hour of music onto the two sides of the LP, so that even its most trivial aspect was a revelation to North American listeners, accustomed to fewer than forty minutes per LP. For those who could get hold of the French pressing, the sound seemed cleaner than they were accustomed to on American pressings of the day. The whole package went a long way toward redressing the twenty-seven minutes of torpid music presented on *Quiet Nights*. Here was a renewal of spirit in Davis's music. Even the working repertoire had been expanded. Besides Davis's perennials, *All of You* (first recorded in 1958, and played frequently ever since) and *Walkin'* (first recorded in

1954, and played nightly ever since), there were the new *Joshua* (recorded two months earlier and not till then issued) and two startling resuscitations: *Autumn Leaves* (recorded by Davis in a band nominally led by Julian Adderley in 1958) and *Milestones* (recorded by the sextet in 1958, and never brought into the working repertoire until this time).

Milestones seemed especially welcome, as one of Davis's finest compositions, neglected by him for more than five years while several other musicians, notably Bill Evans in a trio arrangement (on Milestone 47002) and Gerald Wilson in a big band arrangement (on Pacific Jazz PJ-61), had kept on exploring its modal beauties. Tony Williams was by no means alone in counting it among his favorite compositions, and at the first familiar notes of its fanfare the audience at Antibes burst into applause, a reaction that dozens of Davis's fans shared when they put this record on their turntables a few months afterward.

The recording also clearly established George Coleman as Davis's most effective saxophonist since Coltrane. Coleman shows none of Coltrane's inclinations for teasing apart the formal structure of a song as he plays it, but at his best he comes close to conveying the impression of raw power that Coltrane had, bringing back into Davis's band the basic contrast between the two horns. Coleman also sustains long solos that are seldom repetitive and always swing.

But the essential revelation of this record was the dominance of the new and virtually unknown drummer, Tony Williams. He used his brushes sensitively behind Davis on the two ballads, *Autumn Leaves* and *All of You*, but he clearly preferred the sticks, switching to them as soon as Davis had finished playing and sticking with them until he returned to play the out-chorus. On the faster tempos of *Milestones* and *Joshua*, he chattered along behind the soloists filling all the spaces musically and sometimes threatening to take charge altogether if the soloist did not rise above his level. On the swinger, *Walkin'*, Williams simply thundered along, pushing the other players until they seemingly had to clear out of his way for an extended drum solo, a rare enough occurrence in Davis's music, and removing himself temporarily to allow Coleman and Ron Carter enough room for a duet. The Antibes LP was not Williams's recording debut, but it provided the first revelation of his power.

Williams could make Davis forget his physical suffering and play at close to the top of his form again, as he showed at Antibes, especially in his busy solo on *Milestones* that suggests he was as pleased as everyone else to find himself working over that old composition again. As soon as

Davis heard the tapes from Antibes he knew that his opinion of Williams's talents would very soon be widely shared. "When the test pressings of this album ... reached Miles, he almost wore them out," Ralph J. Gleason wrote in the liner notes for the American release. "It was not a happy time for him in many ways, but these test pressings made it better. I can think of no higher compliment than to point out that Miles called from Los Angeles one morning just to play a passage over several times in which Tony Williams did something particularly exciting."[12] The record met with great critical success, winning kudos as the jazz album of the year in *Jazz Magazine* and other citations when it was released in 1964.

Williams quickly became the most conspicuous young jazzman around. Later that summer, at the Monterey Jazz Festival in California, the Davis quintet were waiting for their scheduled appearance when one of the bands booked for the previous day showed up without a drummer. The band consisted of guitarist Elmer Snowden, 63 and all but forgotten apart from the fact that he had led a band in the 1920s that the young Duke Ellington had taken over, and bassist Pops Foster, 71, and someone suggested, presumably in jest, that Tony Williams should fill in. "He was seventeen and he had never heard of either Elmer Snowden or Pops Foster," Ralph J. Gleason reported some years later, "but he played with them that afternoon and, since Tony is now – and was even when he was seventeen – a musical genius, the result was spectacular. It was one of the finest moments of that whole Monterey festival."[13]

The festival came at the beginning of an extended stay in California for Davis in the fall of 1963. He spent his time working with Gil Evans on the score for a play called *Time of the Barracuda*, starring Laurence Harvey and Elaine Stritch. "Miles and I went to a hotel in L.A., on the Strip, called Chateau Marmont, an old time movie star place," Evans said. "We moved in – we each took as suite and we had two pianos, one in his suite and one in mine. He'd come to my place and we'd play things and I'd go to his and we'd play things. We worked on it for quite a while, a couple of weeks every day. Concentrated – with the script."[14] Harvey came in and consulted with them, and so did the author and director. Davis and Evans finished the score, a suite cued to the script with pieces lasting from forty-five seconds to four minutes, and recorded it at Columbia's Hollywood studio, probably produced by Irving Townsend, with an orchestra comprised of three french horns, bass trombone, three flutes, and rhythm.

Then the problems began. The San Francisco opening was postponed when the musicians' union ruled out the taped score and required a pit band. Then Harvey, a gifted classical actor and notorious misogynist, and Stritch began feuding. The play folded. "Columbia still has the tape," Evans said, and then he shrugged, "It will come out some day."

Evans has recorded some themes from *Time of the Barracuda* on his infrequent LPs. So far the only hints of the collaboration are his 1964 recording of *Barracuda*, a jazz waltz (Verve v6-8838) and *Flute Song* (Verve v6-8555), both credited to Evans alone, and *Hotel Me* (also Verve v6-8555, and recorded again in 1971 on Artists House 14), credited to both Davis and Evans. *Hotel Me* is based on a wicked striptease vamp that Evans says he took from Otis Spann's comping on a Muddy Waters record. On Evans's 1964 recording the vamp is sustained by drummer Elvin Jones and two of Davis's bassists, Ron Carter and his predecessor, Paul Chambers; the most prominent solo voice is Evans's piano, but other voices rise intermittently from the trilled background, notably the bass clarinet of Eric Dolphy. The 1971 recording, a much less effective orchestration, is dominated by a baritone saxophone, either Howard Johnson or Trevor Koehler, and includes a ragged ensemble passage based on Davis's original, and unissued, solo.

Columbia has kept the original tape in its vaults, apparently fearing another fiasco after *Quiet Nights*. For Davis and Evans, *Time of the Barracuda* added another frustrating experience to their collaborations. From then on, they would work together only sporadically, with little conviction. Few of their projects would ever be completed, and none would rival the ambitions or the standards of their earlier work.

In November 1963, President Kennedy was shot and killed in a motorcade going through the streets of Dallas, Texas. The act sent shock waves throughout the world as a first reaction, and it gave breadth and depth to the dissatisfaction with established political and social mores among the young. In the United States and all the industrialized countries of the West, many young adults began advocating political ideals for alternative societies and in some cases undertaking political acts against the status quo for their causes. Political unrest and civil disobedience became part of the maturation rite for the rest of the decade.

Among jazzmen the assassinated president had earned a measure of respect for raising issues involving race relations, and even the most apolitical among them usually found something admirable in the sense of style that he brought to his office. As it happened, one of the last official acts that Kennedy performed was to sign an executive order pardoning pianist Hampton Hawes, who had spent five years in prison for heroin addiction and was expected to spend many more. Hawes returned home to Los Angeles and began playing at a club on Sunset Boulevard, and one of his first visitors was Miles Davis. "He dropped by," Hawes remembered in his autobiography, "threw his arms around me, and said in his husky voice, 'Did they make a faggot out of you?' I said, 'No, but I learned to mop and cook.'"[15]

Presidential politics came under fire in 1964, after Kennedy's vice-president, Lyndon B. Johnson, was elected to the White House on the strength of his association with the Kennedy administration. Johnson almost immediately undertook a massive build-up of men and material in Vietnam, a tiny country in southeast Asia of which most Americans had never heard. Vietnam was locked in a civil war with ideological overtones, as the communist north battled the republican south. The south had originally been supported by France, which had a colonial tie with Vietnam, and China responded by backing the north, but when the intervention threatened to alter the remote civil war into an international conflict, France backed off. In a fateful move, the implications of which became clear only a few years after his death, Kennedy moved American men and materials into the gap left by France, and Johnson then supervised a massive build-up of American troops in Vietnam.

For the rest of the decade, American participation in Vietnam's civil war became the focal point of mass protests and civil disobedience in the United States, as American youth challenged traditional authority. In 1964, the cataclysm was still to come, but the seeds of protest were visible enough to inspire a mock campaign in the jazz world by nominating Dizzy Gillespie for president. As the fantasy of "Dizzy for President" captured the popular imagination, Miles Davis's name inevitably came into it. The satirist Dick Gregory suggested, "How about Miles Davis for Secretary of State?" But Dizzy Gillespie replied, "Miles Davis has offered to serve as Minister of the Treasury, but I've persuaded him to head the CIA instead."[16] The mockery of the political system implied in the campaign was a harbinger of much tougher and much more serious protests soon to follow.

Inside the jazz world, meanwhile, Davis's renewed energy with his young sidemen practically restored him to his position of dominance. Following the release of *Miles Davis in Europe* in 1964, he found himself back on top in most of the polls, including *Down Beat*'s International Jazz Critics poll, ahead of Gillespie, Clark Terry, Art Farmer, and Louis Armstrong, who placed behind him in that order, and his youthful band ranked second, behind Thelonious Monk's quartet featuring tenor saxophonist Charlie Rouse and ahead of Coltrane's band and the Modern Jazz Quartet.

For all that, he still refused to enter the studios in order to record with his band, and Columbia was again forced to capture his music in a live performance early in 1964. The concerts took place at Philharmonic Hall in New York, part of the new Lincoln Center for the Performing Arts, with Teo Macero ensconced in the control booth supervising the sound quality.

True to the temper of the time, the occasion had a political motive. The concerts were benefits to support voter registration drives in the southern states of Louisiana and Mississippi, where generations of black people had never exercised their franchise, either out of ignorance of the registration process or, equally likely, out of fear of reprisals from the local white community. Now, in 1964, just over a century after the Emancipation Proclamation, teams of student-workers and liberal activists were engaged in locating unregistered blacks, who sometimes formed a majority in their local polls, schooling them in the registration process, and encouraging them to turn out to vote. All of this was undertaken at considerable risk, and the registration workers, usually middle-class college students from northeastern states, became targets of abuse and sometimes assault from the hidebound conservatives in the areas. Davis's concerts at Philharmonic Hall, to provide funds for the registration drives, were sponsored by the National Association for the Advancement of Colored People (NAACP), the traditional organizer of black political action, and two upstart organizations, the Congress of Racial Equality (CORE) and the Student Nonviolent Coordinating Committee (SNCC), which were aggressive, youth-dominated groups that threatened to supplant the established NAACP in leading the fight for racial equality.

Davis, as expected, neither acknowledged the political motive of his concerts directly nor observed it in any overt way, choosing instead to use the occasion to run through his regular repertoire in rapid succession. Out of the concerts, Columbia eventually mastered two LPs, the first (CL 2306) released a few months later and the second (CL 2306) a year later. The details are as follows:

Miles Davis Quintet at Philharmonic Hall
Miles Davis, tpt; George Coleman, ts; Herbie Hancock, pno; Ron Carter, b; Tony Williams, dms. Philharmonic Hall, New York, 12 February 1964

So What; Walkin'
(both on Columbia CL 2453)
All of You/The Theme (inc.); *Stella by Starlight; All Blues; My Funny
Valentine; I Thought about You*
(all on Columbia CL 2306)
Four; Seven Steps to Heaven; Joshua/Go Go [theme and announcement];
There Is No Greater Love/Go Go [theme and announcement]
(all on Columbia CL 2453)

Years after these LPs were released, a *Down Beat* reviewer referred to the
second one, entitled *'Four' and More* (CL 2453) as "one of the certifiably
classic live jazz LPs."[17] Certainly they offer a great deal to listen to,
preserving almost two hours of music and showing the quintet off in
long elaborations – the shortest running almost eight minutes – of some
familiar themes. Only *Stella by Starlight* is in any sense unfamiliar,
having finally found a place in the working repertoire after its studio
recording in 1958, no doubt because, as with *Milestones* and *Autumn
Leaves*, Davis was pressed by his young sidemen to play publicly the
music they had admired on his records a few years earlier.

Stella by Starlight gives Herbie Hancock the starring role in a long,
musing solo that spotlights his delicate touch on the keyboard and also
his highly inventive lyricism, which recall Bill Evans's style in the
sextet five years earlier. (Hancock's solo is interrupted momentarily
near the end by a ripple of applause marking Davis's return to the stage
from the wings, where he had shared a bottle of wine with the
announcer, Mort Fega.) Hancock's confidence shines through the
evening, and so does Coleman's; both take long solos on every title,
filling in the long spells while Davis wandered in the wings and
ultimately copping the solo honors with their work.

The chief impression of Ron Carter and Tony Williams, neither of
whom had shown any lack of confidence in their playing in the past and
were certainly not going to start on this night, is one of incredible speed
and endurance. All the uptempo pieces are played at almost the same
blinding speed, a result of the acceleration Davis imposes on his music
in a direct relation to the frequency with which he plays it in public, and
most of the fastest pieces are collated side-by-side on the second LP,
'Four' and More, rather than in the order in which they were played at
the concerts. Listening to *So What, Walkin', Joshua, Four,* and *Seven
Steps to Heaven* in succession, as they come up on the LP, is exhausting
for the listener, let alone for Carter and Williams, who sustain a tempo

that must be close to the physical limits of bass plucking and drumming throughout. For listeners to the LPS, as opposed to spectators at the concert, the acceleration of tempo seems mindless, reducing the individual features of compositions as different as *So What* and *Four* to a kind of sameness, and one might as well be listening to *Walkin'*, Davis's standard fast-tempo number for years, five times in succession for all the difference it makes.

The tempos do not faze the musicians, who respond to the exigencies of the moment with remarkable ease. On *Joshua*, Carter and Williams lead Hancock and Coleman through a series of stop-time intervals, and on *Seven Steps to Heaven* Davis leads the band into an improvised coda, but neither these spontaneities nor any others, and there are several, lead to even momentary confusion. The Davis Quintet had cohered in less than a year together into a strong unit. In that respect, they seemed already to be the equal of Davis's great bands in the second half of the 1950s. The comparison faltered, really, only with respect to solo strength, with Davis himself taking fewer chances in his own playing, and Hancock and Coleman still searching for their individual voices. Davis, presumably, would summon up his resources when the time was right, and the Philharmonic Hall concerts boded well not only for Hancock's future but also for Coleman's. Coleman had established his ability to swing hard, but at the Philharmonic he is no less effective soloing on the ballad *I Thought about You*, playing variations on the melody as interesting as any ballad improvisations of the evening. Although on the ballads the tempo always rises to medium when Coleman's turn comes, he shows signs of developing his ballad style to complement his other strengths.

Unfortunately, Coleman chose to cut off his development in the well-publicized setting of the Miles Davis Quintet. He quit in the spring, a few months after the Philharmonic concert. Carter quit around the same time, but only temporarily and for entirely different reasons. As a New York freelancer, he found himself in demand often enough that he could give up the traveling he was forced to do as a member of the quintet. Carter reconsidered his decision after an interval of playing the mixed bag that freelancers were called for and rejoined Davis's band in time for the summer tour.

Coleman did not return. Ever since, almost every time a fan sidles up to him in a jazz club, he has had to face the question of why he quit. It is not a question that he finds easy to answer, and over the years he has amalgamated several possible answers into one. "Miles was ill during that time – a lot of times he wouldn't make the gigs and it was frustrating," he told Andrew Sussman in 1980. "I would be standin' out front and a lot of people thought *I* was Miles Davis, if you can believe *that*. And I used to stand out front and make a gig some nights after the first set, 'cause he would split – 'cause he was hurtin', you know. His hip was botherin' him – and so there was a lot of pressure on me, and sometimes the money would be late and I'd get it in a check and have to try to get it cashed, so I really got tired of it; so I just decided to leave."

Musically, Coleman always seemed to feel that he was the odd man in Davis's band. Five years older than Hancock and ten years older than Williams, Coleman had set his style by the time he joined the band, but he found that something extra was expected of him. "I began to take more chances, play things that I didn't know how I was going to come out of, whereas before I was always a careful player – always strictly tryin' to play the changes no matter what," he said. "Maybe not succeeding all the time, but always trying. With Miles I began to stretch out a little bit, play some different stuff. He left it more spontaneous – in a creative sense."[18] The difference between Coleman's playing when he joined and that when he left is clearly shown in his original recording of *So Near So Far* and almost everything he played at the Philharmonic concert. He became more adventurous, and he remained so to some extent after leaving Davis, but he never realized the full potential implied at that concert. That discrepancy almost certainly accounts for the persistent question about his leaving, or at least for the fans' expectation that his answer will be worth asking for. Of all the reasons he has given from time to time, the most convincing one involves the direction the music was taking. "He says he left Miles Davis because the band was heading into areas he wasn't convinced about," reviewer Mike Hennessy wrote in *Jazz Journal*.[19]

Both Hancock and Williams kept close tabs on the freer forms of Ornette Coleman, Cecil Taylor, and Eric Dolphy. Those forms were, after all, among the main currents of their formative years, as they had not been for Coleman, and they made their strongest impact on jazz just when Hancock and Williams arrived in New York to begin their professional careers. In Hancock's playing the influence of Taylor and the others is hard to pinpoint, because he works mostly in the harmonically complex but carefully controlled métier of Bill Evans, but he was completely open to innovations of all kinds and felt comfortable in almost any context. His favorite job before joining Davis was a short-lived but influential engagement under the leadership of Dolphy.

In Williams's playing the influence of the free form players is more obvious, as he ranges freely over his drum set apparently unfettered by anything but the limits of his imagination.

Within a few years, Hancock's and Williams's association with Davis would be used routinely by advocates of the avant-garde as evidence that Davis's attacks on Cecil Taylor and the others were hypocritical; Davis was encouraging Hancock and Williams to incorporate freer elements into his band even as he was making the attacks. A.B. Spellman quotes one advocate saying: "When Miles first heard Cecil, back in the 50s, he put him down, right? Well, it's an interesting thing that Miles's present piano player, Herbie Hancock, is trying to go in Cecil's direction, because he thinks that's where the music has to go. And the musicians dig Cecil. Miles's drummer, Tony Williams, does. Tony would rather play with Cecil than with Miles. That would sound strange, wouldn't it? But it's a fact."[20] Fact or not, it had enough credence to be spoken aloud without anyone rushing in to debunk it.

Davis nonetheless kept up his frontal assault on the new music whenever he was cornered for an opinion. Eric Dolphy's playing drew one of his most caustic comments: "He plays like somebody was standing on his foot." The line appeared in *Down Beat* on 13 June 1964, as part of Leonard Feather's blindfold test, and it had the kind of audacity that made it stick in people's minds, whether they were outraged or delighted by it. It was still fresh when news of Dolphy's sudden death broke on 29 June. Dolphy died just nine days after his 36th birthday from a heart attack brought on by an undiagnosed diabetic condition. He left behind a fairly rich discography of works recorded mainly in the four-year span from 1960. The best of his recordings were made with bands led by either John Coltrane or Charles Mingus, and he had made such a strong impression touring Europe with Mingus's band in 1964 that he had decided to try his fortunes there. He died in Berlin.

The elegies following his death naturally drew attention to Dolphy's openness, his easy nature, and his romanticism, all of which shone through in his playing, and amid all the praise Davis's comment lingered like a bad odor. David Baker, the jazz educator who has transcribed several of Davis's improvisations, tried to explain it away by saying, "I really believe very strongly that when Miles uses language like that, that's a language of endearment."[21] Almost no one ever believed that Davis sincerely held such a low opinion of Dolphy's playing, and the rumor circulated that Davis had been trying to hire Dolphy when Dolphy chose instead to join Mingus for the European tour.[22]

If Dolphy seemed an unlikely choice for Davis's band in light of

Davis's public views of the avant-garde, he was certainly no more unlikely than the man who finally replaced George Coleman. He was Sam Rivers, a tenor saxophonist who had moved to Boston at the age of 17 to study at the New England Conservatory and by 1964, when he was 34, had made a formidable reputation in Boston jazz circles but almost none beyond them. Tony Williams pleaded Rivers's case to Davis whenever he got the chance, playing him tapes and lauding his ability. But when Coleman quit, Davis automatically thought first of Wayne Shorter. Shorter had been made the musical director of the Jazz Messengers and felt more committed than ever to Art Blakey. In the end, Davis told Williams to go ahead and bring in Rivers for the spring tour of American clubs that the band were making before heading to Japan for a month of concerts.

Williams located Rivers touring with T-Bone Walker, the old blues shouter, and sent him a telegram saying: "Come to New York, George split. Miles want you to join his group."[23] Rivers arrived in time to spend some hours learning Davis's repertoire with the help of Hancock and Williams before starting the American leg of the tour.

Just before the quintet embarked for Japan, Ron Carter rejoined them at a Birdland engagement. Davis was apparently uneasy about Rivers's playing already, but he had no hope of changing saxophonists at such a late date.

A selection from one of the Japanese concerts, at Kosei Nenkin Hall in Tokyo, has been issued on record. It was produced by Japanese CBS-Sony with characteristic attention to sound reproduction and packaging. It is the only record issued that documents the six-month tenure of Rivers in the Miles Davis Quintet. The details are as follows:

Miles Davis Quintet in Tokyo
Miles Davis, tpt; Sam Rivers, ts; Herbie Hancock, pno; Ron Carter, b; Tony Williams, dms. Kosei Nenkin Hall, Tokyo, 14 July 1964
If I Were a Bell; My Funny Valentine; So What; Walkin'; All of You/The Theme
(all on CBS-Sony [Jap] SONX 60064R)

Even playing this familiar repertoire – all but one of these titles had been recorded at the Philharmonic Hall concert earlier in the year, and all but one had been recorded at the Blackhawk more than three years earlier – this band sounds subtly different. In Japan they were tuxedoed and cosseted, and, perhaps not coincidentally, their music came out careful and considered. The tempos are not accelerated noticeably, and the tenor and piano solos are not distended, perhaps because Davis, on his best behavior for his first exposure to a lucrative new audience, remained onstage all evening.

The subdued jazz they played obviously suited Hancock perfectly. He muses through all his solos and introductions, playing delicate, spare phrases. On the bullish *Walkin'* he slows the tempo to a near stop during his solo, and on *My Funny Valentine*, which gets its finest performance of any of the dozens that Davis has recorded, he stops the rhythm altogether and plays an unaccompanied solo. The mood of the performance works equally well for Davis, although the sound of his muted trumpet on *If I Were a Bell* and *All of You* has a noticeable burr. He is involved enough to take equal time on his solos, and on the ballads he returns after the others not merely to close out the piece but to work out another solo.

Rivers is much less involved, contributing very little to the ensembles, not even the usual saxophone vamp on *So What*. He comes to life only in his solos, which are tidy and compact. For the first time, Davis appears alongside a saxophonist who does not routinely draw on the bebop arsenal of fast runs and broad-toned repetitions in the lower registers, although Rivers's solos here are decidedly within the bebop context. Rivers nudges his solos from a conservative reworking of the melody toward phrases that alter the tonal center of notes. His solos on *If I Were a Bell* and *All of You* take on a vocal quality, which has the same source as Eric Dolphy's style but does not resemble his sound. Rivers's tone is thinner and reedier than the tone favored by bop-influenced players, and for the first time Davis's band lacks the basic contrast between the 'soft' trumpet and the 'hard' tenor. Whatever contrast Davis and Rivers might have generated tonally is lost in any case because Rivers, unlike every other saxophonist Davis has employed, does not rush in immediately after Davis's solos but enters after a pause.

Most of the changes in the quintet's style are positive, or at least have the virtue of novelty. Very few are determined by Rivers's presence. Davis's involvement, his equal participation in the solo sequence, and his care in selecting tempos and limiting the others' solo space all seem unlikely to be responses to Rivers's presence. Perhaps Hancock's liberties with tempo and phrasing are indirectly linked to Rivers, as a response to his freer conception, but some development along these lines was inevitable. Rivers brings to the group a truly distinctive solo voice on saxophone, the most distinctive since Coltrane, and Davis's involvement may well come out of a need, conscious or not, to assert and hold onto his own ground. Rivers's apparent reluctance to participate in the familiar group dynamics, or perhaps his inability to do so because of his natural tone, altered the sound of the band more than anything else, and that might have proven positive in the long run if Davis had been willing to work out the new balance with Rivers. But he was not. By the time the quintet returned to the United States, Davis had given Rivers his notice and was once again searching for a tenor saxophonist.

Rivers left the quintet in August and carried on his highly individualistic course in jazz. The exposure with Davis, though brief and poorly documented, did him no harm. He made his very first recordings as a leader the following year, when he was already 35, on an exclusive contract with Blue Note. He returned to Boston University as a composition major, worked with Cecil Taylor regularly in the last three years of the decade, and in 1971 opened a studio in Manhattan where he fostered the development and dissemination of free form music. Although he never became widely heard or much recorded, he influenced the young experimenters of the 1970s more directly than many musicians who had those advantages.

Looking back on his tenure in Davis's band, Rivers maintains simply that their music was incompatible. "Miles was doing things that were ... pretty straight," he says. "I was there, but I was somewhere else too. I guess it sounds funny, but I was already ahead of that. I kept stretching out and playing really long solos, and that's probably why I didn't last."[24] His incompatibility does not show on the Tokyo recordings, where he is reined in, but eventually it should be documented when further recordings, from Japan or elsewhere, become available.

More than the music, Rivers seemed to find the lifestyle as a member of the Miles Davis Quintet stifling. Essentially it involved traveling with a set band, playing a set repertoire, and working within chordal and modal forms. He had never done those things for any significant period in his life, and now that he was edging into middle age he was reluctant to start. If they were the traditional lot of jazz musicians, and the source of whatever security they had, they still could not tempt him as they might others. "I believe that the musicians who went through Miles's bands were just as impressed with his lifestyle as they were with his music," he told Michael Ullmann. "So if you want to achieve that kind of lifestyle, there's certain things you have to do with the music. You're

[not] going to have it while playing at the frontiers of the music."[25] Rivers has never had it, and apparently he does not miss it.

Earlier in the summer, while the quintet were in Japan, Wayne Shorter had resigned from the Jazz Messengers after five years. He took the summer off, resting and writing music. He gave some thought to leading a band of his own and spent some time talking about it with some of his friends, but he soon abandoned the idea. "I saw that it meant a lot of work and growing old fast," he said, " a hard way to go."[26] When Davis and his sidemen landed in Los Angeles from Japan they apparently did not know that Shorter was available, because Davis prepared to play a series of engagements in California with just his rhythm trio. Rivers maintains that Art Blakey still posed a stumbling block between Shorter and the Davis band. In Rivers's version, Davis and Blakey arranged to trade tenor players but Rivers spoiled the deal by backing out. "I just decided I didn't want to go into any more bebop," he said. "I was already past bebop."[27] Whatever the circumstances, Davis faced the prospect of playing his West Coast dates with Hancock, Carter, and Williams backing him.

It was not a situation that he relished or that he was prepared to accept easily. Shorter soon found himself under some pressure. First he received a call from Jack Whittemore, Davis's agent, explaining that Davis and the others were scheduled to open at the Hollywood Bowl and did not have a saxophonist. Whittemore asked Shorter to phone Davis. He hardly had time to ponder the call because his telephone kept ringing. He remembers: "Ron, Herbie and Tony would call me and talk to me and say, 'Hey, man. Why don't you come on the band? Come on, man. Come on, man.' That's Tony, right? And Herbie used to say, 'Well, I think the opportunity is wide open,' and Ron would say, 'It's all right with me, strictly all right.'" Finally, Shorter decided that he would call Davis and at least listen to what he was offering. "I called Miles then," he told James Liska, "and he picked up the phone and said, 'Wayne, come on out.' Like he was expecting my call, you know? Like it had all been set up. I went and got a tuxedo made, and they flew me out first class. I joined and we opened at the Hollywood Bowl playing *Joshua*. And we had no rehearsal. Miles had said in the dressing room, 'Do you know my music?' And I said, 'Yeah.' He said, 'Oh-oh.' Then we went on. For six years."[28]

11

Circle
1964–8

Coleman Hawkins once told me not to play with anybody old because they'll be hard to bend to the way you want them to play ... I don't tell them what to do, I just *suggest* something and if they don't like it they'll suggest something else. Say, we can do this *and* this. Or they'll know what I mean and add something to it that makes it better.   Miles Davis

"It's quality that makes the music good," Miles Davis once told Don DeMicheal. "If you get the right guys to play the right thing at the right time, you got everything you need."[1] When he added Wayne Shorter to the quintet that already included Herbie Hancock, Ron Carter, and Tony Williams, Davis closed the circle. Surrounded by the young sidemen, he produced four solid years of exploratory small band jazz.

Shorter was the catalyst. He had been John Coltrane's personal choice to replace him in Davis's band as early as 1959, and his instinct, when Shorter finally joined five years after that, proved unerring. Coltrane was originally impressed by the confident young saxophonist when he began turning up at informal playing sessions while he was still a major in music education at New York University, and he grew more impressed when Shorter came into Manhattan on weekend leaves after he was drafted into the army to serve in the army band at Fort Dix.

Picking Shorter out of the crowd of aspiring young jazz musicians was not difficult for Coltrane or anybody else. He arrived already equipped with that indefinable quality that had marked Sonny Rollins ten years earlier among his adolescent peers in Harlem. Shorter was born in 1933 in Newark, New Jersey, across the Hudson River from Manhattan. One of his contemporaries in Newark was LeRoi Jones, the poet and playwright (later known as Amiri Baraka), and although Jones and Shorter were raised in distant neighborhoods and attended different schools, Jones knew a lot about Shorter. He recalled Shorter's stature among Newark teenagers in a profile for the *Jazz Review* in 1959, when Shorter had just finished his stint in the army and was still largely unknown. Jones attempted to define "the kind of aura he cast even as an adolescent, maybe because we were all adolescents ... but I think not. I think Wayne carries that aura around him like an expensive Chesterfield. Talking to him one senses immediately this air of 'invincibility'. Hearing him play, one is convinced that it is no mere air."[2]

Testing himself alongside Coltrane and others as an undergraduate gave Shorter more self-assurance, and he used the two-year stint in the army band not only to hone his playing skills but also to develop his composing ability. He was a member of Maynard Ferguson's sextet when Jones wrote about him, but he stayed only briefly in that band, and when Coltrane's recommendation to Davis was thwarted because Davis persuaded Coltrane to stay with him he joined the Jazz Messengers, forming one of Art Blakey's most formidable front lines with the young trumpeter Lee Morgan. He never developed into the flaming free former that Jones, and perhaps Coltrane too, seem to have anticipated. With Blakey he played and wrote music that carried on Blakey's neo-bop style, extending it somewhat but basically staying within the category. By the time he joined Davis he was as ready to bend the traditional categories as were his colleagues in the band, both in his playing and in his writing.

With Davis as with Blakey, and indeed with the musical associations he formed after leaving Davis, Shorter experimented *with* form rather than *without* form, as a kind of experimenting traditionalist or a progressive conservative. He has never really abandoned the lesson he learned from Coltrane in his youth. "You know, when you're into something, like John, you may make a lot of fluffs and clinkers, but that's in it, too," he told Jones between sets at Birdland. "All that stuff counts. If you're really doing something, you can't be safe. You've just got to blow, and try to take care of some business some way."[3] Because he respects form but needs to take risks with it, Shorter's career looks like a paradox among the jazzmen of his generation: he is a 'tough' or 'difficult' player who has always performed to fairly large, catholic audiences. Shorter has worked throughout his conspicuous career almost inconspicuously, inspiring neither fan clubs nor cults, as a featured player and composer but never a star attraction. His role in the resurgence of the Miles Davis Quintet in 1964–8 (and after that) is crucial, but it is never more than equal to that of the other sidemen.

No other period in Miles Davis's music presents so orderly an appearance. Its key documents are six studio recordings made and released at more or less regular intervals over three years: *E.S.P.* (recorded early in 1965), *Miles Smiles* (1966), *Sorcerer* and *Nefertiti* (both 1967), and *Miles in the Sky* and *Filles de Kilimanjaro* (both 1968). But the period encompasses much more. The last two LPs were selected from a vast store of studio recordings Davis made at the time, some released several years later and much unreleased to this day; most of that music points ahead to the next period of his development rather than substantiating this one. There are also a number of live recordings made early in this period that catch Davis and the quintet reworking the old repertoire rather than working out the entirely new one introduced on the studio recordings. And there are even more intervals of relative inactivity for the quintet than usual, the result of Davis's health deteriorating to the critical point. With enforced absences from performing come increased activity on orchestral projects with Gil Evans, each one destined to be aborted or stillborn. Those that got as far as the recording studio remain there still, in Columbia's vaults, and a whole sub-theme of these years thus remains completely unknown.

With all this diversity, the six studio recordings stand as the touchstones of the period. For reviewers and fans alike, they belong at or very near the apex of Davis's achievements as a jazz musician. The critical consensus is simply stated by Harvey Pekar, in a 1976 article in *Coda*: "When Shorter joined him ... Miles embarked on a new era of exploration that rivaled his 1955–9 period."[4] Ironically, the significance of the quintet's music and its consistent excellence were not widely appreciated at the time, by fans or reviewers. The critics formed their consensus after a gap of several years, not surprising in most art forms but a startling contrast with Davis's earlier peak period, when his music won both the large audiences and the critical plaudits that have stuck with it ever since.

The delayed reaction was partly inherent in the music itself. It demanded new perceptions from its audience and thus required a period of acclimatization before it could be fully accepted. But those demands would not, under ordinary circumstances, have been so great as to require all the time the listeners took. The main reason lay in the times.

Put simply, almost no one was listening. Davis continued to fill concert halls and jazz clubs all over the world, just as he had for almost a decade and would do later. His new records sold well, with only a slight and hardly worrisome falling off in sales compared to his new releases of a few years earlier. But he was almost alone in holding his place with the fans. John Coltrane did too, Thelonious Monk probably could have if he had wanted to, and the Modern Jazz Quartet continued to thrive in Europe, but in general it was a bleak time for jazz.

"Jazz is dead" became a catchword. It was seriously debated in the jazz periodicals, complete with learned-sounding arguments that the music had exhausted itself in the rapid evolution since the turn of the century. Among the most reactionary elements of the jazz audience, as we have seen, the catchword was reinterpreted as: "Ornette and Cecil have killed jazz." However it was phrased, what it really meant was that the audience for jazz was disappearing fast. So too, naturally, were the musicians. At some point or other during the 1960s, Kenny Drew, Art Farmer, Johnny Griffin, Dexter Gordon, Arthur Taylor, Mal Waldron, and many others moved to Europe, Helen Merrill moved to Japan, Randy Weston to Morocco – an exodus in search of a small but loyal audience. Dozens of others disappeared, sometimes irretrievably, into carpentry, sign painting, selling, counselling, teaching, and any other jobs they could find; Eddie (Lockjaw) Davis became a booking agent at the Shaw Artists Corporation, usually with rock bands for clients. Others stayed in music but not in jazz; Hampton Hawes spent these years playing ballads for stockbrokers and their secretaries from 5 to 9 p.m. in a San Francisco bar, and many jazz musicians counted him lucky. Red Garland went home to his father's house in Dallas and sat out the whole decade, playing only occasional weekends at local bars.

In the jazz world, everything seemed to go wrong. "All the clubs were closing and none of the musicians were working," Garland told Len Lyons when he finally returned to jazz in 1978, and he added: "I thought jazz was finished."[5] He was not alone. "The clubs were beginning to hurt," Hawes complained. "The kids were jamming the rock halls and the older people were staying home watching TV. Maybe they found they couldn't pat their feet to our music anymore. Big-drawing names like Miles and John Coltrane were breaking out of the thirty-two-bar chord-oriented structure and into free expression – or 'avant-garde' or 'outside', whatever tag you want to stick on it – charging the owners so much they had to raise the covers and minimums."[6] The complaints of Hawes and the other jazzmen made a long list, and if none of them went far into the heart of the matter all of them had some bearing on it.

Davis complained too, but it was all relative. Max Gordon, the owner of the Village Vanguard, takes some pride in his attempts to hold the line on the fee he had to pay Davis. In one of Gordon's vignettes, probably from around this time, Davis demanded the impossible sum of $6,000 for a week at the Vanguard, and Gordon had no choice but to turn him down. The next day he received a call from Jack Whittemore, saying: "Miles called, said he saw you yesterday ... He said something about a week in May, that you got a week in May open. Right?"

"'Right.'

"'He sounded interested. Maybe I can get him to take it.'

"'How much money?' I asked.

"'Forty-five hundred.'

"'I paid him thirty-five hundred last time.'

"'Miles said forty-five.'

"'Thirty-five,' I screamed.

"'Make it forty and I'll talk to him.'

"'Talk to him. Talk to the bastard. And wrap it up, Jack.'

The next day Gordon found a message on his answering box saying: "You got him for forty – OK?"[7] For Davis and his young sidemen the "death of jazz" had less credibility than it did for many others.

Even so, Davis's fees looked significant only beside the fees commanded by other jazzmen. Performers outside jazz were suddenly commanding stipends unimaginable just a few years earlier. In North America and every other industrialized society, the economies of the 1960s began to show the effects of an inflationary spiral sharp enough to disabuse every citizen of the delusion that prices and wages were fixed things; whereas in the previous decade prices and wages had inched upward almost imperceptibly, now they began to shoot up in annual and semi-annual bursts, and by the time the 1970s arrived they increased in quarterly or monthly bursts. Even with the popular consciousness of inflation in the marketplace, the money paid to star attractions and to "superstars" – a brand-new word for a brand-new phenomenon – seemed astounding, and record-setting grosses were reported in the press with numbing regularity.

Both the swelling prices paid to popular performers and the dwindling audience for jazz and other serious music reflected a new balance of power.At its leading edge were four improbable iconoclasts from Liverpool who called themselves the Beatles. Their first hit records, starting in 1962, were as easy to disparage as most of the pop music of the preceding decade, their lyrics as preoccupied with holding hands, dancing with only one partner, and pledging undying love. That made it easy to overlook the careless charm in their early records and consign them to the pop wastebasket that would come to be known as "bubble-gum music," inanities strung together for "teeny boppers," the new majority. But their music was everywhere, and sooner or later the most hardened critic had to recognize its growing preoccupation with themes such as hypocrisy, self-deception, and loneliness, often expressed in small ironies and neat images.

And the Beatles were not alone. The list of pop songwriters capable of touching a serious theme grew rapidly – Harry Chapin, Bob Dylan, Phil Ochs, Joni Mitchell, Randy Newman, and many others. They harked back not to their pop predecessors such as Jerry Lee Lewis, Bill Haley, and Elvis Presley, purveyors of doggerel notwithstanding the necromancy that surrounds them two decades later, but to Woody Guthrie and the Weavers, the self-styled 'folk' singers of the American labor movement.

The new sophistication of the songs soon found performers of more than ordinary gifts. Singers, not surprisingly, came first, as people such as Paul McCartney, Joan Baez, Art Garfunkel, and James Taylor could span octaves without losing tone or abandoning key. Instrumentalists followed soon after: arranger Sly Stone, organist Garth Hudson, and guitarists – guitars were suddenly everywhere – Keith Richard, Eric Clapton, Jimi Hendrix, Robbie Robertson, Carlos Santana. To all these was added a fringe of performers whose particular gifts seemed strictly limited but whose performances were elevated well beyond those limits, such as Arlo Guthrie, Woody's son, the mild-mannered folkie whose *Alice's Restaurant* dismembered the Vietnam war and reigns as the satirical masterpiece of a satirical era; and Janis Joplin, the vulnerable ruffian who transliterated Willie Mae (Big Mama) Thornton's spirit and some of her style into pop music.

All these elements amounted to a pop explosion, not only in gate receipts and fans per household and concerts per capita but also – unpredictably and astonishingly – in quality. Originally directed to teenagers, already the booming majority, the pop culture found their older brothers and sisters receptive too and spread from there to their uncles and aunts and – like, what a turn-off, man – to their parents. Teenage styles spread like ink on a blotter. Before long, lawyers were wearing colored dress shirts, stockbrokers were wearing flared cuffs on their pinstripes, chartered accountants were wearing blue denims, and professors were wearing ponytails. And most of them were buying the Beatles' records, attending Simon and Garfunkel's concerts, and picking out basic chords on guitars.

Jazz was not alone in losing its audience. Drama withered, trying unsuccessfully to relocate its audience by relaxing its mores on language, nudity, and almost everything else. Musical comedies played to half-empty halls except when they incorporated rock 'n' roll plots, as in *Bye Bye Birdie* and *Grease*, or became topical, as in *Hair*. Symphony orchestras commissioned rococo arrangements of melodies by the Beatles and the other hitmakers for pop recitals. Jazz musicians also tried to adapt to the pop cult by laying pop melodies like a thin veneer over their improvisations. Duke Ellington, in the sixth decade of his life and the fourth decade as America's most self-reliant composer, arranged and recorded some Beatles' tunes to help pay for the upkeep of his orchestra.

Miles Davis's music, for the time being, betrayed no special awareness of the pressures of the pop explosion. His managers at Columbia knew better than to propose anything that sounded like a compromise to him, and, besides, he continued to hold his own – for the time being, and with a slight but perceptible slippage – in the changing marketplace. His autonomy would be respected as long as the Columbia executives who had grown up with him in the organization kept their places and would be questioned only later in the decade when new managers, especially Clive Davis, rose through the ranks to reassert Columbia's dominance in what was, in effect, a new billion-dollar entertainment industry. When that happened, Davis would react not by importing a rock veneer into his music but by altering its very substance. Until then, he piloted his new quintet through a period of growth and change that was internal to the group rather than directed at the changing tastes of the world beyond jazz music.

The internal growth and change were not, of course, unaffected by what was happening outside. They were also guided and inspired by the predilections of his sidemen, entirely appropriate to their youth. In September 1964, when the circle was closed by Shorter's joining, Davis was 38, but Shorter was 30, Hancock 24, Carter 27, and Williams 18. The sidemen carried the confidence that seemed endemic to the under-thirties of the day, and Davis gave them something close to a full share in determining the quintet's direction.

Years later, Ron Carter described the participatory democracy that changed the quintet's direction this way: "Sixty per cent of this was the band taking a new direction and 40% was Miles recognizing this, and, while not being able to predict it would go a certain way, understanding that it was definitely taking a turn. I think he was happy to take a back seat and be an inspiration but not hold the reins too tight, and give the horses their head knowing that it would work out all right."[8] There could be no standing still.

The young sidemen worked together easily and developed an unusual rapport. Davis was soon drawn into it. Contrary to his dark public image, he appeared to his band, Carter told Louis-Victor Mialy, "warm, friendly, open – happy to offer, to share his experience with you, always willing to lend you money or even borrow it for you, always ready to invite you for lunch or dinner, always anxious to show you the good note, the best note to play, to advise you about your problems. I have only superlatives for the man."[9] The others shared his feelings.

The band thrived on the confidence that they were peers on their instruments and ranked among the best players around. They were as willing to challenge one another on the bandstand as Davis had been with his great sextet in the recording studio, and for much the same reason: the challenges might lead to stunning solutions and new directions.

The new directions took a while to assert themselves. In a busy fall schedule that included a sojourn in California and a tour of European capitals, Shorter and the others played Davis's time-worn repertoire. The first of their performances to find its way onto record came soon after Shorter made his debut at the Hollywood Bowl, on Steve Allen's television show from Los Angeles. The details are as follows:

Miles Davis Quintet on The Steve Allen Show
Miles Davis, tpt; Wayne Shorter, ts; Herbie Hancock, pno; Ron Carter, b; Tony Williams, dms. The Steve Allen Show, Los Angeles, September 1964
No Blues
(Teppa 76)
The opening theme is missing from this recording.

Beneath the obscure sound of this unauthorized recording, apparently taken from the impoverished sound system of a home television set, the quintet romp through *No Blues* sounding not much different from any of the other quintet versions of years past. Only Hancock stands out, not so much in his note-filled solo as in his comping for Davis and Shorter, in which he picks up their phrases and tosses them back at them. Many clearer examples of Hancock's growing skill as an accompanist follow this one.

The European tour that followed took them to Berlin (25 September), Paris (1 October), Stockholm (3), Copenhagen (4), and other cities, including Barcelona, and again resulted in an LP issued by a CBS subsidiary, just as Davis's most recent trips to Japan and to France had. This time the producer was German CBS. The details are as follows:

Miles Davis Quintet in Berlin
Miles Davis, tpt; Wayne Shorter, ts; Herbie Hancock, pno; Ron Carter, b; Tony
Williams, dms. Philharmonic Hall, Berlin, 25 September 1964
Milestones; Autumn Leaves; So What; Walkin' / The Theme
(all on CBS [G] 62976)

Three of these four titles were recorded at Antibes more than a year
earlier, with George Coleman in the quintet. The differences between
the performances are subtle, and probably only noteworthy in the light
of what was to come. Certainly Tony Williams does not come close to
his outstanding performance at Antibes; on *Milestones* he enters a
couple of bars late at the beginning and somehow never seems to catch
up. But Wayne Shorter adds an adventurous voice, whether compared to
Coleman or to his own playing with the Jazz Messengers. The elements
of his style, deliberately or not, invite comparisons: the dry tone of
Coltrane, the short, choppy phrases of Jackie McLean, and the sliding
onto and away from the tonal centers of notes of Dolphy. They converge
into an approach that is ultimately his alone.

Herbie Hancock, more surprisingly, alters his role almost completely.
His calm, unruffled solos never beg attention, and yet he quietly
dominates much of the music. On *Milestones* and *Walkin'* he slows the
tempo by degrees to a complete stop before revving it up again to its
original pace, an audacious move that belies the quiet surface of his
solos. In support of other soloists, especially on *Autumn Leaves* and
Walkin', he plays much less than comping pianists were expected to,
instead chipping in dissonant splashes of chords at irregular intervals
and punctuating the soloists' statements like a percussionist rather
than providing a running commentary on them as pianists had done not
only in bebop but also in every older style of jazz. He thus liberates the
ensemble from the steady progression of chords and breaks away from
the pianist's traditional role in much the same way that drummers were
breaking away from their time-keeping role. Although it seemed a
radical departure, it was dictated in the first place by Hancock's
befuddlement with Davis's music. "Herbie wanted to quit when he first
got with me," Davis told Gregg Hall. "He said it didn't seem like there
was enough music for him to play. I said, 'Well, then, lay back,
motherfucker. You just told yourself what to do.' He would play for a
while and could not keep it up and sometimes it just seemed like there
wasn't anything for him to do."[10] Hancock's solution to his dilemma
made an influential precedent for a host of young pianists then coming
into jazz.

By the time the quintet reached Barcelona near the end of the tour, they welcomed some free time to behave like tourists. For Davis, it was an opportunity to seek out some of the Spanish music that he had hybridized in *Sketches of Spain*. He and Ron Carter headed into the Catalan backwaters of the city and found a restaurant far from the tourist paths. "I don't speak Spanish and Miles hardly speaks at all," Carter said later, "but there was no communication problem. I took the waiter by the arm and went back to the kitchen to see what was available. I suppose they could have thrown us out. But the staff seemed flattered at our interest. The result was an incredible fish dinner, followed by two hours of beautiful flamenco."[11] Whether or not the occasion reinforced Davis's feeling for flamenco, it definitely aroused his feeling for fish. A few years later, when he took up cooking, he made bouillabaisse one of his specialties.

Soon after the quintet returned to the United States, again to California, which Davis had been using as his home base as often as New York for a year and a half, they began working on a new studio recording, the first in almost two years. The LP that resulted, called *E.S.P.*, would be an eye-opener, the first of the series of LPs that would reveal the new balance of the quintet as none of their live performances, before or after, ever did. In that new balance, Tony Williams was to be the kinetic force, the hub of action, and, inevitably, the attention-getter. "The dense, complex, polyrhythmic textures of his best performances are wonders in themselves," Martin Williams commented, "yet they are always in motion, always swing, are always responsive to the soloist and the ensemble, and are never interfering or distracting. And for his splashing, complex cymbal work alone, Williams belongs among the great drummers in jazz history."[12]

Williams's drumming forced the rest of the players to react. Hancock told Conrad Silvert: "The difference between what Miles had been playing before the quintet crystallized and what we played was incredible. Like, Tony was introducing rhythms I had never even heard. I think what made the band unique was the interplay of the rhythm section, the way the ball passed around ... and at the same times Miles and Wayne floated on top of the ever-revolving rhythm section sound. And just the way Tony mixed up the roles of different parts of the drums – the focus might be on a snare drum, or another time on the bass drum, or it might be totally the cymbals without any other parts of the drums."[13]

Because of his power, Williams could not be missed, and it is easy to undervalue the contributions of the others in what developed. "I'm

inclined to think that the band was important for all of us to grow in,"
Ron Carter points out, adding: "It is also true that we had all kind of
decided on our kind of groove before we joined the band. Obviously
Miles saw that we had something to offer before we joined, or he
wouldn't have asked us. It's clear that he wasn't picking a bunch of total
beginners in concept and technique."[14]

Carter was probably the most secure player in terms of technique
among the young sidemen, a fact that seems vitally important for
someone faced with holding his ground nightly alongside Williams's
drumming dervish. Carter did just that, holding his ground, and the
combination was stronger than either of its parts. "When Miles Davis
had Ron Carter and Tony Williams," Michael Moore, another technically excellent bassist, observed, "Carter was the anchor, and Williams
tended to rush the beat. That created tension, and tension creates
excitement."[15]

Hancock enhances that tension with his percussive colorations in the
ensembles, but in his solos he more often seems to bring it under control
by dictating the pace to the others. His response to the powerful duo is to
speak softly in their company, the antithesis of the most obvious or
expected response, and in doing so he reserves his own personal space
where he might otherwise have simply been swallowed up.

The rhythm section, in any consensus, rival any other ever assembled
in a working band. They have persisted remarkably, lasting long after all
three players finished their tenure with Davis, so that they remain a set
group for recording sessions and occasional tours more than twenty
years after Davis first put them together. In 1983, Carter told Lee Jeske:
"We have found – and I will speak for them at this point – that we seem
to make the most incredible music with the least amount of effort with
each other. And the camaraderie that's involved – this is our twentieth
year of playing together – both on and off the bandstand has sustained
itself, and I'm sure that it plays a big role in our respect and our response
to each other's musical talents and our ability to sacrifice our personal
needs, musically, to make that music go in the direction that it's going,
without input."[16]

As for Davis, he stirred up his own creative energy with the new
quintet. Perhaps his response really was, as Carter later said, 60 per cent
reaction to the creative juices unleashed by his young sidemen and 40
per cent rediscovery of his own resources, but, when all else is said and
done, the direction taken by his new quintet was truly new only to the
young sidemen themselves and not at all new to him. For him, the new
music was a return to the principles he had already asserted brilliantly

Wayne Shorter (Bernie Senensky)

Ron Carter (Bernie Senensky)

in *Kind of Blue*, almost six years earlier. He reasserted his belief in the modal basis for jazz composition and improvisation, presided over the development of a whole repertoire of original compositions, and reclaimed his position in, as Martin Williams put it, "the advance guard of the period."

There can be no doubt that his imprint was on everything the band produced. "He was the only bandleader who paid his personnel not to practise at home," Shorter says, "so as to avoid the polish that makes even some improvised music sound boring. He always wanted it fresh."[17]

That gambit had been easier for Davis to enforce a few years earlier, when he could simply show up at the recording studio with a completely new set of sketches and compositions for his band to play. Now, in the new band, he was only one of the composers; all five members would contribute, and Shorter in particular made several key contributions. "Herbie, Wayne or Tony will write something," Davis told Arthur Taylor, "then I'll take it and spread it out or space it, or add some more chords, or change a couple of phrases, or write a bass line to it, or change the tempo of it, and that's the way we record."[18] On the first LP he claimed credit as co-composer for his efforts, but thereafter the pieces were credited individually to the sidemen. Several of the very best compositions, in any case, are Davis's own. After marking time for a few years, Davis was rejuvenated.

The first studio recordings took place in Hollywood, under the supervision of Irving Townsend. The details are as follows:

Miles Davis Quintet: E.S.P.
Miles Davis, tpt; Wayne Shorter, ts; Herbie Hancock, pno; Ron Carter, b; Tony Williams, dms. Los Angeles, 20 January 1965
E.S.P.; R.J.
(both on Columbia CL 2350)

Same personnel. Same place, 21 January 1965
Eighty-One; Little One
(both on Columbia CL 2350)

Same personnel. Same place, 22 January 1965
Iris; Agitation; Mood
(all on Columbia CL 2350)
Most discographies list an unissued drum solo by Tony Williams recorded on 22 January, but it is probably the one spliced onto the beginning of *Agitation*.

It is hard to imagine music more unlike, say, *Some Day My Prince Will Come*, the "ofay Disneyland tune" (as Hampton Hawes once called it) which was Davis's hit between *Kind of Blue* and these recordings. Some of the new pieces seem anti-melodic, especially the three by Carter: *Eighty-One* (written with Davis), *R.J.* (dedicated to Ralph J. Gleason), and *Mood*. On *Eighty-One*, the trumpet and the tenor saxophone state melodic phrases with long pauses in between, as if to disguise any melodic coherence. On *Little One*, by Hancock and Davis, Shorter opens with a single phrase, Davis plays the next one, and then they repeat them in turn, again breaking up the traditional coherence of melody.

Agitation, by Davis, *E.S.P.*, by Shorter and Davis, and *Iris*, by Shorter, preserve the melodic line in the opening and closing, although they are "simple in structure and sparse melodically[,] containing relatively few notes," as Harvey Pekar noted in his overview.[19] Even these take liberties with conventional structures, as *Agitation* opens with a drum solo, and all of them shift freely in tempos. Time signatures also move around: *Eighty-One* is basically in 6/8 time but shifts to 4/4 time for parts of the solos, and *Little One* opens and closes as a pulseless mood piece but shifts surprisingly into 3/4 time for the solos.

The music is, as Scott Yanow says, "a total break from the past,"[20] and James Lincoln Collier described Davis's stylistic departures this way: "His playing is thoroughly modal, often interrupted by tempoless stretches. He is inflecting his line with a lot of half-valving and often intentionally letting notes fall off pitch, as if he were mocking his own music. He is using the upper register more. The delicacy and interest in note placement that characterized his work previously is less in evidence, and, at times, as, for example, in *Iris* on *E.S.P.*, his line is filled with vast, empty phrases, like wind in a ruined cathedral."[21]

For Davis's perennial fans, *E.S.P.* served notice not only of a change in direction but also of an about-face in his stated position on Ornette Coleman and the other exponents of freer forms. That change was also implied in the title, *E.S.P.*, which seemed to reflect the cliché current among both the adherents and the detractors of free forms, that the only way bands would play unstructured music together was through extrasensory perception or mental telepathy. Davis offered his listeners music held together by less rigid structural principles than he had formerly used, and he was showing off a new, young band capable of suffusing each piece with a remarkable unity. If they were not exactly appealing to ESP, they were nevertheless giving up the familiar hallmarks of melody and tempo in favor of the much more elusive notions of mood and atmosphere. And *E.S.P.* was only the beginning, though a remarkable one. The next step, however, took almost twenty-two months, as other matters intervened.

In the spring of 1965, Davis's hip ailment hindered his mobility and kept him in constant pain. Thrombosis in the joint had caused the left socket to deteriorate, and the only chance of his continuing to walk unaided was through an operation to replace the dead socket. The surgery and its complications laid Davis up for seven months and kept the quintet inactive all that time. It may have been scheduled for earlier in the year than April, perhaps closer to the end of January, when *E.S.P.* was concluded, but Davis's general health forced his doctors to postpone the operation. "A doctor went to check my blood pressure and he said, Where is it? Do you *have* any blood? Really?" Davis told Cheryl McCall. "He told me to eat some bread so I could get my strength up and have my blood. I had to have a five hour operation and I needed strength for that."[22] The first operation on 14 April replaced the hip ball with a graft from Davis's shin. Davis allowed three months for recovery and booked an engagement at the Village Vanguard in August, but as the date approached he remained hurting and nearly immobile. The bone graft had failed, and in August he went through a second operation to replace the joint with a plastic one. He would not be ready to resume performing until November.

In the meantime, *E.S.P.* was released. If its contents were largely unexpected, its cover at least carried a familar theme. It again depicted Frances Taylor Davis, this time with Davis peering up at her from a chaise longue. It was the third of his covers that she had graced, in alternate years since 1961, and the last. The marriage had become troubled, and it would gradually dissolve, ending in divorce after nine years.

The young sidemen kept busy during the layoff, playing on several recording dates and in pickup bands. All of them took studio calls, and Carter especially was in demand for all kinds of jingles, pit bands, and studio dates, so much so that he occasionally missed Davis's engagements outside New York during his remaining three years with the band. They also played together as often as they could, thus reinforcing the bonds that worked so well for Davis's music. Usually Tony Williams instigated their reunions. On his own debut LP as a leader (*Spring*, Blue Note BLP-4216), recorded in August, he hired Shorter and Hancock. His friend Sam Rivers, also recording for Blue Note at the time, used Carter and Williams on *Fuchsia Swing Song* (BN-4184) and Hancock and Carter on *Contours* (ST-84206). Williams booked a trio engagement at a small club in Boston for Shorter, Carter, and himself, where they collectively worked on free improvisations.[23] When Davis reassembled them, they resumed their work with him without any preliminary rehearsals.

Davis made his return to performing in the week beginning Tuesday, 16 November, at the Village Vanguard. His appearance was eagerly anticipated after the seven-month absence and the cancellation during the summer. Dan Morgenstern, who covered the opening night for *Down Beat*, reported that "the long lines of people waiting outside – not a common sight on today's night-club scene – testified to Davis's drawing power, and the music more than justified the turnout."[24] Ron Carter could not break a commitment and was replaced by Reggie Workman. That change caused no problems. Workman, originally from Philadelphia, had worked with Coltrane in his first bands and had played alongside Shorter in the Jazz Messengers in Shorter's final years with that group. After that, he stuck close to New York rather than traveling regularly with bands, but his reputation among musicians as a power bassist capable of fitting into any context has always been formidable. (When Mal Waldron, long domiciled in Europe, signed a recording contract with the Munich firm ENJA in the early 1970s, he stipulated that the company provide him with an opportunity to record in New York with Workman as his bassist.) The quintet, with Workman filling in, played excellently by all accounts.

If the audiences found little diminution of Davis's music, Max Gordon found none at all in his business acumen. "Miles always liked to get $1,000 front money before he'd open," Gordon recalled. "If I didn't have it, he might open, but after the first set opening night, he'd come to me and, scanning the crowd, whisper, 'Don't forget the grand if you want me to come in tomorrow night.'"[25] Michael Zwerin, part of the audience on the first weekend, recalled that Davis "had been sick and hadn't played much in about six months, so he sounded a little weak," but that was no drawback. "I would rather listen to a weak Miles," he added, "than a strong almost anybody else – especially the way he plays a ballad ... He blew *Old Folks*, and a young girl sitting near me said softly, 'He opens up melodies like a flower.'"[26] Davis had recorded *Old Folks* in 1961 on *Some Day My Prince Will Come* and had seldom played it since.

The rest of his repertoire for this engagement and the tour that followed was similarly retrospective, consisting of ballads and Davis's old standbys. Morgenstern caught the quintet playing *Round Midnight, If I Were a Bell, When I Fall in Love, I Thought about You, Four, So What, All Blues, The Theme,* and "a spontaneous blues, on which Davis dug deeply to roots, toying with phrases from *Royal Garden Blues* and *Easy Rider.*"

The Vanguard comeback, like other comebacks by Davis to follow, was not just an exploratory engagement for testing himself physically and musically, but a full-fledged return to work. It was followed by an engagement at the Showboat in Philadelphia in early December and, immediately after that, by two weeks, from 21 December until 2 January, at the Plugged Nickel in Davis's traditional Yuletide stopover, Chicago. The engagement at the Plugged Nickel aroused even more excitement than the one at the Vanguard, the local demand having been whetted by Davis's canceling three previous engagements scheduled during the year, the most recent in mid-October. Ron Carter had resumed his place in the band, and Davis had updated the repertoire by adding *Agitation,* the first of the quintet's new music to enter the working book.

Davis's high spirits at the Plugged Nickel showed when he agreed to let a teenaged saxophonist sit in with the band, perhaps through the intermediacy of Hancock, a native Chicagoan who knew many of the local musicians. As it happened, the young saxophonist never summoned the courage to take the stand. "I was seventeen or eighteen when a friend of mine set it up for me to sit in with Miles," John Klemmer recalled several years later, "and I just sat there, kept on drinking and holding on to my horn. I never got up. I just tripped out on the idea that Miles was gonna let me."[27] Klemmer moved to California a few years later as a soloist with the Don Ellis orchestra and gained some prominence fusing jazz forms with rock elements in the early 1970s.

Adding to the hubbub at the Plugged Nickel was the presence of Teo Macero and a flotilla of mobile recording facilities hired by Columbia. Davis's long absence from performing coincided with an equally lengthy absence from recording, and Columbia was having little success getting a commitment from him for a return to its studios. It moved in to record the first three nights of his engagement. Ironically, the enormous quantity of music it taped then lay in its vaults until Japanese CBS-Sony mastered two LPS from it in 1976; Columbia finally reissued the Japanese masters as a double album in North America in 1982. The music issued so far hardly makes a dent in the tapes, even though only the second and third nights' performances are apparently suitable in quality, the first night presumably given over to setting up and attuning the recording equipment. With typical assiduity, the Japanese producers listed the recorded materials, set by set, from which their LPS are selected, providing not only an indication of what will eventually be issued but also a document of Davis's repertoire at the time. The details are as follows:

Miles Davis Quintet at the Plugged Nickel
Miles Davis, tpt; Wayne Shorter, ts; Herbie Hancock, pno; Ron Carter, b; Tony Williams, dms. The Plugged Nickel, Chicago, 22 December 1965
Set 1: *If I Were a Bell; Stella by Starlight; Walkin'; I Fall in Love Too Easily*
Set 2: *My Funny Valentine; Four; When I Fall in Love; Agitation; Round Midnight; Milestones/The Theme*
Set 3: *All of You; Oleo; I Fall in Love Too Easily; No Blues; I Thought about You/The Theme*
(*Round Midnight* on CBS-Sony [Jap] 25 AP 291)

Same personnel. Same place, 23 December 1965
Set 1: *If I Were a Bell; Stella by Starlight; Walkin'; I Fall in Love Too Easily/ The Theme*
Set 2: *All of You; Agitation; My Funny Valentine; On Green Dolphin Street; So What/The Theme*
Set 3: *When I Fall in Love, Milestones; Autumn Leaves; I Fall in Love Too Easily; No Blues/The Theme*
Set 4: *Stella by Starlight; All Blues; Yesterdays/The Theme*
(*Stella by Starlight* [set 1], *All Blues, Yesterdays/The Theme* on CBS-Sony [Jap] 25 AP 291; *Walkin', Agitation, On Green Dolphin Street, So What/The Theme* on CBS-Sony [Jap] 25 AP 1)
All titles issued by CBS-Sony are included on Columbia C2 38266 (1982).

Judging by the typical length of the issued titles, Columbia holds enough material from the Plugged Nickel for five or six more LPS. Except for *Yesterdays*, which Davis recorded in 1952 and had never played since, the titles are, of course, familiar, but the music itself contains many innovations when compared to the last live performance recorded by the quintet, twenty-six months earlier in Berlin. It represents a much more decisive departure from the bebop conventions or, put positively, a much more fluid approach to matters of form and phrasing.

Shorter especially seems uninterested in developing melodic variants of the themes. His solos create sound effects, altering tonality and breaking phrases unexpectedly, so much so that when he reins himself in with occasional references to the original melody he makes the melody itself sound incongruous. On *Agitation*, in his first chorus he leads Hancock into a wild pursuit that ends with the usually calm Hancock unleashing a flurry of Taylor-made runs.

All the music is amazingly fluid: tempos and time signatures alter continually, harmonies in the ensembles shift constantly, familiar breaks such as the one on *Round Midnight* between Davis and Shorter become raunchy, and solos turn suddenly into simultaneous improvisations – by Shorter and Williams on *So What* and by Shorter and Davis on *Yesterdays/The Theme*. Nothing at all in this music seems fixed, and, at its best, on *All Blues* and *Yesterdays/The Theme* (both, one notes, from the same set, from which another title, perhaps of comparable quality, remains unissued), the listener gets the thrill of a musical giant slalom where every turn is completely different from the ones before it. The performance, or as much of it as we have so far, seems to be a textbook example of Davis's feeling for leadership, notwithstanding the six months of independent activity by the players. "I give them their heads," Davis told Don DeMicheal, "but I try to tell them what sounds best. I tell them to always be prepared for the unexpected – if it's going out, it might go out more, an extended ending might keep on going."[28]

He now had musicians who were more than willing to "go out more" and to "keep on going." Their six-month recess from the quintet while Davis recuperated clinched that. During that time each of them had become involved with more of the music being played in New York than they otherwise could have. The atmosphere had calmed down by degrees since 1960. Conspicuous opportunities for playing the new music were rare, and livelihoods for those who played it were tentative, but the jazz business was depressed everywhere and so were all the performing arts; the new men hardly needed to feel paranoid or resentful about their poverty when it seemed to be a general condition. In 1960 it had been possible to see the new music as a kind of graft, or perhaps a parasite, on the jazz scene; by 1965, that view had become implausible. The new music remained. It had survived the period of vituperation, and, more important, it had survived a period of critical and popular neglect. And it had taken root.

John Coltrane's conspicuous support, recording with people such as Archie Shepp, Pharaoh Sanders, and Rashied Ali and occasionally adding them to his band increased their credibility with the general audience, and so did his own increasingly free music. The proponents of the new music not only carried on with it but their numbers increased, and they continued to work at their music with the same conviction as any other school of musicians, or perhaps more.

Ornette Coleman reappeared, after an almost complete withdrawal from performing in public that lasted from 1962 well into 1965. He was back, but without Don Cherry, usually playing only with a bassist and a drummer. Cherry, along with a host of new musicians, including Albert Ayler and Marion Brown, was in Europe, where a small but fervid audience for their music developed in France, the Netherlands, Germany, and Scandinavia. Coleman's biggest success since his Five Spot engagement came in November 1965, when he toured Scandinavia with bassist David Izenzon and drummer Charles Moffett. Coleman and almost everyone else involved in jazz were amazed when Coleman's recording of part of a concert in Stockholm, *At the Golden Circle, Vol. 1* (Blue Note BST 84224), was named best album in *Down Beat*'s Jazz Critics Poll for 1966, edging out Davis's *E.S.P.*, the two LPs being not so different from one another in spirit as anyone could have predicted.

Elsewhere in the same poll, Davis's sharp return to form since 1963 and his continuing explorations with the new quintet since 1964, despite the layoffs, were rewarded with wins both for the top small band and for the top trumpeter.

The comeback was cut off abruptly. On the last day of January 1966 Davis was hospitalized again, this time with a liver inflammation. The disorder probably originated as another symptom of the oxygen deficiency caused by the sickle cells, but it was certainly aggravated by liquor. Davis, whose struggle to withdraw from heroin was twelve years in the past, was forced to give up alcohol. "What could be any worse than whiskey?" he asked Cheryl McCall. "It's got my liver all fucked up."[29] Giving up alcohol was no great problem – he would do it, as Mark Twain did tobacco, several times over the next years – but sitting around recuperating for another three months proved harder. On a Monday night in the middle of March, he slipped out to a club called Slug's and sat in with a band led by trumpeter Lonnie Hillyer and saxophonist Charles McPherson, two young Detroiters who had apprenticed with Charles Mingus's band and were trying to put a band of their own together. Soon after, he reassembled the quintet and started back to work.

Again, the comeback tour made no concessions to his health. It included a month-long swing along the West Coast and then a return to the east for the summer. Ron Carter refused to make the western tour, as he usually did in the years to come; in his place, Davis took Richard Davis, the versatile virtuoso who turned up on dozens of recordings and was considered by many musicians to be the best modern bassist of all, and not only in jazz. Included in the itinerary were some college concerts, one at Portland State College in Oregon (on 21 May) and another at Stanford University in California (on 22 May); the one at Stanford was the final concert sponsored by the student union in a series called Jazz Year, a program designed to improve economic conditions for jazz players. After more then twenty-five years of playing his music in jazz clubs, Davis found the college concerts a relief in every respect, and he was not reluctant to say so. "I make more in one night on a college date than you pay me in a week," he once told Max Gordon. "And I don't have to take all that shit! ... I can't stand the whole fuckin' scene. The cats comin' around, the bullshit, the intermissions. I hate intermissions. And you lookin' sore because I ain't up on the bandstand. And the people! 'Play *Bye Bye Blackbird*!' Shit! I don't drink now. I work out in Stillman's Gym four hours a day. I used to have to come down every night. Down to your plantation. Now I come when I want to come. On a college concert I do two short sets and I'm through. I don't have to hang around, listen to a lot of bullshit!"[30]

Whatever attractions the night-life surrounding a club date had once held for him were curtailed by his health problems, at least for the time being. He turned 40 just four days after the Stanford concert, but he spent his birthday playing in another jazz club, Shelly's Manne-Hole, owned by the drummer, in Los Angeles. For working jazzmen, there was really no way to avoid clubs altogether, and the quintet played there from 24 May until 5 June.

Not all the concert dates were a distinct improvement on the club dates anyway. After closing at Shelly's Manne-Hole, the quintet played a one-night stand in San Diego under excruciating circumstances. The details were supplied by Gil Evans, who was in California rehearsing and performing with an orchestra he assembled for the Monterey Jazz Festival and some other California engagements. Evans traveled with Davis to the San diego concert. "This was in a great big ballroom they had converted into a supper club, and the acoustics were terrible," Evans told Leonard Feather in an interview for *Down Beat*. "They had the group down on the floor, maybe ten feet from the stage, on a little platform, with no shell. I asked the woman who owns the club why they weren't playing on the stage, and she said, 'Well, I like to have them down in front of the people, because the people like to see the emotional expressions on their faces.' The whole thing looked like a set for a Hollywood movie." Evans added, "The piano was absolutely impossible – an old, worn-out grand piano – so that all the important things that Herbie Hancock played were almost completely lost."[31]

Evans's California orchestra was the first he had assembled without Davis since 1961, when he fronted a short-lived orchestra, and for the first time in his career he was playing piano in the band. He had enlisted a good lineup, including tenor saxophonist Billy Harper, tuba player Howard Johnson, and drummer Elvin Jones. After their debut at the Monterey Festival, they played at Shelly's Manne-Hole and were recorded playing concerts at both UCLA and Costa Mesa. Evans seemed ready to embark on his career as a full-time bandleader, but for several reasons – bad recording conditions, a strung-out trumpet player, lack of rehearsal time, and so on – none of this music recorded in California was issued on record. One of the sixteen compositions he arranged for his California orchestra, *Freedom Jazz Dance* by saxophonist Eddie Harris, showed up a few months later in a version by the Miles Davis Quintet, probably an unacknowledged adaptation of Evans's arrangement, but otherwise the music he played in California disappeared without a trace.

Both in California and in New York, Evans and Davis continued working together. They had never ceased doing so, although the last public evidence of their collaborations, the *Quiet Nights* arrangements, was now four years old. Whenever Evans listened to Davis with the quintet, his mind was partly on the orchestrations he might devise for him, and he heard lots of possibilities in Davis's work at the San Diego concert. "When he played *All of You*," he told Feather, "he got the most delicate type of sound – his muted sound – you notice the tremendous power behind the horn, even though it is muted. More often than not, when people play with mutes, everything sounds relaxed, but with Miles there's an extraordinary tension; he went past that quiet feeling and into a thing where it just floated. That's what we have to develop on our next album. I want to write accompaniments for just that particular kind of sound."[32]

With Davis's enforced layoffs from performing in the previous year, the two men spent more time than usual working out ideas. They had several projects half-formed with many more to come, and that was perhaps part of their problem.

Back on the east coast for the summer, the quintet appeared at the

Newport Jazz Festival on 4 July, Independence Day. They played *All Blues* and *Stella by Starlight*, both firmly established as favorites by Davis now, although he had ignored them for years after his original recordings of them. *Stella by Starlight* provided a particularly effective showcase for Ron Carter, who had emerged as one of the best supporting players and remained unsung because he so seldom took a solo.

The Newport Festival had become an institution since it began in 1955, when Miles Davis had scored one of the festival's most conspicuous artistic triumphs, but it was suffering growing pains. It had diversified to the point where Davis branded it, to the delight of almost everyone, "a supermarket." In an effort to keep the crowds during the years of the jazz recession, George Wein added the Newport Folk Festival in 1963, capitalizing on the enthusiasm for folk-pop and folk-rock among the young audience. By 1966 the town of Newport was overrun by campers and partygoers at festival time, and Wein added an opera festival that year, hoping to give the crowds a leaven of highbrows. The additional genre only lengthened the party season at the Newport spa. "It takes only one trip to the Newport Jazz Festival – the gentry in the front row with their martini shakers, the sailors squatting in the back, their heads between their knees, upchucking their beer – to remember what a weird mixture is Miles Davis' world," wrote Murray Kempton in the *New York Post*. "Was ever anything in America at once so fashionable and so squalid?"[33]

Jazz would eventually outlast folk music and opera as the festival feature, but the burghers of Newport were growing impatient with the fashionable squalor Wein was planting in their community every summer.

The Miles Davis Quintet finally returned to the Columbia studios in October, this time in New York with Teo Macero in the control room. In the long interim, both Herbie Hancock and Tony Williams had signed recording contracts with Blue Note, and their releases for Davis's recordings had to be negotiated. The resulting LP, titled, lugubriously, *Miles Smiles*, showed even greater cohesion than *E.S.P.* In his 1978 article, Scott Yanow declared it "the essential quintet album from this period." The details are as follows:

Miles Davis Quintet: Miles Smiles
Miles Davis, tpt; Wayne Shorter, ts; Herbie Hancock, pno; Ron Carter, b; Tony Williams, dms. New York, 24 October 1966
Circle; Orbits; Dolores; Freedom Jazz Dance
(all on Columbia CL 2601)

Same personnel. Same place, 25 October 1966
Ginger Bread Boy; Footprints
(both on Columbia CL 2601)
Freedom Jazz Dance is probably arranged by Gil Evans or in collaboration with
Evans.

Any description of the music contained on *Miles Smiles* is bound to be
couched in contradictions, for the music includes a ballad that is not a
song (*Circle*), an unforgettable melody that mimics semi-articulate
speech (*Dolores*), and two funk-gospel pieces that are not funky
(*Freedom Jazz Dance, Ginger Bread Boy*). Even more obviously than
most Miles Davis LPs, this one consists of previously unrehearsed
music; several of the ensembles are rough, especially the closing theme
of *Dolores*, in which Davis and Shorter seem to tempt one another by
playing fragments that leave the other player stranded, and *Freedom
Jazz Dance* where Davis makes a false start. Hancock plays as if his
piano were a horn; on *Orbits, Dolores,* and *Ginger Bread Boy* he is silent
in all ensembles and during Davis's and Shorter's solos, entering as the
third soloist and then, on all three tracks, fashioning his solo out of
single-note lines played by the right hand only.

Notwithstanding the contradictions, *Miles Smiles* is the most consistently interesting album by Miles Davis since *Kind of Blue.* The rough
ensembles matter less than they otherwise might because the compositions are played as multi-part simultaneous improvisations rather than
set ensembles followed by individual solos. Partly, this realignment of
traditional form seems a natural development from Tony Williams's
refusal to be subjugated, and it was implicit from the beginning but only
burst into the open here. Williams is everywhere, including many places
where jazz listeners least expect to hear him. On *Freedom Jazz Dance,*
his rhythm is not metrical but builds around an uneven drum roll. He
marks the time with his high-hat, and the dance rhythm pervades the
track almost in spite of Williams, sustained by Hancock and Carter.

Hancock's reduction of the piano to a single-note instrument in the
treble clef follows from the modality of the writing. When the
harmonies are not pre-set, there is nothing for a comping piano player to
feed to the other players and Hancock eliminates the left hand not only
when the others are soloing but also when he is.

The unity of the pieces and thus their coherence, those elements that
Davis and many others complained about in free form playing by lesser
bands than this one, fall almost by default to Carter, and he responds

brilliantly. On *Footprints* he carries the 6/4 riff throughout the length of the piece, altering tempo and occasionally playing a variant or inserting a bar of 4/4 time but never for a moment letting the time signature slip. He is simply indispensable.

Regardless of these liberties with form, the music on *Miles Smiles* is hardly less accessible to bop-bred listeners than Davis's earlier work. Only *Orbits*, one of three Shorter compositions and the shortest track on the LP, seems to keep its structural secrets hidden after repeated listening. Douglas Clark's explanation that "it is made up almost entirely of minor seconds and perfect fourths, orbiting around its tonal centre (c)" and that it "is dodecaphonic (but not serial)"[34] does not help much for anyone trying to figure out how the solos by Davis, Shorter, and Hancock, all apparently unrelated in mood, style, and melody, are expected to work together. Otherwise Shorter's compositions on this LP, *Footprints* and *Dolores*, are memorable pieces that passed quickly into the repertoires of other bands. They consist of brief, melodic catch-phrases – the entire written portion of *Dolores* lasts no more than eight bars – that get repeated arbitrarily in the opening and closing ensembles. The point of the catch-phrase is to encode the scale that is available to the improviser, but the quality that distinguishes both *Footprints* and *Dolores* is the clarity of the mood that the catch-phrase also encodes. Shorter's compositions thus direct the improviser not only to the form (the scale) but also to the content (the mood) with only a few deft strokes. They do not present a melody in the conventional sense of a paragraph of ordered musical phrases and clauses; that presentation is left to the improviser.

Traditional forms, specifically the twelve-bar blues and the thirty-two-bar song dominant in jazz for decades, provide no precedents for Shorter's modal compositions. They have slightly more influence on Davis's *Circle*, which is decidedly a ballad (by any definition) although not exactly a song (by the formal definition). Davis's tightly muted exposition of the melody over conventional rhythm accompaniment – Hancock comping, Williams using brushes – relates *Circle* to the long line of ballads Davis has recorded since 1948, but is formally weird, consisting of a twenty-two-bar statement with no discernible bridge. The recorded version also catches Shorter playing a more conventional ballad solo than he usually played in Davis's band, as if to guarantee that Davis's oldest fans would find a point of reference.

More surprising are the two blues-based numbers in the gospel-funk style, *Freedom Jazz Dance* by Eddie Harris, the Chicago saxophonist who was experimenting with electric instruments and attracting some rock fans, and *Ginger Bread Boy* by Davis's old friend Jimmy Heath, the saxophonist who was now mainly occupied writing charts for Julian Adderley, Herbie Mann, and others. ("When people like that record an album that sells twenty or thirty thousand copies," Heath told Valerie Wilmer, "that's a nice little taste to come in out of the mails when you're not working."[35]) Both compositions were originally built on chord progressions with strong blues melodies, but Davis strips them down and distends them so that the blues seem to be ejaculated like steam from a geyser. The homely phrases of the originals are bandied about and permuted over and over again by all five players so that they are never quite set aside and never quite in focus. For the listener, the music presents both the conventional and the unexpected not by moving between one pole and the other but by straddling the poles.

Much of *Miles Smiles* balances that same tension between the old and the new. It seemed an automatic choice when it was cited as record of the year in *Down Beat*'s readers' poll in 1967.

Davis's health continued to nag him until he was forced to make some adjustments. He took the quintet into the Village Vanguard early in 1967, but he eased the physical strain of the engagement by playing three consecutive weekends rather than a straight week, beginning on 20 January. He also eased the playing load on himself by expanding the band into a sextet. The sixth man was Joe Henderson, a tenor saxophonist who gained his first professional experience in Detroit. Although he was a few years younger than Shorter – he would turn thirty later in the spring – his background was very similar. He too had put in time with the US army band, serving from 1960 to 1962, and he came into Davis's band after playing a year and a half with Horace Silver's quintet, a band that worked in the same neo-bop style as Art Blakey's Jazz Messengers. Henderson had a warmer, more robust tone than Shorter, his debt more to Sonny Rollins than to Coltrane, but he too was a transitional player capable of moving with self-assurance from bebop to freer forms when he improvised.

So far, Henderson's tenure in Davis's band remains undocumented, but in addition to his weekends at the Vanguard he remained with the band for a tour of fifteen cities in February and March, in a concert package called the World Series of Jazz. The other headliners included Count Basie and his orchestra, Sonny Stitt, Billy Eckstine, and, in keeping with the mood of the time, a South African folk singer named Miriam Makeba and a political satirist named Dick Davy. The promoter of the tour, Teddy Powell, told *Down Beat*, "The receipts are greater from my jazz promotions than my rock-and-roll shows."[36] The hardest of jazz's hard times appeared to be over.

Around this time, possibly beginning with the weekend performances at the Village Vanguard, Davis began playing his nightclub sets and concerts in a single, unbroken continuum. The change was radical but in retrospect seems a straightforward response to the dictates of his new music. Having abandoned prescribed bar sequences for explorations of mood, some of them determined by successions of scales, Davis began to segue from scale to scale even when the scales belonged formally to different compositions. The changes of mood associated with different compositions evolved in the transitions, as did changes of tempo, time signature, scale, and the rest, but just as the structural elements had become increasingly fluid, so too had the mood, almost by definition, being ineffable or at least less effable than structure. The quintet's performances, at their best, became improvised suites organized around a few common themes instead of a sequence of unconnected melodies.

It was an audacious move, but it represented a small step from Davis's usual practice in his performances for more than a decade, when he gave the downbeat and started the next number as soon as the applause for the previous number had begun. That old practice always roused the ire of fans who expected their applause to be acknowledged, but the new practice left them with no intervals for applause at all as the music rolled inexorably onward.

"The things of music you just finish," Davis told Don DeMicheal in 1969, when questioned about his continuous sets. "When you play, you carry them through till you think they're finished or until the rhythm dictates it's finished and then you do something else. But you also connect what you finished with what you're going to do next. So it doesn't sound like a pattern. So when you learn that, you got a good band, and when your band learns that, it's a good band."[37]

Davis's precedent, like the other precedents he set with his controversial stage manner, won hardly any converts among other musicians. One who followed his lead was Max Roach. Charles Tolliver, Roach's trumpeter for the last two years of the decade and, incidentally, one of the few trumpet players whose style seemed completely uninfluenced by Davis, explained that "you can create a concert-type thing in a club" with continuous sets. "A lot of times you want to connect different songs," he told Valerie Wilmer, "and applause in between is a waste of time. Miles is the first person who started doing it, and Max does it too.

It really keeps you on your toes, because the musicians who are working with you know all the things that you're going to do, but they don't know in which order you're going to play them."[38] Even Roach and Tolliver did not persist, and the practice of playing continuous sets remains an idiosyncrasy of Davis's performances.

In April, Davis moved with the quintet to the West Coast, alternating his home base as he had done for four years. This time, the stay lasted five weeks. Joe Henderson left the band, and Ron Carter took another leave. For the first concert on the tour, at the University of California in Berkeley, Davis borrowed bassist Albert Stinson from the John Handy Quintet, San Franscisco's top jazz group. The Berkeley concert, in the hotbed of student activism, also featured the Modern Jazz Quartet and Gerald Wilson's big band, an aggregation of California studio musicians. Originally scheduled for the outdoor Hearst Greek Theater, rainstorms forced the concert inside to the Harmon Gymnasium, which was packed with 8,000 wet fans. Russ Wilson, covering the event for *Down Beat*, provided what was probably the first notice of Davis's uninterrupted recitals in describing "an electrifying set that continued for 62 minutes, almost without pause." He listed the elements of the medley in order as *Agitation*, *Ginger Bread Boy*, *Round Midnight*, *So What*, *Walkin'*, and *The Theme*, a sequence of familiar titles except for *Ginger Bread Boy*. The concert included a public display of feeling so rare that Wilson could hardly leave it out: "So superb was drummer Tony Williams' playing on *So What* that Davis, after ending his monumental solo, walked over and patted him on the back."[39]

For the rest of the West Coast engagements, the quintet was completed by bassist Charles (Buster) Williams, a 25-year-old from New Jersey who had earned his reputation with the Jazz Crusaders, a California band directed by drummer Stix Hooper. Davis first heard about Williams from Hampton Hawes the previous summer. Hawes's tale of Davis's first exposure to the talented young bassist, as he told it to Harvey Siders, remains one of the great nonsequiturs in the history of talent scouting. "I had told Miles, 'There's a young cat in Los Angeles named Buster Williams who can really play.' Miles said, 'Can he really play?' And I said, 'Yeah, he can play.' I was playing one night," Hawes continued, "and Miles was there, and Buster came up and played so good, Miles threw up on his pants. And that's the truth."[40] Talent like that apparently could not be denied, and the Davis Quintet, with Buster Williams on bass, moved into a San Francisco club called the Both/And for the middle two weeks of April.

Hawes was a member of the audience at the Both/And. He was still playing solo cocktail piano in the early evenings and keeping his parole officer happy, if not himself, by doing it. Davis's opening night gave Hawes's spirits such a boost that he later described it, with slight variations, both to Harvey Siders and in his memoirs. "Miles looked at me in my sharp suit and said, 'Where you playin'?' figuring at 9:30 I must be going to work instead of coming." Hawes told him about his "sad gig" and then found a seat in the audience to listen. "They were really doing something," Hawes said, "and ... I walked over to the stand and I said to Herbie, 'Get up, get off the piano.'" He continues: "I wound up in the middle of a tune with Miles' band wondering, what the fuck am I doing up here. Finished the tune and afterwards asked Miles, 'Was it cool?' He said, 'You're a crazy motherfucker. It was beautiful.'" Hawes added, "Now *that*'s all that counts, as long as you mean it."[41]

Hawes escaped the tedium of his 5-to-9 job in the fall of 1967, when he left San Francisco on a catch-as-catch-can global tour that restored some of his confidence and revived some of his reputation. As jazz music in general came on better times, so did Hawes, and he worked productively, though shifting indecisively between milder-mannered bop than he had formerly played and amplified, rock-based music, until 1977, when, at the age of 48, he died of a massive stroke.

The Davis Quintet moved on to Seattle, into a club called the Penthouse, and then in early May to Los Angeles, where they again recorded in Columbia's Hollywood studios. As had happened a few years earlier on the recordings for *Seven Steps to Heaven*, Davis was dissatisfied with the recordings made in Hollywood and chose to re-record the material when he returned to New York a week later. This time he rejected all the Hollywood takes in favor of the New York ones, and so far only one of them has come to light. The details are as follows:

Miles Davis Quintet with Buster Williams
Miles Davis, tpt; Wayne Shorter, ts; Herbie Hancock, pno; Buster Williams, b; Tony Williams, dms. Los Angeles, 9 May 1967
Limbo
(on *Directions*, Columbia KC2 36472)

Shorter's theme for *Limbo* is not particularly attractive, simply a unison run by the trumpet and saxophone up the minor scale and back down it. It suggests motion but goes nowhere, always ending up at the same place, thus making a fair definition of its title. On both the Hollywood and the subsequent New York versions, Hancock is all but nonexistent until he plays his one-handed solo. The main difference in the two versions, apart from the greater length of Davis's and Shorter's solos on the later version, is Tony Williams, who is torrential throughout the New York version but plays the Hollywood one as if handcuffed, giving it a calmer — or 'laid-back,' as the California buzz-word might put it — surface.

Limbo's re-recording took place just a week later, with Ron Carter back in the band, at the sessions for the LP *Sorcerer*. The details are as follows:

Miles Davis Quintet: Sorcerer
Miles Davis, tpt; Wayne Shorter, ts; Herbie Hancock, pno; Ron Carter, b; Tony Williams, dms. New York, 16 May 1967
Limbo; Vonetta
(both on Columbia CL 2732)

Same personnel. Same place, 17 May 1967
Masqualero; The Sorcerer
(both on Columbia CL 2732)

Same personnel, except Miles Davis does not play on *Pee Wee*. Same place, 24 May 1967
Prince of Darkness; Pee Wee
(both on Columbia CL 2732)

None of these titles is composed by Davis; Shorter contributes four (*Limbo, Vonetta, Prince of Darkness*, and *Masqualero*), Hancock the title piece (*The Sorcerer*), and Williams the one on which Davis is unaccountably absent (*Pee Wee*).

On *Pee Wee*, where the young sidemen are left to their own devices and one might have expected an excursion into the further reaches of free forms, they turned out instead a slow, undistinguished ballad, warmly played by Shorter as Hancock comps behind him; it is easily the most conservative music on the LP.

Vonetta and *Prince of Darkness*, also ballads, are more interesting. *Prince of Darkness* begins as a medium fast ballad and continues as such for Davis's long, lyrical solo; then the tempo varies behind both Shorter and Hancock, and the final statement of the theme ends up, perhaps unintentionally, faster than the opening statement.

Vonetta shows a masterly use of the quintet's resources. Essentially a medium ballad, Davis plays a lyrical solo following Hancock's introduction, and Shorter and Hancock preserve his mood in their solos. Carter's walking bass line buoys the solos, making *Vonetta* a ballad performance worthy of comparison to *Circle*. But it is more than a stunning ballad because of Williams, who sustains an undercurrent of quasi-military rolls on his snare drum in the background. The effect is strange and tense, as if the peaceful mood of the ballad might be ripped apart at any moment. The contrasting elements work so impeccably that they seem to be a carefully calculated device, but they came about spontaneously. As Hancock recalled several years later, Williams used the drum roll because Davis turned to him as they were about to record *Vonetta* and said, "Play a *Rat Patrol* sound."[42]

Masqualero, with a Spanish tinge that is almost a bolero and almost a flamenco, in an uncategorizable time signature, and *The Sorcerer*, a medium uptempo number that strains Davis and Shorter by requiring them to solo in alternating eight-bar fragments, vary the pace of the LP. *The Sorcerer* is dedicated to Davis and named for him, "because," Hancock says, "Miles *is* a sorcerer. His whole attitude, the way he is, is kind of mysterious. I know him well but there's still a kind of musical mystique about him. His music sounds like witchcraft. There are times I don't know where his music comes from. It doesn't sound like he's doing it. It sounds like it's coming from somewhere else."[43]

After listening to the piece called *The Sorcerer* on a blindfold test presided over by Leonard Feather, trumpeter Bobby Bryant complained, "The sameness which is occurring on [Davis's] recent records I don't like," and added: "The guys around him are very exciting; they are inventive enough, and certainly a great deal of energy goes into their performances. If it were not for that amount of energy, especially in the case of the drummer, they would really sort of fall flat."[44] No doubt Bryant's complaint stems in part from a nostalgia for the music played a decade earlier, but his observation about the "sameness" picks out a real problem in some of the recordings the quintet made. With the composed themes so concise, amounting to only a few bars, they must perforce be brilliantly constructed to be effective. Nondescript themes, as in *Limbo* and *Pee Wee*, and on *Orbits* from *Miles Smiles*, slip past without asserting any distinctive mood, leaving behind only an expanse of improvisation on minor scales – the sound that Collier characterized as "vast, empty phrases, like wind in a ruined cathedral."

The problem is not inherent in the conception itself: themes for modal improvisation can be longer and more fully explicated, as Davis demonstrated with *All Blues* and *So What*, and they can also be succinct and still effective, as Shorter demonstrated with *Vonetta*, *Dolores*, and *Footprints* and Davis with *Agitation*. The problem arises when they are short and easy, as some are on the *Sorcerer* LP.

The cover of the *Sorcerer* LP featured a striking profile of a black woman. Although few observers could have identified the woman in 1967, when the cover first appeared in record stores, four or five years later she had become one of the best-known young actresses around. She was Cicely Tyson, one of Davis's companions at the time and eventually his fourth wife, marrying him in 1981 when their relationship outlasted an intervening marriage. "I have a thing about helping black women, you know," Davis told Gregg Hall, "because when I was using dope it was costing me a couple of grand a day and I used to take bitches' money. So when I stopped to clean up, I got mad at *Playboy* and I wouldn't accept their poll because they didn't have no black women in their magazine, you know. So I started putting them on my covers. So I put Cicely's picture on my record. It went all around the world." In the same interview, he claimed to have "taught her a lot of stuff" about acting as well. "I taught her about eyes," he said. "You see, black people's eyes are so wide anyway, so I told her not to open her eyes too much. She had a habit of overacting. I taught her to be subtle, you know, and when it comes time to use some volume, she'd know it." He even did some dramatic writing for her. "I wrote a little thing for her," he told Hall. "It was outtasight! Man, it had her subconscience [*sic*] talking to her and her looking at it and doing something else. It was outtasight!!"[45] So far, the playlet has remained out of sight for Tyson's public.

As Davis prepared for an unusually busy summer and fall schedule that would find him recording and performing more frequently than he had done for years, he and Gil Evans continued their sporadic collaborations on several projects. One of these, certainly the one that aroused the interest of jazz fans, was a bigger band that Davis and Evans were hoping to use as a working band in club and concert dates. "I believe that Miles now is going to have a big band," Evans told Leonard Feather in an interview the summer before. "He would like to, and he is about ready. The time is right. Not an enormous band but about a dozen men. We could work out a library together. It wouldn't be that difficult to book him with a band. He could play at the Vanguard, at Shelly Manne's, or in the place where I heard him the other evening, in San Diego." Evans hastened to add that the band was not intended to replace the quintet.

"Of course when I say it's time for him to have a big band," he added, "that's no reflection on the quintet. They're all wonderful musicians."

Evans's conception of the big band scores was derived partly from what he heard in the quintet: "If Miles could get a band to play the kind of accompaniment he gets from that combo – a sort of orchestral parallel to what happens in the combo – it would be really sensational. If Miles just had a few horns doing the equivalent of what Herbie does, he'd have a fantastic band."[46] Most fans reading Evans's description agreed wholeheartedly. But nothing ever came of it. When Davis and Evans finally recorded together the next year, making some tapes for Columbia that have never been issued, it was with a much larger orchestra.

Years later, Evans suggested in an interview with Zan Stewart that the working big band collapsed because he and Davis could not find financial backing, but he also implied that their collaborations at the time were impeded by Davis's arthritic joints as well. "Sometimes I'd be up at his place," Evans said, "and we'd be working on something, because for a while there we were out to do something but it never materialized on account of the money, and he'd be sitting at the piano, trying to play some chords and he'd say, 'Oh, ouch, ouch, ouch!!' It was agony for him to try and play those chords."[47]

Davis and Evans were also trying to put together the material for a studio project, their first in almost five years. "We have so many new numbers half-finished now," Evans told Feather. "In fact, I don't even know how much music we've got. I talked to Miles just the other day, and we decided to put all the music together and get going on another album as soon as we can." Pressed for details about the music already prepared, Evans became vague, saying that they were "just some songs. Not necessarily standards. It's hard to say what we're going to come up with, but we've written a couple of tunes."[48] None of their efforts from late 1962 to early 1968 received performances, either in public or in the recording studio.

Meanwhile, Ron Carter and Tony Williams, with youth on their side, used some of their time off to dig deeply into yet another musical direction. On 26 May 1967, they appeared at Carnegie Hall accompanying the third-stream pianist and composer Charles Bell. Bell's ensemble also included Richard Davis, a bassist gifted, as Carter was, in both symphonic and jazz music, and guitarist Les Spann, who was added to the ensemble for the premiere of Bell's *Second Quintet: Brother Malcolm*, dedicated to Malcolm X, the charismatic spokesman for black nationalism who had been assassinated in 1965.

For both Davis and his sidemen, most outside activities ended in June, when the quintet spent no less than four days in the Columbia studios recording more original compositions written by the sidemen. The material from the first three days was released soon after on an LP titled *Nefertiti*, and it falls clearly within the domain already charted in the previous three LPS made in the studio. The details are as follows:

Miles Davis Quintet: Nefertiti
Miles Davis, tpt; Wayne Shorter, ts; Herbie Hancock, pno; Ron Carter, b; Tony Williams, dms. New York, 7 June 1967
Nefertiti
(on Columbia CS 9594)

Same personnel. Same place, 19 June 1967
Fall; Pinocchio; Riot
(all on Columbia CS 9594)

Same personnel. Same place, 22 June 1967
Madness; Hand Jive
(both on Columbia CS 9594)
The 19 June session is produced by Howard A. Roberts; the other two by Teo Macero.

If the *Sorcerer* LP contained some perfunctory writing and playing, *Nefertiti* resumes the careful innovations of *Miles Smiles* and rivals the earlier LP as a showcase of this quintet's achievement. Davis solos magnificently on the open horn throughout, capturing the broad tone and the grace of his playing on *Porgy and Bess* and *Kind of Blue*; he solos especially effectively on Hancock's *Madness* and on Shorter's *Fall* and *Pinocchio*. *Hand Jive*, by Williams, and *Riot*, by Hancock, are relatively simple exercises, the former a sequence of solos over a steadily accelerating tempo, the latter a short but tidy theme with surprisingly short, but also tidy, solos.

The most conspicuous strengths seem to flow directly from Shorter's contributions, not only – not even principally – as a soloist but as a composer. His three themes, *Nefertiti*, *Fall*, and *Pinocchio*, float over the restless rhythms of Carter and Williams and the occasional bright splashes of Hancock. Their composed phrases, usually played in unison by Davis and Shorter, are wafted aloft by the rhythmic cushion even though they seem detached from its intensity. Shorter's own solos for the first time show a parallel detachment, as Davis's often had. So conspicuous a transformation drew many notices. "Once the hardest of hard bop tenors, Shorter had softened his strident sound, simplified his ideas and abandoned the harmonic structures of the jazz mainstream in exchange for a greater use of scales and subtle coloristic effects," Bob Blumenthal wrote in *Rolling Stone* some years later. "His twisting, haunting compositions were becoming statements in themselves instead of mere frames for solos. All three Shorter tunes on *Nefertiti* use melodic repetition to an unprecedented extent and, as interpreted by the great Davis quintet, ... became hypnotic messengers of something new."[49]

On *Pinocchio*, formally the simplest of the three Shorter compositions, the short theme recurs at the breaks between each of the soloists (Davis, Shorter, and Hancock) as well as at the open and close. On *Fall*, a beautiful ballad exploiting Davis's lyricism in an ode to autumn, Shorter's melody recurs sporadically, but entirely naturally, all through the piece – before, during, and after all the improvised statements – and simultaneously inspires and determines the improvisations.

Nefertiti goes a step further: it includes no solos in any conventional sense. Instead, Davis and Shorter repeat the mournful theme over and over again throughout the long track (almost eight minutes). Yet both in feeling and in fact, the composition remains rich in spontaneity; improvisation is in a sense constant, not only in the play of the rhythm section but even in the theme statements by the horns, which repeat the same basic scale again and again with different nuances each time. It is a remarkable conception, demanding free interplay and controlled license, and one that could be carried off successfully only by players who are gifted individualists and devoted collectivists. Because of this striking performance, Shorter's composition became an instant postbop classic.

With *Nefertiti* and his other two compositions on the *Nefertiti* LP, Shorter took a giant step into the forefront of the jazz of the 1960s in the unanimous view of critics and musicians. One of the musicians who took special notice was Josef Zawinul, Julian Adderley's pianist and composer-arranger, who was busy at the time inventing new uses for electronics in the gospel-funk writing that had sustained Adderley's quintet for several years. "I heard *Nefertiti*," Zawinul said, "and that's when I felt Wayne was the guy I should do something with. He had the new thinking."[50] Together, Zawinul and Shorter would direct some of the most enterprising permutations in the music of the 1970s with their band called Weather Report.

The Davis quintet's later recording session that same month resembles the music of *Nefertiti*, although none of the three compositions by Shorter measures up to any of the three recorded earlier. Presumably for that reason, these tracks were not released until 1976, when they appeared as one side of an LP titled *Water Babies*. The details are as follows:

Miles Davis Quintet: Water Babies
Miles Davis, tpt; Wayne Shorter, ts, ss (on *Sweet Pea*); Herbie Hancock, pno; Ron Carter, b; Tony Williams, dms. New York, June 1967
Water Babies; Capricorn; Sweet Pea
(all on Columbia PC 34396 [1976])

The three pieces strike moods and hold them: *Water Babies* is lazy and carefree, *Capricorn* mysterious, and *Sweet Pea* ruminative. Of *Sweet Pea*, Douglas Clark observes: "The melody had apparently been with Shorter for some time because it appears at more than double the tempo, at the end of his solo on *Madness* from *Nefertiti*."[51] (The uncertainty of the recording date for *Sweet Pea* apparently gave Clark the impression that Shorter had been saving the theme for a while, but the recording dates for *Madness* and *Sweet Pea* may have been within days of one another.)

Shorter records on soprano saxophone for the first time on *Sweet Pea*, and dozens of other reedmen soon followed him by doubling on the 'straight' horn. The soprano had a history of neglect among woodwind players. Among jazz players, it seemed for decades to be the exclusive property of Sidney Bechet, the old New Orleans nonpareil who spent most of his career in Paris. Bechet used it in preference to the clarinet as his main instrument because it gave him enough amplitude to drown out brass players, and a few of Bechet's admirers from Johnny Hodges to Bob Wilber had picked it up occasionally as a second instrument, more in homage to the old master than as a serious alternative.

The soprano carried the stigma of being hard to play in tune. It came into favor among younger players in the late 1960s by a circuitous route. Steve Lacy had been playing the soprano in Dixieland bands when the avant-garde players became conspicuous in 1959–60, and Lacy, a thoroughly uncategorizable New Yorker, joined them in lofts and clubs almost immediately. The soprano was the only horn he owned, and so exotic was it at the time that most of the younger musicians, including other reed players, had to ask him what it was when he took it out of its case. One of the most curious, naturally, was John Coltrane, who promptly got one of his own in 1960 and began playing it soon after in club dates and on records. As Coltrane became the supreme influence in the jazz of the day, the soprano's star rose as well, until virtually every saxophonist under 40 had one. The horn – a fatter, shinier clarinet – quickly became commonplace. "The outcast in the saxophone family," as Humphrey Lyttleton called it in a chapter on Bechet,[52] was an outcast no more. In 1969, *Down Beat* added a category for soprano saxophonists to its polls. Ever since Shorter unveiled his soprano in the recording studio in 1967, every one of Davis's saxophonists – and there have been many – has doubled on that instrument.

A few days after the *Water Babies* recording session, on 2 July, the quintet shared the stage at Newport with a typically cluttered bill that also listed the Bill Evans Trio, the Max Roach Quintet, Sonny Rollins, the Woody Herman orchestra, singer Marilyn Maye, and a rock band with some slim jazz credentials called the Blues Project. The stage was also literally cluttered because the small bands had to work around the set-up for Herman's orchestra rather than taking the time to rearrange the stage for each group. Ira Gitler recalls "Tony Williams playing on Don Lamond's drum set, the wood chips behind the drummer's spot making that part of the stage look like a sawmill."[53] For Davis and his sidemen, the Newport concert was only the first of several dates in 1967 that would be promoted by George Wein; plans were under way for the quintet to join a package Wein was taking to Europe in the fall.

On 17 July, John Coltrane died. He had been playing in public infrequently for the previous five months, but he explained his relative isolation with a variety of excuses, saying that he was tired of playing in nightclubs or that he was busy working on new music. In fact, he was suffering from cancer of the liver. On the day before his death, with the pain so intense he could no longer bear it, he drove himself to a hospital and checked in. The news of his death numbed the jazz world as nothing had since Charlie Parker's death twelve years earlier. For younger musicians, Coltrane's death became one of those iconic events that stays vividly in the mind. "I was coming back from the midwest with Ray Bryant when they announced that John Coltrane had died," drummer Ronald Shannon Jackson remembers. "It seemed like something had burst my bubble – all the feelings I had for music ... When he died, it just took a lot out of me."[54] Jackson quit music abruptly and only returned as a full-time professional several years later.

At the moment of Coltrane's death, the black neighborhood of

Newark was in turmoil, with riots and fires and looting. It was the start of America's long, hot summers, as the black population grew impatient with the slow advances of the civil rights legislation and demonstrated its unrest in open rebellion in the ghetto streets of almost every major city. Malcolm X was dead and Martin Luther King would be assassinated the next year, and John Coltrane's music, as searing, outspoken, and powerful as the man himself was taciturn and meek, captured the rhetoric of human dignity and human aspiration as forcefully as Malcolm's writings or King's preachings. Deborah D'Amico, in an elegy for Coltrane (quoted in full by J.C. Thomas), wrote:

> we are lucky, I suppose,
> that they let you blow at all
> their love is gold
> that turns to dollars
>
> yours streamed from your mouth
> as free as air,
> as rare as free[55]

By the time of his death at the age of 40, Coltrane "had passed," as Whitney Balliett put it, "from mere musician to messiah."[56] Just as the jazz world was showing signs of recovery after years of recession, Coltrane's death took away one of its most inspirational figures.

Two of the other inspirational figures, Miles Davis and Dizzy Gillespie, took their bands into the Village Gate for the entire month of August. It was pairing that kept the crowds lined up outside the Greenwich Village club for the entire engagement, and those who managed to get a seat in the muggy downstairs room for a complete set heard an encapsulated history of the changes in jazz in the two decades since the 1940s, when Gillespie was the bop guru of 52nd Street and Davis was his star pupil. Gillespie's quintet, with James Moody on tenor saxophone, clung to their bebop roots and played some of the repertoire (*Con Alma, Night in Tunisia, I Can't Get Started*, and so on) that Gillespie had played for years. Gillespie's fervor was infectious, and his band played energetically enough behind him, but Miles Davis's young quintet sometimes seemed to overflow with energy. On some of their non-stop sets, familiar themes dissolved before listeners could identify them, and the entire set turned into explorations of completely unfamiliar themes, forms, and balances. Listeners could hardly help but draw comparisons even though the musics were by now different enough to defy comparison.

One night the audience at the Village Gate included Sugar Ray Robinson, the former welterweight and middleweight boxing champion, and Archie Moore, the former light-heavyweight champion. Out of it came a situation that Gillespie likes to cite as proof for his theory that Davis suffers from abject shyness. "Now, Miles is a big fight fan," Gillespie points out, "so one would think that introducing the fighters from the stage would have been his moment ... Anyhow, Miles, whose band was on the stand, came over to me and said, 'Hey, Sugar Ray and Archie Moore are here.' I said, 'So?' and he said, 'Well, won't you introduce them when you go on?' I said, 'Hell, you're on now. You introduce them. You've got it!' But he didn't introduce them. He left it to me."[57]

Davis's and Gillespie's bands again shared a stage four days after they closed at the Village Gate, on 1 September, when they played at the Laurel International Jazz Festival in Maryland, yet another addition to the summer jazz festival circuit. In the parade of musicians playing that night, which included Herman's orchestra, organist Jimmy Smith, and singer Etta Jones, was Gary Bartz, a young saxophonist born and raised in nearby Baltimore who had just made his first LP. Three years later, Bartz would become a member of Davis's band.

The difficult climate for any music that could not attract a teenaged following became clear when George Wein organized the benefit concert to aid the Metropolitan Opera Orchestra. The activist climate on civil rights issues also came clear. Wein lined up Miles Davis and Duke Ellington, whose bands could fill the posh Met facilities at the Lincoln Center, and, while both agreed and ended up performing, Davis found the decision far from easy. "We gave a benefit for the Metropolitan Opera band," he said later, "and they don't even hire Negroes. And I was gonna tell Duke not to do it, but I told George, 'Now, George, you make sure they hire some Negroes.' But a Negro player told me they get their white cousins and all that bullshit in line to play with them. That's some sad shit."[58] Despite the inroads in the civil rights struggle in the 1960s, symphonic music remained a white preserve in 1967. Ortiz M. Walton, in his book *Music: Black, White and Blue*, points out that he was one of only two blacks employed full-time by any of the five major symphony orchestras in the United States until 1969,[59] when several black musicians including bassist Arthur Davis, a conservatory-trained musician whose best exposure had been with John Coltrane's band, brought a civil suit against the New York Philharmonic. Miles Davis and a lot of other musicians were well aware of the inequities long before the suit brought the facts into the public consciousness.

From 19 October until 12 November 1967, the Miles Davis Quintet played concerts in Europe as part of a touring package known as Newport Jazz Festival in Europe. Wein organized the tour, and the complex of sponsors, musicians, itineraries, and locales made it perhaps the most complicated movement of performing artists ever undertaken. Wein had lined up Pan-American Airlines and the US Department of Commerce as sponsors, thus underwriting his own expenses and ensuring first-class travel for the musicians by attracting public and private funds, a flair that Wein has exploited ever since he began promoting the Newport Jazz Festival for the Lorillard Tobacco Company. For the London leg of the tour, 23–29 October, he tied in his musicians with an ongoing concert series called Jazz Expo '67, named after the enormously successful world fair, Expo '67, in Montreal that summer. Wein's line-up of musicians performed in various combinations, with some groups leaving for the next city as other groups were arriving.

The musicians, both in sheer numbers and in the temperaments involved, made an awesome lot: besides Miles Davis and his four sidemen, they included Thelonious Monk, with an octet featuring Ray Copeland, Jimmy Cleveland, Johnny Griffin, Phil Woods, and Charlie Rouse; Sarah Vaughan accompanied by the Bob James Trio; vibraphonist Gary Burton's quartet with guitarist Larry Coryell; a bevy of guitarists of all ages and styles: George Benson, Buddy Guy, Jim Hall, Barney Kessel, and Elmer Snowden; Archie Shepp's avant-garde quintet, with two trombonists, Roswell Rudd and Grachan Moncur III, and drummer Beaver Harris; Clark Terry; and the Newport All Stars, featuring Ruby Braff, Buddy Tate, and, on piano, George Wein. Most promoters might have balked at the prospect of having any two of Davis, Monk, Shepp, or Braff on a tour, let alone all of them, and the tour itself was neither brief nor sedentary. In the span of about four weeks, they mounted concerts in more than twenty cities in Ireland, England, Finland, Denmark, Sweden, Germany, Holland, Belgium, Switzerland, Italy, France, and Spain. Several of the concerts were taped, including Davis's concerts in London (29 October), Stockholm (31), Karlsruhe, Germany (1 November), Copenhagen (2), Berlin (4), and Paris (6), but none of them has yet been made public.

Relations between Davis and Wein, not surprisingly, have often been strained and have sometimes erupted into recriminations, the first coming at the end of this tour. Both are hard-nosed businessmen, but Wein is blustery and extroverted where Davis is taciturn and introverted, and the combination seldom mixes smoothly. For all that, as the top performer and the top promoter in jazz, they are practically forced to respect one another – sometimes grudgingly, at least on Davis's part – and they have often argued bitterly. Their negotiations about money, beginning with this tour, are hard fought and usually end with Davis getting what he considers his due. "He pays enough money and everything," Davis once conceded.[60] But Wein, with his promoter's instinct, apparently believes that if he has to pay Davis top money he can take his consolation by announcing the terms to the press and getting some publicity for his concerts from the news. It is a practice that rankles Davis. "I think George Wein is unfair," he told Don DeMicheal. "I'm on his tour, but I think he's using me. I wrote him a letter and told him. He tells other people how much I make. He kinda glorifies that, y'know."[61]

Davis's complaints on this tour began with the fitness regimen he was trying to keep up while traveling in Europe. He had stopped drinking because of his liver ailment, but the reason he gave to Arthur Taylor, who interviewed him a few weeks after the tour ended, overlooked his health problems entirely. "When you do one-nighters, like we did in Europe," he said, "and you drink every time you eat, you wind up feeling real tired before a concert. You get up early in the morning ... You might have a hangover and it carries on, and you won't be able to think right." The regimen was also supposed to include regular workouts, but Davis figured that Wein prevented him from doing that: "The only thing I asked George was, 'Wherever we go, try to find a gymnasium in the town so I'll have something to do.' He didn't do it. I figured he'd take care of it himself, but he had those in-between guys, the middlemen, who didn't think it was important. But to me it was important. I guess they thought it was a joke."[62] The afternoons of inactivity nagged at Davis throughout the tour.

His consolation came from the concerts themselves. "I had a nice time in Europe because the band played good," he told Taylor. "The band plays pretty good sometimes." Listeners everywhere agreed. Valerie Wilmer, covering the concert at London's Hammersmith Odeon, in which the Davis quintet were billed, as they often were throughout the tour, with Archie Shepp's quintet, called it "a concert that had everyone standing on their ear." She reported that Davis's continuous recital included *Round Midnight* and four or five other melodies; at the concert four days later in Copenhagen, Davis included *Round Midnight, Masqualero* (from the *Sorcerer* LP), and *No Blues* in his recital. "In spite of all his pretensions to the contrary," Wilmer added, "Davis is by dint of both sound and appearance the master showman." She also recognized the crucial role of Tony Williams behind Davis's solos. "He's loud, sure, but Miles likes it that way because it spurs him into moments of starkly screaming beauty," she said. "The excruciating cry of the Davis horn owes more than a little to Williams. The music was bittersweet perfection."[63]

The coupling of Davis's quintet with Archie Shepp's indicates recognition by the promoters of Davis's recent alliance with freer jazz, a recognition not nearly as widespread as it should have been, perhaps because most jazz fans and many reviewers were still smitten with Davis's earlier records and had not caught up to him in the interval. To someone like Wilmer, of course, the coupling just seemed natural. It may or may not have seemed so natural to Davis, so recently an outspoken critic of the avant-garde. He continued to demonstrate his umbrage publicly. At one concert Davis asked Shepp to join his band on stage and then, according to Barry McRae, "stormed off because Shepp had hogged the solo limelight, playing music with which he had little sympathy."[64]

When the tour reached Barcelona on its last leg, Wein, according to Davis, "tried to slip in two extra concerts and told me he'd pay my room rent. I called him and said, 'George, if we're doing an extra concert, give me more money.' And guess what he said: 'Man, like I don't have no bread.' So how you going to talk business like that?" One of Davis's periodic complaints about Wein is that he affects jazz slang when talking to musicians instead of using business terms. It always succeeds in rousing Davis's ire. In Barcelona, Davis replied, "If you don't have no bread, get somebody else, 'cause I'm leaving." "When it gets so you feel like you're being taken advantage of," Davis told Arthur Taylor, "it's best to leave, because he's not treating you like a man." Davis took the next flight back to the United States. Wein immediately told reporters that Davis had left without giving notice to anyone, including his musicians, who played at the Barcelona concert as the Wayne Shorter Quartet. Davis maintained that he had told Wein at the airport that he was leaving. "Oh yeah, George stopped a check because I didn't play in Spain," Davis added. "I was there for two days. So now I'm suing him for what he said. For always dropping all the weight on me."[65] As on other occasions, recriminations and hard feelings flew back and forth and then were forgotten by both parties, until the time came to enter into a new business deal.

As soon as the quintet reassembled in New York, Davis started putting in hours with them in the recording studio, a sharp reversal of his infrequent visits to Columbia's studios for several years and a practice that he would continue long after he disbanded his good young quintet. Many of the recording sessions were decidedly experimental, recorded rehearsals rather than performances, and they show Davis searching for ways of incorporating new elements into his music. The new elements derive mainly from rock and soul music, but at this stage they are relatively mild effects and not at all the full-fledged incursions that would show up in his music with *In A Silent Way* and *Bitches Brew* a little more than a year later. They point in that direction, undeniably, but they consist of electronic instruments, either electric piano played by Hancock or electric guitar played by a guest sideman, overlaid on the style of the regular quintet. Later, after the quintet disbanded, the fusion of jazz and rock-funk-soul elements became part of the fabric of the music.

Of all the music recorded from December to March, only one title was released at the time. Seven more titles were held until 1979 or 1981 and then compiled along with unreleased material from other periods in two collections of Davis's music put out during his years of temporary retirement. These seven titles show clearly that Davis's development of his fusion style was much more gradual than anyone suspected at the time. The remaining unreleased music from this period, which is voluminous if not monumental, will probably not contain many surprises, after the samples from so many different dates spread over these months.

Davis's first attempt at finding richer textures for his music left him bitter. He added a young guitarist, Joe Beck, to the quintet for some recording sessions in December and worked out some arrangements for the altered instrumentation, probably enlisting Gil Evans's aid, but he was dissatisfied with the results. Two titles from these sessions were issued belatedly, and the details are as follows:

Miles Davis Quintet + Joe Beck
Miles Davis, tpt, chimes; Wayne Shorter, ts; Herbie Hancock, celeste; Joe Beck, gtr; Ron Carter, b; Tony Williams, dms; probably Gil Evans, co-arr. New York, 4 December 1967
Circle in the Round
(on *Circle in the Round*, Columbia 36278 [1979])

Same personnel; Hancock plays electric piano. Same place, 28 December 1967
Water on the Pond
(on *Directions*, Columbia KC2 36472 [1981])

Beck was just outgrowing his reputation in the New York musicians'
community as a guitar prodigy. He was 22 now, but he had been in
recording studios almost continuously for four years. He was a new
breed; traditionally, studio musicians had come from the ranks of
experienced pros who had paid their dues in symphonies and road bands.
Beck arrived from Philadelphia fresh out of high school and fell into
studio work. "I was the only guy in my age group that could play at the
time in New York," he told Julie Coryell. "It just happened that there
was a bunch of guys doing jingles who were starting out at the same time
I was. It was a very special time, and I don't think it could ever occur for a
kid again." After about a year he was in steady demand as an arranger as
well as a player, and, in his version, he fell into arranging commercials
by accident too. "A guy approached me in a bar and asked me to do a
demo for a jingle," he recalled. "I said okay because he said he had a
budget of $250, and I figured I'd play all the parts myself and take the
$250 and split, which I did; but they bought it for thousands of dollars. I
ended up doing hundreds and hundreds of commercials for every
conceivable instrumentation, and they paid me very well to learn how
to arrange."[66] Although Beck credits good luck, he had risen to the top in
one of the most brutally competitive music markets anywhere, and it
was his precocious talent that saw him through. On his studio rounds he
inevitably got to know Ron Carter, who may have recommended him to
Davis, but Beck also had a reputation in jazz circles from playing in Gary
McFarland's studio orchestras and in bands led by Paul Winter, Jeremy
Steig, and Chico Hamilton; he worked with Gil Evans a few months
before Davis hired him and continued working with him whenever
Evans assembled a band until 1970.

On *Circle in the Round*, Beck settles into a steady repetitive drone
that maintains the 12/8 time signature all through and functions solely
for keeping the time. The rambling, twenty-six-minute track rides along
on Beck's rhythmic groove, giving a foretaste of the fusion style to come.
Beck's presence frees Carter from his usual time-keeping and allows
him to take a short solo, a rarity in his studio recordings with the
quintet. Hancock's celeste allows his typical chordal colors to reverberate, something he would accomplish more facilely on the Fender
Rhodes piano in later sessions. While the track is interesting as a

foreshadowing of fusion, it is flawed by several abrupt transitions (possibly splices) and by a series of false endings. Musically, its interest resides almost exclusively in Davis's solo choruses on open trumpet – he reappears to solo five times, probably through the dubious magic of splicing – and over the background guitar his playing takes on some of the timbre and the lyricism of his solos over Gil Evans's orchestrations.

Water on the Pond is more of an entity: a simple, self-contained medium-tempo ballad based on a rhythm maintained by Beck and Carter, with good solos by Davis on muted trumpet and Shorter on tenor saxophone. This track marks Hancock's recording debut on electric piano and apparently also his first attempt at playing an electronic keyboard, and he is predictably cautious, asserting himself only mildly when Davis stops the rhythm and plays over Hancock's and Beck's fills.

Hancock's debut on Fender Rhodes piano came about as one of Davis's calculated surprises. When Hancock arrived in the studio that morning, Davis pointed him toward the piano already set up in the corner. Josef Zawinul had been playing an electric piano nightly in Julian Adderley's band, and Davis was fascinated by it. "Miles came to see me and checked it out," Zawinul says, "and then he got an electric piano for Herbie Hancock."[67] Hancock, too, was smitten and spent long hours working on his technique. The instrument would soon alter Davis's music in several ways. "My playing of the electric piano ... gave the music plenty of bottom," Hancock says, "and when the individual band members became more aware of the Rhodes, their writing began to change as a result, and in a subtle way the rhythms began to change."[68] At the time of the recordings with Joe Beck, those changes were still a long way off.

Beck's presence marks the beginning of Davis's long search for richer textures in his music. In the dynamics established by the working quintet, Tony Williams had been mainly responsible for the density – what Davis and the others call "bottom" – while the others kept up an austere surface. Now he wanted to enrich the density of his music by augmenting Williams's drumming with more varied timbres in the rhythm. He has Hancock comping on celeste and electric piano and himself striking the chimes, but the key addition was expected to come from the arranged ostinato of the guitar. The changes are not completely successful. Although the textures on *Circle in the Round* and *Water on the Pond* are altered from those of the quintet's performances, they are not richer. Davis considered the sessions a failure, and he laid the blame squarely on Beck. "I was so mad, they gave me a royalty check and I didn't even look at it," he told Martin Williams at a recording session a month later, when he brought in George Benson to play guitar. Williams reported then that "Davis was still smarting from the experience of a previous session when an otherwise capable studio guitarist had failed him miserably."[69]

It is impossible to know, of course, what Davis expected of Beck, but on the aural evidence of the two tracks released so far the failing – if it can be called that, when the tracks offer so many points of interest – seems to rest partly with Tony Williams as well as with Beck. Beck plays his parts mechanically, without departing from his arranged lines, but Williams allows him to take over the rhythms completely and loses his identity in the restraint he imposes on himself. He seems intent on keeping out of Beck's way instead of sharing in the new dynamics of the augmented band. His dissatisfaction is almost audible in the stilted drumming on these tracks.

Davis blamed Beck, and he attributed much of the problem to the pigmentation of Beck's skin. "When whites play with Negroes and can't play the music, it's a form of Jim Crow to me," Davis told George Benson within ear-shot of Martin Williams. "Studio musicians – they're supposed to know what's going on in our music, too. One, two, three, four – anybody can do that. And if you don't do it, they don't believe the beat is still there."[70]

Before Davis could line up a new guitar player he spent more hours in the recording studios with the quintet, allowing Hancock to work on the electric piano. So far, only an excerpt of these sessions has been issued. The details are as follows:

Miles Davis Quintet
Miles Davis, tpt; Wayne Shorter, ts; Herbie Hancock, electric pno; Ron Carter, b; Tony Williams, dms. New York, 11 January 1968
Fun
(on *Directions*, Columbia KC2 36472)

As its title implies, *Fun* is merely an out-take, a four-minute slice in which Davis plays a few notes at the beginning and then fails to return after Shorter's solo.

Davis added George Benson to the quintet for a series of recording sessions in the next two months. A gifted natural musician, Benson earned his first dollar from music at the age of four, singing on street corners in Pittsburgh. He started picking out tunes on electric guitar three years later, when his stepfather retrieved his old instrument from a pawn shop and brought it home. "I remember sitting with my ear pressed up against the amplifier all night long until I fell asleep," he told Julie Coryell, "and that sound has been with me from that day to this."[71] He left home to tour with organist Jack McDuff when he was 18 and began recording on his own for producer Creed Taylor at 21. He was only a week away from his 25th birthday at his final session with Davis's band, and he was already a highly adaptable guitarist (and singer). He still had to wait a few years before scoring the blockbuster successes that people such as Taylor considered inevitable for him. Those came in the 1970s, notably with a 1976 LP called *Breezin'* (Warner Brothers BS 2919), a million-selling record – 'platinum' in industry argot – in a style best described as middle-of-the-road jazz-rock-soul-funk. When he went into the studio with Davis, his successes were modest and had come mainly in jazz. The details are as follows:

Miles Davis Quintet + George Benson
Miles Davis, tpt; Wayne Shorter, ts; Herbie Hancock, pno; George Benson, gtr (except on *Teo's Bag*); Ron Carter, b; Tony Williams, dms; Gil Evans, co-arr.
New York, 16 January 1968
untitled composition; *Paraphernalia; Teo's Bag*
(untitled composition unissued; *Paraphernalia* on *Miles in the Sky*, Columbia CS 9628; *Teo's Bag* on *Circle in the Round*, Columbia 36278)

Same personnel; Benson on *Side Car II* only. Same place, 13 February 1968
Side Car I; Side Car II
(both on Columbia 36278)

Same personnel, including Benson. Same place, 15 March 1968
Sanctuary
(on Columbia 36278)

Evans's participation has never been credited or acknowledged, but Martin Williams attended the January session seeking fodder for his *Stereo Review* column, and when Evans showed up he explained, "I midwifed a couple of these pieces."[72] He spent the day in the studio, occasionally answering Davis's summons to clear up points in his arrangement.

The first two hours of the January session, called for 10 a.m. and under way by 10:30, were spent on an untitled composition by Hancock arranged by Evans. The band played sixteen takes before Davis was satisfied, and even then his satisfaction was apparently relative, because the track has not yet been released. Williams reported the progress through the takes in some detail, watching Davis and Shorter integrate their phrasing of the "rolling melody" as Hancock advised Benson: "Some of these are chords. Some are just sounds." Tony Williams worked out his part without the guidance of a score, "feeling his way into it," Williams wrote, "in a highly personal manner": "He began with a bit of history, an old-fashioned, regular *ching-de-ching* cymbal beat. By the second or third run-through, he was trying a conservative latin rhythm, executed chiefly with wire brushes on his snare drum. But within a few more tries, his part had become a complex whirl of cymbal, snare and tom-tom patterns and accents, although there was no question of where the beat, the basic 1-2-3-4, was falling."[73]

As the flawed takes piled up, Macero was reminded of the very first band that Davis formed with Gil Evans as arranger. "That line is hard," he said. "It reminds me of those things Miles did for Capitol. Remember them? But this is much freer, of course." After the sixteenth take, Macero announced that Martin Williams considered it a good one, to which Davis replied from the studio, "What the fuck has Martin got to do with it?" But after the playback, he said, "That's all right, Teo."

Shorter's *Paraphernalia* followed and took shape more quickly. Williams watched the sidemen consult with one another over the score and work out its details as Davis sat back, seemingly disinterested. "His presence is authoritative and puts his sidemen on their mettle, and he knows it," Williams commented. "But when the moment is ready for a decision, he makes one. 'Wayne, you don't play the 3/4 bars, and the last 4/4 bar is cut out.'"[74]

Williams left the session after *Paraphernalia*, and Benson apparently did too, leaving the quintet to run through a head arrangement later released as *Teo's Bag*, setting a quick tempo for solos by Davis, Shorter, and an otherwise silent Hancock. The track probably took only a little longer from inception to recording than its actual playing time (almost six minutes) and was tacked on to the end of the reel of tape to fill out the day's work, but it was released before the still-nameless piece with the careful arrangement that occupied most of the session. "That's hard work – making records," Davis told Williams. Made harder, no doubt, when the results of the work are issued so unpredictably.

Paraphernalia was the first music released from any of these sessions, appearing later in the year on *Miles in the Sky* with three quintet tracks and thus finding a place in one of the key documents of the period. The addition of Benson appeared at the time to be a minor whim, and it was more than ten years before the extent of Benson's work with the band became clear. His presence makes little real difference to the quintet's style, certainly less difference than Beck's had made, because all the other players, including Tony Williams, are uninhibited by his presence. *Paraphernalia* is a moody exploration of a minor mode with a very subdued solo by Benson following Davis's and Shorter's solos and a displaced acoustic solo by Hancock following the final statement of the theme. Benson conspires effectively with Hancock and Carter to create the effervescent rhythm line that makes the descending scale of the theme sound strangely doleful.

Davis later told Arthur Taylor that he added Benson for this title because "I wanted to hear the bass line a little stronger." He explained: "If you can hear a bass line, then any note in a sound that you play can be heard, because you have the bottom. We change the bass line quite a bit on all the songs we play. It varies. So I figured if I wrote a bass line, we could vary it so that it would have a sound a little larger than a five-piece group. By using the electric piano [*sic*] and having Herbie play the bass line and the chords with the guitar and Ron also playing with him in the same register, I thought it would sound good. It came out all right. It was a nice sound."[75]

Davis's predilections with the bottom of his music were no mere dalliance. His conception of the fusion to come goes through several phases that thicken the rhythmic density of his music until, finally, in his 1972–5 band, there is virtually nothing left but rhythmic textures.

With Benson, he was less single-minded about the guitar's rhythmic purpose than he would later become. On *Sanctuary* at the March session, the rhythm is largely implied. Benson adds nothing to it and is almost undetectable except for chipping in an occasional chord. Williams, too, is inconspicuous apart from some scattered percussion effects, including a creaky door sound that disrupts the mood. The composition, by Shorter, is a melancholy ballad, played with full respect for its melody and, except for the creaky door, its mood. It will reappear in a definitive version sixteen months later, as part of the *Bitches Brew* LP, but this earlier, unexpected recording of it, a more straightforward jazz version, is as full of feeling. Any comparison between the two is certain to find advocates for the first version in spite of the obvious merits of the later. The differences between them provide a graphic illustration of the changes that Davis was about to make in his music.

George Benson and Joe Beck were only the first indications of those modifications.

The remaining title recorded with Benson in the band, *Side Car*, is a complex composition by Davis. The two released takes suggest that it proved too difficult to execute in the studio time allotted to it. Its theme is stated in unison eighth notes by Davis and Shorter at a fast tempo, with staccato bursts that give it a singsong quality. Shorter struggles with his part in the ensemble, especially in the second version, and on the first manages only a very methodical solo in a strangely thin tone. For Davis, it is an ambitious piece of writing in a period when he tended to leave adventurous composition to the other members of his band.

Later in March, Davis and the quintet spent several hours recording with a large orchestra under Gil Evans's direction. Finally one of the collaborations between Davis and Evans seemed to be coming to fruition.

Evans's charts, as usual, challenged even the experienced pros he had assembled for the studio call. Howard Johnson, Evans's first choice as a tuba player since 1966, told Lee Jeske how he came to learn how to follow one of Evans's directions at these sessions and also, incidentally, supplied one of the few hints of what was played. "There were things Gil requested of me that no one ever asked me to do before and I didn't know how to do some of them," he said. "He used to use the phrase 'a light sound', and I didn't know what he meant by that for years. One time we were in the studio with Miles Davis' quintet and a large orchestra, and there was one part that was very difficult. It wasn't so difficult to play, but I'm not a great reader; I had to play the line with Ron Carter, and it was pretty high up. He was playing with his bow, and we had to be in tune, and the pressure was really *on*. I wasn't sure of myself so I pulled back a lot, and when I heard it back, because I was scared, it was really light sounding and just right. And Gil said, 'Yeah, that's the sound I mean,' very calmly. And it really blew me away because I hadn't heard it myself before. I never duplicated it again on that date, but I learned how to play that way then.'[76]

Most other details remain unknown because none of this material has ever been released, although a few of them might be inferred from the music presented in concert by Davis and Evans a month later, which was also recorded and remains unreleased. These studio dates may have been intended primarily as rehearsals for the upcoming concert, and for Evans it must have seemed like progress just to get as far as a studio appointment and a concert with one of his projects with Davis.

Several of those projects were already gathering dust in Davis's music room. In January Davis had told Arthur Taylor that he and Evans had "been working on something for about three years," but he still could not predict how it might turn out. He showed Taylor some "little sketches," played some phrases from them on the piano, and explained: "We write, and then we take out everything we don't like, and what's left is what we record."[77] Since 1962, the process of taking out "everything we don't like" had left them with almost nothing at all.

They were not getting much help from Columbia's managers, who believed they were doing all they could to unleash the creative energies that had produced *Porgy and Bess*, Davis's best-selling LP. Columbia's most recent proposal to Davis and Evans was to make a jazz version of the score of *Dr. Dolittle*, a 20th Century Fox film directed by Richard Fleischer. The movie, a musical for children about an eccentric old dandy, played by Rex Harrison, who consorts with strange animals and Samantha Eggar, was released in 1967 and perished because of miscasting and – believe it or not – a thoroughly forgettable score. Davis and Evans took Columbia's suggestion seriously enough to listen to the score, and Davis seemed generous to fault in telling Taylor that "*Dr. Dolittle* has about three songs in it that are worth something, but the rest have to be rebuilt." Columbia eventually released a mildly jazzed-up version of *Dr. Dolittle* (CS 9615) by the Dixieland piano player Joe Bushkin, with orchestrations by Billy Byers. Davis and Evans's *Dr. Dolittle* project, predictably and perhaps mercifully, was never completed, like all their projects at that time except for the score of *Time of the Barracuda* and the studio rehearsals for their concert, which went into Columbia's vaults.

The concert was in California, at the second Jazz Festival of the University of California at Berkeley, where the quintet had played the year before when rainstorms forced them to move indoors instead of playing in the Greek Theater. This year, with an eighteen-piece orchestra to accommodate in addition to the quintet, the weather was kinder. The concert was described in a *Down Beat* report filed by Sammy Mitchell.

Davis and Evans appeared in the final performance of the first evening, following Cecil Taylor and Carmen McRae. They used a format similar to their Carnegie Hall concert of 1961, the only other one they had ever presented, with the quintet playing part and then holding their places as featured players with the orchestra for the remainder. But the quintet played most of the concert on their own and the orchestra participated in only three compositions. Mitchell cited as the major "disappointment" "the sparseness, in quantity, of this new collaboration between Evans and Davis."[78]

The quintet, with bassist Marshall Hawkins filling in for Ron Carter, who again stayed in New York, offered extended versions of some of their best recent works; only *Round Midnight* is brought forward from Davis's standard repertoire of a few years earlier, transformed into a duet by Davis and Hancock. The orchestral repertoire was entirely new. The details are as follows:

Miles Davis Quintet with the Gil Evans Orchestra
Miles Davis, tpt; Wayne Shorter, ts; Herbie Hancock, pno; Marshall Hawkins, b; Tony Williams, dms. Greek Theater, Berkeley, California, 19 April 1968
Agitation; Footprints; Nefertiti; Round Midnight (Davis, Hancock only);
Ginger Bread Boy
(all unissued)

Gil Evans, arr, cond; Davis; Shorter; Hancock; Hawkins; Williams; Esther Mayhan, Arthur Frantz, frh; Howard Johnson, tba; Dick Houlgate, Bob Richards, bassoon; Anthony Ortega, flt, ss; John Mayhan, flt, bass clnt; Joe Skufca, oboe, english horn; Herb Bushler, gtr, el b; John Morrell, gtr, mandolin; Jeff Kaplan, gtr; Suzanna England, harp; Tommy Vig, marimba, perc
untitled raga; *You Make Me Feel Like a Natural Woman; Antigua*
(all unissued)
The order of performance at the concert is as shown except that *Ginger Bread Boy* was played by the quintet between *You Make Me Feel Like a Natural Woman* and *Antigua.*

In his report, Mitchell likens the quintet's performances, except for *Round Midnight*, to the evening's earlier appearance by Cecil Taylor, which he called "atonal lightning" and "dissonant thunder," and he makes no bones about preferring Carmen McRae's intervening set to both of them. He complains about Davis's technique, described as "unsteady as a drunk on the fast runs" of *Footprints* and as "fog-drenched" on *Nefertiti*. On the orchestral numbers, obviously much more to his taste, he had no such complaints, and of the untitled raga he says, "Davis' lines were long manicured fingers that reached and expertly flexed inside the silken glove of Evans' subdued orchestration." The raga effect was simulated by a combination of mandolin, electric guitar, and steel guitar, with the marimba carrying the 5/4 time.

Antigua, by Shorter, featured duets by Davis and Shorter over the orchestra's quiet colors. "All good stuff," Mitchell states, "beautifully backed." Of Evans, he declares: "This showing punched no holes in his reputation as a supreme orchestrator. He is the Boswell to Davis' Johnson: illustrating journeys, underlining anecdotes, revealing Davis' personality in full."[79] One can only wonder, even if the performances preserved on tape turn out to be less exquisite separated from the atmosphere of the Greek Theater, why they have been withheld so long.

Back in New York in May, Davis took up where he had left off before the orchestral preparations intervened. He took the quintet into the recording studios and recorded three tracks which, with *Paraphernalia* from a January session, comprised his next LP. The details are as follows:

Miles Davis Quintet: Miles in the Sky
Miles Davis, tpt; Wayne Shorter, ts; Herbie Hancock, pno; Ron Carter, b; Tony Williams, dms. New York, 15 May 1968
Country Son
(on Columbia CS 9628)

Same personnel. Same place, 16 May 1968
Black Comedy
(on Columbia CS 9628)

Same personnel; Hancock plays electric piano. Same place, 17 May 1968
Stuff
(on Columbia CS 9628)

Reviewers of *Miles in the Sky* sensed that something in Davis's music was changing, although they had some difficulty saying what it was. Lawrence Kart, writing in *Down Beat*, said, "This record ... shows the effect of the Coleman-Coltrane revolution even as Miles denies it, for their assault on the popular song has pushed Miles along the only path that seems open to him, an increasingly ironic detachment from sentiment and prettiness."[80] In *Coda*, Harvey Pekar wrote: "The general character of Miles' music seems to change beginning with *Miles in the Sky*. On it he and his sidemen generally play more aggressively and are less interested in improvising lyrically."[81] And yet, in terms of aggressiveness, Tony Williams is hardly more cyclonic here than he was on the three previous LPs, and, in terms of lyricism, Davis and Hancock allow themselves no fewer quiet moments. Change was in the wind, all right, but it does not seem attributable to the Coleman-Coltrane elements or the disavowal of lyricism. Those aspects belonged equally to *Nefertiti* and *Sorcerer*. For the most part, *Miles in the Sky* belongs with them in the style that developed soon after Shorter joined the band and adds very little that is significant to it.

What is new exists in hints, especially on *Stuff* and *Country Son*, both written by Davis. *Stuff* locks Hancock into a little rock vamp on the electric piano and stifles – or at least tries – Williams into boogaloo rhythms that are infectious, toe-tapping, and trite. For Williams, the cadences seem ridiculously easy, and he executes them with a dutiful clarity as long as he can hold himself to them. For Hancock, the vamp may or may not be absurdly easy – it sounds as if it should be – but in either case he is willing to stick with it all the way. In doing so, he gives one of the first indications of the adaptability that in the next decade would permit him to court and find considerable pop fame.

Country Son, a more interesting composition, moves each soloist in turn through a meditative section, a funky rhythm, and a 4/4 striptease shuffle, except in the opening played by Davis, which has no rhythmic developments at all, suggesting that several minutes of the opening have been deleted. Again, Hancock provides a clue to the change that is brewing. In his solo he repeatedly comes up with little funk phrases that sound alien to his style. In the context of the whole LP, they are easily overlooked, and even the more conspicuous amplified vamp and the jolting drums of *Stuff* seem little more than unusual devices. They take on significance in the larger context afforded by the piecemeal release of other material from this period, and still more in the light of Davis's directions after disbanding the quintet, only a few months later.

Those months were spent in the familiar summer rounds of concerts and club engagements, made busier because they had to be fitted into the new regimen of regular recording sessions. In June, the quintet spent the first week at the Showboat in Philadelphia, returned to New York to put in three days recording tracks for their next album, and then left immediately for Minneapolis, where they played a concert at the Tyrone Guthrie Theatre on the same bill as the singer-pianist Mose Allison. Davis squeezed in a short holiday in London, where among other activities he took in a few sets by the Bill Evans trio at Ronnie Scott's jazz club. Back home, the two jazz festivals of the summer – Newport was not on the itinerary, probably because of the stand-off between Davis and Wein following the European tour – brought the quintet together with a baffling mélange of talent, as usual. At the

Randall's Island Festival, Davis and his sidemen shared the first night with Dizzy Gillespie, Ahmad Jamal, organist Shirley Scott, singers Irene Reid and Jimmy Witherspoon, and a comedian named Irwin C. Watson; if the promoters hoped to provide something for every taste they apparently succeeded,. because the first-night attendance numbered almost 20,000. In early September, at the second annual Laurel International Jazz Festival in Maryland, they appeared along with Count Basie's orchestra and singer Joe Williams, the Horace Silver Quintet, and, again, Dizzy Gillespie. In between the two festivals, Gillespie was again their nightly companion as his band and Davis's shared the billing at the Village Gate in July. In early August, the quintet played at Count Basie's jazz club in Harlem, where Davis introduced his new bass player, David Holland, still jet-lagged from his flight from England. As if the regularly scheduled quintet engagements were not enough for the rejuvenated Davis, he then joined Max Roach's band at Count Basie's for a weekend in August, making a rare appearance as a guest soloist.

All the activity kept him from completing the LP started in June, but as soon as his schedule eased off in September he returned to finish it. The LP, called *Filles de Kilimanjaro*, is transitional not only in its style, as *Miles in the Sky* also was, but in its personnel. Davis had used the summer activities to break in replacements for Herbie Hancock and Ron Carter, who moved out on their own after more than five years with Davis. By the time of the September recording session, the replacements, Chick Corea and David Holland, fit easily into the concept of the recording begun by their predecessors. The details are as follows:

Miles Davis Quintet: Filles de Kilimanjaro
Miles Davis, tpt; Wayne Shorter, ts; Herbie Hancock, el pno; Ron Carter, b; Tony Williams, dms; Gil Evans, co-comp, arr. New York, 19 June 1968
Petits machins (Little Stuff)
(on Columbia CS 9750)

Same personnel. Same place, 20 June 1968
Tout de suite
(on Columbia CS 9750)

Same personnel. Same place, 21 June 1968
Filles de Kilimanjaro (Girls of Kilimanjaro)
(on Columbia CS 9750)

Chick Corea, acoustic pno, replaces Hancock; David Holland, el b, replaces
Carter. Same place, 24 September 1968
Frelon brun (*Brown Hornet*); *Mademoiselle Mabry* (*Miss Mabry*)
(both on Columbia CS 9750)
Most discographies, following the liner information on CS 9750, list Corea and
Holland on *Petits machins* in June and Hancock and Carter on *Frelon brun* in
September; however, Holland did not arrive in the United States until August.

Filles de Kilimanjaro presents more elaborate melodic lines than the
quintet had been working on for a couple of years, the palpable effect of
Gil Evans's participation as a composer as well as arranger.

   Tout de suite opens and closes as a ballad and features Hancock's
electric piano throughout. The keening line of the ballad gives way,
inexplicably, to improvisations in free, unsyncopated time – perhaps
intended as the allegro movement of the suite indicated punningly in
the title. Hancock both starts and ends the solo round with Davis and
Shorter in between. *Filles de Kilimanjaro*, a swaying 5/4 tune, has a
strong folk feeling in its written opening, and the time signature is
preserved throughout but the original melody is not reprised at the
close, the piece ending instead with a long coda in which Davis and
Hancock exchange phrases of irregular length. *Mademoiselle Mabry* is
all melody, in a sense. Chick Corea plays its long and complex lines at
the beginning and then repeats them over and over as Davis and Shorter
superimpose variations; by the time Corea's solo turn arrives, the
melody has been repeated so often that it lingers strongly behind his
variations. *Petits machins* sounds almost like a bebop riff, an astonishing sound to hear in Davis's music at this late date, but the connection is
quickly erased by the soloing, which again seems dissociated from the
written opening except when Shorter, like a latter-day Thelonious
Monk, revives its strains to parody them, and again the opening riff is
not repeated at the close. The bop overtones are thus fleeting. They are
more emphatic in a recording of this composition retitled *Eleven* by Gil
Evans and his orchestra around 1972 (on *Svengali*, Atlantic SD 1643) and
in a recording by Johnny Coles, a sometime sideman with Evans, under
its original title (on *Katumbo* [*Dance*], Mainstream MRL 346). Neither of
the later recordings abandons the riff so quickly or submerges it so
thoroughly in the improvisations.

   Petits machins, *Tout de suite*, and *Filles de Kilimanjaro* seem in one
respect to be the apogee of the quintet's development in the four years
after Shorter came along to complete its tight circle. Where the best

pieces on *Miles Smiles* and *Nefertiti* found the quintet using minimal structures in favor of exploring a common mood, the best pieces on *Filles de Kilimajaro* take the further step of releasing the players from the strictures of a common mood as well. The composer's mood is set as strongly here as it was on, say, *Footprints* or *Circle*, but there it was dominant because it was not only established in the theme but also carried over into the solos. Here it dominates only in the sense that it comes first – it precedes the solo statements temporally – but it is not retained. Just as tempos, bar lines, and harmonies had become flexible elements in the quintet's music, now mood is no longer fixed. Listeners must discover the unity of the pieces instead of just locating it, as viewers must discover the unity in a painting with several simultaneous perspectives. The problems caused by requiring such active listening were relieved somewhat by the strength of the composed themes and the sometimes brilliant interplay of the veteran combination that the quintet had become. Listeners did not seem to find *Filles de Kilimanjaro* abstruse when it was released in 1969; *Down Beat*'s readers voted it best record of the year.

Once again, Gil Evans's role – this time a central one – went uncredited and unacknowledged by Davis and Columbia. The first hints of his involvement came three or four years later, with the new versions of *Petits machins/Eleven* recorded by Evans and Coles citing the composers as Evans and Davis in the small print on the label. On Davis's LP, *Petits machins* and all other compositions are credited solely to Davis. In 1977, nine years later, Dan Morgenstern's column in *Jazz Journal International* carried the following notice: "It is not common knowledge that the *Filles de Kilimanjaro* date was largely written and arranged by Gil."[82] Evans had been willing to let decades go by without claiming credit for arranging Davis's 1956 recording of *Round Midnight*, but something stirred him to make public his involvement in *Filles de Kilimanjaro*. He showed something less than temerity in doing so, granting himself no more than a credit line in small print and a single sentence in an English jazz magazine, but at least he put the information into the public domain. After so many years of frustrated projects, unissued recordings, and uncredited arrangements with Davis, he finally seemed to be growing restless by the end of the 1960s.

"I was domesticated," he told Zan Stewart, "I spent all my time with my family. I only got a band together because I was tired of sitting at the piano for thirty years trying to find different ways to voice a minor 7th chord."[83] He formed a band of his own in 1970, at the age of 58, and kept it together more or less steadily for the first time since 1961. In between, he had contented himself with bringing together some players for a weekend engagement whenever the opportunity came his way and with assembling an orchestra for a few weeks in 1967 and a few days in 1968 in California, but he would spend the 1970s developing some projects of his own.

His projects with Miles Davis continued. By now they were part of the way of life for both men, but the new projects had much the same failure rate as the old ones – which might also have become part of their way of life. Neither of them considered simply putting an end to the unproductive collaborations. They were the bond between them. "Oh yeah," Evans says, "he's family to me."[84]

Just as the music of *Filles de Kilimanjaro* served notice of Davis's changing conception and introduced some new personnel in his quintet, so its cover, more circuitously, indicated a couple of other changes, one in the slogan "Directions in music by Miles Davis" printed above the title and the other in the cover photograph.

The photograph, a full-face portrait of a woman with a three-quarter portrait superimposed, probably obscures the face of Betty Mabry, the namesake for *Mademoiselle Mabry*, an aspiring young soul singer. Davis had been divorced from Frances Taylor in February; the divorce was a formality because they had been living apart for some time. Davis's most frequent companion for two years had been Cicely Tyson until Mabry came along. She was 23, and a voluble young beauty who had done some modeling, managed a rock club, and written some soul songs, including one called *Uptown* that was recorded by the Chambers Brothers. She moved among some of the top stars of the rock world and had no qualms about chiding Davis for playing unamplified music without a boogaloo beat. "Miles was dazzled," according to Eric Nisenson in *'Round About Midnight: A Portrait of Miles Davis.*[85]

They were married on 30 September 1968, in Gary, Indiana. Davis and his quintet were playing in Chicago at the Plugged Nickel when he arranged a private wedding to be attended by his brother and sister, their families, and a few close friends. It quickly became public knowledge, because Mabry told a *Down Beat* reporter all about it. "He called me from Chicago and said, 'Sweetcakes, get your stuff together and come to Chicago, we're getting married,'" she told the reporter, and then she announced this pledge: "One of the sexiest men alive is Miles Dewey Davis. We're going to be married forever, because I'm in love and Mr. Davis can do no wrong as far as I'm concerned. He's experienced in all facets of life, has terrific taste in everything, loves only the best, and has taught me many things. I was never really a jazz fan because I lean mostly to rhythm and blues and pop, but Miles's *Sketches of Spain* and *Kind of Blue* really sock it to me. But Miles is the teacher, so I'm going to be cool, stay in the background, and back up my man."[86]

Their marriage lasted little more than a year, although the divorce took three years. Their friendship has been more abiding, and so has Mabry's influence. Davis's listening habits soon reflected her tastes, and still do, and some of the pop and funk elements she exposed him to began to show up in his music, filtered through his sensibility. "Betty would influence Miles musically perhaps more than any of his previous women," Nisenson points out.[87] In the aftermath of their tempestuous marriage, Leonard Feather asked Davis why he got married if he did not believe in families, and Davis replied, "Because they asked me. Every woman I ever married asked me."[88]

The slogan "Directions in music by Miles Davis" was repeated on his next LP, *In a Silent Way*, and then was dropped. The message it was intended to convey, Davis told Don DeMicheal, was a personal declaration of independence: "It means I tell everybody what to do. If I don't tell 'em, I ask 'em. It's my date, y'understand? And I've got to say yes or no. Been doing it for years, and I got tired of seeing 'Produced by this person or that person.' When I'm on a date, I'm usually supervising everything."[89]

Teo Macero, who had been listed in the credits of Davis's LPs starting with *Some Day My Prince Will Come*, the third he produced for him, was now restored to favor after taking the brunt of his wrath for releasing *Quiet Nights*, but Davis intended the new slogan to proclaim – to Macero and everyone else – where the real power in the control room rested. Little or nothing of this message came across, of course, in the slogan itself, and many listeners assumed that Columbia, in displaying it, was simply absolving itself from responsibility for the contents of the enclosed recordings, which had been going through some radical changes and were about to go through many more. Those listeners were wrong: neither Columbia's managers nor Macero were disinterested bystanders in the directions that Davis's music had started to take.

The "directions" flaunted on the LP covers were already a source of bafflement and concern as well as admiration for at least one of Davis's old cronies. Dizzy Gillespie, having spent two consecutive summers alongside Davis's quintet at the Village Gate, told Leonard Feather, "Miles should be commended for going off in a completely new direction. He's just as brave as shit ... I don't think I got that much guts. Sometimes I find myself playing those same old licks I used to play, till I get stale as a motherfuck."[90] He was more baffled than appreciative when Feather played him some of Davis's new music on a blindfold test. "It reminded me so much of Ornette Coleman," he said,[91] but because he knew it was Davis he was willing to concede that it had redeeming qualities, even if he could not figure out what they were. "The guy is such a fantastic musician that I know he has something in mind, whatever it is," he said. "I know he knows what he's doing, so he must be doing something that I can't get to yet."

Backstage one night at the Village Gate, Davis brought in a tape of his most recent recording session. "He played some of it for me," Gillespie told Feather, "and he said, 'How do you like that shit?' I said, 'What is it?' and he said, 'You know what it is; same shit you've been playing all the time,' and I said, 'Have I?' I said, 'Look, I'm going to come by your house and spend several hours and you're going to explain to me what that is.'"[92] A few years later Davis grumbled, "Dizzy asks me to teach him. I say, 'Yeah, come by. I'll show you everything we're doin'. It'll be my pleasure.' And he don't come by."[93] By then, Gillespie may have despaired of ever catching up with Davis's directions.

As soon as Davis disbanded the quintet that had been his workshop for so many innovations since 1964 and had supplied the impetus for them in the first place, the new directions came fast. Sometimes, later on, they seemed to come faster than the speed of sound, but for the next year they brought new life not only to Davis's music but to jazz as a whole.

Miles Davis and Gil Evans (Alan S. Flood, courtesy of *Down Beat*)

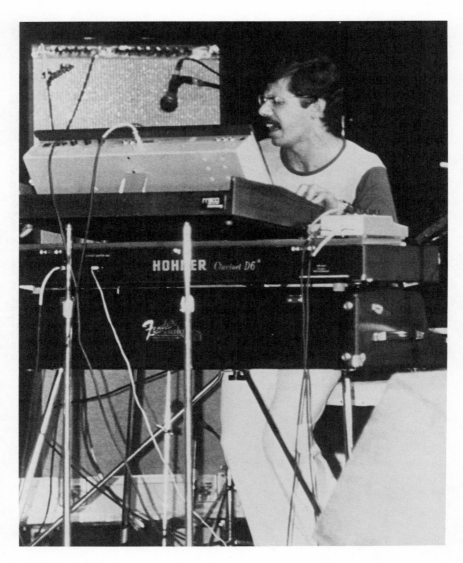

Chick Corea (Bernie Senensky)

12

Miles Runs the Voodoo Down
1968–9

I was telling Herbie the other day: 'We're not going to play the blues anymore.
Let the white folks have the blues. They got 'em, so they can keep 'em. Play
something else.'   Miles Davis

In 1968 Miles Davis faced some inevitable changes. In the spring he
turned 42, an age when most jazz musicians are content to replay the
style they developed in their peak years. The opportunity – and the
inclination – to do just that had presented itself in the early years of the
decade, but somehow he had risen above the temptation and hired the
young men who first pushed him and then followed him along a course
of radical change. Now those young men were entering their own peak
years and all of them were restless. They had spoken among themselves
about moving out on their own, and finally Herbie Hancock and Ron
Carter had taken the daunting step of speaking to Davis about quitting
the quintet. The others would follow them soon enough: Tony Williams
would leave at the end of the year, and Wayne Shorter would leave in
1970. Those changes were inevitable and so, really, were the changes in
his music.

Davis's health, for the time being, was better than it had been for
years, and his energy made him as restless as his sidemen. The hours he
spent in the recording studio, adding instruments to the ensemble,
plugging in amplifiers, reworking arrangements, were the most visible
sign. Nothing he heard in the jazz being played around him seemed to
provide the clues for what he wanted to hear from his own band. "You
can't find a musician who plays anything different," he complained to
Arthur Taylor at the start of the year. "They all copy off each other. If I
were starting out again, I wouldn't listen to records. I very seldom listen

to jazz records, because they all do the same thing. I only listen to guys who are original, like Ahmad Jamal and Duke Ellington, guys like Dizzy Gillespie, Sonny Rollins and Coltrane."[1] More often he listened to records that were not jazz. The day before Taylor interviewed him he had spent some hours listening to *Threnody for the Victims of Hiroshima* by the Polish composer Penderecki.

He was also listening to music categorized at the time as "acid rock," the harsh, dissonant, caterwauling amplifications that were at the leading edge of the rock movement. Tony Williams, who just a few years earlier was credited with infiltrating Davis's music with free-form effects from Ornette Coleman and Cecil Taylor, had transferred some of his boundless enthusiasm to the proponents of acid rock, and before long Davis would speak knowledgeably, and reverentially, about the music of Jimi Hendrix, among others. It would take Davis a few years to incorporate the effects into his music, but the negative lesson from what he heard around him was clear enough: the changes in his music would not be derived from anything in jazz.

He was not the only jazz musician looking beyond jazz for the sources of change. If Ornette Coleman and John Coltrane cast their shadows on the best music of the quintet that was now dissolving, there was never any doubt whatsoever that they were only shadows, never substance, in his music. He accepted their influence only on his own terms. From now on, the shadows of Coleman and Coltrane would recede ever further into the background. For the next year another saxophonist would cast his shadow faintly on Davis's music. His name was Charles Lloyd, and compared to Coleman and Coltrane he was a saxophonist of modest gifts. His influence in jazz was so brief that it is almost entirely forgotten already, and it had much less to do with the music than with its reception. While Lloyd's influence was still fresh, in 1968–9, Davis made two LPs and several individual cuts (with many more still unreleased) that were iconoclastic but popular, and influential but controversial. The two LPs, *In a Silent Way* and *Bitches Brew*, stimulated discussion and debate – and record sales – as few other records have in jazz history.

In 1967–8, Charles Lloyd was a phenomenon. He had played regularly in Chico Hamilton's band starting in 1961, when he was 23, and he moved on into Julian Adderley's band for several months in 1964–5, without attracting any unusual attention from either critics or fans to his soft-spoken style on the flute and tenor saxophone. Then in 1966 he formed his own quartet with three young unknowns: pianist Keith

Jarrett, who was 21, bassist Ron McClure, 25, and drummer Jack DeJohnette, 24. They played at the Monterey Jazz Festival that September and received enthusiastic reviews for their bright, driving performance. As a result, Lloyd was profiled in *Harper's* magazine in an article by Eric Larrabee that focused on the plight of a younger jazz musician searching for an audience when times were tough in jazz. He was also named as the tenor saxophonist deserving wider recognition in *Down Beat's* poll of critics that year.

The wider recognition soon came. Almost by accident, the Charles Lloyd Quartet were invited to play one set on a trial basis at the Fillmore Auditorium in San Francisco, the top rock emporium in the world, and to the surprise of everyone they won a standing ovation from the teenaged audience and were called back for several encores. The event was trumpeted far and wide by the press and the public relations men serving the new youth industry. Charles Lloyd was suddenly 'in.' A live recording by the Lloyd Quartet at the Fillmore a few months later, in early 1967, called *Love-In* (Atlantic sd 1481), became a strong seller in the jazz field and beyond. Lloyd received notices in *Time* and several other magazines, including *Billboard*, which called his quartet "the first psychedelic jazz group," and added, as if by way of explanation, "It really relates to the nostalgia of the war-baby generation." Whatever that might mean, it was couched firmly in the argot of the day – which Lloyd himself spoke fluently. "I play love vibrations," he told the *Time* interviewer. "Love, totality – like bringing everyone together in a joyous dance."[2] With that, the Charles Lloyd Quartet crossed the psychological barriers that had until then kept all but an eccentric fringe of a vast audience of music-consumers away from jazz.

Lloyd's success was a revelation. Almost no one in jazz had really believed that it was possible for jazzmen to play directly to that audience. Certainly several people had been working at siphoning off part of that young audience. Herbie Hancock was one of them. In his independent recordings as a leader for Blue Note records, he spoke of "the concept that there is a type of music in between jazz and rock. It has elements of both but retains and builds on its own identity. Its jazz elements include improvisation and it's like rock in that it emphasizes particular kinds of rhythmic patterns to work off of."[3] In Hancock's recordings such as *Maiden Voyage* (Blue Note bst 84195) and *Speak Like a Child* (bst 84279), the idea of a possible jazz-rock fusion emerges cautiously in some tracks, but generally the rhythms remain mild-mannered and more squarely in the jazz mainstream than the ones

Hancock was playing with in Davis's quintet nightly, and Hancock's piano playing remains more firmly rooted in Bill Evans's delicate lyricism than it often was with Davis. Hancock played music that approximated his description of the fusion on Davis's *Stuff*, recorded for *Miles in the Sky* in May 1968, with its boogaloo drumming and amplified vamp. Just a few days before that, Hancock had recorded *Country Son* with Davis and included in his solo peculiar little melodic touches quite unlike his usual phrasing. When *Country Son* was first released, the most that almost any listener might have noticed was that those phrases sounded unlike Hancock, but within a few years almost every listener could have gone a step further and pointed out that they sounded a great deal like Keith Jarrett. The echo of Jarrett in Hancock's solo on *Country Son* is unmistakeable. Jarrett was then almost unknown, but Hancock was only one of the many jazz musicians listening to him. Probably Miles Davis was too. Actually, they were listening to Charles Loyd, his leader, and inevitably hearing Jarrett as well. And they were listening because Lloyd was the man who had made the breakthrough.

Surprisingly, Lloyd does not seem to have tried very hard, or very consciously, to fuse elements of jazz and rock. He seems to have done little more than hire young men who had grown up in the baby boom generation and let them play their own styles. Keith Jarrett could spin bright, stylish melodies seemingly endlessly, and his technique was as accomplished as his melodies were attractive. When the spotlight fell on the Charles Lloyd Quartet, he thrived, being named the piano player deserving wider recognition by *Down Beat*'s critics in 1967 and going on to become one of the leading lights of jazz in the 1970s. Jack DeJohnette took only a little more time to rise into the top rank of jazz drummers. He propelled Lloyd's music with the drive of a rock drummer, and his work in the group made the most obvious compromises with teenaged tastes, but it soon became evident that his talents were far from exhausted by that style. He was named the drummer deserving wider recognition by the *Down Beat* critics in 1970, after he left Lloyd and joined Miles Davis's band, and from there he too went on to become a respected drummer and bandleader in jazz.

Both became much more conspicuous figures in jazz than their leader. Soon after making the breakthrough at the Fillmore, Charles Lloyd began to devote more of his time to practicing and teaching transcendental meditation in California. By 1971, although he was still occasionally active in music, he was almost completely forgotten by the fans who vote in *Down Beat*'s Readers Poll, many of whom no doubt first became interested in jazz because of his *Love-In* LP.

The breakthrough itself, although fewer and fewer observers would correctly credit (or blame) Lloyd for it, continued to reverberate. One of the movements it stirred up resulted in attempts by largely rock-trained musicians to add some sophistication to their music by using jazz instrumentation, big band devices, and instrumental solos. The first and most successful was Blood, Sweat and Tears, a nine-piece band started in 1968 that included Lew Soloff, later lead trumpeter in the Thad Jones–Mel Lewis orchestra, among its founding members. Blood, Sweat and Tears had three hit records in 1969, and other groups patterned along the same lines soon followed, including Chase, led by former Woody Herman trumpeter Bill Chase, and others such as Chicago and Lighthouse with more remote jazz connections.

A more abiding movement came from within, when dozens of jazz musicians began to notice the possibilities of importing rock elements into their music. When it first gained momentum, in the early 1970s, the movement looked like a stampede. Part of the rush was caused by jazzmen hoping to storm in and make a quick killing as many rock superstars had been doing for a decade, with little regard for their own artistic integrity or for the values of jazz. A few succeeded, but their success soon wore out, as pop fads always do. Some returned to jazz, playing not much differently than they had before, and several others disappeared from music, as last year's hitmakers are expected to in the pop culture. While the amplified compromises of fusion music looked like a majority in the early 1970s and seemed to threaten to become the mainstream, by now enough time has passed for one to look back and notice its diminution, until it looks more like a footnote in the history of jazz.

A few other jazzmen took an entirely different stance. They examined popular music skeptically and disdainfully, but they found in it some genuine sources of energy and inspiration for their music; what they imported remains in their music. One of these was Miles Davis. Ironically, neither his music nor his image seemed suited to fusion superstardom. George Avakian, writing the liner note for Charles Loyd's *Love-In* in 1967, quotes an anonymous rock promoter extolling the virtues of Lloyd for younger fans. "Who else is there?" the promoter asks, and he then answers his own question: "Either you get someone old enough to be their father, or a bunch of angry guys pouring frustration, protest and hate messages out of their horns. That's not the message these kids want to hear."[4] Whether they wanted to hear it or not, Davis was about to give them some protest, and perhaps some frustration and hate too. And it would come from a man old enough to be their father. And if it was not exactly for teenagers, it certainly found an audience among the twenty- and thirty-year olds, to say nothing of the older jazz buffs, some of whom hated it and some of whom did not, but almost all of whom listened to it, at least once.

The dissolution of the quintet allowed Davis to move another step in the direction of fusion by hiring replacements who were – or would become, under his tutelage – more comfortable with amplified instruments. At the time, the change seemed accidental, and Davis probably would have been just as happy to have kept his old band. "It may have been Miles was into electronic music," recalled Ron Carter, who was not into electronic music himself. "It may have been Herbie was into electronic music. It may have been any of these factors. I was leaving the band and we all had talked about leaving. Maybe Miles felt that if he couldn't find guys who carry on the tradition we had set up playing acoustically, he could find a whole different kind of sound from guys who maybe didn't play as well but had enough electronic interests and the control to be able to contribute to his new band."[5] Whatever the reasons, Carter and Hancock were leaving, but Davis would not let them go completely. In effect, they only quit his traveling band. They would join him in the recording studio on several occasions in the next few years. They became members of Davis's studio stock company.

Hancock had found the complexity of the quintet's music harder to come to terms with in the last few years, and his own music on Blue Note reflects his preference for simpler, more straightforward music. "We were always trying to create something new," he told a reporter from *Newsweek*. "It became more and more difficult. Like trying to make conversation never using any words you used before. Miles would say: 'Don't ever play anything straight.' When it worked it was magic. But the music kept getting further and further out and more complex."[6] Davis saw him growing uneasy with the quintet's direction. "Herbie wanted to quit...," he told Jimmy Saunders, "because once in Chicago, he said, 'Miles, sometimes I feel like it just ain't nothing to play.' And I said, 'Then just don't play nothing.' He's a great musician, man, and he knows what's happening. But you can't be a nice guy. He's a nice guy. But me, I ain't nice. I don't care if you don't like me – as long as you can play."[7] The turning point for Hancock was the LP he made for Blue Note titled *Speak Like a Child*. "You know, it's funny," he told Julie Coryell, "when I did that record I knew that was the sound I wanted for my own band. That's when I knew I was going to switch from Miles."[8] The sound consisted of an acoustic piano trio (Hancock, Carter, drummer Mickey Roker) with accompanying colors supplied by a trio of wind instruments (Thad Jones, flugelhorn; Peter Phillips, bass trombone; Jerry Dodgion, alto flute). "Miles suggested a couple of things," he said; "I think he suggested the bass trombone."[9]

Hancock left the quintet in August, soon after *Speak Like a Child* was released. In his first years on his own, he maintained the sextet format of *Speak Like a Child*, using two brass and one reed plus rhythm, but his music quickly divested itself of its conservatism and emulated Davis's movement to more electronics, including a synthesizer, and more percussion, until 1976, when Hancock occasionally returned to acoustic piano and the jazz style he played in the 1960s.

The new piano player, Chick Corea, was just a year younger than Hancock. Davis's attention was drawn to Corea by Tony Williams, who knew him from his Boston days. Corea was playing in Stan Getz's band when Davis first heard him, but by the time he got the call to join Davis he was working as Sarah Vaughan's accompanist. Corea, like Williams, had started in music very young and had been playing professionally most of his life, under the tutelage of a father who was a professional musician. Armando Corea was a jazz trumpeter and arranger around Boston, and he encouraged his son to play several instruments, including drums, trumpet, and vibraphone as well as piano. Davis was delighted by Corea's versatility. "He can play anything he wants to play," he told Sy Johnson, "just like me. He's a music-*lover*, you know."[10]

Beginning with his tenure in Davis's band, Corea became a conspicuous figure in jazz, playing an enormous range of styles from jazz-rock to acoustic duets and free form, all with considerable, and obvious, zeal. His enthusiasm also delighted Davis. "We used to talk about music until late every night," he said.[11]

Until he joined Davis's band, he had never played electric piano and was not certain that he wanted to. "At first, Miles kind of pushed the Fender piano in front of me against my will," he told Conrad Silvert, "and I resisted. But then I started liking it, especially being able to turn up the volume and combat the drummer."[12] His resistance resulted not only from Davis's insistence but also from his dislike for the 'feel' of the instrument. "At first I didn't like it very well because mechanically it's a far inferior instrument to a regular acoustic piano," he told Julie

Coryell. "It still is, but I enjoyed being able to play at a louder volume, mainly so that I could play more comfortably with the volume level of drummers like Tony Williams and other young drummers who were putting out in those days. After that I started liking the timbres of the electric piano and other electronic keyboards and just naturally began using them in my playing, my compositions, and my groups."[13] (The same year that Coryell's book appeared, a very similar dialogue with Corea, except for the point about the Rhodes's mechanical inferiority, was used in advertisements for Rhodes Keyboard Instruments. Asked when he started playing a Rhodes electric piano, Corea replies: "When I started with Miles Davis. We were in a studio, and Miles pointed to this electric piano and said, 'Play it.' I didn't like it." "Didn't like it?" the interviewer asks, and Corea replies: "Not because of the instrument. I just didn't like being told what to do. No musician does. But when I started concentrating on the Rhodes, I came to appreciate all it could do...")

As soon as Corea adjusted to the electric keyboard, he began using it more often than the acoustic piano, and his rapport with Davis, like his facility with the Rhodes, seems to have been almost instantaneous. "We play by sound," Davis said. "I mean I'll give Chick a chord and the sound I want from the chord. He knows I'm musically intelligent enough to give him that. If I don't give him the sound and the approach, he can't play it the way I want to hear it. But there're so many variations on the sound I give him that he's got to get the sound first."[14] Corea's talents were fully exposed during the club and concert engagements the band played during his two-year tenure, but in the recording sessions released at the time he usually found himself alongside one or more other keyboard players where his individual contributions were hard to appreciate.

When Ron Carter left the quintet late in July, Davis hired Miroslav Vitous, a 21-year-old Czech whom he first heard playing with the Bob Brookmeyer–Clark Terry Quintet.[15] Vitous, who later formed the cooperative band called Weather Report along with Wayne Shorter and Joe Zawinul, filled in temporarily while Davis awaited the arrival from England of David Holland, a lanky 22-year-old whom Davis had literally hired off the stage at Ronnie Scott's in June. "Fairytale, wasn't it?" Scott said afterward. "Miles coming in and picking up David Holland like you pick up a girl."[16]

Holland had just finished his final year at the Guildhall School of Music and had taken a job in the band backing singer Elaine Delmar at

Ronnie Scott's for July. "In my last year at college," Holland told Bill Smith in *Coda* magazine, "I was quite active in London. I was doing recordings, some studio work, I was at college, then playing with [John] Surman, and I took a month at the Ronnie Scott club because Bill Evans was going to be there, with Eddie Gomez and Jack DeJohnette, and I had a gig in a supporting band backing a singer. During the last week that Bill was there, Miles came into the club, to see Bill and Jack ... and offered me the job, and that was the beginning of the whole thing."[17]

Davis may have shown up in London because Evans or DeJohnette knew he was looking for a bassist and tipped him off about the talented unknown in the backing band. Whether the recruiting job was by design or by accident, it soon entered jazz folklore. "One night the word went round, 'Miles Davis is in the club,'" John Marshall, the drummer in the backing band recalls. "We did our first set, and Bill went on and we were just going on again when Dave said, '*Miles Davis has offered me the gig*,' and I said, 'Oh really?' and sat down at the drums. But it turned out to be true." And then Marshall adds, "If Miles wants you he doesn't care what color or nationality you are. And his track record is incredible – he can just put bands together. He just *knows*."[18]

Davis phoned Holland at the end of July to confirm the hiring and gave him four days to get to New York for the band's opening at Count Basie's club in Harlem where they were playing for two weeks. "I always wanted to come to America," he said, a few weeks later, still slightly dazed, "but I never dreamed it would be this way." He was barely off the plane before he was playing his first set. "Miles is incredible," he told Leonard Feather. "I feel such strength flowing from him – he's the kind of man that only comes along once in a generation. It's awe-inspiring being around him and these other great players – I feel like I've entered an institution of higher learning. Miles likes to move from one tune to another, without pausing, so we never know what's going to happen next. You've got to be ready to move wherever he goes – usually he'll play an opening phrase that gives just a hint of the next number."[19]

Holland's resilience was quickly tested in other ways as well. Less than seven weeks after arriving in New York, he recorded the final two tracks of the *Filles de Kilimanjaro* LP, and the day after that, on 25 September, the quintet opened a four-day engagement at the Plugged Nickel in Chicago. From there, they went on to play concert and club engagements in California, including a concert at the University of California in Los Angeles, where Leonard Feather inquired about the new bassist. "Miles was so happy," Feather reported, "that he couldn't even put on his surly act for me. 'How about that Dave?' he said backstage ... 'Ain't he a bitch?'"[20] The new band seemed to be shaping up superbly, even in the critical eyes of its leader.

Nevertheless, soon after returning to New York, Davis augmented the working quintet with the two defectors from the old quintet for his next studio session. The recordings, released in 1976 on the LP *Water Babies* along with the old quintet's work from June 1967, extend the stock company concept begun when he added Joe Beck and George Benson earlier. The idea of mixing in various other players with his working sidemen obviously caught his fancy, because he stuck with it every time he made studio recordings for the next four years. The details are as follows:

Miles Davis Ensemble: Water Babies
Miles Davis, tpt; Wayne Shorter, ss (on *Two Faced*), ts (on both titles); Chick Corea, Herbie Hancock, el pno; Ron Carter, David Holland, b; Tony Williams, dms. New York, November 1968
Two Faced; Dual Mr. Tillman Anthony
(both on Columbia PC 34396 [1976])

Considering the extra players added to the ensemble, the music is surprisingly delicate. Hancock and Corea prove to be fully compatible sharing the same instrumental space, as they would again some eight years later when they began presenting duo concerts on acoustic pianos. Here, both play electric pianos, but their roles are clearly defined. Hancock contributes to the bottom on both pieces. On *Two Faced* he plays infrequent chords that punctuate the others' phrases, as he had done with Davis for so many years, and on *Dual Mr. Tillman Anthony* he repeats the staccato rhythmic figure that is the unifying thread of the piece with one of the bass players. Corea ventures more freely, improvising harmonies and feeding the soloists, in the more traditional piano role. He solos on *Dual Mr. Tillman Anthony*, and he and Hancock exchange phrases as simultaneous, but very polite, soloists on *Two Faced*.

The role of the two bassists is harder to divine. One bassist, probably Carter, plays very prominently throughout *Two Faced*, essentially carrying the theme of the piece with a phrase that recurs strategically throughout, and on *Dual Mr. Tillman Anthony* one bassist, again probably Carter, repeats the rhythmic pattern with Hancock all the way through. Through all of this, the second bassist is undetectable, and

Wayne Shorter (Bernie Senensky)

Josef Zawinul (Bernie Senensky)

Miles Davis with Wayne Shorter, Jack DeJohnette, and David Holland
(Trombert, courtesy of *Down Beat*)

whatever space he was supposed to fill cannot be determined from the results. The music is notably high-spirited – relaxed, unfettered, rhythmic, and accomplished – as *In a Silent Way*, with an enlarged stock company, would also be. It obviously leaves a lot to the individual players' discretion. "It's almost aleatory," Ron Carter would say a few years later,[21] and the rewards when the individual players are in such good form radiate from the music.

With the stock company concept justified at least to his own satisfaction, Davis made the move that added a vital dimension to it for the next fifteen months. He invited Josef Zawinul, the Viennese emigré who spoke and acted more 'American' than many natives of New York, his home for nine years, to join the stock company and, as an afterthought, to bring along some music to the recording studio. "Miles called me up one day in the morning," Zawinul told Ray Townley, "and told me to come down to the recording studio at one o'clock. I said fine. After about a minute, he called me back and told me to bring some music."[22]

As it happened, Zawinul had plenty of music stockpiled from a winter he had spent in Vienna in 1966–7 renewing his ties with the family he had left behind him eight years before, when he boarded a steamer from France at the end of 1958 and set sail for the United States. The chance to rest and relax in Vienna came about when he was invited there to serve as a judge at the International Jazz Competition, but the reprieve from the nightly round of jazz clubs soon weighed heavily on him and the best outlet he found was composing. An inveterate composer even when he was working long hours in jazz clubs, he poured all his energies into the task that winter and returned with no fewer than ten charts in his luggage, including *In a Silent Way*, *Directions*, *Early Man*, *Orange Lady*, *Pharaoh's Dance*, and *Double Image*, all of which would find their way onto recordings by either Davis's company or Zawinul's groups or, often, both and would take their place among the hallmarks of the jazz of the early 1970s.

While the number of compositions was unusual for Zawinul or anyone else to write in such a short time, their success was no surprise. Zawinul was already as well established a composer as he was a pianist; any listener who had been paying attention for the previous six or seven years knew something of his accomplishments in both areas. Those who kept a scholarly eye on jazz developments in Europe knew about him long before that.

Zawinul was born in Vienna in 1932 and raised and educated there during the Nazi occupation. He finished his schooling and began working as a professional piano player during the Allied occupation. When the Allies quartered the city in the post-war armistice, Zawinul's family home was in the Russian sector, a geographical accident that prevented him from emigrating as early as he had hoped but did not prevent him from listening to jazz on the military radio stations or watching movies in the adjacent American quarter. George Shearing and Errol Garner, he told Julie Coryell, made the earliest impact on his playing.

Starting in 1952, when he was 20, he played professionally, often as the leader of his own trio. In 1958, he won a scholarship to the Berklee School of Music in Boston and set sail for America, with no intention of studying when he arrived. Almost 27, he was determined to succeed as a jazz pianist in New York. He had been in the city only a few weeks when Maynard Ferguson recruited him into his band for a Birdland engagement, and then Zawinul joined a band led by Slide Hampton, Ferguson's featured trombonist, and kept on playing.

Only a few months after his arrival, probably while he was still with Hampton's band, Zawinul made his first American recording for a label called Strand Records, one of a group of fly-by-night companies known collectively at the time as 'supermarket labels,' because they packaged ridiculously cheap records by generally obscure musicians and displayed them on racks near the check-out counters at supermarkets hoping to catch the eye of impulse buyers on their way home with the week's milk and eggs. On the racks among such gems as *Mediterranean Cruise with Los Españoles* and *Explosive Vocal Percussion with Myra March*, *To You with Love* by the Joe Zawinul Trio (Strand SLS 1007) looked neither more nor less promising in 1959. It was, however, superior to most of Strand's offerings and certainly much better than it needed to be for the supermarket rack. It shows Zawinul with his Shearing and Garner roots well behind him and in debt much more manifestly to Red Garland and Ahmad Jamal. Zawinul, in the company of bassist Ben Tucker, drummer Frankie Dunlap, and bongo player Ray Barretto, plays *Love for Sale*, *Squeeze Me*, and *It Might As Well Be Spring* from the common Jamal-Davis list of standards along with seven other ballads, all neatly arranged for easy listening. He sometimes slips in one of the patented little blues doodles that soon made his style readily identifiable.

Davis was aware of him almost from his first public performance in the United States because Zawinul was playing in Ferguson's band opposite the Davis sextet at Birdland in August 1959, when Davis was involved in the altercation with the police that led to his arrest.

Davis kept tabs on Zawinul's progress after he joined Julian Adderley's quintet in 1961, a job he held until 1970. With Adderley, Zawinul made numerous national and international tours, recorded often, and played many kinds of music. Although Adderley's band made and kept their reputation playing jazz with a blues and gospel tinge, Zawinul co-composed (with William Fischer) *Experience in E*, a symphony for Adderley's quintet and symphony orchestra, and played and composed jazz themes celebrating the civil rights movement (*Walk Tall, Country Preacher*, for the Reverend Jesse Jackson), ballads, bebop, and much more. The Adderley quintet's recording of Zawinul's *Mercy, Mercy, Mercy* in 1967 became a hit single in the pop field. On it, Zawinul played the Fender-Rhodes piano, and if it was not the first time the instrument had been used on a jazz recording it was certainly the first time it had been used so conspicuously. It gave a new respectability to electronic keyboards. It prompted Davis's visit to Zawinul's apartment to tinker around with his Fender-Rhodes, and then he ordered one for Hancock to play on *Water on the Pond* that December. He may also have learned about Zawinul's pile of charts on that visit.

Zawinul was already one of the most interesting composers and players around when he answered the call to join Davis's company in the recording studios, and his presence on the recordings of the next fifteen months gave the kind of edge to Davis's talents that Gil Evans had given them ten years before and had somehow failed to give them since. At 36, he was older than everyone else in the company except Davis, although he was only one year older than Wayne Shorter. Along with his compositions, he brought experience and unflappable confidence into the studio sessions.

Those qualities almost guaranteed that he would never be content, as Gil Evans had been, to lend his talents to Davis's music obsequiously. He used the experience to develop his own approach. "Not from the music," he told Ray Townley, "but from the way Miles handled a recording session I learned a whole lot. They had the tapes running constantly, not to lose certain things. The best things are usually happening when you just get together and try this shit, you know. Miles is a leader, but in such a relaxed way that you never feel like someone is trying to tell you something. There was very little talking going on. It was more just the vibes."[23] In the 1970s, when he entered his forties, Josef Zawinul, the pink-complexioned, balding immigrant, his clear, dark eyes peering out from behind a wall of massed keyboards, would rival Davis as the leader of the fusion movement.

Zawinul first appeared in Davis's recording ensemble in late November on some sessions from which four titles were released belatedly. On the evidence of what has been released so far, Davis clearly wanted Zawinul more for the music he brought along than as a player, although the music seemed to be an afterthought when the invitation was extended. Two of the three titles are Zawinul's, but his contribution to the playing consists solely of adding depth to the rhythms by playing bass notes on the beat on acoustic piano. Were it not for his name on the personnel lists, a listener might never guess he was there. The details are as follows:

Miles Davis Ensemble
Miles Davis, tpt; Wayne Shorter, ts; Chick Corea, Herbie Hancock, el pno; Josef Zawinul, pno; David Holland, b; Tony Williams, dms. New York, 25 November 1968
Splash
(on *Circle in the Round*, Columbia 36278 [1979])

Shorter plays ss; Holland plays el b; Jack DeJohnette, dms, replaces Tony Williams. Same place, 27 November 1968
Directions (take 1); *Directions* (take 2); *Ascent*
(all on *Directions*, Columbia KC2 36472 [1981])

Davis's *Splash* shows his growing fascination with rhythm as the main component for his music. It is organized around the repetition of eight-bar segments at medium tempo, in 5/4 time, with two-bar rests. The soloist constructs his improvisation over as many of these consecutive ten-bar patterns as he chooses, either filling the rests with breaks, as Davis invariably does, or stopping with the rhythm, as Shorter, to good effect, sometimes does. Davis's trumpet playing sounds strangely uneasy with the format, especially considering he wrote it, and he is bothered by sour notes near the beginning of his solo.

Zawinul's *Ascent*, a tone poem similar in its intention to his *In a Silent Way* and *Orange Lady*, fails to find a consistent mood on this playing and remains vague and undefined throughout; it is a failure endemic to this form of composition, which sets up a quiet mood and then seeks to embellish it with sound effects. With no rhythmic pulse to carry the piece, anything less than a concentrated effort by the principal players stalls the implied movement and ends up giving the impression of motionlessness, and the dominant effect is tedium. The success of later recordings of tone poems by Zawinul and Davis elevated the form to the status held by ballads in other jazz genres, but *Ascent,* in this version, would not have provided much incentive for others to take it up.

Zawinul's *Directions,* a pulsating swinger that Zawinul was already playing in Adderley's band, is here revealed in its first, but far from its last, version by Davis. *Directions* became Davis's set-opener almost immediately, and snatches of it occurred in live recordings by Davis's bands long before these studio recordings were issued. *Directions* later became the set-closer for Zawinul and Shorter after they formed Weather Report in 1971, making it one of the most conspicuous strains of the fusion movement. Its appeal is obvious in these recordings. Drummer DeJohnette swats out the 4/4 beats, and his muscular pulse is reinforced by Zawinul and Holland, while the horns play the quick ascent and descent of the theme. The issuing of two takes, a rare event after so many years of Davis's insistence on recording in a single take, indicates how deliberate was his quest for new effects. The two takes show a clear development: on the second, a unison introduction has been added to set off the theme, which then seems to explode following the quieter opening. But the rhythm is much more crisp and the solos are more effective on the first take, suggesting that between the two issued takes there was a long, tiring process of change. Since, by all accounts, the tapes were running continuously throughout Davis's recording sessions, that process of change might someday be documented.

None of these tracks ends with anything that could be called an arranged ending, not even a reprise of the theme. Davis was obviously already planning to 'compose' the final releases from pieces recorded at various times in the studio. His use of post-production splicing, editing, and overdubbing, aided and abetted by Teo Macero, became significant in Davis's releases from this time on, in an increasing degree that at its more extreme did not always, or perhaps often, have happy results. Davis was by no means alone in his reliance on post-production devices, although he was one of very few artists in jazz to pick them up, and he remains to this day the jazzman who took those devices to the greatest extremes. An influential precedent for heavy post-production reworking came in 1967, when the Beatles announced that they would no longer perform in public but would exist solely as recording artists. (A few years before that, Glenn Gould, one of the world's leading concert pianists, had made the same decision.) The Beatles then released *Sgt. Pepper's Lonely Hearts Club Band*, a magnificent pop album by any standards. Its success had conspicuous consequences for the recording business: the Beatles' producer, George Martin, became something of a celebrity in his own right, tagged the "fifth Beatle," and the use of post-production devices was considered to be vindicated in the frenetic quest for hits that has always been the main objective of the pop industry. The fact that those devices contributed very little to the quality of *Sgt. Pepper* got lost in the rush.

In jazz, extensive use of post-production editing hardly outlasted the heyday of fusion music, and even then it was practiced only on a few dozen recording artists in the genre (Davis, Hancock, Donald Byrd, Weather Report, and some others) and by a few 'slick' labels such as CTI, a New York company owned by Verve's former producer Creed Taylor, which routinely added solos and extra rhythm to its releases.

Any discussion of the legitimacy of post-production devices ultimately raises the issue of whether a recording can be an art object in itself, with its own esthetics determined by the manipulation of sounds and textures by a composer-producer – or perhaps by a team of composer-producers that includes the musicians who made the inventory of sounds to be manipulated – or whether a recording is only a means of documenting a performance, which is the true art object and the source of whatever esthetic pleasure the recording can convey.

This controversy has never arisen about other 'packaging' media for art forms, but both possibilities are found. On the one hand, publishers and printers might make novels and poems harder or easier to read and enjoy, but they can scarcely alter or pre-empt the esthetics of the performance – the novel or the poem – they are conveying; printers and publishers, by the nature of their medium, must be artisans not artists. On the other hand, film is a "director's medium" precisely because it can be used to document an actor's performance in the purest sense only by making the most prosaic and boring use of the medium – by, say, training a camera on a stage and making a visual record of a stage play; its most effective use requires heavy post-production editing, elevating the director from artisan to artist.

Sound recording developed primarily to freeze performances in time, as does print, and only later developed the technological flexibility – first mastering onto tape, then multi-tracking, and then 'hot-house' sound effects (pitch manipulation, wah-wah, fuzz-wah, and the rest) – to afford a producer the kind of scope required to 'create' a performance in a workshop, as does a film director. Recordings of classical symphonic music can probably never rely heavily on post-production tinkering and be taken seriously, so revered is symphonic music as a performer's art, and recordings of pop music might well be fabricated entirely in a workshop, because pop artists are so little respected as performers (and so highly regarded as icons) that their audiences often drown out the sound from the stage anyway.

Jazz music has been a highly individualized performer's medium throughout most of its history, and traditionally any post-production alteration with esthetic (as opposed to acoustic) purposes of an arrangement by Duke Ellington, or an ensemble by the Modern Jazz Quartet, or a solo by Charlie Parker would have led jazz fans to dismiss the recording as flawed and unworthy of attention. Those standards seemed to be breaking down in the 1970s. Neither Macero nor Davis seems to have had any qualms at all about what they were doing to Davis's music, and the post-production finalizing became part of their studio routine. "We don't stop the tape machines like we used to do in the old days – they run until the group stops playing," Macero told Chris Albertson. "Then we go back, listen, and decide between us what should be tacked to what – it becomes a search-and-find routine, and finally it's all there, it's just a matter of putting it all together."[24] Many jazz fans accepted recordings at least partly created in the editing room with the same equanimity Macero and Davis showed in producing them.

The period did not last long, but it subsided because of changing tastes rather than popular protests, and the use of post-production devices in jazz recording is likely to arise again as long as listeners show the same tolerance. The music of Miles Davis that was recorded and released in the first half of the 1970s exacts a toll on the listeners' patience and confidence. We now have the takes of *Splash*, *Ascent*, and *Directions*, flawed perhaps but unspliced, because they were released later, on the 1979 and 1981 LPs (neither produced by Macero), after the post-production excesses had become passé, but we get their counterparts released 1969–75 in fragments, with a piece of one spliced onto a piece of another and a solo from one superimposed on another. It is sometimes impossible to know if we are listening to the music of Miles Davis, the trumpeter, or of Davis-Macero, the composer-producer.

Jack DeJohnette's presence in Davis's ensemble with Zawinul and the others for the recording of *Directions* and *Ascent* marked another change in the working band. Tony Williams had handed in his notice with Hancock and Carter but stayed reluctantly for three more months at Davis's request. He told Lee Underwood: "His music was changing. I was a low man on the totem pole, too, and I felt it. He wasn't offering me anything better, and he was talking about using two drummers, which I couldn't see happening. When Herbie left, I figured it was my time, too. Better for me to jump then and make all my mistakes while I was young."[25] He was unbelievably young, still a few weeks away from his 23rd birthday, but he was already a veteran after five and a half years in Davis's band. Since May 1963, when the rejuvenation of his music began, the only drummer besides Williams to play behind Davis was Max Roach, on the weekend at Count Basie's when Davis had sat in with Roach's band.

Finally Davis had to find a replacement, not only because Williams was demanding that he do so but also because Davis's thirteen-concert tour of Japan, scheduled to begin on 6 January, was being held up by Japanese immigration authorities, and Williams was thought to be one of the causes. According to a news item in *Down Beat*, Japanese officials had been reluctant to grant visas to touring American jazzmen since 1967, when several touring drummers were arrested and convicted; Williams had been in some unspecified trouble in Japan.

The tour was finally cancelled even though the promoters had already sold all 2,400 tickets for the opening concert in Tokyo. "They had us on tenterhooks right up to the end," Jack Whittemore, Davis's manager, announced. "The Japanese promoters kept cabling us that things looked 'favorable,' but the visas never came through. When we got the final refusal, the only explanation given was 'personal reasons.'"[26] By then, Davis had replaced Williams with DeJohnette.

For Williams, the release gave him the freedom to fulfill his first ambition. "I knew I was going to leave someday and get my own band," he told Lee Underwood. "Even before joining him, I had dreamed of being what he is. I looked up and saw stars, and I wanted to be a star too. I wanted to be a bandleader. I wanted to make my own music." He felt he had postponed that ambition long enough. "Miles is a very strong personality," he said. "He has definite ideas about what he wants. Therefore, you live in *his* world. Living in somebody else's world is not easy. I was subject to his whims and desires and caprices. It took me a long time to realize that and to get out of it."[27]

He rejoined Davis a few times as a member of his studio stock company but most of his energies were devoted to his own trio, called Lifetime, which he formed in February 1969, three months after leaving

Davis's band. Lifetime's brand of fusion, marked by high-amplitude energy and Williams's shouted vocals, attracted some attention from promoters and record executives but excited less attention from fans. Nothing that Lifetime played on its own found anything close to the success, in either the short or the long run, that its members had while playing in Davis's stock company. For Williams, whose raw talents shone so brilliantly from the moment he was seen playing publicly, the first years as a leader after leaving Davis were successful, but much less so than Hancock's were and Shorter's would be, and less even than Carter's, when he led a non-fusion jazz band between his busy outings as a freelancer.

Williams regained some of his stature among jazz drummers in the second half of the 1970s, when he joined forces with a small and mutable nucleus of star players for record dates, concerts and festivals, and sometimes tours, especially when his rhythm section mates were Herbie Hancock and Ron Carter.

Williams's replacement, Jack DeJohnette, had become peripatetic since leaving Charles Lloyd's group late in 1967, after two years, when Lloyd had elected to curtail his touring activities. His exposure with Lloyd and with Stan Getz in early 1968, with Bill Evans on a European tour in the summer, and with Jackie McLean and Getz again in the fall built his reputation quickly. He was playing with McLean's band when Davis started scouting him, as Tony Williams had been six years before. "Miles started to come around to hear Jackie to hear me," DeJohnette says. "Jackie said to me, 'You're going to be Miles' next drummer, and I know, because I always get the drummers first.'" Then Davis managed to persuade Williams to stay with him, and DeJohnette waited impatiently for his turn. When the opening came, he applied directly. "I had just quit Stan Getz," he told Chip Stern, "when Dave Holland called me and said that Tony had just quit to form Lifetime. So I called Miles, we haggled about price, and I joined them for a gig the next week in Rochester."[28]

The rock-flavored studio recordings of *Ascent* and *Directions* took place soon after, but DeJohnette found the live performances more taxing. "That band was a lot more avant garde than people were ready to admit," he says. He stayed with Davis for two and a half years, supplying his bands with the rock-solid, showy beat that Davis's fans had grown accustomed to with Williams, who was three years younger, but playing a much less unbridled style. DeJohnette's style seemed much more like an updating of Philly Joe Jones's than a perpetuation of Williams's.

Davis's recordings with the growing stock company had so far remained unissued, even though they had been going on since December 1967, when guitarist Joe Beck had joined the quintet in the studio. Starting with some sessions in February 1969, all that began to change. These sessions would be issued, not only because Columbia needed a new release from Davis for its fall catalog but also because the music finally came together in a strong amalgam of talents, so that even though it was novel in approach and style, there could be no mistaking its merits. The novelty preoccupied the fans and critics at the time of its release more than its merits, largely because the long buildup to this music had all gone unheard.

The February recording band were made up of familiar names except for the guitarist, John McLaughlin. He was completely unknown beyond a small coterie of musicians in England, and he was only slightly better known when the recordings were issued a few months later. His presence among the others in the stock company, as it turned out, was as big a surprise to him as it was to the fans who bought the new LP, *In a Silent Way*, on its release. McLaughlin had been in the United States for only a few weeks when the first session took place. He arrived to join Tony Williams's trio, Lifetime, which also included the organist Larry Young. He was 26, and his background as a musician in England was probably more diverse than almost any American player could have had at the time, including classical piano studies, dance bands, professional Dixieland, avant-garde jazz, and highly amplified rock. He came to Williams's attention, and probably Davis's too, through David Holland, who loaned Williams a tape of McLaughlin's playing and extolled his playing to anyone who would listen.

McLaughlin's introduction to New York musicians came in December, when he joined Williams and Young in Lifetime at Count Basie's club. "After thirty seconds of his first solo," said Larry Coryell, then considered to be the most promising young guitarist, "I turned to my wife and said, 'This is the best guitar player I've ever heard in my life.'" Coryell was not the only musician who was impressed by what he heard. "That night," he recalled, "everybody was there – everybody from Cannonball's group; I think Miles was there; Dave Holland – and we were all totally knocked out by that fantastic debut of John."[29] Davis immediately invited him into the recording studios with his stock company. "I found myself after two days in the same recording studio as Miles Davis," he told Julie Coryell, "and I was nervous simply because this man had lived inside of my imagination, inside my record player for so many years."[30]

Many listeners hearing McLaughlin on *In a Silent Way* for the first time assumed that he had been conscripted from the rock ranks, and even those who learned something about his background thought of him as a rock musician. As the fusion movement spread, someone with McLaughlin's credentials would be less anomalous, but at the time his presence aroused curiosity. "I didn't use John as a rock player but for special effects," Davis explained to Don DeMicheal. "John's no more a rock guitar player than I'm a rock trumpet player."[31] Those "special effects" were, however, largely rock effects. The full range of his capabilities would take longer to expose, because his most conspicuous work for the first two years in the United States came on records with Davis, and he played fusion music nightly with Lifetime, but there he had a chance to expand. "While I was recording and playing with Miles," he says, "I was working with Tony Williams's Lifetime, which was a completely new form and which I felt very happy about. It was a new direction which I was really a contributor toward, and this constrasted working with Miles, where I wasn't a contributor except under his own terms. This was fine, because his own terms were very educational to me – so I had the best of both worlds."[32]

In February, Davis brought McLaughlin into the studio with an aggregation that included Zawinul, whose composition *In a Silent Way* would provide the title for the LP and also its centerpiece, and a group of musicians from his past and present working quintets. The details are as follows:

Miles Davis Ensemble: In a Silent Way
Miles Davis, tpt; Wayne Shorter, ss; Chick Corea, Herbie Hancock, el pno; Josef Zawinul, el pno, org; John McLaughlin, gtr; David Holland, b; Tony Williams, dms. New York, 18 February 1969
SHHH/Peaceful
(on Columbia CS 9875)

Same personnel. Same place, 20 February 1969
In a Silent Way; It's about That Time
(both on Columbia CS 9875)
Zawinul plays electric piano on *In a Silent Way* and organ on the other titles.

These recordings shocked the jazz critics and many fans late in 1969. The effect was calculated. "This one will scare the shit out of them," Davis told Don Heckman just before their release, and he insisted that

Heckman listen to some of the mixed tapes over the telephone while a Columbia engineer dutifully played them at the other end.[33]

Compared to the music to come, it is hardly shocking. It seems, in retrospect, to be Davis's valedictory to the careful, lyrical trumpet playing that had brought him such adulation in the 1950s. At the time, no one could guess that what would follow would make it look relatively conservative, but it is beautifully lyrical when compared with both what followed and what came before.

Davis's admonition to his working quintet of a few years earlier, that they should never play anything "straight," has obviously been withdrawn. There is a great deal of straight playing here, with tempos and time signatures sustained throughout each segment, harmonic roles well defined, and, above all, melodies grasped and refined. Listeners whose attention was not completely distracted by the unfamiliar electronics that form the background discovered in *In a Silent Way* a reaffirmation of Davis's venerable musical values. The context is, of course, entirely different. "The music here is static harmonically," Harvey Pekar points out. "It depends for interest on the inventiveness of the soloists and the contrapuntal and textural blend that the players can create while improvising simultaneously."[34] In those respects, it is perhaps not so different after all from the music of the Davis quintet that preceded it. But it is more tightly organized.

Almost nothing is left to chance. Tony Williams is reined in most obviously. He is silent on *In a Silent Way*, and on both *SHHH/Peaceful* and *It's about That Time* he maintains a metronomic pulse, the former on cymbals and the latter on snare, that is bright, elastic, and ingenious but never spontaneous or impulsive, the other characteristics usually associated with Williams's drumming in Davis's bands. Corea, Hancock, and McLaughlin meld their tones into a remarkably self-effacing blend. All contribute sparingly, sensitive to the amount of space that the others require, and collectively they build a rhythmic-harmonic cushion in which individual contributions count for very little. On *SHHH/Peaceful*, they share two interludes on either side of Shorter's solo that amount to pauses in the motion of the piece rather than solos of any conventional sort.

Zawinul stands apart from the others. His organ drone is the principal accompaniment for Davis's solos on *SHHH/Peaceful*, which state the theme at the open and close of the extended recording, and on *It's about That Time* his organ joins Holland's bass in stating the pattern of the quicker, second theme that recurs throughout. On *In a Silent Way*, he states his own indelible melody first, on electric piano, before Shorter enters to restate it on soprane saxophone and Davis and Shorter state it a third time in unison. Those three separate interpretations of the melody comprise the complete take of *In a Silent Way*; there are no solos, no variants, and no developments, but Zawinul's tone poem, a melody that magically finds a sound parallel to silence, insinuates itself into the memory more powerfully than the two lilting, assertive ballads.

Almost as distracting as the amplified undercurrents of this music when it was first released was its form. The LP presents two sidelong tracks, entitled *SHHH/Peaceful* and *In a Silent Way/It's about That Time*, as unbroken twelve-inch expanses of vinyl. Davis had been playing his concert and club performances as single, unbroken sets for years, but his recordings had taken the conventional shape that jazz records had always taken. The appearance of the new record was novel, and so was its organization. Each side was selected from music recorded in a three-hour studio session, with some splicing and other manipulation to make the finished issue. *SHHH/Peaceful* contains a single theme, notwithstanding its double title, and could possibly even be a continuous take on the aural evidence, although it probably is not. *In a Silent Way/It's about That Time* leaves no doubt at all about its provenance. It opens with the quiet strains of *In a Silent Way*, which lasts four minutes and twelve seconds, and then swings into *It's about That Time* as soon as the last reverberation of the electric pianos has faded; after about eleven and a half minutes, and no more than a second or two of real silence, *In a Silent Way* returns, in exactly the same take that had opened the side. It may be the only instance in the history of the recording industry when record buyers were sold the same take of a piece twice on the same record, but Davis's orchestration of Zawinul's striking melody not only works well as an entity but also works well as a frame for Davis's *It's about That Time*, and no one complained about the duplication.

Viewed in the line of development of Davis's experiments with the studio stock company since late 1967, the LP appears as a culmination. The two sessions managed to balance the ensemble and control the colors of the instruments, many of them relatively new in Davis's musical concept. The rock elements in the drumming and in the electric pianos and guitar were mild importations, and the context remains essentially jazz. Davis was bringing all these features into his studio work of the past year and a half, and they finally came together strongly. But none of the developmental work had been released, or would be for several years, and *In a Silent Way* appeared not as a culmination at all but as an abrupt shift. Its polish and precision made it appear remarkably mature, and Davis was hailed as the prime mover in the fusion movement by a public that could not know – had no way of knowing – that the concept did not spring fully grown one day in February 1969, or that several others hands, including Hancock, Zawinul, Williams, and others, had worked patiently along with him in developing it.

In format and intention, the studio sessions were collaborations that Davis presided over and directed, but the released material, beginning with *In a Silent Way*, not only listed Davis most prominently and failed to mention the cooperative system behind the music, but also unabashedly listed Davis as composer on some themes rumored to have been developed in the studio by Corea, Zawinul, Shorter, and the others. It was a practice that predictably drew some comment from the others, especially Zawinul. "We were already playing new things with Cannonball's band," he pointed out ten years later. "We played *In a Silent Way* two years before I gave it to Miles to record."[35]

Zawinul received full credit for composing *In a Silent Way*, but Davis transformed it in the studio. McLaughlin says, "He has a genius for bringing out in musicians what they want to do which corresponds to what he wants. *In a Silent Way* is a perfect example. When Joe Zawinul brought it in originally, there were many more chords. What Miles did was to throw out the entire chord sheet. He took Joe's melody and turned it into something that was far from what we'd been rehearsing in the studio. He made that piece into something of lasting beauty."[36]

That kind of credit to Davis did not sit comfortably with Zawinul, although he was willing to concede that his composition was altered by Davis. "I cut it later myself," he said, referring to his 1970 recording on Atlantic (SD 1579), "and I played on my album the whole version like I wrote it originally. Miles only played the last part ... Miles stayed on the tonic, while I on my recording changed the bass notes."[37] Those bass lines were the chief difference McLaughlin noted between the written version and the version Davis recorded, but Zawinul claimed that Davis later restored much of the original score by overdubbing. "Well, Miles was doing something different, but you've got to consider one thing," he told Larry Birnbaum. "On this first album, *In a Silent Way*, he had a lot of bass lines added on and they were my bass lines. I put them on there, to give it a certain feeling."[38]

When he could be persuaded to say anything at all on the subject, Davis seemed willing enough to credit Zawinul. In the brief notes that

Davis wrote for Zawinul's 1970 Atlantic LP, he said, "Zawinul is extending some thoughts that we've both had for years. And probably the thoughts that most so-called now musicians have not yet been able to express." To that, in a postscript longer than the note itself, he added: "In order to write this type of music, you have to be *free inside of yourself* and be Joe Zawinul with two beige kids, a black wife, two pianos, from Vienna, a Cancer, and cliché-free."[39] For those who saw the tribute and realized how rare it was from Davis, the short statement implied a mountain of praise for Zawinul's contribution.

The other players were never as vocal as Zawinul in claiming credit for themselves because of Davis's mastery over the collaborative process. "Miles directed," John McLaughlin said, "and without that, it wouldn't be what it is, that's for sure." Asked directly by Lee Jeske about Davis's pre-empting credit for arranging and composing several themes that should have been credited to Corea or Zawinul, McLaughlin said, "It happened to me too with certain things – you make a suggestion and then it's rearranged in form. But I can only give credit to Miles because he puts a print on it that's particularly him and particularly whole."[40] Certainly Teo Macero, from the vantage point of the control booth, agreed wholeheartedly. "That influence was so potent and so strong every time they went in there that [they] couldn't afford to screw around," he told Gregg Hall, "and, in fact, none of the musicians do. When they're in the studio it's like god coming – oh, oh, oh, here he comes. They stop talking, they tend to business and they listen, and when he stops, they stop. When he tells the drummer to play, the drummer plays. When he tells the guitar players to play, they play and they play until he stops them. This is a fact, not hearsay; I've seen it ... They got more out of him than they have given to him. He is the teacher. He's the one who's sort of pulling the string. He's the professor. He's the god that they look up to and they never disagreed, to my knowledge, in the studio. If they did, they got a goddam drumstick over their head and I've seen that happen too."[41] Every one of the players involved in *In a Silent Way* absorbed the lessons thoroughly enough to become a leader in the fusion movement.

If Davis was hoping to attract the attention of rock fans and rock musicians, at least those who took their music seriously, in attempting the fusion, he succeeded. *In a Silent Way* was received by at least a small group outside jazz as expressing what Davis called "the thoughts that most so-called now musicians have not yet been able to express." What he may not have been fully aware of was the extent to which some of his previous music was already being listened to by some of the better popular musicians. Joni Mitchell, a songwriter who eventually tried to incorporate some jazz elements into her music, admitted that "*Nefertiti* and *In a Silent Way* became my all time favorite records in just any field of music. They were my private music; that was what I loved to put on and listen to – for many years now. Somehow or other I kept that quite separate from my own music, I only thought of it as something sacred and unattainable." Mitchell did not try using Davis's concept in her own work for several years, until 1979, when she recorded an album of jazz vocals based on melodies by Charles Mingus, who had died at the beginning of the year. By then, she had grasped some of Davis's methods as had few of his contemporaries in jazz. "Miles always gave very little direction, as I understand," she said. "It was just 'Play it. If you don't know the chord there, don't play there,' and that system served him well. It was a natural editing system. It created a lot of space and a lot of tension, because everybody had to be incredibly alert and trust their ears. And I think that's why I loved that music as much as I did, because it seemed very alert and *very* sensual and very unwritten."[42] She applied those methods and made a musically interesting fusion of jazz elements in pop that is in some ways the pop counterpart of the neat fusion of elements in jazz represented in *In a Silent Way*.

With all the recording activity by augmented personnel, Davis still kept up his full schedule of performances with his working quintet, now made up of Wayne Shorter, Chick Corea, David Holland, and Jack DeJohnette. Their summer round of festivals included concerts on both nights of the Antibes Jazz Festival, 25 and 26 July, and one night at the Monterey Jazz Festival in late August, almost half the globe away. Reviews of the new quintet were as effusive as they had been for the old one. "The group is an intellectual experience," Harvey Siders wrote in his review of the Monterey performance. "Miles and his alter ego, Wayne Shorter, are gravitating ever closer to a free Nirvana, basing their improvisations on arbitrary scales and/or modes, rendering all conventional frames of reference obsolete. Tempos change and moods shift almost subliminally. The rhythm section follows with an uncanny instinct." Siders adds, ominously, "He left many of his listeners behind."[43] The disaffection of a segment of the jazz audience had barely begun; it would grow in the years ahead.

Siders's account of the live performance implies that the music was a direct descendant of the previous quintet. Certainly it had the same spirit, perpetuating the spontaneous solutions that Davis had long required of his sidemen as the current studio sessions, with their protracted rehearsals and assigned roles, no longer did. No recordings by this quintet have been issued. In the studio, they always shared the floor with guest players, and Columbia, holding what they considered a superabundance of Davis's studio sessions, felt no need to add to it by recording his concerts. "The live stuff really should have been gotten on tape," Corea says, "because that's when the band was burning ... That quintet developed some really beautiful improvised stuff. We would do two or three pieces that were just strung together, one right after another for the whole concert, and we would make this wonderful, wonderful composition."[44]

Corea holds a cache of tapes accumulated on its tours, and several performances exist in other private collections. Notable among them is the concert recorded by Radio-diffusion, France, at Antibes (26 July), which catches the quintet moving glibly through several themes. Two of them, *Spanish Key* and *Sanctuary*, were not recorded in their approved versions until a month later, for *Bitches Brew*, and the performance of music prior to its recording date probably has no precedent in Davis's career. For the first time Davis was spending hours with his band rehearsing; they were working on new themes all the time in Columbia's studios and were ready to play them outside the studio. *Directions* opens the concert, and it too was completely unknown to the audience. By the time Davis's 1968 recording of it was released in 1981, it was well known in a 1972 version by Weather Report (on *Live in Tokyo*, CBS-Sony [Jap] SOPJ 12-13-XR, and edited to one-fifth its length on *I Sing the Body Electric*, Columbia KC 31352) and indirectly from Davis's concert recordings of 1970 (where it was never named). The other themes invoked at Antibes are *Masqualero* and *Nefertiti*, both recorded in 1968, and *I Fall in Love Too Easily*, first recorded by Davis in 1963 and played frequently since but hardly one of his signature ballads. The burst of studio activity led him to eradicate the familiar repertoire he had clung to since the 1950s – *Walkin'*, *So What*, *My Funny Valentine*, *Stella by Starlight*, *Green Dolphin Street*, and all the others. They clung to him, too, and he continually fielded requests for them. Occasionally in the next year he gave in and played a request, but after that he never played them again, much to the consternation of his oldest fans.

The concert tapes reveal the talents of Corea, Holland, and DeJohnette as the studio recordings never do. There their individuality was subjugated to the augmented rhythm sections that formed the purée of fusion music. Here, they function as individuals always have in small-band jazz: they toy with time signatures, comp for soloists, and construct solos of their own. Corea plays the Fender-Rhodes piano with Zildjian instincts and Steinway dexterity; few electric piano players – and there would soon be dozens of them – succeeded so well in imprinting their own voices onto its circuitry. Holland plays electronically too but switches to the old upright bass whenever his solo turns come around, and in the ensembles and his solos – that is, on both electric and acoustic instruments – he shows the nimble technique that made him stand out on the Soho stage when Davis recruited him. DeJohnette proves harder to admire, perhaps because he has to combat the echoes of Williams that linger in Davis's music. Williams played tough, but DeJohnette sounds tougher as a basic 4/4 drummer hitting cymbal splashes on every beat. In Davis's band even more than in Charles Lloyd's, he sticks to the beat single-mindedly, as no other drummer of Davis's did until Al Foster, his successor. Together, the new rhythm team leave no doubts about the underlying pulse in Davis's music, which had become a more fluid element with the previous quintet. Now the beat became the only fixed point, and, in the bands that succeeded it, it often became the whole point. Before that happened there was a lot to listen to, but so far none of it is available. Corea says, "With Miles I hope they release everything I've ever done with him. I only remember going into the studio quite often and hardly hearing anything."[45]

With all his recordings and concerts in 1969, Davis cut a large swath in the jazz world. The activity was reflected in all the polls and awards by which a small segment of the audience makes its opinions and impressions known. In *Down Beat*'s poll of its readers, Davis was conspicuous even for someone who had dominated several categories for decades. He was named top trumpeter ahead of Gillespie, Clark Terry, and Freddie Hubbard; his quintet was named top small band ahead of Elvin Jones's, the Modern Jazz Quartet, and Gary Burton's; he was named Jazzman of the Year as well, over Buddy Rich and Duke Ellington; and three of his LPs were cited among the top eleven: *Filles de Kilimanjaro* was first, *In a Silent Way*, although released so late in the year that it had not made its full impact, was third, and *Miles in the Sky* was eleventh.

With those honors and many others to show for his year's work, both Davis and Columbia should have felt satisfied. Instead, Davis found himself under increasing pressure from Columbia to plunge further into the youth market.

The pressure was not exactly new to him, but lately it had become more intense. *In a Silent Way*, with its creative and tasteful use of rock elements, represented Davis's first serious response. If it seemed a blantant compromise to a few purist fans and critics, most saw it as a strikingly innovative and artistically successful use of new instruments and new textures in jazz. It caught the attention of jazz fans as no other LP by Davis had for almost a decade, and of a small but significant segment of the rock audience, the ones willing to stretch their imaginations and raise their sights.

The broader response still fell short. "It didn't sell well at all," Teo Macero said. "It sold 80–90,000 units."[46] That figure was excellent for jazz sales, but it only whetted Columbia's appetite when it was thinking in terms of hundreds of thousands of sales. Its perspective was shaped by its enormously successful popular music division, where aggressive recruiting and promoting had vaulted Columbia into the forefront of the teenage music market.

The man credited for Columbia's surge was Clive Davis, a Columbia lawyer who became vice-president and general manager in 1966 and hoisted himself into the presidency soon afterward. Under Davis, Columbia's image was transformed from the safe, familial face that had long made it the General Motors of the record industry, with a safe, familial roster that included Mitch Miller singalongs, Andy Williams, and the Ray Conniff Singers, to the showcase for the baby boom counterculture, with recording stars such as Bob Dylan, Donovan, Janis Joplin, Simon and Garfunkel, the Byrds, Sly Stone, and Carlos Santana, each of whom could sell a million new records for the company annually with a little luck and a lot of promotion.

Clive Davis's transformation of Columbia started as a make-it-or-break-it risk for the hustling young executive. "If a revolution came," he declared in his memoir of his Columbia days, *Clive: Inside the Record Business*, "it would require new faces and new minds, not a cosmetic job by past masters."[47] As a corporate philosophy, Davis's view posed a threat to every officer in the company; the "new faces and new minds" he was looking for were not confined to the roster of recording stars. More than a few of his peers in the executive suite expected him to self-destruct when he started lighting the fuses for the "revolution," and more than a few hoped he would when the shrapnel spilled over into their departments.

The marketing department was one of the first to feel the impact; Davis recalls that the introduction of the new young personnel he placed in marketing put "some radical thinkers" into the department, a description that hardly does justice to the impact in the corporate corridors of mutton-chopped dropouts with hair down their backs.

Columbia, and Davis, thrived. For Davis it was a mission. He hopped planes to the farthest reaches and threw open the doors of his paneled office in order to hear a new group that someone somewhere had tipped him about; he negotiated contracts and listened to unmastered tapes; he was a president in shirt-sleeves, who had the gall to make million-dollar decisions guided by his gut reaction to music made for, and often by, people more than two decades younger than he.

At the end of 1968 and beginning of 1969, he made some decisions that aggrandized even his impressive portfolio. He signed a newly formed band called Blood, Sweat and Tears, and then he signed a band called Chicago. Both groups played rock, but it was musically literate rock compared to almost all the successful bands of the day. It was, in the perception of almost everyone, rock with a jazz bias, and although the jazz elements were milder in both groups than the rock elements were in *In a Silent Way*, they were sufficient to separate the bands from the main currents of commercial rock and thus to make their signing a heavy risk.

The risk turned into a windfall profit. In 1969, both bands scored huge hits with pop singles and best-selling LPS. Their releases on Columbia diverted the pop currents and left most of the competition high and dry. If he was not before, Davis certainly was now the champion of the fastest waters.

His successes with pop music that flirted with jazz strengthened his resolve to get Columbia's jazz division moving at a pace that came closer to matching the other divisions. It was already, of course, healthy, with an incomparable vaultful of classic jazz from Bessie Smith to Thelonious Monk and a current roster, admittedly sparser and aging after several years of retrenchment during the bad times, that included Charles Mingus, Stan Getz, and Bill Evans as well as Miles Davis. But Clive Davis was not inclined to compare his jazz division to those of other companies; he compared it instead to the other divisions at Columbia, and he was thoroughly dissatisfied. "I am very eager to allow Columbia to be used by the most forward-looking American jazz artists, to explore what kind of synergy can come out of jazz and rock," he told Chris Albertson in 1971. "What do the jazz giants, the leading figures of today, have to say? What is their reaction to the fact that, in attempting to fuse jazz and rock, Chicago and Blood, Sweat and Tears have reached millions of people all over the world while they, without such an attempt, only reach a few thousand with their music?"[48]

The target of many of Davis's pleas to broaden the musical ground was Miles Davis. That seemed to contradict his principle about "seeking new faces and new minds, not a cosmetic job done by past masters," but Clive Davis knew about Miles Davis's gift for self-renewal – Miles Davis had never allowed himself to be pegged a "past master" anyway – and he may also have sensed that the real fusion, if it were to happen, would require a masterly musician. One thing he never wavered on was Davis's ability to reach a larger audience. "When I took over the Presidency of Columbia," he said, "he was one of the company's mainstays. His albums *Sketches of Spain*, *Kind of Blue* and *Porgy and Bess* were landmarks. But his sales in recent years had fallen off; he sold between forty and fifty thousand albums now – he'd once sold more than a hundred thousand, sometimes a hundred and fifty thousand."[49] Those were the credentials that convinced Clive Davis that he already had the right man under contract.

His program for Miles Davis's breakthrough went well beyond his recording activities. "I suggested that he play the Fillmore – or places like it – if he wanted to reach a larger audience and raise sales. Youth was ready for Miles Davis, but he had to play where they went for their music." Miles Davis was infuriated by the suggestion. After fourteen years with Columbia, years when his records made with complete autonomy had won honors and compiled sales figures undreamed of for any other jazz artist, he was not likely to accede to the suggestions – or the dictates, as he saw them – of a Columbia executive who had been around for only four or five years. Clive Davis felt his fury when he pressed the suggestion by telephone. "He wasn't going to play for 'those fucking long-haired white kids,'" he was told. "He would be 'ripped off'; Bill Graham [owner of the Fillmore] wouldn't pay him enough *money*. The audience would be prejudiced because he was black. And further-more, if the head of Columbia was espousing this, he wanted off the 'fucking label.' And he hung up on me."

Soon afterward, Clive Davis received a telegram stating that Miles Davis would make no more records for Columbia and demanding that he be released immediately. The day after that, Jack Whittemore called and offered him a chance to back down from his position and patch up the affair, but he did not take it. "Miles's manager called the next day," Clive Davis recalled. "Wow, Miles was really heated up! What in the world had I said to him? I told him what had happened and I added that I was *still* convinced we had the same objective. Young audiences were getting into sophisticated fusions of jazz and rock; they could easily get into Miles – but they had to be exposed to him. The way to do it was for him to play Fillmore. I added that I had nothing to apologize for; I wasn't giving Miles his release."[50]

Détente was obviously impossible. What had so far been a private disagreement between the president of Columbia and the leading jazz artist became public and grew nastier.

Several New York newspapers and the wire services they feed carried stories announcing that after almost fifteen years Miles Davis would leave Columbia for Motown Records, a Detroit-based company founded by Berry Gordy that rose to prominence on the strength of soul hits by Diana Ross and the Supremes, Smokey Robinson and the Miracles, the Four Tops, and other groups. Motown was revered by many jazz musicians as well as pop singers as a corporation that epitomized black initiative. (The bloom did not last long; reservations were soon being voiced, as when Elvin Jones, in 1971, told Arthur Taylor: "Motown Records is supposed to be a black company – well, I know that it is not. Maybe originally Berry Gordy conceived the idea, but the time has long since passed where he has anything at all to do with that company other than being a front-office man. I think it probably belongs to the Bank of America ... I'm sure it's not controlled by the finances of Negroes. It's controlled by the established finances who control everything."[51] Whatever the facts about Motown's corporate control, the perception of its 'blackness' that made it an ideal in the 1960s faded in the cynicism of the 1970s.) Whether or not Davis discussed his move seriously with Gordy or others at Motown has never been corroborated. His reason for making the move, according to the newspaper accounts, had nothing to do with his artistic autonomy, a reason that might have raised some eyebrows among those who knew that Motown's output had a homogeneous rhythm-and-blues veneer, called the 'Motown sound,' widely attributed to Gordy's overwhelming influence in its studios. Instead, according to Davis, he was leaving because Columbia exploited its black artists.

Now it was Clive Davis's turn to be infuriated. He made an angry denial and demanded a public retraction from Davis. The retraction, predictably, never came. "Clive asked me why I had said that," Davis told Albertson several months later, when the furor had died down, "and I said, 'Was I telling a lie, Clive? If you can say I'm a liar, I'll retract that statement.' You see, all those records I have made with them have been a bitch, and they come out being rich behind all this token shit." Davis began referring to himself as "the company nigger."

"You would think he's not grateful," Clive Davis said when Albertson passed along Davis's remarks, "but I just know he is. I'm not sure that it's his mind he speaks; I'm not sure that he doesn't tell people what they want to hear, because it takes a certain amount of research before you go off making such statements. I do mentally treat him differently, not because he's black – we have a tremendous number of black artists – but because he's unique among people, and you expect the unexpected from Miles Davis."[52]

Not only did Miles Davis not retract his statement, but he repeated it several times in the years to come, well aware that he had hit a corporate nerve. "I think they're the saddest record company in the world," he told Gregg Hall in 1974, long after he had resettled comfortably into Columbia's roster, "But the greatest ... They don't do nothin' for niggers – nothing!"[53]

Clive Davis could not respond publicly to that statement because by then he had been ousted at Columbia after being charged with procuring narcotics for his recording stars; the charges were eventually dismissed – with much less publicity than when they were laid – and he started his own record company, Arista, which gained some prominence in the second half of the decade for its avant-garde jazz division under producer Michael Cuscuna. Had he still been at Columbia, he probably would have responded to Davis's charges with the same mixture of bitterness and resignation he showed earlier. "It bothers me," he told Albertson, "because I think we have really done a tremendous amount to be creative along with him, and we work very closely with him so that we make sure he sells not only to jazz audiences and to contemporary rock audiences, but to rhythm and blues audiences as well."[54] He connects, as he apparently always connected, the idea of "being creative along with him" with expanding his audience from jazz into rock and rhythm and blues.

When Miles Davis announced his imminent departure from Columbia, the reality of that departure was closer to fantasy than fact, for reasons that had nothing to do with artistic autonomy, race prejudice, incompatibility, or anything else that impinged on the creative process. The plain fact was that Davis's finances were bound to Columbia almost inextricably. Clive Davis knew that; Miles Davis's threat to leave, he said, "both disturbed and amused" him – disturbed him that he would consider it and amused him that he would think it could be accomplished so easily. "In the process of becoming a star in the jazz world," Davis wrote in his memoirs, "he'd acquired some expensive habits: exotic cars, beautiful women, high-fashion clothes, unusual homes. He's also gotten in the habit of calling Columbia regularly for advances."[55]

Miles Davis took the financial arrangements for granted. "The Internal Revenue Service is always after me," he told Albertson, "but I just send their bills on to Clive. I got one for $39,000, but he took care of it." "Miles Davis is treated very well by Columbia Records," Clive Davis said. "I think he's really appreciative of it too — we don't get Internal Revenue bills from Chicago or Blood, Sweat and Tears."[56]

Columbia's decision to subsidize Davis with advances against his future earnings was made before Clive Davis got there, but he perpetuated it. In his version of the high finances of modern record production, "fifty thousand albums barely takes you out of red ink," and he adds: "We began to give Miles additional money each time he recorded an album; we weren't making any money at all." As Davis's sales hovered around 50,000 throughout most of the 1960s, a period when most jazz artists would have been delighted by sales of 10,000, the advances and tax payments became a sizable investment by Columbia on future sales or, looked at from the opposite direction, a nearly perpetual bond on Davis's career. "Miles nonetheless called constantly to ask for more," Davis says. "He has a raspy, low voice—a fiery whisper that conveys heat over the telephone while you are straining to find out how much money he wants. He is spell-binding, and he can talk. After a while, the money business got to be sort of a joke. For Miles called often — sometimes urgently — and I had to figure out each time if he was serious. Walter Dean [Columbia's head of business affairs] got some of his calls too — fortunately — and he handled them well; sometimes he spent *hours* on the phone listening to that hoarse, almost demonic voice and dodging its monetary thrusts."[57] Despite his well-publicized threat to leave Columbia, Miles Davis had been too successful too often with his "monetary thrusts" for it to consider releasing him.

The facts are clear: after publicly repudiating Clive Davis's suggestion, Miles Davis's music became increasingly hybridized, soon finding the broader audience that would fill the largest rock concert halls. The interpretation of these facts is not so clear. Many jazz critics and fans made the obvious interpretation that Davis bowed to pressure from Columbia. Bill Cole, in his 1974 biography, stated that Davis "relented," and he concluded: "Miles Davis became a household word at the expense of his own creativity and the intrinsic value of his whole band."[58] That interpretation finds little credence among other commentators. Dan Morgenstern, in his book *Jazz People*, dismissed the notion altogether, saying: "Critics who think his recent direction, which has brought him closer to rock and soul music than to their idea of what jazz should be, is the result of record-company persuasion simply demonstrate their ignorance. Miles is his own man; his need to be up-to-date, to change, to move on, is not dictated by outside pressure but by inner needs."[59] Teo Macero, closer to the situation than almost anyone else, agreed. "He has never been bound by convention," he pointed out.[60] Sonny Rollins, normally as taciturn as Davis himself, also rose to his defense. "He was always a resourceful musician who was able to use whatever was around for his own sound," Rollins pointed out. "He doesn't like to be typecast, so what you would call his rock period was very natural ... The music had gotten to a standstill insofar as a lot of guys were playing clichés other people had done over and over again. The music that Miles was playing was perfectly compatible with the guys that were coming up at that time, like Billy Cobham, John McLaughlin and Chick Corea, and I'm sure he was a hero figure to them."[61] Rollins's point about Davis changing his music in order to find the idiom of the young players makes sense for a man who filled his bands with young musicians rather than men of his own jazz generation, and it is a point that Gil Evans later used to explain a parallel change in direction for his own music.

Davis had been flirting with disparate musical elements for two years, so that his new emphasis was not the complete turnaround it once seemed. Now he moved into fusion music in earnest.

In August, Davis assembled his stock company with several new faces to record the music that would be released six months later under the title *Bitches Brew*. The two-record set proved commercially successful probably beyond even Clive Davis's hopes, selling 400,000 copies in its first year and going on eventually to sell more than 500,000. But *Bitches Brew* takes the fusion music only one small step beyond *In a Silent Way*, recorded six months earlier. Like *In a Silent Way*, *Bitches Brew* presents a transitional conception of music, the difference being that the fusion elements of *Bitches Brew* are more robust, especially in the density of the percussion. The details are as follows:

Miles Davis Ensemble: Bitches Brew
Miles Davis, tpt; Wayne Shorter, ss; Chick Corea, el pno; David Holland, b; Jack DeJohnette, dms; Jim Riley, bongo. New York, 19 August 1969
Sanctuary
(on Columbia CS 9996)

Miles Davis, el tpt; Wayne Shorter, ss; Benny Maupin, bass clnt; Chick Corea,
Josef Zawinul, el pno; John McLaughlin, el gtr; Harvey Brooks, el b; David
Holland, b; Jack DeJohnette, Lenny White, Charles Alias, dms; Jim Riley, perc,
dms. Same place, Same date
Bitches Brew
(on Columbia CS 9996)

Add Larry Young, el pno. Same place, 20 August 1969
Spanish Key
(on Columbia CS 9996)

Omit Zawinul, Davis plays trumpet. Same place, Same date
Miles Runs the Voodoo Down
(on Columbia CS 9996)

Add Zawinul, el pno; Shorter plays ts and ss on *Pharaoh's Dance*; omit Davis
and Shorter on *John McLaughlin*. Same place, 21 August 1969
Pharaoh's Dance; John McLaughlin
(on Columbia CS 9996)

"It was really free," said drummer Lenny White, describing to Julie
Coryell the process that ended up as *Bitches Brew*. "Miles would say
play and he'd play something, then he'd say stop. Then he'd say, now,
Benny Maupin, you play something and we'd be playing and he'd say,
stop. There weren't any real roles. There was a sketch and everybody
would play to the sketch for a minute or however long the sketch was,
eight or twelve bars. There would be a tonal center and the rest was left
up to everybody else. He got all these people who were great improvisers
and put them together. We all played and there was just a blend; it was
like a palette of a lot of different colors. Everybody was adding a lot of
different things. For that time it was really different. To this day it still
is."[62]
    Lenny White was 20 when he joined the small battalion of drummers
to make *Bitches Brew*, an art student at the New York Institute of
Technology who played drums to pay his way through college. He had
worked with Jackie McLean before and after DeJohnette worked with
him, and his presence in McLean's band caused a lot of half-serious
comment about Davis automatically recruiting him, as he had Williams
and DeJohnette before him. For three days in August it came true. White
was playing with another drummer, Rashied Ali, when a friend of
Davis's introduced himself and took White's telephone number, and a

few days after that White received a call from the same man inviting him to join the recording ensemble.

Benny Maupin, who went on after *Bitches Brew* to play his bass clarinet in Herbie Hancock's fusion bands for several years, joined the stock company for *Bitches Brew* with no more preparation. "It came about as a result of Jack DeJohnette talking to Miles about me," he told Elliot Meadow in *Down Beat*. "Jack was in the group at the time and Miles was considering hiring me but that never happened. However, I did make *Bitches Brew* and I'm sure that exposure helped me."[63]

The large number of players and the unfamilarity of several of them with Davis's methods caused some problems that show in the finished LP, notwithstanding the scrupulous editing that turned at least nine hours of studio time into a little more than an hour and a half of music. The LP includes many stretches in which nothing happens apart from the constant burble of the dense rhythmic mélange. Zawinul's *Pharaoh's Dance* suffers most noticeably, in a performance that never seems to come into focus over the chugging beat of the drums and grows more diffuse throughout its unconscionable length (20 minutes and 7 seconds); almost the entire second half of that length is a colorless rhythmic ramble. Davis's *Bitches Brew*, even longer (27 minutes), is more successful, with interludes of echoing trumpet electronics at the beginning, middle, and end separating a brighter theme, but, again, much of the second half is turned over to what sound like background rumblings. The track titled *John McLaughlin*, although credited to Davis as composer, is just a slice of tape from the intervals between takes that catches McLaughlin, Maupin, and one of the pianists, probably Corea, bouncing ideas off one another while the rest of the ensemble (minus Davis and Shorter) keep up a steady beat. (The title of the short piece flattered McLaughlin when he saw it. "That was the biggest surprise to me," he said. "I mean, I saw it on the record. I was shocked, really shocked."[64])

These long rhythmic passages may or may not have delighted Davis's new fans who bought the record in such numbers, but they predictably left his old fans unmoved. "To me jazz has to stimulate [and] this is not necessarily stimulating," Clark Terry said, when Leonard Feather played him the track called *Bitches Brew*. "It's something to listen to as far as new sounds are concerned, but it could just as easily have been background for a scene in a jungle movie ... an Australian setting with the foo birds running around and the kangaroos making love to each other." And then he added, appeasingly, "I'm not necessarily putting it down; it's different."[65]

Still, the rhythmic passages do not fill the recording; far from it. There is, in what is left over, a great deal for jazz fans to listen to once they adjust themselves to the new textures, dense rhythms, and amplified instruments. When *Bitches Brew* was first released, the shock of all that was new on it definitely impeded any broadly based appreciation of what it had to offer for jazz listeners, but in a few years – with denser rhythms clouding Davis's music and electronics becoming common-place – the LP became easier to hear somehow; that fact alone may account for its continuing sales long after the initial burst of sales had died down, a commercial history very different from pop albums.

Jazz fans who returned to it after a pause found a haunting modal ballad, Shorter's *Sanctuary* (in which Shorter is heard only in the background, playing the melody behind Davis's dominating trumpet). The ballad develops from almost complete silence, as Davis and Corea alone play the theme, to high intensity as the rhythm trio builds relentlessly to a climax; like so much else on this LP, the development is repeated twice in its entirety, as if Davis were afraid that his listeners might not be capable of figuring out his formal devices if he played them only once, but this time the repetition avoids the undirected rhythmic intervals.

Spanish Key, composed by Davis, may be the most completely successful track, considered as an orchestration of diverse elements capable of sustaining interest from start to finish. Its organization, typically loose but no more so than most of the music played by Davis's previous quintet, offers two recurring and apparently unrelated themes. The first, played repeatedly by Davis and referred to obliquely by both Shorter and Maupin in their solos, is an ascending run of one bar with the last note held through a second bar. The other, played in the bass clef, is a quick rise and fall that momentarily freezes the thumping drums. The first theme, as the tonal center of the piece, is readily available and recurs continually, but the second theme, as a kind of rhythmic sub-theme, recurs irregularly and infrequently; when it does it alleviates the percussive pulse remarkably. One of the pianists, probably Zawinul on the aural evidence, determines the occurrences of the sub-theme, and the same player also dominates the sequences in which the guitar and pianos intermingle without superimposed horns. *Spanish Key* also features a beautifully clear-toned, unamplified solo by Davis, but it is the piano player in the background who seems to hold the piece together so effectively.

Notwithstanding its silly title, *Miles Runs the Voodoo Down*, another memorable theme by Davis, inspires the best solos on the LP, with good ones from Shorter and McLaughlin and a splendid one from Davis. It sound like an exotic dance except for a turbulent, but brief, explosion of percussion near the end, and the theme cajoles the players into fashioning rich and melodic variations. Davis's solos on *Miles Runs the Voodoo Down* and *Spanish Key* alone should have vindicated the LP for most of his fans.

All of Davis's solos follow the canon of jazz improvisation established, in jazz legend, when Louis Armstrong first overpowered an ensemble and superimposed his own inventions on collective improvisations. Davis stands apart, "the soloist," as Barry McRae wrote in *Jazz Journal*, "showcased by the seemingly dense backgrounds he had chosen."[66] The other soloists do not stand apart in the same sense. Shorter enters into his solos unobtrusively, slowly rising out of the backgrounds, and McLaughlin hardly rises at all, so that his solos always seem to be shared with one or more of the piano players. The group remain an ensemble in the root sense of the word.

The separateness of Davis from the others was felt physically as the music was being made. "On *Bitches Brew* Miles wasn't even playing that much," Zawinul told Larry Birnbaum. "Miles was inside the booth with Teo Macero and he just came steppin' out here and there and played a couple of notes, but mainly he just let us play. It was Chick and me playing and Wayne was back there with Benny Maupin. We had this music, man, and we played and we rehearsed and we put things together."[67] The new collectivism of fusion music, a throwback to the old collectivism of New Orleans jazz bands but one that seemed separated from it by millennia instead of decades, was one more adjustment that listeners were expected to make.

"We were better off when 'Miles smiled,'" said one of his fans, who rued the day Davis left bebop behind but had managed, finally, to tolerate his modal music. Now he and hundreds of others faced moving another giant step, and many of them balked. "This was probably one of the most controversial records and jazz personalities of the past century," Clark Terry said two years after it was released, and he shook his head remembering the reactions Davis provoked with it: "The way he's been ostracized and criticized – and probably rightly so ..."[68]

Not all of Davis's peers reacted negatively. A few noticed that *Bitches Brew* did not in any way pander to teenaged tastes. It was probably more unlike anything that rock fans had ever heard than it was unlike what jazz fans were used to. It caught the public ear but was resolutely in

Miles Davis's – not Clive Davis's – own idiom. "The value of what Miles is doing now," Herbie Hancock said, "is that he is, in effect, setting up a criterion of excellence in the direction of rock that nobody else has achieved, in terms of instrumental efficiency, interaction, and all of those things that just hadn't happened too much in rock before."[69] Shelly Manne, the drummer who learned his trade on 52nd Street when Davis was learning his and later helped transliterate Davis's 'cool' experiments into the West Coast sound, agreed. "The performer can't concern himself with bending to play something he thinks people will like," he told Leonard Feather, "because by doing that he's subconsciously killing his own creative powers. He has to play what he feels, and just hope it will be liked ... Miles Davis did that and his latest LP sold close to a quarter of a million."[70]

Miles Davis, of course, needed no lectures on the value of pursuing his own star. In 1968, when he was feeling the pressure from Columbia's managers, he told Feather: "Anybody can make a record and try to do something new, to sell, but to me a record is more than something new, and I don't care how much it sells. You have to capture some feeling – you can't just play like a fucking machine ... You are what you are, no matter what you do. I can be loud and no good, soft and no good, in 7/8 and no good. You can be black and no good, white and no good ... A guy like Bobby Hackett plays what he plays with feeling, and you can put him into any kind of thing and he'll do it."[71] In the final analysis, perhaps the most important aspect of *In a Silent Way* and *Bitches Brew* is that they both manage, in no uncertain terms, "to capture some feeling."

Soon after recording *Bitches Brew*, Davis made his peace with Clive Davis. He called him and said he would consent to play at the Fillmore East, Bill Graham's New York counterpart of his San Francisco Fillmore (which now became "Fillmore West"). Clive Davis immediately proposed billing the Davis quintet with Laura Nyro, one of his favorite young rock ballad singers on the Columbia label. They were given equal billing, but in the show business pecking order there was no doubt about their ranking on the night of the concert: Davis opened the show and Nyro closed it. For Miles Davis, one of the greatest players in jazz for two decades, opening for youngsters with few musical credentials turned out to be a situation he had to live with as long as he made forays into their territory.

Instead of arousing his outrage and causing a further disruption of his relations with Columbia's president, the Fillmore billing filled him with anticipation and led him to make yet another peace offering. "A week before the Fillmore East concert...," Clive Davis recalls, "a package arrived at my hotel one day containing black and gray striped flared pants, a black and gray striped vest and a long-sleeved black silk shirt. A note from Miles asked if I would wear the outfit to the first performance. 'I want you to look special,' Miles wrote. I was very touched. It wasn't a typical outfit for me, but everyone needs a change of style now and then; and so I took it to a clothing store for a fitting. Miles played a beautiful set that night, and he was terribly pleased to see me in the outfit. We posed for pictures, which eventually appeared on the cover of *Cashbox*."[72]

And with that, Miles Davis crossed the invisible, but once impregnable, barrier between jazz and rock audiences. He also absorbed another lesson in humility that would become commonplace for him in the years ahead. "During the first Fillmore concert, some of Laura's girlish fans had trouble getting into him,"[73] Clive Davis says. So would the fans of Crosby, Stills, Nash and Young, and The Band, and Santana, and many of the other bands for whom he would open at the Fillmore and elsewhere. But Davis seems never to have considered that he might have been out of his natural element. Instead, he was determined to conquer the new world.

PART FOUR
PANGAEA

In a whirl of thighs
Jazz concert dollies
Cool us Miles
Warm eyed
Beneath the sleek
Cheek to cheek
Explosive
Like the music

Norman Humphreys *Concert* (1970)

13

Funky Tonk
1969–71

One thing about Miles and his music, in working with Miles, you can experiment as much as you wish. You can take his music, you can cut it up, you can put the filters in, you can do anything you want to as long as he knows who it is. I mean, he's not going to let just anyone do it.   Teo Macero

The dark underside of the bright ideals of the 1960s cast its shadow gloomily as the decade came to a close. It was not that those ideals were inverted into cynicism, at least not right away. The cynicism was held in abeyance for a few more years, closer to 1974, when President Richard Nixon resigned his office before he could be impeached for improprieties that had helped him score a landslide victory in the presidential campaign of 1972, and it did not set in irrevocably until the second half of the decade, when a long economic recession caused the piecemeal dismantling of many of the social, cultural, and educational programs that had been erected in response to those ideals. But by 1970 no one could carry his or her ideals with utter conviction any longer; no one could pretend that the world would become a fairer, freer place simply by willing it to be so, or even by marching and singing and demonstrating against the inequities and the injustices. "You gotta sing *loud*, if you wanna end wars and stuff," Arlo Guthrie had declared in *Alice's Restaurant*, but by the end of the decade the singing had grown faint.

No single event crystallized the growing gloom more powerfully than a demonstration at Ohio's Kent State University in America's heartland early in May 1970, which ended with National Guardsmen firing their M-1s into the crowd of about 500 unarmed students protesting President Nixon's decision to move troops into Cambodia and further escalate America's undeclared war in southeast Asia. Four students, two men and two women, aged 19 and 20, no different in most ways from thousands of other bright, middle-class achievers who populate universities all over the world, were killed on the grassy knolls of the campus, and people everywhere were numb with disbelief.

The Kent State students were counted as four more victims of the Vietnam War. By now, even the diminishing group favorably disposed to the American presence in Vietnam – the 'hawks,' as opposed to the 'doves' – had to admit the terrible toll that that war was taking on Americans. The number of young people maimed and dismembered and killed in combat was appalling, but the body counts really had to go beyond that. The war was reviled and despised not only, or even principally, by the young people but by many older people as well, enough of them altogether to form a sizable minority at odds with civic authority. Opposition to the war had spread even to the troops already in Vietnam, to the extent that some percentage of the long casualty lists was routinely attributed to sending dispirited and demoralized troops into combat.

For many of those troops, coming home took its own toll. Many young men and women had embarked for Vietnam in the same spirit in which their fathers had embarked for Korea and for Europe one or two decades before them, but the Vietnam veterans returned to find no ticker-tape parades or hometown celebrations but only quiet relief from parents and sullen disinterest from some of their peers; they soon discovered that in putting their lives on the line against an elusive foe they had earned no more respect from their peers, and often much less, than had their classmates who had dodged the draft and were living in napalm-free self-exile in Toronto or Amsterdam or Stockholm. That realization, dawning while the horrors of war still invaded their sleep, wounded many of the young people whose limbs were unscathed.

By the end of the decade, almost no American escaped some deep personal torment as a result of Vietnam. Miles Davis's sons, Gregory and Miles, both attained draft age as the buildup of American troops under presidents Kennedy and Johnson grew deadly serious. By 1969, Gregory, the elder of the two, had been discharged from the army. Davis introduced him to Don DeMicheal in Chicago in the fall, where father and son were honing their boxing skills in a gym. "'Greg won three [boxing] titles while he was in the Army,' says the young man's obviously proud father. 'Plays drums too.'"[1] But his sons were suffering, and Davis blamed the system. In 1970, he told an interviewer from *Zygote* magazine: "There's so much graft and shit, you wouldn't believe the shit going down with dope. The dope goes in and the judges know about the dope, so subsequently the dope comes up to Harlem and the Spanish people. Both of my sons are hooked because there's nothing else for them to do. There's nothing for them to go to school for 'cause they're gonna get fucked over by the system."[2] Ten years later he was more guarded when he spoke to Cheryl McCall. "They took my son," he told her, "fucked *him* up in the war. I don't even want to say which son."[3]

The war was the main issue, but hundreds of other issues, great and small, percolated into public consciousness, and few of them failed to show a dark side. Another one that touched Miles Davis, at least indirectly, was the government's response to sickle cell anemia, the disease that hobbled Davis and hundreds of other black Americans. In 1970, Senator John V. Tunney of California declared: "It is fair to say, and research figures prove the fact, that if sickle cell anemia afflicted white people, we would have made a commitment long ago to end this disease."[4] Tunney sponsored the National Sickle Cell Anemia Act declaring the condition "a targeted disease for concentrated research" and quickly won executive approval for allocating several thousand dollars to research.

When the act reached the Senate, it presented senators from urban districts with an apple-pie issue, and they tripped over one another to broadcast their approval to their black constituents by upping the ante. By the time the act cleared the Senate in 1972, it carried allocations of $25 million in federal research grants for 1973, $40 million for 1974, and $50 million for 1975.

What the politicians apparently never considered was that sickle cell anemia, a genetic disease, has no foreseeable cure – no vaccine or serum can eliminate sickle-shaped blood cells without eliminating normal blood cells too. The research investment might improve palliative treatment for the sufferers, but the only way to eliminate the disease is by blood-typing the black population and counseling carriers against producing offspring.

When teams of counselors set up clinics in the ghettos with federal funds and began dispensing their advice to one out of every ten blacks – potentially affecting one black couple in five – against raising a family, the outcry was predictable. "I can't tell any of my patients not to have children because of sickle cell anemia," said one black, female obstetrician. "Most of them regard birth control as a white plot against black people. I'm not certain they're wrong."[5]

The talk of genocide, long a topic that concerned black intellectuals, quickly drowned out any talk there might have been about government largesse in sickle cell research, adding its bitter taste to the brewing cynicism. "I don't know about the world," Davis said, "you can see it's already fucked up. They're still practicing genocide with the black people, nobody ever says anything about that, they always talk about the Jews. They never talk about the black people getting fucked up."[6]

For jazz, the social movements of the 1960s brought an unexpected bonus when dozens of universities and other institutions recognized "black studies" – history, sociology, arts, including music, and other facets of the participation of Afro-Americans in the world – and devised curricula and programs. Jazz had been held in low esteem by educated blacks as well as educated whites for most of its history, until it moved into the cultural citadels as the keystone of black studies and acquired an air of institutional legitimacy that was long overdue. Dozens of jazz artists were appointed to teaching posts, among them David Baker, Billy Byers, Jerry Coker, Richard Davis, Alan Dawson, John LaPorta, Ralph McDonald, Jackie McLean, Bob Northern, George Russell, Bill Russo, Billy Taylor, and Cecil Taylor. Miles Davis had his chance to join them. "They asked me did I want to be dean of Howard University's music department," he announced, and then he reported his predictable answer. "Hell, no! See, I don't think like that, man. I don't like them bourgeois niggers. That's why they're rebelling at Howard. For a long time they wouldn't even have jazz concerts on the campus of Howard University."[7] A few years later, asked about Howard University's offer by Gregg Hall, he was less bellicose about his reason for rejecting it. "I can't do that shit," he said, "I teach my musicians."[8]

Davis had grown jaded about using jazz, or at least about using *his* jazz, for social purposes. Recalling the benefit he had played for voter registration drives in 1964, he said in 1981, "I just did one concert. It was a double concert, but I'm not going that way again. I think the government should take care of their own people."[9] Now he had other, less idealistic goals.

"I could put together the greatest rock and roll band you ever heard," he boasted to Don DeMicheal late in 1969,[10] after *Bitches Brew* had been recorded but still months before it was released. During the first five years of the 1970s, he seemed to be trying to make good on his boast, although, naturally, there was always something *sui generis* in his music and it never convincingly stood as "rock and roll" anyway. Neither did the music inspired by and sometimes dedicated to Miles

Davis that many other jazz musicians were playing for the next six or seven years. But if the music that came to be called jazz-rock fusion was never really rock it seemed to many listeners in the jazz community to be not quite jazz either.

The conventional labels had seldom seemed so imprecise, and Davis deplored all of them. "I don't like the word 'rock' and all that shit," he said, just a few minutes after boasting about putting together "the greatest rock and roll band you ever heard," and rock was not the only one: "'Jazz' is an Uncle Tom word," he added; "it's a white folks' word."[11] A few years later, he declared, "There's no such thing as 'bebop.' It's a white man's word to sell black music."[12] And he was quoted in *Melody Maker* saying: "Rock is a white man's word. Blues is a white man's word. Jazz is a white man's word." Davis's diatribes were hardly surprising when he was playing music that defied those labels, and even less so when he had always maintained that music should not be discussed, even when it was more readily categorizable.

Whatever else it was, fusion music was undeniably an assault on a mass audience, and the audience materialized en masse as soon as *Bitches Brew* was released. Davis kept silent about the ulterior motive in his plunge into fusion music, but others did not. Herbie Hancock, only 29 at the end of the decade but already an established jazzman after his years with Davis had made him a poll winner and a conspicuous name in the field, admitted that his own fusion music, which would be the most lucrative of all in the short run, began as a search for the masses when his musical ideals clouded over. "I started thinking of the great masters I know – Miles Davis, Charlie Parker, John Coltrane, those guys to me, more than anybody else, seem to be the giants of my era – I'm none of those guys, or anywhere near them," he told Leonard Feather in *The Pleasures of Jazz*, "so I might as well forget trying to be in that category. Forget trying to be another genius or legend in my own time. Once I got the idea of becoming a legend or genius out of my head, then I felt satisfied in just making some nice music and making people happy."[13]

Hancock's greatest commercial success, a 1974 LP called *Headhunters* that had almost nothing to do with jazz, sold more than 500,000 copies in a few months, but Hancock had been building toward that commercial peak for four years. Along the way, he was yoked into concert bills as the opener for acts like the Pointer Sisters, a rock-gospel trio, and ingenuously observing to the press that the most gratification he ever hoped to get out of his music was a standing ovation like the one he had seen the Pointer Sisters get. Even before *Headhunters* was released, the Pointer Sisters had fallen in popular esteem to the point where they would have been happy to find themselves opening for Hancock, and by the time *Headhunters* completed its quick heist they were no longer filling the biggest rooms in Las Vegas. Perhaps their decline helped Hancock appreciate how fickle were the hands that gave adoring ovations, because soon after *Headhunters* he resumed displaying his delicate touch on acoustic piano on records and in concerts, something that many listeners assumed he had forgotten entirely after his years of synthesized fuzz-wah. He has done so regularly ever since, in an all-star jazz band called VSOP, duets with Chick Corea, and other outings. At the same time, he has carried on recording funk.

Davis's history in fusion music misses both the commercial highs and the artistic lows of Hancock's, but not by much. In the sixteen months following the *Bitches Brew* sessions, Davis put himself through an extraordinarily productive period, even by the standards of his own highly productive career. He recorded so often that Columbia's managers, who a few years earlier were trying to cajole him into the recording studios, shook their heads in despair at the prospect of mastering his enormous backlog. He led his working band, still comprised of some talented young individuals despite the changes in personnel, through a dizzy round of concert and club engagements, some of them at the large rock emporiums favored by Clive Davis, and he proliferated his recording backlog by getting Columbia to tape his performances at Fillmore West, Fillmore East, the Isle of Wight Pop Festival, and at a club in Washington, DC. (His music from this period is also documented on an unauthorized recording of a performance at Philharmonic Hall.)

As if that were not enough, he also became what is known, in agentry circles, as a "more visible personality," appearing at Columbia's publicity bashes, on televison talk shows as a non-talking guest, and at other 'image-making' functions. With it came a new image ready to be made. Gone was the Italianate wardrobe, the pinstripes and patent leather elevator shoes that were his cachet for *Gentleman's Quarterly*, and in their place came buckskin jackets with fringes, embroidered dashikis, and clogs or boots with three-inch heels. The new look did not arrive suddenly. It came by degrees in the late 1960s, and by the end of the decade Davis was a trend-setter in the anarchic fashion show of those times just as he had been in the charcoal-grey button-down days a decade earlier. Some fans mourned the change, and one of them was his daughter Cheryl. "I loved it when he used to dress so cute in those suits," she told David Breskin, "when I was a teenager. Those Italian suits. Polka-dot ties. Those cute suits. Oh, he was so cute."[14] The difference in style was obvious, but the effect remained the same. Davis's audiences had always included a fringe of idolators who were just as interested in what he wore as in what he played, and his new look just kept them coming.

The differences in his music were greater. After making his reputation as a master of melody with the experimental nonet at the end of the 1940s and the great quintet and sextet of the 1950s, and then moving on to become an ingenious manipulator of harmonies with the modal and tone-centered compositions of the long-lived quintet of the 1960s, Davis moved now to highlight percussion. He had given the piano player less and less to play in ensembles for years now, and he reached a point where some of his recording contingents omit the piano player; in his next phase, beginning in 1972, he would form his working band with two guitarists and no piano player at all. His trumpet playing usually rides above the rhythmic current, but more and more, especially in the live performances, it is reduced to only a few notes, often with heavy electronic inflections; in the next phase of his development, he plays the trumpet even less and often abandons it for the organ or piano. These aspects of his music become dominant later, when he settles into the fiercely percussive style, but they are already broad tendencies in the flood of recordings that followed *Bitches Brew*.

That outpouring is remarkably diverse, spanning a stylistic range that occasionally approaches the control he exercised over *In a Silent Way* or seems to be lurching out of control altogether, a kind of wild ride impelled by flailed drums. While the diverse range is perceptible in the music that has been made available, the character of the music remains far from clear. Several hours of it have been issued, but probably scores of hours have not been. Compounding the problem, most of the music released is obscured by splicing, overdubbing, tape loops, and other post-production devices. The live performances show the heavy hand of editing no less than the studio recordings. Many of the recordings obviously combine fragments of several different recording sessions or concert sets that might someday be unscrambled by issuing complete takes or continuous performances. In the meantime, the character of the music remains nebulous and the discographical puzzles are legion. Davis's most prolific months in an incredibly productive career have so far left his listeners with some strangely unrewarding music.

Those months came perilously close to being snuffed out before they got underway. On the night of 10 October 1969, Davis was sitting in his Ferrari in Brooklyn in the small hours of the morning with a woman named Marguerite Eskridge when he looked out his window and saw a man with a pistol pointed at him. The man fired, shattering the window and grazing Davis. "I don't know what it was all about," Davis told Cheryl McCall. "The agency knew, 'cause they were having an agency war. I didn't know it. I was talking to Marguerite. If she had gotten out of the car she'd have got killed. But I had just kissed her in the car, you know? And I look around and this guy is staring at me, and I said *shit* this is [it]."[15]

In the aftermath, police investigators searched Davis's car and said they found marijuana. He was arrested, but the charges were later dismissed for lack of evidence.[16] It was his first arrest since the Birdland incident in August 1959.

Davis denies any knowledge of the gunman's motives, but no one, not even Davis, has ever suggested that he might have been a mistaken or innocent target. Lunatics are not completely unknown on the streets of Brooklyn, and a black man in a white Ferrari might make as conspicuous a target as anyone else for someone in search of a target, but this gunman had an accomplice driving his car, and the notion of lunatics traveling in pairs strains credulity. He was not the near-victim of a crime of passion either. Asked if he thought the gunman might be the woman's husband, he replied, "I don't mess with married women."[17] Davis's explanation that he was caught in "an agency war" might account for the fact that the gunman missed him from point-blank range, if the shooting was intended only as an underworld warning. He had recently signed a marketing deal with a black-owned public relations firm called New Wave Communications after complaining about Columbia's and Jack Whittemore's work on his behalf, with unknown repercussions.

Rumors of Davis's associations with underworld figures have occasionally surfaced throughout his career, sometimes encouraged by Davis himself. When his interview with Sy Johnson was interrupted by a telephone call, Davis identified his caller as "one of my old gangster buddies."[18] Art Pepper, the alto saxophonist who spent several years in San Quentin and other prisons for crimes related to narcotics, admired Davis for allegedly defying the underworld, especially for informing on narcotics peddlers – "burning connections" in Pepper's jailyard argot. "Miles Davis is basically a good person and that's why his playing is so beautiful and pure," Pepper says in *Straight Life*. "This is my own thinking and the older I get the more I believe I'm correct in my views ...

He's tried to give an appearance of being something he's not. I've heard that he's broken a television set when he didn't like something that was said on TV, that he's burnt connections, been really a bastard with women, and come on as a racist. The connections probably deserve to be burnt; they were assholes, animals, guys that would burn you: give you bad stuff and charge you too much, people that would turn you in to the cops if they got busted. Most of the women that hang around jazz musicians are phonies. And as for his prejudice, ... that's what he feels he should be like. He's caught up in the way the country is, the way people are, and he figures that's the easiest way to go."[19] For someone like Pepper, who lost more than he won in his battles with both the underworld and the police, the rumors about Davis, a clear winner, increased his esteem almost boundlessly.

The shooting incident launched new rumors, which probably gave the incident its dénouement. Joachim Berendt reported: "Miles set a reward of $10,000 for the capture of the two assailants. Nobody collected the reward, but a few weeks later the two gangsters were mysteriously shot."[20]

Just a few days after the shooting, Davis was playing music again, appearing with his quintet at the restored Apollo Theater on a bill titled Midnight Concert in Harlem. The concert also featured Bill Evans, Herbie Hancock, Donald Byrd, Milford Graves, and the Thad Jones–Mel Lewis orchestra, all part of an international fund-raising campaign for a jazz center in Harlem.

A week later, the quintet left for Europe on a two-week tour of nine cities. The tour began in Milan with two concerts (on 26 October), and moved to Rome (27), Vienna (31), London (1 November) and Ronnie Scott's club (2), Paris for two concerts (3), Copenhagen (4), Stockholm (5), Berlin (7), and Rotterdam (9). Despite the crowded schedule, Davis somehow found time to circulate in some of the cities. After finishing his London concert, he turned up in the audience in Ronnie Scott's club, where he was scheduled to play the next night. The entr'acte at Scott's was Professor Irwin Corey, an American comedian who played a crazy genius in his act. Scott, an enthusiastic raconteur, told Kitty Grime, "Miles came in with a whole entourage – girl friends, barber, lawyer, shoe shine boy, you know. And they all sat down front. And he had these huge wrap-around sunglasses on. And Corey suddenly bent down and whipped the glasses off Miles and put them on. And said, 'No wonder you're smiling – everyone looks black.'"[21]

Davis was treated almost as irreverently when he phoned Jack

Whittemore from Paris during the same tour. "I needed a few albums, a cut of my latest record," he told Max Gordon. "Friends, critics, broads wanted one. So I called up Jack in New York. 'Call CBS,' I told him, 'and tell 'em to call Paris and have their wholesaler here deliver a dozen albums to me in my hotel.' So what do you think Jack said to me? 'Who do you think you are, Frank Sinatra?'" Davis was not amused. "I'm getting rid of that bastard," he told Gordon. "What's Sinatra got I haven't got?"[22] For Whittemore, Davis's agent for some fifteen years, Davis's threat to change agents was nothing new, and a few more years passed before the change was made.

Back in the United States, Davis kept up the pace. The quintet played at the Garden State Jazz Festival in Holmdel, New Jersey. Chris Albertson, covering the Festival for *Down Beat*, filed a report filled with superlatives about their non-stop performance. "Davis and Wayne Shorter expressed themselves eloquently," Albertson wrote, "stepping to the back of the huge stage between chill-provoking solos as the rhythm section exploded in a pulsating orgasm of hip sounds, pianist Chick Corea embroidering electrical embellishments that lent a tinge of rock to this memorable piece. During the second minute of the tumultuous ovation that followed, the young lady seated behind me was still gasping, 'Oh God, oh God, oh God.' Her reaction was understandable. She had just witnessed contemporary jazz at its peak of perfection."[23]

Audience reactions were not always so effusive. When the quintet moved into the Plugged Nickel in Chicago, Don DeMicheal listened impatiently to the grumblings of a longtime Davis fan who shared the elbow space at the bar with him, and the grumblings were only silenced when Davis brought forward some of his old familiar titles – *Walkin'*, and especially *Stella by Starlight*, which Davis played, according to DeMicheal, "much as he has for the last several years – with an inner pain that touched the heart."[24] It was probably the last time he made that concession.

The Plugged Nickel engagement was followed by a week at the Colonial Tavern in Toronto, 1–6 December, and it turned into an especially notable engagement for local fans who watched Davis's public audition of Toronto guitarist Sonny Greenwich. "One day I got a phone call," Greenwich told Mark Miller in *Jazz in Canada*. "I had seen Miles before in New York, but I'd never spoken to him. He'd never heard me play; he'd heard *of* me, I guess, through Wayne and the guys. I just got a call one morning. 'Sonny? ... Miles.' You know, with his voice? I thought somebody was joking." Greenwich, then in the most active phase of his playing career, has emerged sporadically and unpredictably to display fervid improvisations that evoke memories of Coltrane.

During his week with Davis's band Greenwich continually wrestled with sound problems from his cheap amplifier, but he held his own on the stand and Davis discovered off the stand that he was a boxing fan as well. At the end of the week Davis invited him to join the band, but Greenwich, who had had immigration problems a year before when he played a week-long stint at the Village Vanguard, was skeptical. "I told him he'd have problems getting a lawyer to get me down there," Greenwich recalled. "He said he could do it. But nothing ... I didn't hear from him."[25] Greenwich slipped back into his silent ways, and he has broken his silence less frequently in the years since, barely often enough to fuel the legend that surrounds his playing.

After the week in Toronto, Davis and his sidemen finally took some time off. What was a Christmas break for most of them was a more decisive break for Wayne Shorter, who ended his long tenure in the working band. His departure at the end of 1969, after five and a half years, ended the musical associations that Davis had formed in the 1960s. Shorter had no alternative plans, quitting mainly just to settle down for a while. "I spent the next year moving all over New York, getting a family started and basically doing no music," Shorter says.[26] He played on two of Davis's recording sessions early in the new year, and he recorded an album of gentle, impressionistic music for Blue Note in August (*Odyssey of Iska*, BST-84363), but mainly he was content to compose and practice out of earshot of audiences.

He grew restless only months later, and then he made a significant move. "At the end of 1970 Joe [Zawinul] and I got on the phone – he wasn't with Cannonball anymore – and talked about starting something up together rather than doing it individually," he says. Their band was called Weather Report, and Miroslav Vitous joined them as co-leader but left after two years. Several bassists, drummers, and percussionists have completed the personnel over the years. They signed a recording contract with Columbia, made a couple of innovative recordings in their first two years, and then progressively diluted their jazz content in favor of funk, becoming one of the conspicuous commercial successes as the fusion peaked. By the end of the decade, they had increased the jazz content in concerts and, less noticeably, on records, and kept going strong.

Shorter's replacement in Davis's band was Steve Grossman, a

Brooklynite who turned 19 in January 1970, soon after he joined. Grossman is white, an unremarkable fact except that Davis seemed preoccupied with racial stereotypes in music at the time. "It's social music," Davis said of rock in a long interview with Don DeMicheal for *Rolling Stone* that took place while he was playing at the Plugged Nickel, and then he launched into a diatribe on music and race. "There's two kinds – white and black, and those bourgeois spades are trying to sound white and the whites are trying to sound colored. It's embarrassing. It's like me wearing a dress. Blood, Sweat and Tears is embarrassing to me ... They try to sing black and talk white."[27]

"I can tell a white group just from the sound, don't have to see them," he added, repeating a claim that had occasionally been made by jazz musicians for years without ever being substantiated. Leonard Feather's blindfold tests, a regular feature of *Down Beat* for decades, have piled up several instances where a jazz musician casually labeled an unidentified record racially and was wrong. Sometimes Feather deliberately tested a musician on his perceptions of race when he was known to have made claims on the topic. Roy Eldridge was the first, and he failed miserably at it in the 1950s, but of course his failure did not lay the issue to rest. Davis, too, had made several wrong guesses on various blindfold tests. Listening to a record by Buddy Colette, Davis said, "All those white tenor players sound alike to me," and more than a decade later he labeled Sun Ra's Arkestra a "white" band.[28]

Davis's version of the myth is not segregationist. "You got to have a mixed group – one has one thing, and the other has another," he told DeMicheal. "For me, a group has to be mixed. To get swing, you have to have some black guys in there." Davis, of course, often included white players in his band from the time he chose Lee Konitz for his nonet in 1948, with Bill Evans in 1958, Chick Corea and David Holland in 1968, and now Steve Grossman, and he had the long association with Gil Evans as well as more recent ones with Josef Zawinul and John McLaughlin. Few musicians should have been in a better position to realize that the racial stereotyping was nonsense. Earlier in the interview with DeMicheal, he praised the drumming of Buddy Rich, but he now said: "See, white guys can only play at a certain tempo. They can play here [taps finger], but they can't play here [slightly faster tapping] or here [faster tapping] ... For me, if I listen to a white group, they got to have some spades in there for me to like them in more than one tempo. Spades got that thing – they can tighten it up."[29]

Davis's remarks have no real bearing on his music or on his recruiting;

in practice, he continued to select his sidemen by choosing the best musicians for the job. But his remarks were well publicized when the interview was published, and they no doubt helped to perpetuate the ignorance and the hatred that fastens itself to racial stereotyping within jazz and beyond it. If exactly the same remarks had been made by a white jazz musician and published in *Rolling Stone*, the outrage of fans and critics – both black and white – would have been deafening, and rightly so.

Around the time that Grossman replaced Shorter, Davis added another musician to his working band, making it a sextet. He was Airto Moreira, a 29-year-old Brazilian percussionist. Moreira, who later went by his first name only as Brazilian soccer stars and other celebrities do, had emigrated to the United States in 1967, arriving in California, where he hoped to establish his reputation in jazz as he had already done at home. During his first year, he saw two concerts by Davis in California and made up his mind that he would someday play in his band. After the second concert, he managed to make his way backstage to Davis's dressing room door, where he stood and, in faltering, almost incomprehensible English, attempted to explain to Davis his admiration for his music and his ambition to join his band. After a few minutes of the monologue, Davis, perplexed and perhaps embarrassed by the flowery sentiments, said, "So what?" and closed the door in his face.

Moreira had better luck after he moved to New York in 1969. He was befriended by Walter Booker, the bassist in Cannonball Adderley's band, and through Booker he met and played with Adderley, Zawinul, and others. In Brazil, Moreira played drums as well as congas, bongos, and maracas, but his first chances to play in New York were on the latin percussion instruments only. Davis had already used Don Alias and Jim Riley as percussionists on some recording sessions, and late in 1969 he asked Moreira, probably on Zawinul's recommendation, to show up for a recording session. For the next two years, Moreira worked for Davis.

With his highly visible role in Davis's working band, the use of percussion in jazz underwent a dramatic increase. Dozens of bands began using a percussionist, a term that denoted a non-drumming percussion player or a person who played any number of percussion instruments other than the conventional drum kit. Moreira, encouraged by Davis, led the way for percussionists to proliferate their instruments. To the expected congas, bongos, and maracas, Moreira added instruments at a wild rate, until by the time he left Davis he counted 32 different noise-makers. He described some of them in an interview with

Lee Underwood: the berimbau, a single string with a movable gourd as a resonator capable of making a non-electronic wah-wah sound; the cabacas, a gourd wrapped with beads that slide against its surface when it is turned; the reco-reco, a bamboo stick with ridges that resonate when stroked with a stick; the ganza, a metal tube with pebbles inside, in various sizes to make various pitches; and all sorts of other exotic devices, most completely unknown to jazz audiences, plus a few not so exotic, such as the wooden soles of clog shoes, then fashionable, which Moreira banged together like non-resonating cymbals.

In Davis's live performances, Moreira made a spectacular show, sitting onstage on a blanket with his array of noise-makers spread out around him. Even Davis was impressed. After his solos he often crouched down beside Moreira's blanket and stared intently at his every move. Moreira's impact on the jazz world was enormous. As more percussionists appeared, percussion, as Moreira put it, "became an instrument instead of just background," and *Down Beat* responded by adding percussion as a category in its polls in 1974. It was a category that Moreira automatically won year after year.

Moreira, trained as a drummer, did not arrive in the United States with his talents as a percussionist fully formed or even clearly defined. He had to teach himself how to use most of his unconventional instruments, and the only useful lessons he ever received, he has said many times, came from Miles Davis. "He was the most profound influence that I ever had in my career," he told Underwood, "meeting him and listening to the very little he had to say. He once came to me and said, 'Don't *bang*. Just play.' That's all, 'Don't *bang*. Just play.'" Those imperatives turned into a long learning experience. "When I asked him, 'What do you mean, don't bang, just play?' he said, '*You* figure that out,'" Moreira remembers. "He was a beautiful guy, and a nice guy, too, but I was terrified for the first month."[30]

Moreira described to Dan Morgenstern what happened after that. "At first I didn't understand what he meant, and then I realized that he wanted me to hear the music and *then* play some sounds. So then I'd listen and not play at all, and then he came to me after a few concerts and said [imitating Miles's voice]: 'Play, man – play more!' So then I'd start to play more, but in the right places, and then I really got into the thing of listening to the music and picking up the right instrument at the right time and playing the right sound. Miles doesn't say very much, but when you understand him, everything he says means a lot."[31] Moreira's contribution to Davis's music, apart from the long solo spots that he was allotted in concert performances while the rest of the band retreated to the wings, was felt rather than heard. He added another layer to the growing density of the bottom, the undertone of Davis's music that was becoming its focus.

Davis's crowded performing schedule was matched by an equally crowded recording schedule, and Columbia was growing concerned about the amount of material it now held. "When we met [around 1966], he felt underpaid and was producing relatively few albums," Clive Davis recalls. "After that, we had trouble slowing him down. He started recording three albums a year, sometimes right on top of each other. He would call Bruce Lundvall [head of marketing], Bob Altschuler (another jazz aficionado) [head of publicity], or myself and play long passages. Then he'd want *that* album released, despite his backlog. If we had just had a release in December, he'd record an album in January and want it out immediately. And we'd protest, saying that the December one needed time for sales and exposure. Then he'd call in March telling us to forget the January album — he had a new one."[32]

Beginning with *Bitches Brew*, all of Davis's records on Columbia except two (*Jack Johnson* and *On the Corner*) until 1981 were issued as double albums, called 'twofers' (from the advertising claim, never literally true, that one was buying "two for the price of one"). Even so, the music that was released represents only a fraction of what was recorded, consisting of one or two titles from several dates and a staggering assortment of bands, the permutations and combinations of Davis's stock company. But the increased production, marketed in the more expensive twofers and sold to a larger audience in the wake of *Bitches Brew*, still did not succeed in balancing Davis's accounts with Columbia, at least not during Clive Davis's term of office. "At no time did Miles ever fully recoup his advances," Davis says. "Yet our relationship remained warm because I dealt with his financial problems on the assumption that he was good for Columbia in the long run, both on commercial and cultural levels."[33] If he hoped that increasing his production would eventually free him from the company, he was stymied, and he has remained with them ever since.

The first recording session following the *Bitches Brew* sessions took place in November and introduced Steve Grossman and Airto Moreira, among others, into the ensemble. The first significant issue, amounting to nearly half an hour, was held until 1974, when it appeared on the *Big Fun* LP, but a hint (2 minutes and 42 seconds) was issued in France the year before as a 45-rpm bonus in a three-album boxed anthology, *The*

Essential Miles Davis (CBS [Fr] S66310); the B side of the 45-rpm gave a hint, the only one so far, of the music from a session nine days later. The details are as follows:

Miles Davis Ensemble
Miles Davis, tpt; Steve Grossman, ss; Benny Maupin, bass clnt; Herbie Hancock, Chick Corea, el pno; John McLaughlin, gtr; Harvey Brooks, el b; Billy Cobham, dms; Airto Moreira, perc; Khalil Balakrishna, Bihari Sharma, sitar, tamboura. New York, 19 November 1969
Great Expectations [*Great Expectations/Orange Lady*]; *Great Expectations* (45 rpm)
(first version on Columbia PG 32866; second on CBS [Fr] 4927)

Omit Corea; add Josef Zawinul, Larry Young, el pno, and Ron Carter, b. Same place, 28 November 1969
The Little Blue Frog (45 rpm)
(on CBS [Fr] 4927B)
Orange Lady, composed by Zawinul, comprises the second half of the long version of *Great Expectations*.

Great Expectations consists of a single phrase repeated over and over by Davis, sometimes with Grossman's soprano and Maupin's bass clarinet playing in unison, as the percussion ensemble, eight men strong and laced with the exotic sounds of Indian instruments, rumbles and roars underneath. The point of the exercise is apparently to stimulate the rhythm players because the melodic surface is unrelieved, and perhaps purposeful, monotony. Although it is hard to be certain when the music consists only of a simple, repeated refrain, the short version of *Great Expectations* from France does not sound like an excerpt from the longer version but instead seems to be another slice of the master tape.

Davis's use of the sitar in this and later sessions reflects the discovery of Eastern music and also of Eastern cuisine, dress, and especially mysticism that took place in the late 1960s. The new interest made Ravi Shankar, the sitar virtuoso, a cult figure who played his music in packed bars and concert halls and inspired George Harrison of the Beatles and other rock guitarists to take up the instrument. Harrison's sitar accompaniment on *Norwegian Wood* in 1966 and the next year on *Within You without You* on the influential *Sgt. Pepper's Lonely Hearts Club Band* LP gave rise to a fashionable affectation in the pop music of the day, and Davis was one of the few who followed the lead in jazz. For

Davis, the Eastern instruments came along opportunely as he was searching for more varied percussion colors.

The second half of the long version of *Great Expectations*, separated audibly by a pause but not visually by the usual band of vinyl, is Zawinul's beautiful theme, *Orange Lady*. Davis allows himself to embellish the theme, but the musical elements are otherwise much the same as for *Great Expectations*, the main difference coming from Zawinul's writing, which attracts attention to itself as Davis's theme never does. Zawinul was surprisingly philosophical about being uncredited. He simply said, "There was some kind of mess up with the titles, so it was not mentioned it was my tune." By the time Davis's version was released, *Orange Lady* had already appeared on the inaugural Weather Report LP of 1971 (Columbia C 30661), in a version incomparably more subtle and graceful than Davis's.

As with much of Davis's work of this period, the music itself is often less interesting than the process involved in making it. Davis was experimenting, trying to control musical elements complex both in their diversity and in their provenance. The experiments seldom failed to reward the musicians. "The unifying spirit was Miles," said Billy Cobham. "He brought together a lot of musicians from different parts of the world and then would scream at them in a soft whisper, 'I want you to do this! No, don't play, play this, don't play,' that kind of thing, and out of it came this concoction, this brew. I mean, it was like he was stirring a big, black pot of notes."[34]

Cobham's presence in the studio when DeJohnette was Davis's drummer in the working band underlines his different intentions in the two settings. As a jazz drummer, DeJohnette gave Davis the solid backing for his quintet's improvisations, but Cobham, a self-taught drummer born in Panama and raised there and in Brooklyn, brought a broad, uncategorizable background and helped make some broad, uncategorizable music. At the time of these recordings, Cobham played regularly with the fusion band Dreams. Davis once suggested that he should join his band, and Cobham was willing. "I really loved to play with him," he told Brian Priestley; "I *never* had any hassles with that cat over *nothing*. Sometimes just being in his presence can really cool you out – he doesn't have to say anything. You know, it's not like I consider him a god or anything, but there's a charisma or something about the cat that I wish there were words for."[35] But Davis did not renew his suggestion, and Cobham played with him only in the studio.

Besides the hours he spent in Columbia's studios, Davis also began spending some of his time at functions designed to circulate his name more widely. He visited a recording session by Laura Nyro, one of Columbia's best-selling young ballad writer-singers and a special favorite of Clive Davis's, where he was encouraged to play as a guest star in her backing band, but after listening to the arrangements he decided that there was no space for him to play.[36] He also donned his tuxedo to attend a formal party for the singer Janis Joplin, hosted by Clive Davis to "offset ... some of the more scruffy stories" about the hard-living diva of rock.[37] Miles Davis found himself among many of the other luminaries of the Columbia roster: Tony Bennett, Bob Dylan, Laura Nyro, Johnny and Edgar Winter, among others, as well as Earl Wilson and Leonard Lyons, show business columnists in New York newspapers.

He was probably more in his element being interviewed by Dwike Mitchell, the pianist in the Mitchell-Ruff Duo, for the soundtrack of a film documentary called *The Legacy of the Drum*, with music by Dizzy Gillespie and the Duo.

The recordings with large ensembles continued in January and early February, at some sessions with Wayne Shorter back in the ensemble. The details are as follows:

Miles Davis Ensemble
Miles Davis, tpt; Wayne Shorter, ss; Benny Maupin, bass clnt; Chick Corea, el pno; Josef Zawinul, el pno, org; David Holland, b; Harvey Brooks, el b; Billy Cobham, Jack DeJohnette, dms; Airto Moreira, perc; Khalil Balakrishna, sitar.
New York, 27 January 1970
Lonely Fire; Guinnevere
(*Lonely Fire* on *Big Fun*, Columbia PG 32866; *Guinnevere* on *Circle in the Round*, Columbia 30278 [1979])

Omit Maupin, Brooks; add John McLaughlin, el gtr. Same place, 6 February 1970
Gemini/Double Image
(on *Live-Evil*, Columbia 30954)

Lonely Fire, by Davis, opens as an anticipatory, pulseless call, repeated over and over by Davis, and then alternately by Davis and Shorter, like a soundtrack for a suspense movie, except the suspense is never resolved. After some eleven minutes, with the listener's patience sorely taxed, and perhaps the musicians' too, David Holland introduces an insistent bass riff that carries along the rhythm and breaks open the musical stalemate; Davis solos, and then Shorter, and then Corea and Zawinul together. During this nine-minute sequence, before the band returns to the monochromatic suspense motif for the final minute, *Lonely Fire* cruises along with some of the infectious drive and plain-spoken joy of *It's about That Time.*

The other two recordings from the same time have more in common with its suspenseful phase than with its looser segment. *Guinnevere,* based on a ballad by David Crosby, the lead singer of the Byrds who had just joined three other lead singers from other bands to form a 'supergroup' called Crosby, Stills, Nash and Young, lacks the lyric of the original, a love song to the first lady of King Arthur's Round Table, and gains only a plodding beat; Davis occasionally directs a few notes outside the repeated melody statement, but the only real relief from the repetition comes in an incongruous passage dominated by the whining sitar and some jungle percussion.

Gemini/Double Image, a medley of Zawinul compositions, yokes the two themes together almost imperceptibly and recites them repetitively, again without any solos, over a backdrop dominated from beginning to end by John McLaughlin's guitar accents, in a milder imitation of Jimi Hendrix, the lefthanded rocker who used his guitar as a lightning rod.

All this music, which fills more than three-quarters of an hour in the form in which it is issued, pares down the music into its simplest components – the beat is constant or nonexistent, the tonal centres are narrow, and the melodies are repeated single phrases – as if Davis were struggling to maintain control of his unwieldy ensemble.

Immediately after, at least in the sequence of events reconstructible from the music released to date, Davis began recording with smaller groups, although he continued to form recording bands rather than merely calling in his working band. The reduced ensemble helped to free his music somewhat and allow the individuals more room to play. The details are as follows:

Miles Davis Ensemble
Miles Davis, tpt; Wayne Shorter, ss; Benny Maupin, bass clnt; John McLaughlin, gtr; David Holland, b; Billy Cobham, dms. New York, 17 February 1970
Duran
(on *Directions*, Columbia KC2 36472)

Miles Davis, tpt; Steve Grossman, ss; John McLaughlin, gtr; David Holland, b; Jack DeJohnette, dms. New York, 27 February 1970
Willie Nelson
(on *Directions*, Columbia KC2 36472)

Same personnel. Same place, 3 March 1970
Go Ahead John
(on *Big Fun*, Columbia PG 32866)

Duran might have given Davis the hit that Clive Davis thought he needed if it had been released at the time instead of eleven years later. It uses the fusion vocabulary more blatantly than anything he had recorded so far, with a simple bass riff providing the unity of the piece and brash chords from the guitar punctuating the easy rhythm. It is no more sophisticated, and no less accessible to teenaged audiences, than most of the hits of Blood, Sweat and Tears. Davis plays an electrified funk solo, McLaughlin an acid solo, Maupin and Shorter a helter-skelter duet, and Cobham a bumptious interval; judicious editing of any of these pieces onto two sides of a 45-rpm single might have sent the kids scurrying.

If it had been released at the time, it would have had a different title. *Duran* refers to Roberto Duran, the welterweight boxing champion from Panama, Cobham's native land, who rode roughshod over other welterweights in the late 1970s, earning the epithet *manos de piedra* ('hands of stone'). But Davis's use of Duran's name was not clearly an homage when it appeared on the 1981 release: in 1979 Duran had defeated Sugar Ray Leonard, an American hero in the 1976 Olympics whose image was as pristine as Duran's was nasty, but in their 1980 rematch Duran walked away from Leonard in the middle of the eighth round, conceding his championship for reasons that never really stood up to scrutiny. As a boxing fan, Davis might have named his tune *Duran* either to honor the 1979 champion with fists of stone or to deride the 1980 pug with feet of clay; if the latter, Davis probably intended the title to be a critical comment on his little rock ditty of years before.

For *Willie Nelson* there can be no doubt about Davis's intentions in naming the piece for the rough-voiced middle-aged country balladeer. Soon after it was released in 1981 Davis told Cheryl McCall, "I *love* the way Willie sings; the way he phrases is great. He phrases sometimes like I do."[38] The next year he proved his fanship by detouring to Las Vegas and visiting Nelson backstage at Caesar's Palace, where according to rumor the two of them wrote a country song called *Expect Me Around*,[39] and after that Davis continued his tour wearing a cap with "Willie Nelson" emblazoned on its crest.

The piece bearing Nelson's name seems somewhat less than idolatrous. It consists of a stretch of music that catches the pianoless quintet working over an uptempo riff, but, despite its liveliness and Holland's amazingly supple accompaniment behind McLaughlin's solo, it is a head arrangement of no special distinction, lacking a beginning and an end (though credited to Davis as the composer).

Go Ahead John, with exactly the same band in the studio four days later, includes more interesting moments, although it was obviously composed in the editing room. Its first eleven minutes and its closing four and a half minutes resemble *Willie Nelson* as a head arrangement built on a riff, with the riff sustained this time by McLaughlin's steady wah-wah in the background. Spliced into it is an unrelated theme that opens with two minutes of a slow blues unaccompanied except for occasional notes from Holland; Davis's blues solo becomes a duet with himself by overdubbing, and then builds into a quintet performance lasting ten more minutes. The overdubbing effect is made by superimposing part of Davis's solo on other parts of it, in what Teo Macero calls a "recording loop." "You hear the two parts and it's only two parts, but the two parts become four and they become eight parts," Macero told Gregg Hall. "This was done over in the editing room and it just adds something to the music ... I called [Davis] in and I said, 'Come in, I think we've got something you'll like. We'll try it on and if you like it you've got it.' He came in and flipped out. He said it was one of the greatest things he ever heard."[40] In spite of the gimmickry, the blues segment manages to state some old verities in a new context, and state them powerfully. Most jazz listeners can hope that someday *Go Ahead John* will be unscrambled and re-presented to them as, among other things, an unhurried blues by Davis accompanied only by Holland.

On the night of 3 March, Davis again ran afoul of the law. He was sitting in his red Ferrari with an unidentified woman in a no-standing zone on Central Park South when a patrolman approached to ask him to move, noticed that the car had no inspection sticker, and asked Davis for his license and registration. Davis, wearing a turban, a sheepskin coat, and cobra-skin pants, began rummaging through a handbag and exposed a pair of brass knuckles. The patrolman booked him on charges of carrying a deadly weapon and driving an unlicensed, unregistered, and uninspected vehicle. The next day he was fined $100 for being an unlicenced driver and cleared of the other charges.[41]

A week later, Davis and his working band again appeared at the Fillmore East. Davis's band played the opening set at a concert that featured the Steve Miller Band – "how's that for *noblesse oblige*?" James Isaacs remarked – and Crosby, Stills, Nash and Young. The concert realized one of Davis's fears about entering the rock circuit. "The audience, at least in my section," Isaacs reported, "nattered incessantly, passed contraband and generally ignored Miles and his cohorts throughout their open-ended fusion set."[42] Soon after, Davis rebuked the quality of the musicians who topped him on the bill in his forays into the rock world. "In rock groups the guys know so little about harmonies," he complained to an interviewer for *Zygote* magazine. "It's a shame because they don't study. They deal in visual appearance and loudness, and in sex ... All the jazz musicians can play in any school of music because they have the knowledge. It's usually the rock musicians that don't have a musical background. They just pick up on something. They just play a regular triad kind of sound."[43] Some rock musicians were willing to concede that point. A few years later, the manager of an English band called the Clash refused an interview with a music magazine by stating: "We know nothing about music. If you want to know about music, ask Miles Davis or somebody like that. We're all trying to find out what it is."[44] Despite Davis's disillusionment with the company he kept at the Fillmore, both in the audience and on the stage, he kept on playing the Fillmores and other rock halls.

Davis's enlarged circuit exposed him not only to the teenaged audience but also to America's bourgeoisie when he began appearing on Nielsen-rated national network television shows. He and his band performed on the televised Grammy Awards show for 1970 from Alice Tully Hall in the Lincoln Center, as one of the music acts that broke up the seemingly endless parade of recording personalities being presented with awards. The show barely missed televising a spontaneous news happening when its host, Merv Griffin, a singer with swing bands in the 1940s now grown roly-poly and ingratiating as the host of a televison talk show, broke protocol and rushed up to Davis after his short piece, grasping his hand and directing a supercilious comment into the television camera. "Merv Griffin is embarrassing to me," Davis told Chris Albertson a year later, still smarting from the incident; "I felt like yanking off his arm."[45]

Davis knew that the large, middle-class, middle-aged audiences courted by Griffin and the other talk show hosts made no real contact with his music and that the hosts themselves were incapable of bridging the gap. "The trouble with those cats," as he put it, "is that they all try to come off to those middle-aged white bitches."

Aggressive promoting by Columbia nevertheless got him several spots on the talk show circuit, which had become the prized promotional vehicle for publishers and movie distributors as well as record companies. Once or twice a year from 1970 until 1972, by which time either Davis could stand it no more or the mass audiences could no longer tolerate even a few minutes of his increasingly percussive music, Davis appeared before millions of television viewers late at night, decorously garbed as he pointed his trumpet at the floor and squeezed out a few tortured notes, a taciturn mystery man who acknowledged neither the audience nor the smiling host.

After the Grammy show incident, he never consented to appear on Griffin's show, but he made his brief appearances with Johnny Carson, Dick Cavett, and Steve Allen. He explained his refusal to talk on the talk shows this way to Albertson: "Dick Cavett and Johnny Carson don't know what to say to anybody black, unless there's some black bitch and she's all over them. It's so awkward for them because they know all the white facial expressions, but they're not hip to black expressions, and – God knows – they're not hip to Chinese expressions. You see, they've seen all the white expressions like fear, sex, revenge, and white actors imitate other white actors when they express emotions, but they don't know how black people react. Dick Cavett is quiet now when a black cat is talking to him, because he doesn't know if the expression on his face means 'I'm going to kick your ass,' or if 'Right on' means he's going to throw a right hand punch. So, rather than embarrass them and myself, I just play on those shows and tell them not to say anything to me – I have nothing to say to them anyway."[46]

He was less philosophical about it all when he told Don DeMicheal, "I can't be on none of those television shows, 'cause I'd have to tell Johnny Carson, 'You're a sad motherfucker.' That's the only way I could put it. If I did that, right away they'd be telling me, 'You're cursing.' But that's the only way I can say it."

Davis's revulsion eventually included even Steve Allen, television's original talk show host in the 1950s whose feeling for jazz made his *Tonight* show the only regular showplace for jazz groups on the commercial networks. Allen had turned his talents to songwriting and other less public forums but returned to television hosting for a while in the late 1960s. "I was supposed to be on Steve Allen's show," Davis said, "but I sent him a telegram telling him he was too white, his secretary was too white, his audience was too white. And he wanted me to play for scale! Shit. I can't be standing there in front of all those middle-aged white broads – and all of them got maids. I can't be associated with that kind of shit. I got a maid myself. See, whatever they're trying to do, they're trying to get those middle-aged white bitches to watch it."[47] But Davis kept appearing sporadically for a couple of years, probably because his managers felt it was good for his image.

In between his celebrity turns, Davis took another small ensemble into the Columbia studios to record music for the soundtrack of a feature film called *Jack Johnson*. Although the film, with unconventional cinematography and controversial subject matter, stood little chance of finding a mass audience, it is an unequivocal artistic success. Director William Cayton turned scant and often flawed photographic resources into a coherent and dramatic documentary, juxtaposing still photos, boxing footage, and newsreels to evoke the life and times of the first black heavyweight champion (1908–15) from the early years of the century until his death in 1946. Teo Macero, credited as musical director for the film as well as producer for the LP, patched together snippets of Davis's music to accompany the shifting images. If the music was unspecified for the visual images at its inception – and there is no feeling that Davis tailored his improvisations to the finished film, as he had to Louis Malle's *Ascenseur pour l'échafaud* in 1957 – Macero's marriage of music to image brought them together ingeniously. The music forms a legato undercurrent for the film, quickening its still images and smoothing its stroboscopic motions.

In its own right the music on the LP, which bends the literal meaning in proclaiming itself the "original soundtrack recording," makes a self-contained continuum of shifting moods. The editor's hand is always evident, and the LP poses so many discographical puzzles that the music on it may never be identified in all its parts, but it is for all that one of the more effective, and certainly one of the more listenable, pastiches composed by Davis-Macero. The details are as follows:

Miles Davis Ensemble: Jack Johnson
Miles Davis, tpt; Steve Grossman, ss; Herbie Hancock, el pno, organ, probably synthesizer; John McLaughlin, probably Sonny Sharrock, el gtr; Michael Henderson, b; Billy Cobham, dms. New York, 7 April 1970
Yesternow

Same personnel. Same place, date uncertain, but probably the same or similar
Right Off
(both on Columbia s 30455)
The recording date for *Right Off* was originally given as 11 November 1971, but Davis and his band were in Europe on that date; Ruppli silently emends the

date by bringing it forward a year, to 11 November 1970, putting the second session, with its identical personnel and similar music, seven full months after the first. Besides the music from these sessions, the LP includes some music from other sources. *Yesternow* incorporates one and a half minutes of *SHHH/ Peaceful* (18 February 1969), starting at 12:30, and 1 minute and 40 seconds of Miles Davis and a large orchestra at the end. The orchestral sequence also includes a 12-second recitation by Brock Peters, the actor who speaks Jack Johnson's lines on the film soundtrack.

The two sides of the *Jack Johnson* LP consist essentially of two different fusion riffs, the one on *Yesternow* a quiet, suspenseful phrase and the one on *Right Off* a rocking medium-uptempo phrase, with interpolated material interrupting the basic riffs or altering their tempo. Because of the editing-composing process, one can seldom trust one's ears about the music. Sonny Sharrock is listed as the second guitarist because he told Valerie Wilmer that he heard himself on the recordings; neither the personnel nor the recording dates were listed on the LP itself, and Sharrock was not included in the information that Columbia eventually gave out. "I am on the *Jack Johnson* album on the *Yesternow* side, near the end," Sharrock said. "I'm soloing using an echoplex. My solo was mixed down low under Miles."[48] The second guitar is indeed heard momentarily late in *Yesternow* (at 22:30), but a second guitar is heard much more prominently near the end of *Right Off* for several minutes (beginning at 20:44 and showing up throughout Hancock's organ solo and Grossman's soprano solo for the next four minutes). The second guitar in those instances may be Sharrock's, or an overdubbing of McLaughlin. Similarly, a second bass is heard clearly in *Yesternow* (in the seventh minute). The synthesizer parts, probably contributed by Hancock, are concentrated in the second half of *Yesternow*, following the interpolation of *SHHH/Peaceful*, and showing up off and on until the end, when the fragment of Davis and the orchestra breaks in.

Davis's selection of musicians for the soundtrack includes only Grossman from his working band. The others make an unpredictable mix, with Hancock, McLaughlin, and Cobham all at various stages of the fusion crossover, Sharrock a Coltrane-based free former, and Michael Henderson, who in five months would join Davis's working band, a funk bassist from Stevie Wonder's backup band.

Davis kept a tight rein on the disparate elements. "On *Jack Johnson*, Miles instructed almost everybody individually about what he really wanted from them," Cobham recalls. "He tried to show me, physically, what he wanted." In a later interview, he emphasized that Davis's attempt to take over his drum set did not irk him. "And it was *not* in an obnoxious way," he told Brian Priestley, "it was not meant to degrade. I always felt that he always got the most out of the cats that worked with him because everybody loved him, if only for the musician that he is and what he stands for." Cobham even found Davis accommodating when he did not follow his instructions: "He said, like in *Jack Johnson* [hoarse whisper], 'I want this and I want that' and I said, 'Oh yeah? o.k.' and I didn't do it the way he wanted me to do it, and then he just left me alone. He sorta knew just when to let me be, because maybe he felt he was beating a dead horse, you know. But yet when I heard the record, man – if you can't make the adjustment to him, he will adjust to you quite naturally."[49]

Davis directed the musicians almost wordlessly. "It was nice to play with him without having him speak to you verbally," Cobham told Gregg Hall, "because you could learn so much from what he said through his instrument. It's another way of communicating. And one of Miles's major attributes is that he knows how to do that first nature, rather than second nature."[50]

Three days after the *Yesternow* session, Davis flew to San Francisco with his working band to play a concert at the Fillmore West. David Holland was absent, and Michael Henderson filled in for him, the studio sessions apparently serving as his audition. The concert was recorded – Davis's first live recording since his engagement at the Plugged Nickel in 1965 – and released as a double album totalling eighty minutes by Japanese CBS-Sony in 1973. The details are as follows:

Miles Davis Sextet: at Fillmore West
Miles Davis, tpt; Steve Grossman, ss; Chick Corea, el pno; Michael Henderson, el b; Jack DeJohnette, dms; Airto Moreira, perc. Fillmore West, San Francisco, 10 April 1970
Black Beauty I [medley includes *Directions*]; *Black Beauty II* [medley includes *Sanctuary*]; *Black Beauty III* [medley includes *Bitches Brew*]; *Black Beauty IV* [medley includes *Spanish Key*]
(all on CBS-Sony [Jap] SOPJ 39–40)

The sound quality is mediocre, and the playing includes very few moments of distinction. Davis apparently had some reservations about releasing this material on record, but the liner insert (in Japanese) attempts to vindicate the release by arguing that he was seldom satisfied with any of his records. With this one, he had good reason to be dissatisfied. Steve Grossman shows up particularly poorly, especially on the first two sides, with a nervous downpour of notes that is narrow in range and unimaginative. The long, continuous, apparently unedited concert ends with desultory applause.

The main value of the record is in documenting Davis's format for his live performances, using the repertoire of his most recent recordings exclusively, something he had never done before. Many of the themes that surface in the medley had not yet been released in their studio versions, and the only familiar old strain comes at the very end when Davis plays four notes of *The Theme* as a signal to his sidemen to wind up the proceedings.

The themes that do appear are sometimes difficult to identify – so difficult, in fact, that they are unidentified on this recording and all the live recordings to come, appearing instead under cover terms (in this case, *Black Beauty* i–iv) credited to Davis as composer (even though Zawinul and Shorter composed some of them). They are introduced obliquely, by a few notes by Davis or a few repetitions of the bass riff or the rhythm motif, any of which are sufficient to lock the players into the tonal center of that theme for the indeterminate period during which it serves as the improvisational base. The format is loaded with risks. It can inspire creative bridges and emotive playing melded into a spontaneous suite or degenerate into a babble of voices bogged down in search of the musical means to get from one theme to the next.

Although Davis was already experimenting with bands that did not include a piano in the studio and would eventually form his working band without one, he remained convinced enough of the piano's role in his music to expand the band by adding a second pianist. Keith Jarrett, who turned 25 around the time he joined Davis's band in May, now shared the keyboards with Corea at Davis's concerts. He had successfully used two (or more) keyboardists in several of his recordings, notably *In a Silent Way* and *Bitches Brew*, and now used them in his live performances for the first time. The pairing of Corea and Jarrett could hardly be expected to last very long, when both were emerging as leaders in their own right, but Davis got them to stretch out their overlapping terms in his band for four months.

Corea was already considering moving out of Davis's band with David Holland and forming his own band, but he postponed his departure until after the summer round of concerts. Jarrett had been leading his own trio, with Charlie Haden on bass and Paul Motian on drums, since leaving Charles Lloyd's band at the end of 1968, and he kept the band together, expanding them to a quartet with the addition of reedman Dewey Redman, while he played regularly in Davis's band.

Jarrett's quartet lasted for several years after he left Davis, when he began splitting his time between working with his quartet and playing solo piano concerts. The concerts became the touchstone of his reputation, as he spun out continuous melodies with dazzling displays of taste and control. Jarrett's solo concerts, preserved in great numbers on the Munich label ECM from 1973 on, comprise some of the brightest moments in the jazz of the time, and they are as thoroughly individual, consistently swinging and harmonically inventive as any jazz piano music past or present. Toward the close of the 1970s, buoyed by the success of his piano recitals, Jarrett grew more ambitious, producing unwieldy orchestrations that seemed to satisfy his drive to create music beyond category but also seemed, even to listeners predisposed toward his music, designed to satisfy an audience of one.

Even before Jarrett's ambitions led him away from the jazz mainstream, he seemed to be undervalued by part of the jazz audience. One complaint was that his piano performances often lacked intensity and ended up being easy recitals that hid as many of his gifts as they revealed. More often, the complaints centered on his stage manner and had the same nitpicking illegitimacy as the ones that dogged Miles Davis's career for so long. Like Davis, Jarrett presents himself to his audience as a brittle, arrogant character. He occasionally interrupts his performances to lecture audiences on their coughing, or plays a brief, and loose, adaptation of Mozart as the entire second half of a concert for jazz listeners, or refuses to play at all because of some flaw in the piano imperceptible to all but himself. Critics offended by Jarrett's arrogance as a performer have easily found more extraneous aspects to criticize in his extravagant body movements on the piano bench and his adamant opinions about almost everything. As Jarrett became better known in the mid-1970s, such criticisms often appeared to hinder the appreciation for his achievement, a body of solo piano music that celebrates, as he put it, "one artist creating spontaneously something which is governed by the atmosphere, the audience, the place (both the room and the geographical location), the instrument; all these being channelled consciously through the artist so that everyone's efforts are equally rewarded."

Almost forgotten by the time he reached the height of his success a few years after leaving Davis's band was the fact that a younger, more flexible Jarrett had so recently been willing to bend one of his most adamantly held opinions in order to play beside Davis. Jarrett despises electronic instruments and considers his solo concerts to be part of "an anti-electric-music crusade.""Electricity goes through all of us," he declared in 1973, "and is not to be relegated to wires."[51] His view probably had a salutary effect by encouraging other young players to impose some restraint on the use of electronics in jazz, which became such a fad in the early 1970s that it threatened to supplant deeper musical values, but for the year and a half that Jarrett stayed with Davis he played electric keyboards exclusively. "If I wanted to play with him, which I didn't mind the idea of at the time, I wasn't going to be able to change his music to suit me," he told Ted O'Reilly. "I did it with that knowledge so I was not upset about it."[52]

He later told Julie Coryell that Davis had been asking him to join his band for a few years, but that he had resisted his offers only partly because he would have to play electronic keyboards. "Actually, more than the electric thing," he said, "I couldn't stand his preceding band and I wondered if I could do anything, if I could save anything, and if I couldn't, I'd leave right away." And then he added, "It turned out very well because the whole band kind of changed around the time I joined." In fact, the band remained intact for four months after Jarrett joined, and even then only three of the six members changed, Corea, of course, among them. The only attraction Jarrett found in the band, he says, was Davis himself. "With Miles, fortunately, I liked his playing throughout the change of personnel he had," he said. "The time I had heard the band that made me feel bad about it, the only person who I thought was playing music at all was Miles. So I realized that, if I would play with the band, at least I would have that camaraderie with him, that I could trust his playing and maybe he could trust mine." He shrugs off his compromise with electronics, saying, "the music wouldn't sound like anything at all with acoustic instruments ... But I knew it was temporary and I told him it was temporary."[53]

Jarrett's stay was temporary, but it was not brief, and it was the prelude to his rise to prominence. "I just put him at the piano and let him go," Davis told Leonard Feather, and then he added: "Keith wasn't playing the piano like that before he joined me."[54]

Jarrett joined Davis's recording ensemble for two sessions, one in May and the other still undated; only one title from each date has been released. The details are as follows:

Miles Davis Ensemble
Miles Davis, tpt; Benny Maupin, bass clnt; Keith Jarrett, el pno; John McLaughlin, gtr; Jack DeJohnette, dms; Airto Moreira, perc. New York, 21 May 1970
Konda
(on *Directions*, Columbia KC2 36472)

Miles Davis, tpt; Steve Grossman, ss; Keith Jarrett, Herbie Hancock, keyboards; John McLaughlin, gtr; Michael Henderson, b; Billy Cobham, dms; Airto Moreira, perc. New York, 1970
Honky Tonk
(on *Get up with It*, Columbia C33237)

Neither piece resolves into a well-defined concept, and neither makes any special use of Jarrett's presence in the ensemble. *Konda* attempts to work out an arrangement for a written unison passage by Davis and Maupin played over a non-jazz rhythm in which Moreira's plucked berimbau is conspicuous. The attempt fails, ending up in a non-swinging oriental dance cadence, and DeJohnette enters for the first time about halfway through, leading the rhythm players into a conventional funk sequence unrelated to the preceding part.

Honky Tonk is more interesting, as an attempt to get a group of jazz sophisticates – the same band that recorded the *Jack Johnson* soundtrack, with Jarrett and Moreira added – to play the unsophisticated funk of a bar band from, say, Chicago's South Side so that Davis can play a low-down blues over it. "I listen to James Brown and those little bands on the South Side," Davis told Don DeMicheal. "They swing their asses off. No bullshit."[55] Davis's band, intentionally or not, makes a wry abstraction of the whole idea, like a troop of models striking poses against a Skid Row backdrop.

Leonard Feather used *Honky Tonk* on a couple of blindfold tests and found a consensus. Ron Carter conceded that "this leaves a lot to the players' own discretion and levels of musicianship ... and that will work if the players involved are all at the same level." But, he said, "It seems that the levels of the players involved are very different." He added: "It seems that ... the basic rhythm – the percussion, the guitar player and the keyboard – are all playing at random, and, for me, at a loss of something that's really quality."[56] That remark seconded the opinion of trumpeter Blue Mitchell in an earlier test: "It doesn't sound like a composition; it just sounds like somebody blowing ... trying to kill some time till the set's over." And he added: "I hope it ain't anybody I know."[57]

Both *Honky Tonk* and *Konda* simply fade out when the length of vinyl allotted for them on their belated releases is filled.

In a unique event replete with symbolic significance, Davis joined somebody else's recording ensemble on 29 May, when Flying Dutchman Records brought together jazz musicians from all eras to pay homage to Louis Armstrong, recording a vocal album called *Louis and His Friends* that would be released on his 70th birthday on 4 July. Besides Davis, the friends included Eddie Condon, Ornette Coleman, Bobby Hackett, and a dozen others.[58] The collected ensemble sang *We Shall Overcome*, the anthem of popular protest in the 1960s, behind Armstrong's lead, giving Davis his first discographical entry as a vocalist. His voice in the chorus went undetected, making his vocal debut less than auspicious, but the gesture counted more.

The feelings between Armstrong and Davis, the two dominating trumpeters in jazz's historical oligarchy, had always been surprisingly congenial considering their differences in age, style, and attitude. On the few occasions when Davis has said anything about Armstrong, he has been full of praise. "You know you can't play anything on a horn that Louis hasn't played – I mean even modern," he told Nat Hentoff in 1958. "I love his approach to the trumpet; he never sounds bad. He plays on the beat and you can't miss when you play on the beat – with feeling. That's another phrase for swing."[59] He was almost as effusive with Alex Haley, in the *Playboy* interview of 1962, when he said: "I love Pops, I love the way he sings, the way he plays – everything he does, except when he says something against modern jazz music. He ought to realize that he was a pioneer, too." Around the time that Davis gave this mild rebuke to Armstrong for scorning bebop, he himself was publicly scoffing the avant-garde styles of Ornette Coleman, Don Cherry, and Cecil Taylor, but the parallel apparently did not strike him. His comment about Armstrong's disdain for bebop led him to recall an early meeting, probably around 1950, when Davis was in his early twenties and Armstrong in his late forties. "A long time ago," he said, "I was at Bop City, and he came in and told me he liked my playing. I don't know if he would even remember it, but I remember how good it felt to have him say it."[60]

Apart from their mutual admiration, the two men have almost nothing in common apart from the instrument they play, and no two figures in the rapid evolution of jazz make such an instructive contrast. Some of the rich implications were drawn by Leonard Feather in his book *From Satchmo to Miles*, a title that in itself evokes a universe of fascinating diversity for jazz listeners. "Miles' personality has built a mystique around him and has contributed to the hold he has on the public," Feather began. "The irony lies in the fact that three or four decades ago Louis Armstrong, whose attitudes were antithetical to Davis' in almost every conceivable way, also owed his commercial achievements in large measure to his personality. Armstrong, accepted first by musicians as the supreme instrumentalist, later reached the masses by being, onstage, exactly what they wanted him to be. Davis, after gaining similar in-group acceptance, went on to acquire his material luxuries, and massive income tax problems, by doing precisely the opposite: defying the public to like him, insisting that he be accepted solely for the instrinsic value of his music."[61]

Jazz musicians separated by stylistic chasms have occasionally managed to collaborate effectively: one thinks of Sidney Bechet and Martial Solal, Pee Wee Russell and Thelonious Monk, Duke Ellington (as pianist) and Charles Mingus, and a few others. Davis and Armstrong might have found a common ground playing ballads together in the 1950s – indeed, the thought of that missed opportunity might be enough to make some grown-up jazz fans weep – but by 1970 the most that anyone could wish for would be to have Davis singing inaudibly in Armstrong's chorus. A year later Armstrong died, while Davis was engrossed in exploring his electronic frontier.

Early in June, Davis assembled his aggregation in the studio to record some curious little miniatures written by Davis and arranged by the Brazilian multi-instrumentalist Hermeto Pascoal, an old colleague of Airto Moreira's who had been his co-leader in a Brazilian band called Quarteto Novo. The details are as follows:

Miles Davis Ensemble with Hermeto Pascoal
Miles Davis, tpt; Steve Grossman, ss; Chick Corea, Herbie Hancock, Keith Jarrett, keyboards; Ron Carter, b; Jack DeJohnette, dms; Airto Moreira, perc; Hermeto Pascoal, voice. New York, 3 June 1970
Selim; Nem Um Talvez [Selim]
(both on *Live-Evil*, Columbia G 30954)
Selim and *Nem Um Talvez* are different takes of the same composition.

Miles Davis, tpt; Steve Grossman, ss; Chick Corea, Herbie Hancock, Keith Jarrett, keyboards; Hermeto Pascoal, el pno, whistling; John McLaughlin, gtr; David Holland, b; Jack DeJohnette, dms; Airto Moreira, perc. New York, June 1970
Little Church
(on *Live-Evil*, Columbia G 30954)

Davis's melodies are little set pieces played slowly by the ensemble, which forms an instrumental choir. In the mastering, the other players are mixed low beneath Davis's trumpet, which is distorted electronically, and Pascoal, who moans the melody on *Selim/Nem Um Talvez* and whistles it on *Little Church*. Both melodies are doleful, unrelieved by rhythmic pulse or harmonic variety. The title *Selim*, which is 'Miles' backwards, somehow seems appropriate for the monochromatic dirge that it represents.

As dirges, *Selim* and *Little Church* work better than *Nem Um Talvez*, because *Nem Um Talvez* adds Moreira playing a pitter-pat percussion line that has the effect, roughly, of a tap dancer in a funeral procession. If Moreira's role on *Nem Um Talvez* was a miscalculation, it was probably emphasized by the release of these short, strange pieces of petrified melody on the LP called *Live-Evil*, where they stand among long, mostly live performances of heavily amplified fusion music.

A few days later, Davis played an engagement at the Fillmore East again, with both Chick Corea and Keith Jarrett in his band. Columbia recorded the concerts on four consecutive nights, from Thursday to Saturday, and released the edited materials – each evening reduced to one side of a record – as quickly as possible, hoping to catch the tide that was carrying *Bitches Brew* into six-figure sales. Helped along no doubt by the name of the rock palace in its title, *Miles Davis at the Fillmore* became another big seller. The details are as follows:

Miles Davis Septet: at Fillmore East
Miles Davis, tpt; Steve Grossman, ss; Chick Corea, el pno; Keith Jarrett, org; David Holland, b; Jack DeJohnette, dms; Airto Moreira, perc. The Fillmore East, New York, 17 June 1970
Wednesday Miles [medley includes *Directions*, *Miles Runs the Voodoo Down*, *Bitches Brew*, *The Theme*, and other titles]
(on Columbia G 30038)

Same personnel, same place, 18 June 1970
Thursday Miles [medley includes *Directions*, *Pharaoh's Dance*, probably

Milestones, It's about That Time, The Theme, and others]
(on Columbia G 30038)

Same personnel, same place, 19 June 1970
Friday Miles [medley includes *Pharaoh's Dance, I Fall in Love Too Easily, Sanctuary, Bitches Brew, Miles Runs the Voodoo Down, The Theme*]
(on Columbia G 30038)

Same personnel, same place, 20 June 1970
Saturday Miles [medley includes *I Fall in Love Too Easily, Sanctuary, Bitches Brew, Miles Runs the Voodoo Down, The Theme,* and other titles]
(on Columbia G 30038)
Medley identifications are by Nils Winther-Rasmussen and Jan Lohmann; few of the identified themes are complete performances from the concerts.

Compared to the relatively orderly performances on *Bitches Brew*, the music that attracted most of the young fans to the Fillmore, these concerts presented Davis's new fans with fleeting allusions to dozens of themes and restless inventions of wholly new music. The presentation had nothing in common with any other rock or pop concerts, which attract their audiences mainly on the expectation that the performers will reprise their greatest hits, current or recently past, allowing the audience the noisome delight of recognition.

Davis's music for these concerts, in a real sense, did not exist before he played it, leaving the audience little or nothing to recognize, even for those listeners who knew every phrase on *Bitches Brew*. For fans willing or able to alter their concept of how concerts worked, Davis's were bright and flashy happenings. Dave Liebman, a 24-year-old saxophonist just beginning his professional career with a fusion band called Ten Wheel Drive, had no trouble altering his concept, and he could hardly contain his enthusiasm. "I saw him at the Fillmore, man, with Keith Jarrett and Chick Corea, the first time they ever played together, on organ and electric piano," he said. "I mean they didn't even know each other, know what I mean? And Miles is sittin' there playing right in the middle of it. You know? 'cause he likes the unpredictability."[62]

The unpredictability is preserved on the recordings, and perhaps even enhanced. The editing needed to reduce an hour or more of performing to less than half that length on record takes the hard course of condensing the entire performance by snipping and splicing parts from here and there rather than selecting a continuous sequence containing highlights. The editing strategy probably gives a truer sense of being there, although its compression taxes the listener's concentration even more than actually being there ever would.

The few critics who have looked back on Davis's music of the 1970s all hear in the *Fillmore* recording the seeds of many of the properties yet to come. "On balance, the Davis concert at *Fillmore* is an artistic triumph," wrote Barry McRae in *Jazz Journal*, "but the frantic, electronic ending to *Thursday Miles* and the ludicrous opening of *Saturday Miles* bode badly for the immediate future."[63] Scott Yanow concluded that "too much of this set is consumed by endless 'battles' between Chick Corea on electric piano and Keith Jarrett on organ. *At Fillmore* has several other faults that would be present on Davis's future albums: overlength, an occasional lack of direction, and poor editing." But he adds: "Still, there are moments."[64]

Davis's band toured the United States playing rock halls with the band Santana, led by (and named for) guitarist Devadip Carlos Santana. Davis eventually adjusted to his new milieu, feeling comfortable playing as an opening act and performing in front of noisy teenagers. "The audiences didn't always know how to deal with him," Clive Davis reported, but " he has a sense of arrogance about him that speaks out to an audience."[65]

Some musicians caught on more quickly. Santana was one of the first, as Davis's tour companion and Columbia stablemate. Davis began attending Santana's concerts, talking to his musicians backstage, and showing a keen interest in Santana's *Abraxis* LP in all phases of its production. "Back when Miles used to come hear us every night at the Fillmore East," Santana says, "I began to realize that maybe – just maybe – we had something important to say." The main lesson that Santana learned from Davis was the same one that hundreds of jazz musicians had learned over the years. "Through Miles Davis, I learned about the use of space between the phrases," Santana told Lee Underwood in a *Down Beat* interview. "Silence gives people time to absorb the music. Otherwise you sound like a machine gun."[66]

The young musician who fascinated Davis most of all was Jimi Hendrix, the powerful guitarist who overlaid screaming electronics on a basic blues style he had learned when he played in the backup bands of Little Richard and the Isley Brothers. Hendrix was a particular favorite of Betty Mabry, and Davis soon shared her enthusiasm. As he had always done, he passed along his enthusiasm to Gil Evans, and Evans, whose music seemed worlds removed from Hendrix's, became as rapt as

Davis. "I bought all his records and I realized what a good songwriter he was," Evans said. "He was the kind of person who'd write a song every time something would happen to him. A true songwriter."[67] Davis was more impressed by the high-volume, electronic theatrics of Hendrix's guitar sound, and he began searching for a guitarist who could bring that sound into his band. Dominique Gaumont, one of the guitarists who later filled that role, recalled that Hendrix's LP *Band of Gypsies* "traumatized Miles."[68] Although Hendrix's music had blues roots and used improvisation, he never aspired to play jazz and made no conscious efforts to fuse his music with jazz. The respect he gained among some members of the jazz audience, which crested with his election to *Down Beat*'s Hall of Fame in 1970, seemed a spontaneous response to his strikingly distinctive style. "Hendrix, as a guitarist, was an innovator," Evans said. "He set the tone for guitar." As fusion blurred the hidebound categories, Hendrix's originality hoisted him to a status he neither sought nor exploited in what was, to him, an alien genre.

The fusion of jazz with rock, soul, funk, and other pop elements was itself perceived as an alien genre by much of the jazz world, including some of the younger musicians. "Miles is a beautiful cat and I love him, but he's gone off in a strange direction," Freddie Hubbard told Leonard Feather. "Now that I'm getting my shit together, Miles is gonna have to change. As far out as he's gone now, it sounds like a bunch of noise. Not so long ago a lot of young trumpeters were following Miles; now they're trying to play what I'm playing."[69] Those were bold words, but the challenge they implied fizzled out. A few years later Hubbard too began dabbling in fusion, at least on record, and for several years he bobbed back and forth between commercial funk and modal jazz so capriciously that it was hard to guess where his convictions lay.

If Davis's involvement in fusion had an uncertain effect on jazz, there can be no doubt that it had a salutary effect on the rock audience. Whitney Balliett points out: "People tend to get locked into the music they grow up on; whatever comes later is threatening and foreign, and whatever came before is quaint. This insularity is particularly true of the first rock generation, which, with unwise revolutionary fervor, slammed the door on the past. But jazz musicians like Miles Davis and Buddy Rich and Joe Zawinul and Gil Evans have chipped away at the kids' armor, and, from all reports, they are beginning to pay attention."[70] Pianist Ramsey Lewis saw Davis's use of rock elements as the key to expanding the vocabulary of jazz. "It was not until the late sixties when Miles Davis gave his stamp of approval by incorporating some of these

Jimi Hendrix (courtesy of *Down Beat*)

Paul Simon, Clive Davis, and Miles Davis at the Anti-Defamation League luncheon, 1971 (Clive Davis personal collection, courtesy of Helen Merrill)

ideas into his albums that musicians accepted the fact that rock rhythms and influences other than the traditional ones could be integrated with jazz," Lewis wrote in his preface to Julie Coryell and Laura Friedman's *Jazz-Rock Fusion*. "Now with Miles's blessing, it was no longer taboo to venture beyond the traditionally accepted structures, harmonies and rhythms." Lewis added: "Davis extended the harmonic concept, employed polyrhythmic patterns, added electronic instruments and devices to his trumpet along with his highly unique and creative ability, and set the pace for what has come to be known as fusion music."[71]

Coryell's book also included a jazz-rocker's parody of the Lord's Prayer by guitarist Larry Coryell that said, in part, "Our Father, who art a cross between Miles Davis, John Coltrane, and Jimi Hendrix, hallowed be thy name ... And lead us not into disco, but deliver us from commercialism."[72] In spite of Coryell's petition against commercialism, one of the forces that fostered fusion was purely commercial, and many observers saw *Bitches Brew* more as a commercial coup than a musical one. In the immediate aftermath, numerous jazz musicians seemed prepared to pursue their commercial quarry as far into the pop side of the fusion as the audience deemed saleable, and many attempts at fusion music in the first half of the 1970s are grab-bags of rock excesses, unworthy of serious attention except as period pieces.

As Davis's backstage involvement with Santana and others developed, he still remained curiously aloof. In the summer of 1970, New York newspapers made considerable to-do about rumors that Davis would play as a guest soloist with Cream, a supergroup comprised of three top British rock musicians, guitarist Eric Clapton, bassist Jack Bruce, and drummer Ginger Baker, at the Randall's Island Festival. The rumors were quashed at the last moment, after considerable publicity, when Davis announced that he would play only with his own band at the festival. "I don't want to be a white man," Davis told reporters, in a circuitous answer to their question about playing with Cream. "Rock is a white man's word."[73]

He also avoided a meeting with Jimi Hendrix, under strange circumstances. Betty Mabry held a party for Hendrix at Davis's house in 1969, and the guest showed up but the host did not. Eric Nisenson says: "Miles, who hated parties, especially ones for men in his home, conveniently arranged to be working at a late recording session and never showed up at all. However, he left a score for Hendrix to look at, and called him from the recording studio. Unfortunately, Hendrix could

not read music, but the two had a lively musical discussion anyway."
Davis's absence proved fateful for his marriage; according to Nisenson,
Mabry and Hendrix began seeing one another regularly.[74]

Davis resisted meeting the rockers on their own terms, musically and
socially, but he became more involved with their audiences. On 29
August 1970, he played for a gigantic crowd, variously estimated from
100,000 to 400,000, on a 165-acre farm near East Afton on the Isle of
Wight, off the south coast of England. The Isle of Wight Festival was an
attempt to replicate the rock "happening" of the previous summer at
Woodstock, New York, which had attracted 500,000 fans in a similar
setting. There the size of the crowd had been totally unexpected, and the
inadequate food supplies, toilets, and other amenities were further
complicated by downpours of rain that turned the farmland into a
quagmire, but the vast crowd kept its high spirits and turned the
four-day festival into one of the signal events in the baby boom
hagiography. Reports trumpeted the camaraderie that prevailed over the
awful conditions; "Woodstock nation" was held up as a symbol of the
peace-loving citizenry fostered by the ideals of the 1960s. The Isle of
Wight Festival, blessed by fair weather, brought teenagers from all over
the world who filled the rolling fields in front of the scaffolded
bandstand like stalks of wheat. Besides Davis's sextet, the lineup
included a contingent of rock and pop stars including Jimi Hendrix, Sly
and the Family Stone, David Bromberg, Leonard Cohen, Kris Kristoffer-
son, Procol Harum, and Ten Years After. A tightly edited sampling of
Davis's performance, amounting to seventeen and a half minutes, was
released a few years later with selections by other featured performers at
the Isle of Wight and some from the Atlanta Pop Festival in a three-LP
package called *The First Great Rock Festivals of the Seventies*. The
details are as follows:

Miles Davis Septet at the Isle of Wight Festival
Miles Davis, tpt; Gary Bartz, as, ss; Chick Corea, pno; Keith Jarrett, org; David
Holland, b; Jack DeJohnette, dms; Airto Moreira, perc. Isle of Wight, England,
29 August 1970
Call It Anythin' [medley includes *It's about That Time, Spanish Key, The
Theme,* and other titles]
(on Columbia G3x30808)

The medley, in the form preserved on record, is heavily percussive, with
especially forceful electric bass by David Holland often leading the

assault. The Isle of Wight performance marks the first appearance on record of Gary Bartz with Davis's band, replacing Steve Grossman. Grossman's contributions to Davis's concerts seldom survived the transition onto records; on the *Fillmore* LP, his presence is almost undetectable. Bartz fares little better on the Isle of Wight recording, being heard mainly in a brief solo near the beginning, but long enough to make a more aggressive and more melodic impression.

When the music issued from Davis's festival performance offers little to interest jazz listeners, the band's experience of playing before hordes of young people in an open field affected the musicians powerfully. Airto Moreira later cited it, in the interview with Lee Underwood for *Down Beat*, as the turning point in his career. "They covered all the mountains and the hills," he recalled.

It was like an ocean of human beings everywhere. They were all young people in the sun, and everybody was crazy and happy, drinking wine, tripping on acid and laughing to be alive. We started playing and everybody started liking it. They got into the music more and more. We were improvising, of course, and everything was *burning*, man. Then one guy dropped out. As the music played, another guy dropped out, and then another, until everybody had stopped but me. I was playing *cuica*, the 'talking drum'. All of a sudden I was playing by myself. And there were 400,000 people out there waiting for me to play. Miles was standing on my right side holding his trumpet, looking into my face. 'Play!' So I started to play a solo on the *cuica*. Never before in Europe had they ever heard this drum that talks and squeaks and laughs and cries. I played, and played more, and I got into something really strong. And I was cooking, man! One guy in front stretched his arms over his head and began to sway in time to the rhythm, and then another guy and another guy and another guy. And then *everybody* started to wave their arms like that in rhythm. I looked out and there were 400,000 people swaying together like waves in the ocean. 'Wow!' I thought. 'What is this? ... Me, by myself, doing this ... and playing with Miles Davis!' That was the turning point in my career. I could communicate to 400,000 people – 400,000 people *in Europe*! If I could do that then, I knew I could do that anytime, anywhere.[75]

Most reviews of the festival simply passed over the Davis band's performance, listing their presence among all the other acts and dwelling on the huge, polyglot crowd that camped out in the farmer's field. Only *Melody Maker*, Britain's pop music newsmagazine, took much notice of Davis, and the gist of its comment was bafflement at

Davis's aloof stage manner. The notice brought a swift rebuke from Davis by long-distance telephone from Milan. According to Leonard Feather, Davis told *Melody Maker*'s editor: "What kind of man can call me 'arrogant'? I know where you're at. You shouldn't be a critic. You are a white man looking for white excitement, but there are more subtle forms of excitement."[76] He went from there to blast the whole world of rock music.

Davis's riposte seemed as far out of character as did his appearances at Columbia's publicity luncheons and on television talk shows. For decades, he had maintained a stony silence about his critical notices. In 1962, in the *Playboy* interview, he had stated his view on critics clearly. "I don't pay no attention to what critics say about me, the good or the bad," he told Alex Hailey. "The toughest critic I got, and the only one I worry about, is myself. My music has to get past me and I'm too vain to play anything I think is bad."[77] Now, as he courted rock stardom, he gave up the pretence and was willing to take on the critics.

Whenever he talked to jazz writers, he made a point of letting them know that he held the rock world in low esteem. "We're not a rock band," he told Dan Morgenstern. "Some people get that idea because we've amplified, but with amplification, we can be heard and we can hear each other ... Our music changes every month."[78] But those changes all seemed to be taking him in the same direction, and he began to fit in more easily with the company he kept at the Fillmores, the Isle of Wight, and elsewhere.

In the aftermath of the Isle of Wight Festival, while Davis and his band were making a short tour of Europe, Jimi Hendrix settled into London for a series of playing engagements. Hendrix's two most recent LPs had failed to become best sellers, and although he was only 28 he was feeling the strain. In the accelerated grimace of the pop culture, one was not allowed a modest success after a bonanza without arousing a chorus of whispers among managers, bookers, record executives, and the trade magazines. Davis had been involved in one of the plans for reviving Hendrix's appeal. "You know they came to me to reorganize Hendrix's band," Davis told Gregg Hall.[79] Producer Alan Douglas had tried to bring Davis and Hendrix together in the recording studio earlier in the year, but one or the other had repeatedly backed off, coming up with an excuse to cancel the date. Finally, Davis had demanded $50,000 as his share in the collaboration and Douglas ended the negotiations. Instead, Douglas turned to Gil Evans, and plans got underway for an album. "Jimi would just play the guitar and I was to write the charts," Evans reported. "Alan had played Jimi a couple of the Miles albums that I had written for and he liked them."

Hendrix was expected to return to New York for his first meeting with Evans, but he died in London three days earlier, choking on his vomit when he was unable to wake himself after a night of drinking capped by sleeping pills. "Nobody ever told him not to mix barbiturates and alcohol," Evans told Zan Stewart. "Funny, you'd have thought the word would have gotten around because some famous people have died like that: Dorothy Kilgallen, Tommy Dorsey. It's a loser."[80] Evans carried on with the orchestrations of Hendrix's music on his own, becoming the greybeard of the fusion camp when the LP, *The Gil Evans Orchestra Plays the Music of Jimi Hendrix* (RCA CPL1-0667), appeared in 1974.

Hendrix's body was returned to Seattle, his home, for a spontaneous but well-publicized wake. Davis, who had grieved privately when Parker and John Coltrane, his chief mentor and his greatest pupil respectively, were buried, attended the funeral at the Greenwood Cemetery in Seattle on 1 October, his presence publicized by an Associated Press wirephoto.

As soon as Davis's band returned from the European tour, Chick Corea and David Holland resigned. They shared some ideas about music that they felt were stifled as long as they were playing Davis's music. "We were buddies in Miles's band," Corea explained, "and shared a liking for acoustic music, forms not based on the usual influences. We were listening to people like Stockhausen, John Cage, Ornette Coleman, Paul Bley, Messiaen and Varese."[81] "We both wanted to leave the group," says Holland. "I didn't feel there was anything more to be done with Miles, for my own taste, for what I wanted to do."[82]

In spite of all the changes in Davis's music during Corea's and Holland's tenure, both felt that it had not changed enough to suit them. "The premise on which Miles' music is built is still largely the old-fashioned one of a soloist and a rhythm section," Holland said. "I feel that the most positive direction for him to take now would be to go into the concept of playing a supporting role, as well as a supported one, and into more interaction between the players on a somewhat subtler level."[83] Corea agreed, at least as far as saying that Davis's music changed very little. "To me Miles's playing didn't change that much," he said. "He was essentially playing similar ways, only the music around him had changed."

Still, neither of them could deny the large-scale transformation of Davis's concept, if not of his soloing, in the transitional band of which

they were members. "It's interesting in retrospect," Corea acknowledged to Kitty Grime. "Miles is a good example because his music is
very well documented on record. But, like any musician that's moving
on, it's always in a period of transition. Like, when I came with the band,
it was the *Nefertiti* period with Wayne and Herbie and so on. Then the
electric elements got added to the band, and Miles had some ideas about
some rock rhythms that he wanted to play, and the music gradually
tended towards that. Until, at the end of my stay with the band, the
music was very heavily rock-oriented." Corea also observed the
transition in a later stage, after he left the band. "About a month after I
left the band, I heard the group. It was playing some very, very strong
rock music, but very creative, very nice. So that was a whole trip that's
still moving."[84]

Corea and Holland immediately formed a trio with drummer-
percussionist Barry Altschul and tried out at the Village Vanguard. One
of the spectators was the young reedman Anthony Braxton, who had
already been discussing with Corea the directions in music in which he
was interested. "When I first met him," Braxton says of Corea, "he was
fixing to quit Miles because Miles was doing more commercial music.
Chick was interested in more contemporary kinds of music, with more
open forms. Another use of language."[85] Braxton joined the group, to
form a high-minded quartet called Circle that lasted until 1972. After
Circle, Corea formed his own band called Return to Forever and began
playing rock-influenced jazz again, but relying on more subtle, or at
least more subdued, effects than were being used by either Davis's band
or Weather Report. Braxton, Holland, and Altschul often played
together afterward in concerts and on records in free form settings and
became stalwarts, along with Sam Rivers, Oliver Lake, Kenny Wheeler,
and the members of the Art Ensemble of Chicago, in the revitalized
avant-garde of the 1970s that formed a strong counter-trend to the
thickening fusion movement.

Davis already had Keith Jarrett on hand to replace Corea. He briefly
brought in Miroslav Vitous to play bass, as he had in 1968, but Vitous
left to become a founding member of Weather Report, and Davis hired
Michael Henderson, whom he had often conscripted for his recording
ensembles to give the patented funk bottom to some of his records.
Henderson was the bassist in Stevie Wonder's soul band and had
apprenticed with Aretha Franklin and the Motown lineup. He became
the first, but not the last, funk musician to join Davis's working band,
and his hiring marked a decisive change in Davis's live performances. It

also, incidentally, earned Davis the enmity of Stevie Wonder, the top-selling black pop singer of the day. "Stevie Wonder, now there's a sad motherfucker," Davis told Gregg Hall. "He thinks I stole Michael Henderson from him, but Michael came to me. I never did anybody like that in my life."[86]

Henderson had just turned 19 when he joined, and he stayed five years. Throughout, he gave Davis's audiences the kind of show they had come to expect from the backup bands of pop stars, and Davis apparently valued his contribution to the band even when his youth and his onstage style made things difficult. Davis described the problems for Sy Johnson: "Michael fartin' around, showin' off, not being a group player. He'll do that shit two nights and I'll tell him, 'Michael, you been fuckin' around for two days. Settle down!' And he'll say, 'I knew you were gonna say that!' And I'll say, 'Man, bitches make you act funny.'"[87]

With Gary Bartz replacing Steve Grossman on reeds in the summer, Henderson replacing Holland, and Jarrett taking over solely on keyboards in the fall, Davis's band ended the year with a revamped look. The changes were not as significant stylistically as they might have been or as they would be in later personnel changes, notwithstanding the loss in jazz virtuosity from changing the bassists. DeJohnette and Moreira remained from the band that had begun the year, and the other changes balanced the gains and losses. Bartz was, if anything, a more willing soloist than Grossman, standing apart from the ensemble more, as Davis also did. Jarrett, left to his own devices now, could range more freely away from the organ, but with Davis he remained, as Corea also had, essentially an ensemble player.

The burst of recording activity that had begun near the end of 1967 and kept Davis and his coterie of musicians busy almost constantly in the studios began to peter out in the spring of 1970. Apparently satisfied that he had worked out most of the problems he faced in fusing electronics and funk rhythms with his music, and perhaps deterred from the extra musical activity by Columbia's distress about his overproduction, Davis settled back into the more familiar routine of earlier years. He had recorded several times with various groups from January to May, but since then his only studio appearance – the only one to come to light in Columbia's releases so far – was the minor session with Hermeto Pascoal. His other recordings for the year were live performances at the Fillmores and the Isle of Wight festival. So far, no studio recordings by the band with Bartz and Jarrett have turned up at all, even though that band stayed together for more than a year.

Columbia recorded the new band extensively during an engagement at a Washington club called the Cellar Door in December, but after several nights of taping Davis was dissatisfied with their performances. "Miles was looking for an element he hadn't quite nailed down," according to Mort Goode, in a promotional newsletter printed on the inner sleeve of some Columbia LPs, including Davis's *Live-Evil*, the LP on which excerpts of the Cellar Door performances were eventually issued. "Now it was Saturday morning," Goode continues. "And the thought came clear. 'Let's get John McLaughlin down from New York. For tonight.' Phone calls. To friends. To acquaintances. Seeking John. Locating him at last. 'Come on down. The first set is at 9:00.' The first set began without McLaughlin. He hadn't arrived in time. Came in halfway through. Unpacked. Set up. Fitted in as though he had been there forever." The addition of McLaughlin, in Goode's view, represents "Miles' instinct for the right touch, his understanding of talent, his ability to make use of it brilliantly."[88]

The tapes of the evening's performance with McLaughlin in the band were then added to the pool of tapes from the other nights, "an original working pile of thirty reels," according to Teo Macero. Davis and Macero then selected "ten to fifteen" of the reels and made what Macero calls a "distillation" for the *Live-Evil* LP, where they were collated with the short studio tracks involving Hermeto Pascoal. "The album is partly live, and it has an ethereal evil, where the mind is clouded and all these things are happening," Macero told Chris Albertson, before the LP was released. "It's like a wild dream."[89] The music from which Davis and Macero concocted the "wild dream" has never been released in unedited versions, and its character remains unclear. The details, such as they are, are as follows:

Miles Davis Sextet, plus John McLaughlin: Live-Evil
Miles Davis, tpt; Gary Bartz, as, ss; Keith Jarrett, pno, el pno; John McLaughlin (19 December only), gtr; Michael Henderson, el b; Jack DeJohnette, dms; Airto Moreira, perc. The Cellar Door, Washington, DC, probably 16–19 December 1970
Sivad; What I Say; Funky Tonk; Inamorata and Narration by Conrad Roberts (all on *Live-Evil*, Columbia G30954)

Whatever the purpose might have been in editing the tapes, it had nothing to do with making the performances more coherent. All the live tracks on *Live-Evil* involve ear-wrenching shifts of mood and tempo, most of them caused by splicing.

Gary Bartz's contributions emerge from the chaos unusually effectively. he dominates the first third of *Funky Tonk* and the first half of *What I Say* with solos that sound as if they have been preserved whole, and he proves more assertive than either Steve Grossman or Wayne Shorter in the same situation. Like Shorter prior to 1969, Bartz liked to develop a melodic idea rather than play with effects fed to him by the rhythm section, as both Shorter in his final year and Grossman had contented themselves with. Both *Funky Tonk* and *What I Say* swing wildly throughout Bartz's solos, but both tracks continue long after Bartz grows silent, and both lapse into ambivalent, unfocused passages in his wake.

Funky Tonk later springs to life again during an unaccompanied solo by Keith Jarrett on electric piano, in which he builds momentum until he is playing a sort of psychedelic fugue, providing one of the best interludes on the LP and one of the few effective examples of his work on the amplified instrument anywhere. According to Mort Goode, Jarrett's wild invention sprang partly from a malfunction in the piano: "The electric piano wasn't functioning perfectly [and] Keith Jarrett had to improvise around the mechanical problems. The improvisation brought forth the Far East sound, the feeling of gamelin music."[90]

Davis's use of a wah-wah trumpet effect also drew a favorable notice from at least one critic. Barry McRae, writing about Davis's rock music in *Jazz Journal* in 1972, cited Davis's reverberations on *Funky Tonk* as "his excellent solo in this genre" and went on to say: "His now strong commitment to rock music has become more aesthetically credible and throughout *Live-Evil* he matches his surroundings with artificially assisted sound in a way that is both apt and compatible."[91]

Out of the astounding variety of sounds spliced together to make *Live-Evil*, then, it is possible for listeners to isolate bright moments for Bartz, Jarrett, and Davis, but the dominant impression is the befuddling variety itself. *Sivad* – 'Davis' spelled backwards – perhaps shows it most of all, as it moves from Davis's amplified sound over an insistent beat into a pretty ballad introduced by Jarrett as a feature for Davis's muted horn and finally into a slow blues by McLaughlin. All three phases are well defined in their own right, but the transition from one to the next is abrupt and disquieting. The listener must puzzle through three unrelated themes under one title on an LP that includes also *Selim* and *Nem Um Talvez*, the same theme under two different titles.

Live-Evil seems to have purged Davis's impulse to compose his music almost entirely in the editing room. His music had been heavily edited before and would continue to be for the next two years, but never again would some thirty reels of tape be reduced to a little more than 100 minutes of playing time. For Macero, the hefty editing jobs on Davis's music provided a challenge that he accepted eagerly. "The music needs to be played with," he contended, and he saw his post-production duties with Davis as a vote of confidence from the man who a few years before had rejected his services altogether. "Both of us have learned from the things we've done together," he told Gregg Hall. "I learned from the standpoint of editing, shifting the compositions around so that the front becomes the back, the back becomes the middle, the middle something else. It's a creative process being a producer with Miles. In fact, it's more of a creative process than it is with any other artist. You have to know something about music. You really need to be a composer, because for a lot of it he relies on you and your judgement."[92] What the manipulations contributed to the performances that served as the raw material can be known only when some of the unedited reels of tape finally become available.

Around the time of McLaughlin's guest appearance at the Cellar Door, Davis asked McLaughlin to quit Tony Williams's Lifetime and tour with him. After giving some thought to the proposition, McLaughlin turned him down. "I had too much music invested in Lifetime," McLaughlin told Lee Jeske more than a decade later. "I had a freedom there that was irreplaceable. But when I started chafing at the bit in Lifetime, it was Miles who suggested that I put my own band together."[93] That happened a few months later, when McLaughlin formed his Mahavishnu Orchestra, an electronic quintet that quickly joined Zawinul and Shorter's Weather Report, Corea's Return to Forever, and Hancock's Mwandishi among the most popular bands in the fusion movement, along with the bands of Davis, whose touch was obvious in the music that all of them played.

Although Davis could not persuade McLaughlin to join his band, he was now convinced that he needed a guitarist, and he began keeping a watchful eye out for the right player. It would take him more than a year to find one, and then his choice would move his music further from its jazz roots. In the meantime, his sextet remained intact throughout 1971 except for Airto Moreira, who defected to join Corea and then strike out on his own, in a band featuring the vocals of his wife, Flora Purim. Moreira's replacement was James Foreman, who became better known as Mtume, a congas player who made sparing use of the more exotic rattling and scraping devices Moreira had introduced but later added a synthesizer to Davis's ever-increasing percussion backdrop.

Although Davis's band remained strong in individual jazz talents, he seemed no more satisfied with it than he had at the Cellar Door. He carried on playing his full complement of concert and club appearances, but he neither recorded any of those performances nor took the band into the studio. The lack of activity may also have had an extramusical cause, for Davis's hip ailment was again causing him pain. The only documents of this band's work after the Cellar Door engagement at the end of 1970 are private tapings, which are relatively copious because the itinerary included a busy European tour in the fall, and one unauthorized record of a concert performance late in the year in New York.

If Davis remained unconvinced about his band's prowess, the jazz audiences did not. *Down Beat*'s readers voted him Jazzman of the Year for the derring-do of his fusion experiments in the poll results announced at the end of 1971 and also gave first place to both his touring band, with Weather Report second and Herbie Hancock third, and to his trumpet work, ranking him ahead of Freddie Hubbard and Dizzy Gillespie. His LPs of the previous twelve months also placed well in the popularity poll, with *Jack Johnson* third behind Zawinul and Shorter's debut LP *Weather Report*, a strikingly original fusion with a delicate edge, and Duke Ellington's *New Orleans Suite*. Significantly, Davis's *Live at Fillmore* LP, more representative of his current music than *Jack Johnson*, placed only ninth; that low ranking was an early harbinger of the jazz fans' growing dissatisfaction with Davis's further dilutions of the jazz element in his music. His 1971 awards looked pretty much like a continuation of his career-long mastery of the poll system, but they would turn out to be his last significant showing for the entire decade.

His itinerary for 1971 had been partitioned geographically with unusual neatness: he spent most of the spring around Los Angeles, the summer in New York, and the fall in Europe.

The Los Angeles sojourn began with a concert at the immense Hollywood Bowl, where Davis's sextet opened the concert for the main attraction, a countrified rock 'n' roll band called The Band. One of the most musicianly rock groups of the day, The Band, a quintet comprised of Levon Helm, from Arkansas, and Robbie Robertson, Garth Hudson, Richard Manuel, and Rick Danko, from Ontario, first gained recognition as Bob Dylan's backup band and then attracted a discerning audience with their own understated songs. Their music was, even to the most catholic tastes, leagues apart from Davis's.

Predictably, The Band, according to Leonard Feather, "was wildly received; Miles, opening the show, played continuously for 45 minutes and walked off to tepid applause."[94] The press notices reflected the same mismatch of tastes. "The critics wiped [Davis] out in the papers the following morning," Morgan Ames reported. But Ames, in his liner note for *Miles at Fillmore*, claims that Davis's reception at the Hollywood Bowl was at least more tolerant than many observers believed. "In amphitheaters as large as the Hollywood Bowl," Ames explains, "a roaring ovation can sound like a polite coming-together-of-hands, unless you listen closely and look around you. I did. Hippies were on one side of us, non-descripts were behind, a black couple was on the other side. Front-to-back it was a happily received evening. People liked what Miles was about, even if they couldn't grasp his free-form display. They felt his honest effort, his adventure, his openness, and they took him in without asking why."[95]

Davis faced crowds more conversant with his music when he moved into Shelly's Manne-Hole with his band for a week. He earned $4,000, the largest fee that Shelly Manne had paid since opening the club in 1960, but Davis's band sold out most of its sets all week and gave Manne's club a much-needed boost. Davis was well aware of the Manne-Hole's precarious finances when he accepted the booking. "I worked Shelly's just to help keep the place open," he told Leonard Feather. "I lost about ten pounds in that motherfucker. I made $4,000 a week there, but I went in weighing 139 and came out weighing 129."[96] Manne recognized the gesture by Davis. "Everyone puts him down, and sure, he has his faults," he told Harvey Siders. "But he also took care of business. The back room would be full of friends and hangers-on, but Miles would keep checking his watch, and when the next set was supposed to begin, he'd say, 'Okay, let's go.' And one Saturday night, when there was a tremendous crowd waiting to get in, Miles actually split the last set in order to play an extra one."[97]

Among the friends crowding into the musicians' room night after night were dozens of other musicians. They turned out in unusual numbers nowadays wherever Davis was playing, and the Manne-Hole hosted jazz players all week long. Their interest was precipitated by rumors of his defection from jazz, which preceded him wherever he traveled. "I had to go and see if it was true what the guys on the street were saying," J.J. Johnson said, and, on finding out it was indeed "true," Johnson could only give his assent: "It's out there, what he's doing. But I approve. Listen, Miles is doing his natural thing, he's just putting it in today's setting, on his own terms. If you put Miles and his new group in the studio and record them on separate mikes and then you cut the band track and you just played the trumpet track, you know what you'd have? The same old Miles. What's new is the frame of reference."[93]

Most musicians reacted the same way, usually betraying more than a little bafflement at the sound of Davis's band but finding some reassurances in Davis's own sound. "If he ever plays something that I don't enjoy," Maynard Ferguson said, "I tend to wait and think, well, pretty soon I'll probably *hear* him, because he is also in his directions a believer in change. Otherwise he'd still be doing nineteen-piece versions of *Sketches of Spain* or pretty tunes with a mute." And Beaver Harris, the avant-garde drummer, said: "Miles Davis – whatever he's doing, you can bet he's advanced. He's played with all the advanced players in the world, and now he's dealing with the advanced electronics of the world. But he's still playing Miles Davis."[99] Art Pepper, the alto saxophonist whose return in 1971 after years of wasting away in prisons turned into one of the highlights of jazz in the 1970s, could hardly help comparing what he heard from Davis on his return with the seminal works of a decade earlier. "Yeah, I loved all those things," he told Hal Hill, referring to the collaborations with Gil Evans, "but now Miles has gone way beyond that, and some people don't like him at all. Miles has eliminated the space that I liked about him before," said Pepper, and then hastily added, "but now the space is even greater, every note is like a gem, he has reached the epitome of music."[100] A lot of musicians were thinking aloud about Davis's music, and many of them seemed to be covering any doubts they had with a layer of tact. No one wanted to be a 'moldy fig' or a reactionary as the jazz world faced some new directions.

Davis's fans mixed curious regulars, some of them recalling two decades of his changing music, with a new breed attracted by *Bitches Brew*, and there would always be enough of both to fill a hall or a club even after many critics and musicians began expressing their doubts more openly. Shelly Manne counted on that when he paid Davis the record-high stipend and earned a reprieve for his jazz club. But Manne's business acumen backfired when he booked Davis a year later. The new owners of the building that housed the Manne-Hole built a recording studio adjacent to the club, and Davis's music not only could not save the club this time but inadvertently closed it. "The studio, unbeknown to us, had an echo chamber right above our club," Manne told Sinclair Traill, "but they told me everything was fine. They were going to renew our lease, they loved having us there. So I figured everything was O.K. until one day right out of the blue [they] served us with an eviction notice! Thirty days to vacate because the music, especially with groups such as Miles Davis, was feeding into the echo chamber and lousing up their recordings. They said they had done a record the night before and it had screwed up the whole record because Miles's music had infiltrated the echo chamber."[101] The Manne-Hole closed early in September 1972.

After his week at the Manne-Hole in the spring of 1971, Davis, feeling fatigued and complaining about his weight loss from the constant performing, turned down an engagement in Boston and stayed in Los Angeles for several weeks, as he often had since the 1960s. His residence there, as usual, was the Chateau Marmont on Sunset Boulevard, described by Leonard Feather as a "fading relic of the old Hollywood." He spent his days, according to Feather, working out at a gym with "his own personal trainer and watching baseball on the black and white television set at the Marmont with his "lissome girlfriend."[102]

Davis's divorce from Betty Mabry became official in the third year of their marriage, although they had not been living together for some time. Their relationship had been stormy, but they remained friendly. Mabry launched her singing career under her married name, Betty Davis, and she sought her ex-husband's advice on her recording ventures, including his active participation on one track of her 1975 LP (Island ILPS 9392), a song called *You and I*, written by Mabry, with Davis credited as "director" and Gil Evans as arranger and conductor of the brass backing.

Soon after the divorce she scored a modest success with her first LP, entitled *They Say I'm Different* (Just Sunshine Records 3500). Her songs, all written by her, explore the familiar blues-soul-pop themes of broken hearts, unfaithful lovers, and spent emotions in straightforward, if sometimes strained, lyrics. In *Your Mama Wants You Back*, she sings:

Can you hear your mama callin'?
She's a-callin' you on the phone.
Can you hear your mama cryin'?
A girl said you weren't at home.

Occasionally she breaks away from the safer pop territory for more unorthodox subjects, as when she roughs up her clear, girlish timbre in *He Was a Big Freak* to deliver such lines as: "I used to beat him with a turquoise chain; ... He used to laugh when I'd make him cry." Fans who imagined that her ex-husband might be the target of these barbs could also imagine that Miles Davis framed a musical reply to her when, a few years later, he titled on of his themes *Back Seat Betty*. But Eric Nisenson asked Davis about *He Was a Big Freak* and Davis said: "Well *she* was the biggest freak I ever met, but the song wasn't about me, it was about Hendrix. I'm a big freak myself, but I don't want anybody beating me with a lavender whip."[103]

Davis returned to New York in May 1971 and immediately led his band into a club called the Gaslight for a five-night stand. Once again he was kept busy in a social whirl of promotional events by Columbia. At Clive Davis's urging, he attended a party at Tavern-on-the-Green celebrating the end of a week of SRO concerts at Carnegie Hall by Chicago. Most of Columbia's stars dutifully turned out, including Stevie Wonder, to honor the seven young Chicagoans who had found the crest of the commercial wave in orchestrated rock. Says Clive Davis, "They were star-struck at meeting Miles and Stevie and were knocked out by the entire evening."[104]

Davis also attended a luncheon of the Anti-Defamation League at the Waldorf-Astoria, where Clive Davis was presented with the League's Man of the Year award. "It was not a typical scene for Miles," Clive Davis recalled, "but he viewed it as a personal responsibility and sat with me, Paul Simon, André Kostelanetz and others on the dais."[105] As much as anything else, the occasion was probably an object lesson for Davis as he watched the man he had once accused of racism receive the highest honor from a respected civil rights organization.

The summer rounds again included the Newport Jazz Festival, which Davis's band played on 5 July, a Monday. The parade of bands at the concert seemed dizzying in its variety. The concert opened with a quintet led by Gene Ammons and Sonny Stitt; those two reedmen had been Davis's closest friends in Billy Eckstine's band in 1946 and were still playing the swing-inflected bebop that they had all played then. Two other bands were working in Davis's more recent directions: one of them, Soft Machine, a short-lived group looking for the commercial potential in jazz-rock, and the other, Weather Report, gathering momentum for a long life playing not only jazz-rock but, in their turns, funk-rock and disco-rock and, occasionally, jazz as well. Davis's touch was evident all afternoon.

The European tour in the fall of 1971 looked like a hit-and-run affair, with concerts in twelve cities in three weeks. Some taped performances exist in private collections from the concerts in Zurich (22 October), Paris (23), Brussels (26), Paris again (27), Rotterdam (29), Belgrade (3 November), Vienna (5), Berlin (6), Uppsala (7), Copenhagen (8), Oslo (9), Cologne (12), and Festival Hall, London (13). Jack DeJohnette had left the band in the summer to form his own fusion band, called Compost, and although they started with the obvious advantage of a Columbia recording contract they struggled to find an audience and steady work; they were destined not to join the long line of successful bands spawned by Davis's stock company. DeJohnette returned to Davis's band whenever their schedules permitted in the next months, but on the European tour Davis tried out Leon Chancler.

Davis put his European tour into the context of his performing schedule for Leonard Feather, in *From Satchmo to Miles*. "I got a tour in Europe," he said. "I'll make about $300,000 on it. Then I won't work again until the spring and I'll make a spring tour. No more week here and three weeks off and a week there. I'm through with that shit." When Feather asked how he expected to keep his band together through the long periods of inactivity, he replied, "I can always get a group. The men I need I can keep on salary while I'm laying off."[106] Noting Davis's indifferent attitude about performing, Feather concluded that the light schedule amounted to "a policy of semi-retirement." Feather must have been aware also that Davis's recording activities had become even lighter, practically nonexistent. He predicted that Davis schedule might well become "almost total inactivity" before much longer. Feather's remarks, which appeared in print in 1972, proved to be prophetic, and Feather was one of the few observers not completely surprised when Davis limped along in something that might be described as semi-retirement from 1972 to 1975 and then retired fully for more than five years after that.

At least one other observer noted in retrospect that Davis seemed less than fully involved with the music of his band at his European performances. "In his London concerts in November 1971," Barry McRae wrote in *Jazz Journal* in 1975, "we began to hear too much of the hot declamatory outburst and less of the natural lyricism. The Davis who had swept along with the rock sounds had become bogged down by them. His use of wah-wah trumpet was less effective and, of all things, it lacked the rhythmic subtlety that had always seemed the trumpeter's birthright. This could be construed as moving back into the ensemble but the outcome was strangulation, not inspiration."[107]

On 26 November 1971, less than two weeks after returning from Europe, Davis and his band performed a concert at Philharmonic Hall in New York. Don Alias was added to the band, and Jack DeJohnette returned for the concert, which proved to be the last gasp for the working band with Keith Jarrett and Gary Bartz, and, for that matter, the last gasp until 1981 for a band of Davis's in which a majority of the sidemen were schooled in jazz.

The concert drew more than the usual advance publicity when Davis telephoned Jack Whittemore from Paris a month before and told him to spend half of his fee buying tickets for the concert and to distribute them among young people who could not afford them. "Miles has never done anything like this before," Whittemore told Chris Albertson, "but nothing he does surprises me." For Whittemore, the main problem was "how to go about distributing more than $2,000 worth of free tickets to the right people."[108] Davis's largesse came as a response to his new awareness of his stature in the black community, where his broader, younger audience of recent years saw him not so much a musician as a hero. "I like when a black boy says, 'Oohh, there's Miles Davis,' like they did with Joe Louis," he told Gregg Hall in 1974, recalling an incident at a concert in the American south around this time. "Some cats did me like that in Greensboro. They said, 'Man, we sure glad you came down here.' That thrilled me more than anything that happened to me that year."[109] For his concert at the Philharmonic, he was hoping that some of those youngsters could be in his audience.

The concert was taped privately and later released in part as an unauthorized LP proclaiming itself a "special limited anniversary issue for collectors." The details are as follows:

Miles Davis Septet at Philharmonic Hall
Miles Davis, tpt; Gary Bartz, as, ss; Keith Jarrett, el pno, org; Michael Henderson, b; Jack DeJohnette, dms; Don Alias, James Foreman, perc. Philharmonic Hall, New York, 26 November 1971
Bwongo [medley: *Directions, Sivad, What I Say*]; *Ananka* [medley: *What I Say* (cont), *Sanctuary, Miles Runs the Voodoo Down, Yesternow*]
(both on Session 123)
Identification of the medleys is by Jan Lohmann.

The final ten minutes of the recording, identified as the *Yesternow* theme from the *Jack Johnson* LP, features Davis's incantatory amplified sounds over percussive accents and Bartz's down-home blues on the alto saxophone over the same percussive accents, making a stylish conclusion to the record. Almost everything that precedes it – and the record logs a generous forty-seven minutes of the concert – highlights a percussive barrage that overwhelms the music and in effect becomes the music.

One of the regrets about this band's lack of recordings arises from the interest in Keith Jarrett's work, but on this recording (and on the European concerts as well) Jarrett goes largely unheard, his ensemble contributions swallowed up in the percussion and his solo efforts, on this record no more than one minute of electric piano on *Directions*, lost in the mix. Long before Jarrett took off on his own singular course, Davis had relegated him to the backdrop in his band, a missed opportunity for Davis's music as well as Jarrett's.

In relegating him so, Davis obviously implied no disrespect. After all, he had now relegated himself in the same way.

14

Sivad Selim
1972–5

Alone

for Miles Davis

A friend told me
He'd risen above jazz.
I leave him there.
  Michael S. Harper

As the wall of percussion moved out of the background of Miles Davis's music and into the foreground, numerous critics, fans, and musicians began to balk at the direction his electronic experiments were taking. They had been laying back for three years, waiting to see what he would do, and stifling their doubts because Davis had led the way so often before. That period of grace was now over.

Davis chose musicians with diverse backgrounds to replace the jazzmen of his last band, and their limitations seemed obvious to the jazz audience even if they successfully filled the roles Davis assigned them. His studio recordings of the period, as they came out at irregular intervals, laid bare those limitations, and, because the recording ensembles sometimes imported musicians of proven abilities, the new LPs seemed proof positive that the limitations lay not so much in the music's execution as in its conception. Either way, the band's failings were pinned on Davis.

The recordings of the period showed much more diversity than Davis's critics seemed willing to concede, but their common element was a bumptious, domineering rhythm. *On the Corner* (issued in 1972) sounded like a crass attempt at funk; in the words of a reviewer in *Coda*, it presented "nameless, faceless go-go music." *In Concert* (1973), recorded live at Philharmonic Hall, preserved remarkably little of Davis's trumpet playing and perhaps even less of his guiding hand. *Get Up with It* (1974) featured long, listless rambles and little else, with Davis playing sustained chords on an organ most of the time. *Dark Magus*, *Pangaea*, and *Agharta*, all concert performances released after Davis retired in 1975, showed more spunk in the onstage give-and-take but not much more definition. Davis repeatedly expressed his admiration for James Brown and Karlheinz Stockhausen, musicians so far removed from one another that they seemed irreconcilable, but Davis's bona fide masterworks of this period, easily overlooked in the musical morass, drew on both sources: *Rated X* (recorded in 1972, released in 1974) unleashes seven minutes of distilled tension in an idiom that defies category, and the *Maiysha/Jack Johnson* segments of *Agharta*, a 1975 Japanese concert performance, magically bring into focus the musical forces over which many thought Davis had lost control.

He seemed to be struggling for control physically as well as musically. His arthritic hip kept him in constant pain and forced him to abandon his regimen in the gym. He had more run-ins with the police, leading to a variety of charges, including alleged narcotics and weapons offenses. The abstinences of a few years earlier were replaced by indulgences. He drank more heavily, perhaps hoping to kill the pain, but succeeded only in aggravating a peptic ulcer. He began receiving injections of morphine in order to keep moving. And, in the end, he collapsed and stayed down for a long time.

Until the collapse, Davis swaggered through his public appearances, conducting his bombastic rhythm sections autocratically onstage and damning both his old peers and his young disciples offstage. But the tumult of his life and his music could not drown out the chorus of critics.

"Maybe he's doing it sincerely," Clark Terry told Leonard Feather, "but I do know that it's a much more lucrative development for him. I happen to know that there was a period when in spite of all his many possessions – investments, home, car – there was a period when he needed to bolster these: he really needed to get into a higher financial bracket. And there was an opportunity for him to get into this kind of thing, and he took the opportunity to jump out and do it."[1] Betty Carter lumped Davis with Herbie Hancock and Donald Byrd as a musician abusing his talent. "He did the same thing, for money," she said. "It's all about money ... They have a 'reasonable' excuse for the why of what they're doing, but the only excuse is money."[2] John Hammond, long

associated with Columbia, agreed: "The musicians who are selling out voluntarily are succumbing to the worst instincts of the capitalist system," he said, and he added, "For Miles Davis, who was a real original, to be putting out crap – repetitious crap – that's a disgrace."[3]
"Miles Davis is a consummate blues player," Archie Shepp commented, but then he felt the need to qualify that remark: "I don't mean what he's playing now; what he's playing now impresses me as something very antithetical to the blues. It depresses me when I hear formerly good blues players in a certain context merely pandering their artifacts for money's sake, for commerciality, because they cheapen the genuine product."[4]

Overlooked in these criticisms were the facts that Davis's music was not commercially successful, at least not by the standards he had set with *Bitches Brew*, and was no more readily accessible as soul music than as jazz. It was a different species, or perhaps several of them.

Other commentators rose to Davis's defence. "Miles isn't up there to please everybody, or anybody," Herbie Hancock said. "He's there to be honest, that's all; and he has to be taken for what he is."[5] Cecil Taylor explained to Nat Hentoff the difference in Davis's musical orientation that seemed to be disorienting his critics. "As Miles Davis's European technical facility becomes sparser," Taylor said, "his comment from the Negro folk tradition becomes more incisive. He's been an important innovator in form in jazz, but again not out of theory, but out of what he hears and lives."[6]

What Davis was hearing – and apparently living – had changed, as Taylor notes, but it was not so much "Negro folk" music as black pop music, and not in any sense a "tradition" but only the most current samples. Dave Liebman, who played reeds and flutes in the band for much of this period, told Gene Perla: "Every time I've been with him on the road or at his house, I've never heard a tape in the machine – and there's always something on – that is older than a few days or a week. He doesn't listen to anything that's in the past, of his own music ... I've never heard him listen to anybody else's music, except maybe a particular track of Sly [Stone] or James Brown. Of the music the group is doing, he won't even listen to a tape of two weeks ago. That's already old to him. So when you see that in him, it's really understandable why, to me, the music has moved in another direction."[7] Gil Evans, who was making similar, though less radical, changes in the rhythms of his infrequent music, stated simply, "Jazz has always used the rhythm of the time, whatever people danced to."[8]

Davis's most direct incursion into what he saw as the musical space charted by Sly Stone, James Brown, and the rhythm bands of Chicago's South Side, the studio recordings released as *On the Corner*, was scheduled for the Columbia studios early in 1972, but it had to be postponed when Davis was rushed to the hospital suffering from gallstones in April.

The sessions finally took place around June, after a long layoff, and when the music was released in November it got a harsher reception than anything Davis had ever recorded. Reviewers savaged it, and many fans ignored it. Most of Davis's Columbia LPs have stayed in print continuously, but inexpensive copies of *On the Corner* were available in delete bins at record stores within sixteen months of its release.

Everything about the LP seemed blatant. Its cover, inside and out, was festooned with ghetto caricatures by cartoonist Corky McCoy: prostitutes, gays, activist, winos, and dealers. Apart from them there was only (as Jérome Reese described it) "une grande photo du beau Miles en star 'sexy'." None of the other musicians was identified. And, it turned out, both the cover design and the missing credits were Davis's brainchild. "I didn't put those names on *On the Corner* specially for that reason, so now the critics have to say, 'What's this instrument, and what's this?'" Davis explained to Michael Watts. "I told them not to put any instrumentation on ... I'm not even gonna put my picture on albums anymore. Pictures are dead, man. You close your eyes and you're there." Watts asked him what would appear on future covers and was shown a stack of cartoons. "Things like that, man," Davis said.[9] Mark Zanger, in an overview of Davis's music of this period in *The Real Paper*, commented: "The album is best seen, rather than heard, as Miles's manifesto."[10]

The instrumentation varies from track to track, and the music probably comes from several sessions in and around June. Tentative lists of personnel, all slightly different, have appeared in at least four different sources, indicating a befuddling parade of musicians through the studios, and the music gives those players few opportunities to identify themselves. The details are as follows, with the collective personnel listed first and the instrumental breakdown for the titles listed separately:

Miles Davis Ensemble: On the Corner
collective personnel: Miles Davis, el tpt; Dave Liebman or Carlos Garnett, ss, ts; Benny Maupin, bass clnt; Chick Corea, el pno; Herbie Hancock and/or Harold I. Williams, el pno, synthesizer; David Creamer, el gtr; Colin Walcott,

sitar; Michael Henderson, b; Jack DeJohnette and/or Billy Hart, dms; Badal Roy, tabla; Don Alias and/or James Mtume Foreman, congas, perc. probably June 1972

Davis; Liebman; el pno; synthesizer; Creamer; Henderson; dms; congas; perc
On the Corner; New York Girl; Thinkin' One Thing and Doin' Another; Vote for Miles
(all on Columbia KC 31906)

Davis; Garnett; other instruments as for *New York Girl*
Helen Butte
(on Columbia KC 31906)

Davis; synthesizer; Walcott; Henderson; dms; Roy; congas; perc
Black Satin
(on Columbia KC 31906)

Omit Davis; add Garnett, ss, and Creamer; other instruments as for *Black Satin*
Mr. Freedom X
(on Columbia KC 31906)

Garnett, ss; Maupin; el pno; org (perhaps Davis); Henderson; dms; perc
One and One
(on Columbia KC 31906)
Some discographies list John McLaughlin, el gtr, in addition to, or instead of Creamer.

The music, notwithstanding the changes in personnel and instrumentation, humps along on electric discharges, like a man walking barefoot on a field of broken egg shells. Stan Getz heard the first three titles, which form a continuous track, as part of a blindfold test with Dan Morgenstern and commented: "Is that a Miles offering? If that's Miles, where is Miles? He was directing. It sounded like they were gathering at the elephant graveyard. I didn't hear any elephants screech, though." And then he grew serious: "That music is worthless. It means nothing; there is no form, no content, and it barely swings. The soloists are playing a half tone above and a half tone below so it'll sound modern, but there's nothing to build on or anything logical – nothing."[11]
    The feeling of monotony arises from the simple harmonic foundation

of each piece, what Clark Terry called "the one-chord modal bag." Ron Brown, reviewing the LP for *Jazz Journal*, said, "It sounds merely as if the band had selected a chord and decided to worry hell out of it for three-quarters of an hour. Also the solos are practically nonexistent; Miles wanders over to spit a hasty note into the rhythmic wodge every now and again, like he did on his last visit to London."[12] Terry viewed the simple harmonies as a cynical expedient in Davis's search for a mass audience: "Miles is smart enough to put something where they can reach it on their own level. If they're not hip enough to know what's happening ... they're going to grasp whatever is simple enough for them to cop. And the simple thing for them to cop happens to be that one-chord modal bag that is so fashionable."[13]

Terry surmised correctly that Davis had a specific audience in mind. Davis told Michael Watts in *Melody Maker*, "I don't care who buys the records as long as they get to the black people so I will be remembered when I die. I'm not playing for any white people, man. I wanna hear a black guy say, 'Yeah, I dig Miles Davis.'"[14] That admission added insult to injury. Bill Cole, in his biography of Davis, called *On the Corner* "an insult to the intellect of the people."[15] Brown concluded his review by saying, "I'd like to think that nobody could be so easily pleased as to dig this record to any extent." But Davis was not willing to concede that *On the Corner* was a miscalculation. Questioned about it, he became defensive, as when Sy Johnson told him he was having trouble "following the music" with the extra rhythm players. "You can't understand me 'cause you're not me," Davis said. "In the second place, you're not black. You don't understand my rhythms. We're two totally different people. That's almost an insult to say you don't understand."[16]

Davis's apparent reluctance to play his trumpet also drew comments from the reviewers. Beginning with *On the Corner*, he seemed content to play few notes and short interludes. When Watts asked him about it he said, "Because you have technique you don't have to use it. You use it when you feel like it. I mean, you can run, but if you can walk you walk, right? You do what you gotta do. It's called good taste. I play whatever comes into my black head, man."[17]

The only other music to be released from these June sessions, a long piece that filled one side of the *Big Fun* LP two years later, shares some of the main characteristics. The details are as follows:

Miles Davis Ensemble: Big Fun
Miles Davis, el tpt; Sonny Fortune, ss, flt; Carlos Garnett, ss; Benny Maupin, bass clnt; Lonnie Liston Smith, el pno; Harold I. Williams, synthesizer;

Michael Henderson, b; Al Foster, Billy Hart, dms; Badal Roy, tabla; James
Mtume Foreman, perc. New York, 12 June 1972
Ife
(Columbia PG 32866)

The music moves along over a simple, repeated bass riff, its progress
charted mainly by the percussionists, whose interplay seems somewhat
less jittery than it is on *On the Corner*. The rhythm is suspended
altogether in the last third while Davis muses over sustained organ
chords; this section gives a foretaste of the style that Mark Zanger
would call "pseudo-trance music" when it appeared in abundance on
the 1974 LP *Get Up with It*.

In these June studio sessions, Davis used seventeen different sidemen
in various combinations. Many were unknown and untried, members of
a loosely knit contingent of young musicians who gravitated to New
York with high aspirations, enormous self-confidence, and unpredictable talents. Davis had regularly recruited his sidemen after hearing
them play publicly with other bands, but now he began looking for them
before they had a chance to establish their reputations beyond their own
circle of acquaintances. He relied on people such as Herbie Hancock, Gil
Evans, Sonny Rollins, and a few others, including friends of friends, to
relay the names of youngsters heard by chance in a loft jam session or on
a one-night stand. Usually he phoned the potential recruit himself and
told him to appear in the recording studio at an appointed hour; on one
memorable occasion in 1974 he would tell two new recruits to meet him
onstage at Carnegie Hall during a concert.

The parade of players did nothing to stabilize the conception Davis
was working on in his music. Only bassist Michael Henderson and
percussionist James Mtume Foreman were retained from the working
band of the previous year. To replace Gary Bartz on reeds, he had brought
three different musicians into the recording studio in June. Although
Dave Liebman became his first choice for the next two and a half years,
he also used both of the others, Carlos Garnett and Sonny Fortune, from
time to time. All three were relatively experienced, although only a
little better known than most of the other sidemen. Garnett, born in
Panama in 1939, had played in rock bands in the 1960s before joining
Freddie Hubbard and Art Blakey. Fortune, a Philadelphian, was a year
older; he had played for years in local bar bands before going on the road
with Mongo Santamaria's band and was a regular member of McCoy
Tyner's quartet when he first recorded with Davis. Liebman, from
Brooklyn, was first noticed in Ten Wheel Drive, a jazz-rock band in the

shadow of Blood, Sweat and Tears in 1970, when he was 24, and he was playing regularly in Elvin Jones's quintet, where he shared the front line with Steve Grossman, when he first recorded with Davis. Davis's sporadic playing schedule required him to keep all three on call, because between his playing dates they were busy with other commitments, often with bands they led themselves.

He often used Jack DeJohnette as the drummer in his studio ensembles, but DeJohnette was also working as a leader. For *Ife*, he borrowed Billy Hart from Hancock's band, whose talents were well known to Davis. Hart recalled their first meeting. "One time I was working with Herbie at the Vanguard, and after the set I sat down at one of those chairs next to the drums," he said. "I was soaking wet. I guess the music had been satisfying. I'm sitting there dripping. I couldn't even open my eyes. Suddenly I heard this voice in my ear – 'You played your ass off.' I looked up and it was Miles. He startled me. The very next thing he said was, 'You know, sometimes you can play behind the beat, and that shit swings. And sometimes you can play on top of the beat, and *that* shit swings. But sometimes you can play right over the beat, and *that shit swings.'*"[18]

The second drummer on *Ife* was Al Foster, an athletic-looking young man with a ready smile. He was just starting to work professionally, and the recorded evidence of *Ife* reveals nothing about his ability, but he became Davis's regular drummer not only in the band of 1972–5 but also in the new band formed in 1981, after Davis's emergence from retirement, making his association with Davis the most enduring of any sideman. Compared with the pyrotechnical fireworks of Philly Joe Jones, Tony Williams, and DeJohnette, Foster is an elemental player whose main strengths are in setting up a rhythmic pattern and sustaining it for long stretches. None of the other personnel changes reveals as tellingly Davis's changed conception. From the beginning, he instructed Foster, according to Dominique Gaumont, to "copy the simplicity of Buddy Miles,"[19] Hendrix's drummer on *Band of Gypsies*, and Foster has done that, with muscular ease, ever since.

Foster joined Henderson and Foreman in the rhythm section of the working band, and they were its only fixtures. Either Liebman, Garnett, or Fortune was usually available to fill the reedman's spot when Davis accepted performing engagements, and the other players were recruited as he needed them. Davis no longer maintained a working band, for the first time in years, but he had a pool of players on which he could draw. Many musicians came into the band as unknowns and remained unheralded both with Davis and afterward. The pattern broke the spell of Davis's reputation as a star-maker.

The band had a built-in instability, and several critics began to question the abilities of some of the sidemen. Asked by Harriet Choice how he knew what musician was right for his band, Davis retorted, "The same way I know what girl I want to screw."[20] To many jazz fans, that recruiting policy seemed much less selective than it had once been. Dave Liebman, who was, with Sonny Fortune, probably the best jazz player associated with Davis in this period, suggested that Davis's critics were looking for talents in the sidemen that they were never intended to have. "Miles has picked these people to achieve the sound that he wants," he said. "Some are not experienced in jazz. This band is made up of so many different elements that only a few of the cats have swung in the jazz thing for a long period of their musical life. The other cats are coming out of funk or something different."[21]

Davis himself seemed content with the challenge of adjusting to the youthful mix of disparate backgrounds he had put together. "I'm 48," he told Sy Johnson. "I never feel that shit. I'm not vain. As long as I'm not draggin' the musicians I'm with – and I pick the best ones I can find, that are available to me – then I figure I'm pretty alright. That's the way *I* judge."[22]

For all that, the young sidemen treated him as a grey eminence. When Johnson arrived to interview Davis, he passed Al Foster and Michael Henderson in the foyer and said, "I'm off to see the master." "Do you call him that too?" Foster asked. "Some of the guys in the band call him the master." Davis once complained facetiously, "They think I'm their father! [They say,] 'We don't see *you* fuck around on the road.' I say, 'I told you I used to have a bitch for every night I went to work, and one night I went to work and all seven of them were there.' Shit!! *That*'s why I don't fuck around."[23]

On the Corner fell far short of Davis's commercial expectations, but he saw that not as a failure of the musicians or the music itself. He blamed his manager and Columbia. He replaced Harold Lovett, his manager for seventeen years, with Neil Reshen. He renewed his feud with Columbia, this time over its apparent failure to sell *On the Corner* in black neighborhoods. "You know," he told Michael Watts, "I will make $500,000 in a year, but I will do it for $5 if my music would get to the black people, and Columbia couldn't get the albums into Harlem ... That's what I'm told by the vice-president. He don't talk to me on the phone for nothing."

While Watts interviewed him, they were listening to tapes that Watts described as "the next step from his *On the Corner* music." "I've been up for three days writing this fucking music," he complained, "and Columbia ain't going to sell it, anyway. They sell all the pretty, little faggot-looking white boys, that's their thing. I just got an offer from Motown for this new album." He claimed that he was being taken for granted at Columbia. "When I make a record and it sounds good, they say, 'Well, that's Miles.' Y'know, it's supposed to sound good. That's why I'm leaving Columbia, man, I'm not going to give them this latest album ... I'll erase it ... I told Clive [Davis]. Sent a telegram, told him he should get a black – he should use his sources all over the country to get a black man who thinks black to sell the music to black people, 'cos the white people seem to know about it ... I been exploited for ten years, man."

When Watts called Bob Altschuler at Columbia to check the story, Altschuler told him calmly that Davis could not terminate his contract. "This is his way of pressuring Columbia," he said. "We talk to him every day. He needs reassurance."[24]

A few weeks after his June studio dates, Davis was involved in controversy at the Newport Jazz Festival, now transplanted from the Rhode Island resort to New York. He was listed as the featured performer at afternoon and evening concerts in Carnegie Hall on 4 July, but did not appear. In his place Freddie Hubbard led a quartet, sharing the bill with Sonny Rollins's quartet. Davis had warned the New York newspapers that he had no intention of showing up and supplied them with the kind of caustic comments that gave the festival some sensational publicity. He was not offered enough money, he said, and he had never agreed to play the concerts in the first place. Besides, in his opinion the festival catered to older styles by booking musicians such as Dizzy Gillespie and Sarah Vaughan.

His comments brought a sharp rebuke from Mary Lou Williams. "You know what evil is?" she asked Roland Baggenaes. "What Miles just did ... If you and I know someone, well, we could talk about him but to say it in the paper like that – that's very bad. Selfishness and bitterness will make you evil ... He can stop bookings of those people." As for Davis's claim that he was playing more current music, Williams said: "I hear what he's playing, he's playing practically the same style he always has played. But he's got the modern thing in back of him, the guys who make the noise ... Listen to his tone, listen to his chord changes and you'll hear it. So Miles Davis really has no reason to say anything about Dizzy Gillespie or Sarah Vaughan."[25]

If Vaughan heard about his remark, she was apparently not upset enough to say anything publicly, and Gillespie remained magnanimous when Leonard Feather gave him the chance to respond by asking for a comment on Davis's fusion music. "Whether it'll last, what he's doing now, that's not up to me to judge," he said. "Time alone judges that, so I just sit here and wait until – well, if he's hooked that far out in front, wait for time to catch up with it ... The guy's a master, so I wouldn't come out and say that I don't like what he's doing now." And then he slyly added, "Besides it would be out of line. Could the King of England criticize the King of France?"[26]

Davis's refusal to appear at the Newport Festival in what would have been his first concert date in months set in motion some speculation about whether or not the fee was the real issue, as he had claimed. Whitney Balliett, in his review of the festival for the *New Yorker*, suggested that "the real reason may have been fear, for he has played little in recent months, and a trumpeter's chops, if not used, can deteriorate in a week."[27] But Davis had spent several hours in the recording studio in the weeks leading up to the festival. The studio work was planned partly as preparation for his return to performing, both to restore his embouchure and to assemble a new band. Rather than the embouchure, it was probably the failure to fashion a working unit from the passing parade in the studio that kept him off the Carnegie Hall stage.

He kept trying. On 7 July, just three days after he was to have played at the festival, he led another group into the recording studios. The personnel remains unknown, and the only music released from the session came out on a 45-rpm single for the teenage market. The scant details are as follows:

Miles Davis Ensemble: Molester
Miles Davis, el tpt; rest of personnel similar to *Ife*. New York, 7 July 1972
Molester, part 1; part 2
(Columbia 4-45709 [45 rpm])

The release of *Molester* on 45 rpm inaugurates a set of releases of Davis's music for the pop market, probably as Columbia's response to Davis's charges that it was not marketing his music properly. In the instances to come, the 45-rpm release is usually a slice of music from an LP currently in preparation and can safely be ignored in favor of the longer LP versions in charting Davis's music. *Molester* so far has shown up exclusively on the 45-rpm release.

Its title may ironically commemorate Davis's latest run-in with the police. Just two days after he recorded it, he was arrested and charged with "unlawful imprisonment and menacing" of a woman named Lita Merker at his house. The woman accused Davis of shouting insults at her and preventing her from leaving. The arresting officer reported no evidence of assault. Davis pleaded not guilty, and the case was adjourned to 22 August.[28] Privately, Davis maintained that the incident started as an argument between his girl friend and Merker, whom he had known as a neighbor for several years, and that it ended out of court with apologies all round.

By September, he had gathered more players for his working band and returned to the studio with them. Carlos Garnett was probably the reed player at this recording date, but he is not heard on the music that has been issued so far. With Davis playing keyboards more than trumpet, the recording ensemble became a rhythm band, and they produced, in *Rated X*, one of Davis's most striking percussion pieces. The details are as follows:

Miles Davis Ensemble: Get Up with It
Miles Davis, org (on *Rated X*), el tpt, el pno (on *Billy Preston*); Cedric Lawson, el pno (on *Rated X*), org (on *Billy Preston*); Reggie Lucas, gtr; Khalil Balak-rishna, sitar; Michael Henderson, b; Al Foster, dms; Badal Roy, tabla; James Mtume Foreman, perc. New York, September 1972
Rated X; Billy Preston
(both on Columbia C 33237 [1974])

Billy Preston, dedicated to the veteran soul musician who had been imported by the Beatles to lend some weight to their final album, *Let It Be*, belongs to the genre of *On the Corner*, with layers of wah-wah modulations from the trumpet, guitar, and organ reverberating through the hefty rhythmic bottom.

Rated X, however, bursts out of the confines of Davis's current conception. It defies category – certainly not jazz by any known standard, and at least as far removed from soul-funk-rock pop music, yet made from components of both. Davis pits himself on the organ against the bumptious rhythm band. He plays sustained, two-fisted chords that sound like a soap opera soundtrack in the unaccompanied opening. Then the rhythm starts fretting beneath him. Whenever the rhythm threatens to become the focal point it is stopped abruptly; it is cut off for a few seconds at a time, irregularly, isolating the awful drone of the organ. The mood is strangely menacing, with the rhythm band boogying like dancers at a high school sock hop while the Prince of Darkness looms over them like the grim reaper. It is taut, unpleasant music, and it could do nothing to revive the interest of jazz fans in what Davis was pursuing, but it is also a simple, audacious concept with great integrity and power. And it is Davis's most conspicuous success in adapting the values of European avant-garde composers, especially Karlheinz Stockhausen.

Davis occasionally cited Stockhausen in his terse and mostly unenlightening comments to interviewers seeking an explanation for his music, and in 1980 he was joined by the German composer in Columbia's recording studios in a collaboration that is still unissued. The best information on the unlikely pairing, and on the role of a young English cellist-composer named Paul Buckmaster, who also joined them on the 1980 studio date, comes from Ian Carr in *Miles Davis: A Critical Biography*. According to Carr, Davis first met Buckmaster on his English tour in 1969, when he was played a tape of a Buckmaster composition featuring bass and drums distorted electronically to create moods. "Definitely space music," Buckmaster told Carr. Davis was so impressed that he kept up his sporadic acquaintance on subsequent tours. In 1972, Davis summoned him by phone to New York in order to work on some new music. Buckmaster stayed with Davis for about six weeks in May and June, when Davis was working on the music for *On the Corner*, and he was present in the studio when that music was recorded. As Carr puts it, "It is ironical that after his discussions with Paul Buckmaster, and after his immersion in the music of Stockhausen, Miles should have produced an album so alien to the European tradition."[29] But Buckmaster's influence, if not immediate, became clearer with the recording of *Rated X* and soon began to show up in many smaller ways.

Carr reports that Buckmaster spent hours during his stay at Davis's practicing Bach's cello suites, often under the critical gaze of his host. Soon Bach's name also began to crop up in Davis's conversation, as in his description of unconventional melodic organization for Sy Johnson. "I think it's time people changed where they put the melody," he said. "The melody can be in the bass, or a drum sound, or just a sound. I may write something around a bass line. I may write something around a rhythm ... I always place the rhythm so it can be played three or four different ways. It's always three rhythms within one, and you can get some other ones in there too." And then he looked quizzically at Johnson, a well-schooled composer in his own right, and asked, "Do you know what I mean? It's almost like Bach. You know how Bach wrote."[30]

Buckmaster brought Davis a recording of Stockhausen's *Mixtur* and *Telemusik*, Carr says, and for the next days Davis's house reverberated with the strains of Stockhausen's electronic recomposition of symphonic orchestrations. Davis also bought several cassettes of Stockhausen's music to play in his Lamborghini.

The effect of Davis's study of Stockhausen could not be repressed for long. He passed along some of the cassettes to Gil Evans, as he had Rodrigo's *Concierto* and his other enthusiasms over the years. For Davis, the discovery of Stockhausen and the avant-garde European composers must have seemed like a vindication of the post-production composing he had been doing with Teo Macero for at least four years, and also of the reorganization of conventional musical values — harmonically, melodically, and now rhythmically — that had attracted him ever since the days of his 1949 nonet. *Rated X*, Davis's own "space music," shows Stockhausen's influence compositionally, but his influence would soon show, more tangentially, in Davis's concert format as well.

On 10 September, just a few days after the recording of *Billy Preston* and *Rated X*, Davis led his working band onstage at the Ann Arbor Blues and Jazz Festival in Michigan. "Miles Davis was to end the festival, but instead he began the night's festivities," Bill Smith wrote in a *Coda* photostory. "ZAAAPPPP ... just like that. Dressed in his finest silks and satins, the Prince of Darkness simply overpowered everything. Incredible." Smith then posed a question that other members of the audience were thinking: "Why does it sound so crappy on his last three records?"[31]

The records Smith refers to are *At Fillmore*, *Live-Evil*, and *On the Corner*. Certainly one reason they seemed less satisfying to most fans than Davis's live performances was because they lacked the physical presence of Davis, a charismatic performer now no less than in his tailored days of ballad musings. Ralph J. Gleason offered a novel theory to account for the discrepancy. "The kind of music Miles Davis plays now," he contended, "stretches the capability of stereo to its limit and finds it failing. There is more sound here than stereo can handle on record ... I have heard Miles's band ... and the effect was overwhelming. So overwhelming that in retrospect the stereo records he has made sound pallid by comparison, even granting the ordinary distance between live and recorded performances."[32] The difference in feeling between his records and his performances seemed to mark another reversal from the late 1950s and early 1960s, when Davis seemed sometimes to save the band's peaks of originality for the studio, in recordings such as *Milestones* and *Kind of Blue*, while he continued to play the well-worn repertoire – *Round Midnight*, *Bye Bye Blackbird*, *Four*, and the rest – on their nightly round of club dates.

Dave Liebman, who was gaining recognition as a jazz saxophonist in work he was doing outside Davis's band, became something of an apologist for Davis with members of the jazz audience. "This band is a combination of almost all the free elements that have been used in the last ten years, the avant garde elements of music [which are] the free association of ideas, and the thing that rock has brought to the music which is the steady vamp bassline or rhythm to work off of," he told Gene Perla. "It's a combination of those two things with all the other elements taken out here and there from jazz: the use of lyricism, straight ahead – like Miles will play a really pretty melody once in a while, quiet everybody down, and it'll be just him playing alone sometimes. It seems to me that he's using all the things he's gone through in little packages almost." He saw Davis less as a leader in the time-honored sense than as a spontaneous composer. "It's like a concerto where you have your adagio and allegro sections," he continued. "Now he's manipulating the controls in a way more than he did when he was playing the straight jazz thing. It's like one long piece or suite every time we play. Within it there is always the texture of drums, then the quiet latin thing, then the psychedelic thing. It goes through maybe five, six or seven moods."[33] Again, the convergence of Davis's goals with avant-garde European composition becomes clear, but transformed into a jazz-derived format in which composition is spontaneous and improvised.

Little of the live vitality of Davis's band was preserved in the recording, later in the month, of a Philharmonic Hall concert. The four-sided Columbia release relied less heavily on extensive editing and fanciful remixing than other recent releases of live performances, but the new band members were undeniably less talented jazz players than their predecessors on the *Fillmore* and *Live-Evil* performances, and the new LP did little or nothing to assuage jazz listeners, who again found themselves greeted by Corky McCoy's caricatures on the package. The details are as follows:

Miles Davis Nine: In Concert
Miles Davis, tpt, probably org; Carlos Garnett, ss; Cedric Lawson, el
keyboards, synthesizer; Reggie Lucas, el gtr; Khalil Balakrishna, sitar; Michael
Henderson, b; Al Foster, dms; Badal Roy, tabla; James Mtume Foreman, perc.
Philharmonic Hall, New York, 29 September 1972
side 1 [medley includes *Rated X*]; side 2 [medley includes *Black Satin*]; side 3;
side 4
(all on *In Concert*, Columbia KG 32092)

The reviewer for *Coda* concluded: "*In Concert* exudes more vitality on
any one of its four sides than the sapless *On the Corner* could muster in
any one bar ... Its vitality is probably a direct result of Miles Davis's
continuous participation in the music, although it may also be
connected to the fact that there are fewer drummers this time."

Throughout its hour and a half playing time, there are several
attractive moments. Side 1 closes with a lush ballad by Davis and
Garnett; side 2 is dominated by *Black Satin*, from the previous LP,
exploited here for its interesting melody, in a context where melody is
rare. Side 4 includes a funereal blues by Davis over a one-bar motif
carried by the bass and organ.

Much of the rest seems unexceptional. On side 3, Henderson repeats
three notes on his bass with scarcely a variation for almost fifteen
minutes, which is, as the *Coda* reviewer notes, "pure torpor." Side 1
meanders through multiple moods and tempos so rapidly that none of
them makes a point. Side 4 includes a hard rock number featuring
Reggie Lucas that depersonalizes Hendrix's sound woefully. "Almost
everything sounds like something that Miles has recorded before," one
reviewer said, "but little of it is identifiable and its parts seem more or
less interchangeable."

John Toner, reviewing the LP in *Jazz and Blues Journal*, gloomily
concluded of Davis: "He has always consciously attempted to simplify
the lines of his music to allow freedom of expression, but this time he
has created a prison rather than open musical spaces. Davis has got
nothing but the cluttered and static form which he once professed to
hate so much." And Scott Yanow, in *Record Review*, wrote: "Up until
1972, it could be truthfully stated that every Miles Davis album was
worth owning. *On the Corner* and *Live at the Philharmonic* are
exceptions."[34]

Davis continued touring with his new band in October, playing at
Paul's Mall in Boston and at a club in Denver. In between, he was

scheduled to play a concert at Painters Mill Theater, but the concert was cancelled, *Down Beat* reported, due to lack of advance ticket sales.[35]

In the early morning hours of 21 October, after returning to New York from his concert in Denver, Davis ran his Lamborghini into a concrete island and broke both his ankles. "I was cruising, y'know, but I was still up from that gig in Denver," he told Michael Watts. "I musta hypnotized myself 'cos I went right up fast ... I was only doing about thirty miles an hour. I ran up on an island. I was just tired." During the long layoff while his ankles were encased in casts, Davis tried to deal lightly with the accident. "I'm all right," he told one reporter. "I'll just have to stop buying those little cars."[36] And to another he said, "I fucked the car up, but it wasn't a mess. I got a new one. A Ferrari."[37] He was immobilized for two and a half months, and when he returned to playing he still had to hoist himself around on crutches with the ankles swathed in walking casts. More serious in the long run were the strain that the casts placed on his deteriorating hip joint and the debilitating effect on his general health of the enforced inactivity.

While he was sitting idle, the jazz periodicals published their year-end poll results for 1972, and Davis, coming off a year in which he was largely inactive in the first four months and completely inactive in the last two, with only a controversial LP and concerts by an untried band in between, fared poorly. The *Down Beat* poll of international critics placed his band fourth, after the Dixieland collective called the World's Greatest Jazz Band, Ornette Coleman, and the Modern Jazz Quartet. *Down Beat*'s readers' poll showed his band seventh; the top three places went to bands spawned by Davis's fusion experiments of 1969–70: Weather Report, John McLaughlin's Mahavishnu, and Chick Corea, and the next three were the MJQ, McCoy Tyner, and the World's Greatest Jazz Band. *On the Corner* was left off all the lists of new albums, although *Jazz Journal* listed two Prestige twofers of Davis's 1954–6 music (seventh and eighth) among the best reissues. Most telling was his fall from grace among the trumpeters, possibly his worst showing in twenty-five years. The *Down Beat* critics placed him fifth, after Dizzy Gillespie, Clark Terry, Don Cherry, and Roy Eldridge; the *Down Beat* readers made him a distant second behind Freddie Hubbard.

The *Down Beat* editorial accompanying the readers' poll results noted Davis's poor showing and commented: "It's Miles who opened the door for most of these younger players [who supplanted him]." If that was intended to console Davis by putting him in the role of patriarch, Davis soon showed that he was feeling anything but patriarchal toward his former protégés. In interviews, he unloaded venomous views. Of Hubbard, his replacement not only in the top spot in the readers' poll but also at Newport in New York, he said, "He don't have no ideas and no talent. All he does is run up and down the scales. I used to teach Freddie ... Man, he doesn't have any imagination. If you don't have no imagination, then you don't have no talent, right?"[38] Of Weather Report, he concluded, simply, "Foggy. It's foggy." Wayne Shorter, so long his right-hand man, was blasted gratuitously for what seemed to be sexual rather than musical misdemeanors. "He fell in love, man," Davis told Jimmy Saunders in *Playboy*. "He started playing pretty, syrupy music. Ain't no fire there no more ... You can't come, then fight or play. You can't do it. *I* don't. When I get ready to come, I come [laughs]. But I do not come and play." Of Josef Zawinul, who had complained that his contribution to Davis's early fusion music remained largely unacknowledged, Davis said, "Zawinul is like Sly and Mingus. They write things and they fall in love with them. You know what I mean? I don't write things for myself. I write for my band. When you write things for yourself, your ego takes over."[39] Herbie Hancock, who remained in closer contact with Davis than most of the others, almost escaped Davis's venom altogther. "Herbie tries to be too intellectual," Davis told Gregg Hall for *Down Beat*. "He needs to be edited." And then he added, "But he's the only one out there."[40]

The younger players were not the only ones to feel Davis's bitter mood. He had unloaded on Dizzy Gillespie and Sarah Vaughan in his defence of his cancellation at Newport, and now he maligned Max Roach, whom he would describe a few years later as "my best friend." "When I was with Bird," he told Michael Watts, "Fats Navarro used to say I played too fast all the time, but I couldn't swing with Max Roach 'cos he couldn't swing."[41] As an attempt to revise the history of bebop, the comment is simply ludicrous.

It was probably during the enforced idleness following his accident that Davis recorded *Red China Blues*, one of the anomalies of his recorded works. A conventional down-home blues gussied up with riffs by a brass section, *Red China Blues* is devoid of the imprint of Davis. It appears to be an attempt to break into the middle-of-the-road music market served by FM-radio. The details are as follows:

Miles Davis Ensemble: Get Up with It
Miles Davis, el tpt; unidentified brass section arranged by Wade Marcus; Wally Chambers, harmonica; Cornell Dupree, gtr; Michael Henderson, b; Al Foster,

Bernard Purdee, dms; James Mtume Foreman, congas; rhythm arranged by
Billy Jackson. New York, possibly early 1973
Red China Blues
(on Columbia c 33238)
The date is controversial; Priestley lists it as "possibly January 1973," Ruppli
as "June 1974." An excerpt was released on 45 rpm (3-10110) backed by an
excerpt from *Maiysha* (recorded 19 June 1974).

The dominant sound comes from the amplified harmonica; Davis
contributes only a few notes, mixed into the background. Horace Silver,
on hearing the piece in a blindfold test with Leonard Feather, simply
said, "It ain't my particular cup of tea, to tell the truth. I wouldn't
venture forth to buy it. I doubt if it was given to me that I'd play it." So
alien was its sound from anything Silver recognized that he mistakenly
took it to be part of Davis's new direction, and he was willing to be
charitable under the circumstances: "We all have to open our minds,
stretch forth, take chances and venture out musically to try to arrive at
something new and different, and he's doing it – and I give him credit for
that."[42] But *Red China Blues* stands apart from Davis's music in this
period or any other. Far from being venturesome or new or different, it is
just a blatant attempt to win friends, something Davis otherwise never
felt impelled to do in his music. It lacks all conviction.

In January 1973, Davis re-formed his band with Dave Liebman on
reeds and flutes for a new round of concerts. The reviews were
devastating. In Montreal on 24 January, John Orysik called it "a most
unusual concert": "The percussion section, Mtume in particular, was
the only highlight. Miles distorted everything he played and I couldn't
hear Dave Liebman for the overamplification of the other instruments.
Most distressing to hear Miles, I wish I'd stayed home."[43] The concert
was sold out, and so were two concerts on 28 January at the Guthrie
Theatre in Minneapolis, but the reviews from Minneapolis were even
worse. "The critics' views were unanimous – Davis stunk up the joint!"
Ron Johnson reported in *Coda*. "The sound was loud, almost cacophony, and there were just very few occasional approaches to jazz
music. It was probably the worst jazz concert in Guthrie history."[44]

On returning to New York, Davis took his band into the recording
studio for rehearsals, with producers and engineers present and tape
running. They spent all day on 13 February in the studio and probably
other days around the same time, but so far none of the music has been
issued. Dave Liebman described the process: "We go into the recording

studio there's no, like, take one. Light goes on, they miss it [the beginning], they miss it. [Davis] is aware of the light, but it's, you know, no cutting, no outtakes, nothing like that. Just play. Rehearse on tape." The extra hours of exposure to one another were absolutely crucial to the band members because of the way Davis was letting the music evolve. "I mean there *are* some melodies," Liebman confessed, "and they're made up on the gig and after a few nights we play the same thing and I say, 'All right, that's a new melody, I got to get something that goes with it.' It's totally improvised and loose."[45]

Davis again ran afoul of the law. He was arrested early in the morning of 23 February and charged with possession of cocaine and a .25-caliber automatic pistol. Davis and an unidentified woman were apparently trying to arouse someone in his house to let them in when neighbors called the police to investigate the commotion. Police found a purse thrown behind a bush containing three packets of cocaine and the loaded pistol. Davis spent the night in jail and was charged in the morning. On 1 March, he was fined $1,000 for possession of a deadly weapon, but the cocaine charge was dropped for insufficient evidence.

After all the run-ins, several offices of the New York Police Department had files on Davis. His home address and his automobile license plates appeared on the police blotter often enough that few narcotics officers or patrolmen needed special instructions on receiving a late-night complaint.

Davis's Ferrari was temporarily inactive because of the walking casts he wore, but otherwise his driving attracted police attention regularly. "I did that shit once in front of a brother; I did one of those things that only a Ferrari can do," Davis told David Breskin. "He stopped me and said, 'God*damn*, Miles, why do you do that shit?' I said, 'What would *you* do if you had this motherfucker?' And he said, 'Okay, go ahead.'"

"The white cops, they all know me by now," he added. "Mother-fuckers say, 'Oh, that's just *him.*'"[46] On their house calls, the police entered the dim sanctum of the brownstone to find the once-stylish decor going to seed. Davis admitted three interviewers – Harriet Choice, Sy Johnson, and Michael Watts – to his home, and all of them described the music blaring from the speaker system, television sets flickering in dark corners, and pieces of the expensive wardrobe strewn about. He complained to the interviewers that he felt isolated and alone – "Dizzy asks me to teach him. I say, 'Yeah, come by' ... And he don't come by" – but he seemed to be surrounded by people and activity. His gofers, male or female, emerged at the first hoarse shout, on call night and day to give him a rubdown or run an errand. He spent hours on the telephone, calling his sister and his acquaintances on the slightest pretext, often playing them tapes by long distance. Once he carried a tape to Sly Stone's apartment that he thought Stone should hear. "I took a gun over there one day and put it right to his head," Davis told Gregg Hall. "I said, 'Man, sit down, we *will* listen to this!'" And then he laughed and added, "Of course there were no bullets in it."[47]

Davis's life seemed more orderly when he was on the road, ensconced in hotel suites. He made another personnel change in his band for a pair of concerts in western Canada, in Edmonton on 29 March and Calgary on 1 April 1973. He replaced Cedric Lawson on keyboards with Lonnie Liston Smith, who had played keyboards for him on the recording of *Ife* almost a year before, but instead of transporting the Fender-Rhodes electric piano, Davis took along a Yamaha organ for Liston to play. The rest of the band remained intact, with Liebman, Reggie Lucas, Balakrishna, Henderson, Foster, Mtume, and Badal Roy.

It was a rare occurrence for Davis's concerts during this period to find a sympathetic reviewer, but *Coda* magazine assigned the task to Eugene Chadbourne, the free-form guitarist then based in Calgary. Chadbourne approached Davis's new music with an open mind, much as he approached his own spontaneous performances, and filed a report far removed from the perfunctory dismissal accorded to Davis by most reviewers at the time. His account is one of the few that capture in prose the elements that Davis was unabashedly promulgating.[48]

Chadbourne duly noted the disaffection of most of the audience, from Davis's older fans – one of whom spent the intermission yelling, "Where's Dizzy?" – to the rock fans who did not return after intermission. But Chadbourne waxed enthusiastically about the percussive elements that were driving others away. "As far as percussion sections go," he said, "this is IT. The blending of congas and tablas, with Al Foster's rough-and-ready, runaround drumming in back of it, has to be one of the most inspiring sound arrangements Miles has come up with ... Everything is rhythm! The electric guitar chops away, often sounding like an African log drum. Henderson's bass work is percussive, often resembling the sound of a wet finger rubbed against the top of a conga drum. The organ fills up any spaces in the music like hot, melted wax poured onto cheesecloth. The music has been called amelodic, and it might be – but somehow you find yourself humming along to it. Sound, pure sound and sensation, are the main components." He compared Davis as an innovator with the Art Ensemble of Chicago and Ornette

Coleman, noting that his music now had similar "aspects," but he added that "it is still Miles' thing, an approach to sound that no one has attempted before."

Noting that Liebman seemed to have difficulty finding space for himself in the ensemble, as other critics would also note, Chadbourne sought an explanation from Liebman. "You don't get the same feedback, with the rhythm responding to everything you do," Liebman told him. "You are sort of playing *over* it, almost beside the point. Like a vocalist singing over a bunch of horns. It's really a pattern behind you." Chadbourne contrasted Liebman's and Davis's voices in the ensemble this way: "Whenever Miles played, the music was not a pattern at all – there was response, encouragement from the group, and small, subtle examples of give-and-take. But with Liebman – nothing. His winding, sonorous sax warbled over a glass wall." Chadbourne's own explanation for the problems Davis's reedmen were having was that "this music may be so personal to Miles that no one else can find his own voice in it."

Davis himself seemed to be enjoying the performance immensely, notwithstanding the fetters that remained from his automobile accident more than five months earlier. Chadbourne described him "hobbling around on a walking cast with two shiny metal crutches, sitting on a high black stool, his feet surrounded with mute, wah-wah pedal, a hundred different wires ... Constantly signalling, conducting, cueing, waving his crutches around like grotesque batons."

Chadbourne also offered an insight into the critical and popular outrage that so often greeted Davis's music. "If you don't like Miles," he said, "you'll hate this new music, because his career can be summed up as a struggle to tone down his arrogance into terms an audience can feel comfortable with. His new music is pure arrogance. It's like coming home and finding Miles there, his fancy feet up on your favorite chair."

Lonnie Liston Smith's tenure with Davis's working band began and ended with this brief western tour. Although he was a veteran member of bands such as Art Blakey's and Rahsaan Roland Kirk's, Smith had trouble fitting into Davis's ensemble. At the concerts, Chadbourne noted, "Several times Miles, perhaps dissatisfied at the sound of the organ, limped over to the instrument to demonstrate what he wanted." Smith's problems were not unexpected, because he was, in effect, learning to play his instrument on the bandstand. When Davis called to offer him the job, Smith assumed that he would be playing electric piano. "[I] haven't played the organ since college," he told Chadbourne, in an interview published in *Coda* nine months after the concert, "and there is a wah-wah pedal, and this thing, it isn't exactly a moog but it's like one, and I've never used any of that stuff either. So it's all new."

Smith's job was made all the more difficult because Davis's ideas about what he wanted from the organ, as well as from the electric piano, were so specific by now that only Davis himself could supply them. After trying Smith, Davis stopped carrying a keyboard player in the band, and he spent as much of his performances playing keyboards as trumpet.

Smith remained undaunted. "It's a gas playing with Miles," he said. "The first thing I realized was, he's really serious about this stuff! That knocked me out, the way he's really into it. I heard him on that wah-wah pedal doing some amazing things, and I thought, well, I'll try that too. We can still all learn from Miles, that's what I mean. He's a master. Other people are growing – we are all growing – we'll be the Tranes and the Birds and the Miles of the future, but he's it right now."[49] A few years later, Gregg Hall passed along some of Smith's flattering remarks to Davis, and Davis said, "Oh yeah, I taught him a lot of shit."[50]

Smith left the band at the same time as the exotic percussionists Balakrishna and Roy, and Davis added a rhythm guitarist, Pete Cosey, to the band. Cosey, a stolid, Buddha-like figure, sat almost motionless on the stage during Davis's performances for the next two years, strumming out chords that melded into the rhythmic bottom of the music. The percussion elements grew even denser.

Davis had been playing keyboard instruments in the recording studio for some time and had occasionally played them in performances even when he carried a keyboard player in the band. Now, he became the band's only keyboard player. "Well, I only play to get the idea how it's supposed to go but it always turns out that my piano playing – I hate that word 'better' but it brings out the band, and doesn't clutter too much either," he told Michael Watts. "When I play piano in my band, they swing. When my piano player plays they swing sometimes but they don't swing all the time. I don't worry about anything 'cos I have Reggie [Lucas], y'know, the rhythm swings, but you have to watch a musician and anticipate it."[51] About his organ playing, he was more modest. "I can't play it the way I want it," he told Sy Johnson. "I know guys who can show their technique and all that stuff. I just play it for Dave [Liebman, when he is soloing] and difficult little sounds and shit. Reggie can play the same things [on guitar] that I can play. I taught him to make the same sounds."[52]

Davis's critics were aware of his limitations as an organist. "About the best thing that one can say about Miles's organ playing is that sometimes it works out like a delicate Japanese wash," Mark Zanger commented. "At its worst it sounds like daytime TV. Miles on organ reveals what most great instrumentalists reveal on secondary instruments: intellectual concepts stripped of the technique that would grab one emotionally."[53]

The attention to keyboards shifted Davis's attention even further from the trumpet, which he had been playing much less in concerts and on recordings both in the sense that he used it less frequently and that when he did use it he played very few notes. Woody Shaw, a forceful young trumpeter just reaching maturity as a jazz soloist in the early 1970s, speculated: "He's a little older now, and I guess he's sort of tired of blowing his lips away, which you do on trumpet."[54] Others, Davis among them, saw the sparse trumpet calls as a response to the "pure sound and sensation" aesthetic of his music. Charles Fox commented that Davis's "cluster of notes ... struck the ear like separate images, the conception pointilliste instead of linear."[55] Liebman agreed that Davis's parsimony was the best method for coping with the rhythms. "Using short rhythms, playing one note, dit-dit, and letting them [the rhythm section] have it," Liebman explained, was one of the lessons he was learning from Davis. "When the rhythm section is happening, he hardly plays. He'll play the least and yet most. Also, it's not quite stage presence, but it's a way of drawing the powers that are up there and dispersing them ... It's a much more compositional thing than I had thought of. Where is it going? It's not just going to the end of the tune because there's no such thing as that any more."[56]

The first public appearances of the reorganized band took place in California. They played in Los Angeles at the Dorothy Chandler Pavilion as part of a week-long program sponsored by Columbia Records to promote the breaking down of barriers between musical categories. Clive Davis was behind it, and his enthusiasm for a project so close to Miles Davis's expressed wish suggests again that the two men were listening to one another. Columbia assembled its artists from different genres in threes for the concerts, with the profits turned over to charity. The night before Davis appeared, McLaughlin's Mahavishnu Orchestra had shared the stage with Loudon Wainwright III, a folk-cum-novelty singer, and Anthony Newman, from classical music. Davis's band appeared alongside Earth, Wind and Fire, a rock band, and Ramsey Lewis, the pianist.

Davis's California tour also included concerts at the Santa Monica Auditorium and back in Los Angeles at the Shrine Auditorium, with Nina Simone sharing the bill. A ten-minute segment of one of these concerts was filmed for a television–FM radio simulcast on a public network series called "Midnight Special." The film clip opens abruptly with a rollicking rhythm sequence and follows the musicians in their detached machinations through two mood changes as the concert ends. Compared with conventional clips in the series, Davis's band seem to be engrossed in surrealistic music-making.

Davis spent much of the second half of 1973 playing in Europe on two separate tours, his first since October 1971 because of his health. Although he had resumed touring, he still suffered from various ailments. He wheezed slightly from the nodes on his larynx which had grown back – they had probably never been completely removed – since the operation that inadvertently altered his voice in 1956; he suffered from stomach aches and occasional vomiting from an ulcer, which was especially aggravated by liquor; and he still walked stiffly because of the arthritic hip, which had grown much more painful after the strain of wearing casts on his ankles.

The first tour, in July, took him on a round of jazz festivals in Pescara and Verona, Italy, and Montreux, Switzerland, and to London for a concert at the Rainbow. Ron Brown, reviewing the London concert for *Jazz Journal*, saw some advances in the way Davis had unified his young band: "He's managed to whip his line-up ... into an exciting, swirling rhythmic unit, as recognizable as a Miles Davis 'sound' as were the quintets with Coltrane and Shorter." But Brown, like most other reviewers, regretted Davis's almost complete withdrawal from soloing. "The amazing and almost heart-breaking crunch lies in the fact that Miles himself hardly plays at all," he said. "He spits a strangled bleep into the action every couple of minutes, and we're left with an efficient backdrop with nothing to back up." The result, he said, was "a Miles Davis concert that had everything but a substantial helping of Miles Davis."[57]

Before returning to Europe in the fall, Davis and his band again spent several hours in the recording studios. On at least one of these sessions, Davis did not show up at all. After everyone else was assembled and set up, ready to play, he phoned Teo Macero to tell him he would not be coming, and Macero got Davis's permission to tape some music by the sidemen, with Liebman on flute. Liebman began leading the band through something he calls *Slow Vamp* when Macero interrupted them with the message, "Miles says play a lot. Do something." He had apparently been listening on the telephone from the control booth and decided to let the band add more hours to Columbia's huge accumulation of his music, even in his absence. Asked by a reporter whether he had played well on the occasion, Liebman said, "It was *out*, y'know, but I don't know. Miles got it. I'll hear it. It was out. It could be good, it may have come out great. I don't know."[58] So far nothing has been released under the title *Slow Vamp*, and none of Davis's releases credits Liebman as composer, but parts of the session may turn up spliced into other titles – may already have turned up – in the cut-and-paste process.

Liebman's flute is heard fairly prominently on a track called *Calypso Frelimo*, which fills one side of the *Get Up with It* LP almost to overflowing. At thirty-two minutes, it runs very close to the limits of microgroove technology. The details are as follows:

Miles Davis Ensemble: Get Up with It
Miles Davis, tpt, org, pno; Dave Liebman, flt; John Stobblefield, ss; Pete Cosey, Reggie Lucas, gtr; Michael Henderson, b; Al Foster, dms; James Mtume Foreman, conga. New York, possibly September 1973
Calypso Frelimo
(on Columbia C 33238)
Two sides of a 45-rpm single (4-45946), *Big Fun* and *Holly-Wood*, were recorded in September 1973, possibly at the same sessions as *Calypso Frelimo*; the excerpt *Big Fun* is not related to the music on the LP *Big Fun* (Columbia PG 32866), although both were released in early 1974.

Calypso Frelimo is divided into three parts. It opens as a frantic exercise for the rhythm team, with Davis on electric trumpet, Liebman on flute, Davis again, and Stobblefield on soprano saxophone taking turns playing above the wall of rhythm. Then the rhythm stops abruptly after Stobblefield's contribution (the only time he is heard) and resolves into an eerie stasis, the only motion at the beginning supplied by a recurring bass riff; as the rhythm players re-enter one by one, Liebman's flute and Davis's trumpet again take turns playing above them. Then the rhythm rises again, making a long crescendo back to the frantic pace of the opening. The only unifying element is a two-bar calypso phrase stated by Davis on organ near the beginning of each of the three parts and heard at unpredictable intervals throughout. Davis's organ and trumpet overlap in several places, indicating overdubbing, and the whole piece was probably composed in the editing room.

As a composition, *Calypso Frelimo* simply seems disjointed. The calypso phrase is too sporadic to give the listener a focal point, and probably too insignificant for that in such a long exposition. Yet Davis apparently pinned his hopes on this track making a breakthrough. "My next thing, *Calypso*, will set a new direction," he told Gregg Hall in 1974. "The entire record will be one track."[59] He changed his mind, or was talked into changing it, about filling both sides of an LP with it – surely he was not considering filling four sides with it, although most of his LPs were now twofers – and even as an overlong single side its rudimentary melody and one-chord harmony are spread thin.

The return trip to Europe lasted three weeks and sent Davis and his band on a taxing itinerary to Malmo (24 October), Stockholm (27), Copenhagen (29), Berlin (1 November), Bologna (10), and Paris (15), with two concerts in many of the cities. Davis was in excruciating pain from his hip, and it was probably near the beginning of this tour, perhaps in Malmo or Stockholm, that he received an injection of morphine to kill the pain. Davis told Cheryl McCall: "A doctor told me in Sweden – *he shot me right in the leg* – he said I know how many girls want to come over here and give you a *shot*. I said fuck that if I don't feel better. He said tomorrow you'll feel better, or the next day."[60] Davis continued the tour feeling more comfortable than he had for a long time, but he began to rely on more injections to keep going. The pain-relieving benefit of morphine exacts a well-known price from the user, not only because it induces a dependency, as do all products of the poppy seed, but also because it dulls the sensation of pain without altering the cause of the pain in any way. When Davis collapsed in 1975, he blamed the morphine for preventing him from realizing how far his health had declined.

The year-end poll results for 1973 again revealed that Davis was losing his grip on the segment of the audience that bothered to vote. *Down Beat*'s critics' poll named Dizzy Gillespie top trumpeter and Jon Faddis, a 20-year-old very much in Gillespie's mold, top new trumpeter. The readers' poll named Freddie Hubbard, for the second year in a row, ahead of Davis. For Davis, that result may have seemed especially ominous because Columbia had just signed Hubbard to a long-term contract. Hubbard certainly saw it that way and so, according to him, did Columbia's executives. "When I first went there in 1973," Hubbard told Steve Bloom, "this is what they told me: 'We're gonna make you the number one trumpet player at Columbia because Miles isn't playing.'"[61] Hubbard made eight albums for Columbia in the next seven years and then moved to Fantasy Records.

If Davis felt any pressure from Columbia's hiring of Hubbard or his poor notices, he did nothing to alter the course of his music or his influences. He listened to Stockhausen, but more often he listened to black pop performers. Harriet Choice entered his inner sanctum for an interview and spent most of her time studying the decor – "Miles' records, plaques, art, trinkets, various musical instruments, and huge plastic plants" – while Davis wailed away on a drum set to a loud James Brown tape that repeated over and over again. Davis wore a black patch over his eye but the co-habitants of his house, two young women named Loretta and Ruby, assured Choice that there was nothing wrong with his eye. "He just likes to wear the patch sometimes. He's got a bunch of different ones," Ruby shouted over the din of the drums.[62]

The influence of Stockhausen, as Davis finally assimilated it, showed more in his approach than in his technique or composing. Certainly Stockhausen's influence is felt more directly in the work of younger jazz musicians, especially Anthony Braxton and the later work of Keith Jarrett. For Davis, two years older than Stockhausen, the German composer's example seems mainly to have reinforced his conviction that conventional form – the beginning, middle, and end prescribed by Aristotle – is an artificial limitation. Stockhausen has expounded a theory of "process compositions," the basic notion that "what one hears in music is only an excerpt, what I call a window, in an unlimited time." He derided conventional form, the converse of process composition, in an interview with John Diliberto: "Though sometimes a composer is pounding on the table like Beethoven at the beginning of the *Fifth Symphony* and gives the impression of 'Now I start,' or when they hit the last two chords five times or more to say, 'Now I really stop, are you aware of this?,' still this is fake because he could have started before and he could've gone on if he had wanted to because the basic truth in every spirit is that there is nothing like limited time. To present a work of art with a particular beginning and end, and to reinforce the impression is only an illusion. It is one proposition of an excerpt of time, the timeless time."[63]

Davis shared that basic concept and had incorporated it years earlier into records that splice tapes made months or even years apart and concert performances that move imperceptibly from one musical nonsequitur to another. Encouraged by Stockhausen's example, he now declared: "I'm through with playing from eight bars to eight bars. I always write in a circle. I never end a song. It just keeps going. The public likes starts, confusions, and happy endings."[64] But the elements of their music could hardly have less in common. For Stockhausen they are symphonic components filtered through acoustic devices, and 'found' sounds such as short-wave bands. For Davis they are the trappings of black pop music, arranged densely and amplified deafeningly.

"You know what he listens to at home, man?" Liebman asked an interviewer. "You think he listens to what those traditionalists always hounding him to listen to, classical, even *jazz*? Shit, he's into the same kind of stuff guys our age are into – rock and roll, man, whatever, Sly, James Brown, Hendrix, *music*, man. He absorbs what is around. He *is* what's happening."[65]

Davis seemed inclined to agree. "I'm 48 but so what?" he told Jimmy Saunders. "Am I supposed to stop growing?" To Harriet Choice he said: "I'm never into anything *new*. What's the evolution? In music, you take out what you don't like any more, and what's left is what you like. And you've got to keep doing that." He was willing even to recall his early development to point out how it matched his current temper. "I looked at all the other trumpet players, the way they held their horns, the way they fingered the horn," he said. "And I paid attention to how each would play a different phrase. Seventeen different trumpet players are going to play the same phrase seventeen different ways. You've got to eliminate some of it. But you've got to see all the possibilities."[66]

This process of elimination threatened to resolve into nothing at all. He claimed that he was working toward performances in which nothing happened. "We might get up there and just hold hands," he said. "We have rehearsals, like a five-hour rehearsal of nonreaction ... Like, if I say, 'Ba-bop-ba-ba-ba,' you don't say, 'Bop.' You don't do that. You don't say nothing."[67] And again, "Yes only means something after you've said no. We had a five-hour rehearsal one day, and I gave the band a certain rhythm and told them to stay there. Not to react. To let me do all that. Afterwards, they said, 'Thanks, Miles.'"[68] Liebman was apparently describing one such rehearsal when he said, "Even playing E^b for four hours, which is what we did most of the time, even within the context of that very limited area and beat, and four guitars and an amazing amount of sound – even within that I was able to discern the subtleties of Miles's playing."[69] And what of the other band members? Liebman said nothing, but Davis said, "My ego only needs a good rhythm section. I mean, my band now, man, they have so much fine energy and I got to bring it out of them or it don't work."[70]

As for jazz, Davis no longer liked even to hear the word, which he considered racist. "It's a white man's word," he told Hubert Saal in

Newsweek.[71] So, in his view, was almost every other word that had been applied to a musical category. "I don't play rock. Rock is a white word," he railed. "And I don't like the word jazz because *jazz* is a nigger word that white folks dropped on us. We just play *Black*. We play what the day recommends ... You don't play 1955 music or that straight crap like *My Funny Valentine*." When Harriet Choice asked him about playing jazz, he scoffed, "Don't use that word with me. That's an Uncle Tom word. Clues for white folks in theaters and the dine-and-dance places. They know what they're going to get, except with my band or Chick's or Herbie's. Otherwise it's the same old shit." Choice pointed out that his audience, and Hancock's and Corea's too, were largely white, whereas Sonny Stitt and Gene Ammons drew black audiences, but he just scoffed again. "They draw the pimps and all that shit," he said. "The young blacks don't have enough money to see Herbie and Chick. You gonna print that?"[72]

In the band's performances, the jazz elements became secondary, and accidental. "The jazz swing," Liebman told Gene Perla, "happens completely spontaneously. None of our songs are planned that way. There are a few times that it presents itself, mostly between Al and Michael, the bass and drums. Sometimes between Al and Mtume, like they'll kind of signal each other in a way and swing out. There have been a few times that they have been unbelievable, the lift that it gives to the music. Miles gets so excited he suddenly gets a whole different personality. He'll start to move around a lot. One time it happened we were playing a funky thing and suddenly it went into 4/4 double time. He took the mute out, threw it off the stage, and started burning eighth notes. It was incredible, really a lift." But it remained far from the core of Davis's music. "That doesn't seem to be near the main sound of the band," Liebman added, " and I think this is due largely to the people who are playing and the way Miles has picked these people to achieve the sound that he wants."[73]

The performances had turned into a process, with no pre-set sequences and few replicable patterns. Davis conducted the process with a kind of mephistophelian glee. "I could make the cats in my band play by just looking at them," he told Julie Coryell. "I'd look at them and not say anything. They'd wait and watch. Finally, I'd say, 'Motherfucker, will you get down!'"[74] He no longer left the stage when the band were playing, but spent most of the evening at stage center, facing Foster's drum set, occasionally inclining his head or raising his hand, and sometimes sweeping his hand grandly to stop the rhythm dead. For the sidemen, the conducting style became an advanced test in interpreting body language. "He doesn't tell you how to play," Liebman explained. "I mean, he'll sometimes get very general, conceptual about it. He doesn't say, 'You gotta play the first bars with me, then skip four' – you know, like a *head* – no such thing. You gotta be able to *read* Miles. That's the thing. And that's one of the things he judges musicians on: the ability to translate what *Miles* wants ... Nothing is ever said. You know? It's totally physical movement. And sometimes not even overt physical movement, it's just a vibration you get if you study the man and if you're – you know – aware. That's all. With Miles, part of the playing is the watching. That's playing, you dig? You gotta know what's happening, and everybody does, all the people that are there."[75]

In spite of his waning health, Davis performed more frequently than he had for years, putting on display not only his latest transmutation of the music but also some new idiosyncrasies in his stage manner. At the end of 1973 he played a concert at Carnegie Hall; "he was forty minutes late, he spat on the stage a few times, and his trumpet, some said, was lost in the electrics," Choice reported.[76]

In January 1974, he embarked on a tour that would conclude with another concert at Carnegie Hall on 30 March. The first stop was supposed to be the Outremont Theatre in Montreal, but the concert was cancelled because, according to a rumor reported in *Coda*, he decided to attend the heavyweight championship bout between George Foreman and Joe Frazier that night.[77] So the first stop was Massey Hall in Toronto on 27 January. The reviewers, predictably by now, were torn between the power and conviction of the rhythms and the inscrutability of their succession. "Miles' attitude toward the world of listeners ... seems to say, 'Here it is. You need the music more than it needs you, so take it like it is or split,'" Alan Offstein wrote in *Coda*, and then he added, "Plenty of people did split from Massey Hall after the first set; however, a sizeable portion stayed on and dug the music of a still-reigning master of jazz."[78] In the *Toronto Star* Peter Goddard noted: "Davis kept his own contributions last night to a minimum of notes, even if they seemed to have been wrenched, screaming, from his electronically amplified trumpet ... Davis constantly goaded and coaxed his players last night, keeping his back turned on the audience much of the night."[79]

As at the Carnegie Hall concert the month before, he started about forty minutes late and projected a stream of spit toward the drums. The spitting, apparently an unconscious habit, was all the more noticeable because Davis removed his robin's-egg-blue cashmere jacket and placed it neatly beside the pedestal for Foster's drums, where it absorbed more than a little of his spit as the evening wore on.

From Toronto, the band traveled to Chicago for a 1 February concert, Davis first appearance there in three years, and to Minneapolis, where they played two concerts at the Tyrone Guthrie Theatre on 5 February. In San Francisco later in the month, they settled into the Keystone Korner for two weeks, playing a rare nightclub engagement. The sound level in the small club was deafening, but Ralph J. Gleason, for one, not only learned to live with it but found it the main source of strength in the music. "In a nightclub the sound completely surrounds you," he wrote in *Rolling Stone*. "The bass produces tones you can feel in the air around you and in the pit of your stomach. The synthesizer, the guitars, the wah-wah effects of Miles's trumpet, all combine to deluge you in sound from all corners of the room. But the bottom pulse, which is really at the same time a kind of melody of different tones, keeps the emotional feeling building and carrying you along so that at the end of a set you are emotionally exhausted but exhilarated, out of breath but not tired."[80]

Gleason's reaction was evidently shared by the Japanese producers of Davis's *Pangaea* LP, a 1975 performance with the same rhythm team, because they included on the liner this piece of advice: "We suggest that you play this record at highest possible volume in order to fully appreciate the sound of Miles Davis."

When the band returned to New York at the end of March for the closing Carnegie Hall concert, Davis's spittle was finally brought to his attention. Sy Johnson had attended the concert with Thad Jones, where they sat in the third row. "Thad got so upset that you kept spitting on the stage that he left," Johnson told Davis. "He kept saying, 'Miles shouldn't spit on stage at Carnegie Hall.' And finally he said, 'I'm sorry, Sy, but if he spits one more time I'm gonna have to go!' And you spit, and he went." Davis looked embarrassed and said, "Didn't he know I just got over pneumonia?"[81] But he brought the habit under control soon afterward.

The Carnegie Hall concert was recorded by Columbia and released in Japan on CBS-Sony in 1977 as *Dark Magus*. The performance is comparable in most respects to the other concerts from this tour (of which the Massey Hall concert is preserved in a low-fidelity tape in some private collections). The presentation at Carnegie Hall, described by Noë, began with the house lights on: "Musicians began setting up nonchalantly and Miles strolls on *ever* casually, making the whole thing look like a sound check. All of a sudden, without obvious reason, Miles starts to play, and the band follows with a wall of heavily larded rhythm. It seems he is trying to make it look as if it didn't matter when he started, it was all his whim." To that, Liebman responded, "It *is* his whim ... That's the thing! ... Miles can do that and have three thousand musicians follow him. Right? So what I learned in that respect from Miles was to be able to watch him and be on his case – which I am, 'cause I don't *play* a lot. I'm the only one in the band who doesn't do something all the time. Miles, when he's not doin' something, he's directing, so I'm the only cat that's standing there, keeping his cool. Sometimes I'll hear something to play. Or sometimes *he'll* call *me* in. In other words, my gig is to follow him."[82]

While this extraordinarily complex process was unfolding at Carnegie Hall, Davis auditioned two musicians who had never played with him. Whatever the intended effect on his music, in the end the impact was negligible. The music was already so dense, and the roles of the regular members, who had been together almost a year, were so tightly circumscribed, that a listener would hardly know that two extra players had been added to the ensemble. But Davis's audacity in adding them is the stuff that legends are built on. Liebman says, "What he was doing – which he often does at big kinda gigs like that – is change the shit up, by doing something totally out. Totally unexpected. I mean, we had been a band together on the road for a year ... And then, suddenly, a *live* date, New York city, Carnegie Hall, the cat pulls two cats who never even *saw* each other. I mean, you gotta say, 'Is the man mad or is he – he's either mad or extremely subtle.'"[83] The details are as follows:

Miles Davis Ensemble: Dark Magus
Miles Davis, tpt, org; Dave Liebman, ts, ss; Reggie Lucas, Pete Cosey, gtr; Michael Henderson, b; Al Foster, dms; James Mtume Foreman, perc. Carnegie Hall, New York, 30 March 1974
Moja; Wili
(both on CBS-Sony 40 AP 741-2)

Add Azar Lawrence, ts; Dominique Gaumont, gtr
Tatu [ends with *Calypso Frelimo*]; *NNE*
(both on CBS-Sony 40 AP 741-2)
Davis plays trumpet on *Moja* and trumpet and organ on the other titles.

This music is distinguished by a long ballad sequence introduced by Liebman and sustained by Lucas and Davis in the second half of *Moja*, and by a short blues by Davis near the end of *NNE*.

The unexpected guests, saxophonist Azar Lawrence and guitarist Dominique Gaumont, make their presences felt somewhat in *Tatu*, where Gaumont follows Lucas's solo with a long, nebulous passage muddied by heavy use of the fuzz-wah, and Lawrence skirmishes briefly with Liebman in a duet and then plays a choppy, disjointed solo. As Noë remarked, they "seemed to be following different orders than those the band were picking up on" – through no fault of their own, he might have added.

Azar Lawrence, who was just 20 when he auditioned at Carnegie Hall, was the most highly regarded young saxophonist around. From Los Angeles, he arrived in New York the year before to join Elvin Jones's band when Liebman left it for Davis's, but he switched to McCoy Tyner's quartet a few weeks later and was still playing with that band when he appeared with Davis. *Esquire* magazine, in an article profiling the young people it considered to be future leaders in business, law, and the arts, had singled out Lawrence as the rising star in jazz just before his audition. That early promise remains largely unfulfilled; after his Carnegie Hall audition, Lawrence returned to Tyner's band for a while, and he occasionally played as a competent sideman, but seldom as a leader, since then.

If Davis was hoping to rouse Liebman's competitive instinct by bringing Lawrence onstage, he certainly succeeded. "Azar Lawrence played with Miles for the first time at this concert, and Miles didn't keep him for one minute longer," his fellow auditioner, Gaumont, said, and he added, "Liebman, on the other hand, took care of himself very well; he was very attentive."

Gaumont himself, though the recorded evidence scarcely suggests that he fared any better, was hired and stayed with the band for the rest of the year, apart from a brief return to his home in Paris. He harbored no illusions about Davis's motive for bringing him onstage, because he was completely unknown to jazz audiences not only in America but also in France. "Miles had no need of me," he admitted, "but he wanted to make Lucas flip [*faire flipper Lucas*]."[84] Lucas, Gaumont says, wanted a raise, and Gaumont's presence was Davis's way of telling him that he was not indispensable.

For Gaumont, it seemed an unbelievable break. He had attended both of Davis's concerts at the Olympia Theatre in Paris just four months before and become star-struck. "That's the guy I'm going to play with," he told himself, and through a complex chain of acquaintances that started with Oliver Lake, the St. Louis reedman who, like many other free-form jazzmen at the time, was living in Paris, got an introduction to Pete Cosey, who in turn introduced him to Al Foster. Foster, whom Gaumont calls "truly *la crème* among men," took him in when he arrived in New York from Paris and twice played Davis a demonstration tape by Gaumont over the telephone. The tape had Gaumont playing with the Black Artists Group, a Paris coalition of St. Louis avant-garde players including Lester Bowie, Charles Bobo Shaw, and Lake. Davis was impressed enough to tell Foster to bring Gaumont over to meet him, and one week later he met him for the second time, on the Carnegie Hall stage. Gaumont had been in the United States exactly two weeks on the night of the concert. He was 18.

Gaumont attributes whatever success he had at his audition to his briefing at the Olympia concerts. "I had seen what Miles did in Paris at the two concerts I went to," he told an interviewer for *Jazz Hot*, "and since I'm a child of music I could play with them." Davis was no doubt attracted by Gaumont's rough approximations of Jimi Hendrix, his main influence. He had first heard Hendrix's records two years before he journeyed to the United States and the impact was greater than Davis's. He said, "After I discovered Hendrix at fifteen, I still had another year of school, but I spent the year in my basement practising the guitar like a madman."

More than anyone else, Gaumont exemplifies Davis's predilection for sidemen who were relatively unschooled and unsophisticated. "I teach my musicians," he told Gregg Hall. "I taught my drummer everything he knows about playing drums. I play drums myself. I'm teaching a young boy now that I have in the band. His name is Dominique. He's about nineteen and he's from Bahia. He's a baddd motherfucker. He's like Hendrix. I have to show him the different chords. You know, Hendrix never did learn any chords."[85] Though his tenure with Davis was short and, as we shall see, not always pleasant, Gaumont concedes that he learned a great deal. "It was Miles who helped me understand, when at the beginning I considered his methods less valid than Hendrix's," he said. "In playing with him, I learned the differences of phrasing, tempos, and silences."[86]

"So Miles had me on his hands," Gaumont said later. "Two days after the concert his office called me with a firm offer of employment and said they would arrange to get my working permit. We then went on a tour across the country. Every night was different ... That's how Miles is, never the same, he has such power."

In May, Columbia released the first new LP by Davis in eight months, and it pinned some hopes on the LP recouping some of the listeners who had passed up *On the Corner* and *In Concert*. It was called *Big Fun* (PG 32866), and it again featured Corky McCoy's cover caricatures, this time somewhat subdued. Each of its four sides was filled with a single composition recorded a few years earlier. The most recent music was *Ife* (recorded 12 June 1972), with three of the men in the current band (Henderson, Foster, Mtume) among its eleven players; the other sides were *Great Expectations* (19 November 1969), *Lonely Fire* (27 January 1970), and *Go Ahead John* (30 March 1970), with more recognizable names among the studio stock companies such as Wayne Shorter, Chick Corea, Herbie Hancock, and Josef Zawinul. The selection seemed a calculated move by Columbia to strengthen Davis's recent showings with his comparatively anonymous sidemen, but Teo Macero told Gregg Hall that he had been actively working on these releases for years. "*Big Fun* didn't just happen overnight," he said. "That thing has been brewing for a long time. There has been trial and error in the editing room, trial and error in the studio. There are a lot of things that have been done since then that haven't come out. But this one has been [produced] over a period of at least three years. Some of it went back – I was just looking at the sheet today – to 1969 ... Five years later, and I'm just now putting it together. I'm telling you, it's like a composition."[87]

Most reviewers, and also those listeners who were still paying attention, were relieved to discover its relatively lyrical bias, especially on *Great Expectations* (which turns into Zawinul's *Orange Lady*, unannounced, as its second half) and *Lonely Fire*, but the LP fell far short of Columbia's commercial expectations. Davis did not share those expectations at all. When Gregg Hall, interviewing him around the time of its release, told him that Columbia thought it would be "bigger than *Bitches Brew*," Davis, dumbfounded, replied, "How??? I did *Big Fun* years ago."[88]

Davis then told Hall about his expectations for *Calypso Frelimo*, the most recent music that he and Macero were working on, which he hoped would eventually come out as a whole LP. Sometime between then and its December release, Davis changed his mind about issuing so lengthy a version, and one factor in that decision was Davis's subsequent recording of another long composition that he was anxious to release as quickly as possible. The new piece was titled *He Loved Him Madly*, and it appeared on *Get Up with It* (Columbia KG 33236), the

December release, as an overlong single side, as did *Calypso Frelimo*; the remaining sides of the double album were filled out by the evocative *Rated X*, the jejune *Red China Blues*, the 1970 *Honky Tonk* with Keith Jarrett in the band, and some other short pieces.

He Loved Him Madly eulogized the death of Duke Ellington on 24 May 1974. Although Davis and Ellington had had very little personal contact – surprisingly little, considering that their careers among the leaders of jazz had overlapped for 25 years – Davis was deeply moved by Ellington's death, and within days he assembled his working band in the studio to record his memorial. The details are as follows:

Miles Davis Octet: Get Up with It
Miles Davis, tpt, org; Dave Liebman, flt; Reggie Lucas, Pete Cosey, Dominique Gaumont, gtr; Michael Henderson, b; Al Foster, dms; James Mtume Foreman, conga. New York, probably 27 May 1974
He Loved Him Madly
(on Columbia KG 33236)

There can be no doubt that this music is deeply felt. Whether it succeeds in matching the feelings to the man whose death evoked them is a separate question, and one that would be debated hotly. It is a dirge, carried by long, motionless organ chords, with occasional drum rolls as punctuation and long, spacey interludes by guitar, flute, and trumpet that add color to the organ drone without distracting the listener from it. The organ dominates, although it seems more appropriate as a background for a spoken elegy or perhaps for a musical allusion to Ellington's style. The anticipation that something will arise to fill the empty foreground is the listener's main response on the first listening, but the foreknowledge that it never comes affects further listenings. *He Loved Him Madly* thus reduces to a passionately understated individual response to Ellington's death. At that level, it is articulate enough, even affecting, but as a composition it is too monochromatic to justify its half-hour length.

If Davis misjudged the length, he nevertheless fully intended it to be nothing more or less than the highly personal, almost private, statement of his feelings that it is. His original title for it was *He Loved Us Madly*, according to Sy Johnson, and that title obviously designates Ellington. The published title, *He Loved Him Madly*, connotes Ellington but designates Davis, a subtle shift of emphasis that is more appropriate for the music.

In spite of its apparent simplicity, the elegy aroused Davis to revive his arranging skills, which had not only been set aside but had become antithetical to his music since 1971. "We really rehearsed!" Gaumont reported. "Miles sat at the piano and showed Al and me the melodic line of *He Loved Him Madly*." But Gaumont was not convinced by the result. "It's not my favorite," he added; "I find it's the sort of thing you listen to only once."[89]

Sy Johnson was scheduled to interview Davis on the morning of the recording, but when the interview had to be postponed Macero suggested instead that Johnson drop into the studio for the end of the recording session. When he arrived, "the control room was full of thick Spanish funereal music and solemn men filling out w-4 forms ... Miles came out of the studio wearing a big jaunty hat, looking pinched and tired beneath it. He leaned on the console for a few minutes, lost in the music. Then, smiling wanly and touching a few hands, he slipped out the door." As Johnson listened to the playback, he noted that "the band sounded sure of itself on the slow, treacly tempo. I was sorry I hadn't seen them record it."[90]

Davis's elegy for Ellington pays homage to him not as a direct influence but as a man who followed his own star and enriched the jazz spectrum enormously. Although Ellington was easily the most honored and respected jazz figure of all, Davis felt that he did not receive his due. "The public completely ignored Duke," he told Julie Coryell. "He was a great man. I'd put him and Stravinsky in the same category. He was trying to teach everybody something."[91] When *Down Beat* solicited tributes from people all over the world to commemorate Ellington's death, Davis offered the one that has become the most widely quoted: "I think all the musicians in jazz should get together on a certain day and get down on their knees to thank Duke."[92] *He Loved Him Madly* attempts to transform that sentiment into music.

How well it succeeds became a minor controversy. Even Jérome Reese, whose assessment of Davis's "electronic" music is seldom critical, notes that on *Get Up with It* Davis's "sonority tends to deteriorate," and from that he concludes that "Miles is fatigued and his 'personal problems' are becoming a handicap for his music."[93] Barry Tepperman, reviewing the LP for *Coda*, labeled it "identifiably personal, rhythmically involved background music, compressing the limitations of his [Davis's] horn to their ultimate closure, with absolutely nothing to project it into consciousness." As for *He Loved Him Madly*, Tepperman states: "The only vague interest in this bonsai album comes in an artistically absurd dedication 'For Duke'."[94] Poles apart, Burnett

James listed *Get Up with It* among the best records of 1975 in the year-end tabulation for *Jazz Journal*, specifically because *He Loved Him Madly* "remains the finest and most profound tribute in music yet paid to Duke."[95] That opinion fanned the flames that had been raging through *Jazz Journal*'s letters section, where readers had hotly expressed their opinions on the matter for the past months.

Ralph J. Gleason, writing in *Rolling Stone*, saw the controversy as a positive sign of Davis's integrity, which had occasionally been impugned on the evidence of *On the Corner* and *Red China Blues*. "The greatest single thing about Miles Davis is that he does not stand still," Gleason wrote. "He is forever being born. And like all his other artistic kin, as he changes, leaves behind one style or mode and enters another, he gains new adherents and loses old ones ... It is a tribute to artists like that when the pages of publications steam from the anger of thwarted fans. It is a measure of their artistic value and integrity."[96]

In August, Davis replaced Dave Liebman in the working band with Sonny Fortune, and while Fortune was finishing his commitment to the Buddy Rich orchestra he replaced Liebman on a recording session in June on one of the pieces that would fill out the *Get Up with It* LP. The details are as follows:

Miles Davis Ensemble: Get Up with It
Miles Davis, tpt, org; Sonny Fortune, flt; Reggie Lucas, Pete Cosey, Dominique Gaumont, gtr; Michael Henderson, b; Al Foster, dms; James Mtume Foreman, perc. New York, 19 June 1974
Maiysha
(on Columbia KG 33236)

Omit Fortune and Gaumont. 20 June 1974
Mtume
(on Columbia KG 33236)

Mtume is a rhythmic ramble with layered wah-wahs from trumpet, organ, lead guitar, and rhythm guitar; it settles into its bumptious groove early and keeps going for fifteen minutes, long enough to fill the left-over space on side 4 of *Get Up with It*.

Maiysha is more carefully made, and it became a fixture in the concert repertoire, one of the few fixed points that listeners could latch onto in the disorienting process of the live performances. Gaumont recalls, "It had no title until Miles met a woman named Maiysha. She was a real *conne.*"[97] The piece has two distinct and apparently unrelated parts: the first is a conventional samba, played softly and, in this studio performance, almost politely; the second is yet another rhythmic ramble, played loudly, with a whinnying guitar, probably Gaumont's, cantering above it. Even in the polite samba sequence, Fortune's flute, in its only turn, seems lost amid Davis's thick organ chords, which pose a challenge for any soloist; it is a challenge that Davis, when he picks up his trumpet, is spared, and perhaps one that he would have spared his reedmen if he had had to cope with it himself.

Both *Mtume* and *Maiysha* feature abrupt, momentary stops in the rhythm, a device first used, with extraordinary effect, on *Rated X*, also released on this LP. On the two new pieces, the stops seem otiose, and their frequency merely cheapens the dramatic effect, but within the limits of sonority and harmony in this rhythm band Davis apparently could find very few other options for relieving the music.

Onstage, the device was visually impressive. With congas beating, guitars wailing, and cymbals crashing, Davis would raise his finger and stop the commotion dead. Gene Williams, reviewing a concert in Washington, DC, in the fall, viewed Davis as a bwana leading his safari through "a dense electric rain forest": "Sensing a clearing, Davis extends his fingers in a signal and his group halts motionless as a soprano sax or electric guitar or even the leader's trumpet slips ahead alone, reporting what he sees. The leader listens, choosing a path. He arches his body, nodding his head to the desired pulse, beckoning the rhythm guitar, and his group falls in, resuming their journey. Echoing, reverberating electronically shaped notes and phrases form the strange beautiful foliage and strong life rhythms of Davis's musical world."[98] It was all in a night's work.

Davis took part of August off, his first complete break from recording and performing for over a year. Filling in time during the layoff, Sonny Fortune and Al Foster joined a quartet formed by bassist Buster Williams, with Onaje Allan Gumbs on piano, for a week-long engagement at Boomer's in New York. In the same period, Reggie Lucas assembled all the members of the working band except Davis for a recording session. "What cacophony!" Gaumont remarked. "We were obliged to face the fact that, without Miles, our getting together was totally useless."[99]

The busy schedule resumed in the fall with concerts at the Artpark in Lewiston, New York, and Washington, DC (September), club dates at the Bottom Line in New York (November) and the Troubador in Los

Angeles (December), and a tour of South America (November–December). Fortune had to adjust not only to the music he found himself playing but also to the audiences he faced. "The audience was mostly rock as opposed to jazz," he noted. "I've seen him [Davis] in two different settings. In the jazz situation he wasn't necessarily as visual as he was in the rock or fusion. For example, in the jazz situation, I remember Miles would play and walk off the stage after he had finished. But certainly when I was working with him in the band, he would never walk off the stage. The band was louder and Miles played fewer notes but whether all this was because of the rock setting or a matter of ifs, I can't say. Those things did happen but they may have more or less evolved to that."[100]

Gaumont was finding his adjustment difficult, but not because of the audiences. "I thought Henderson and Foster were fantastic," he said, "but when it came to playing the guitar, I told myself I could do better [than Lucas or Cosey]. I didn't even get the chance; there was too much vying for space among the guitarists. Still, it didn't stop Miles from keeping me on for a year. Miles had nothing to do with my leaving; I just couldn't transcend all the fuss. The guitarists would go and tell Miles that I couldn't play well, that I made them uncomfortable, when in fact I had done nothing. Well, they were wrong if they thought I was going to waste my talents by joining them in their pettiness."[101]

Gaumont quit several times, usually only for a few hours or a few days, but once more decisively. "It's for this reason that he kept me on for so long," he says. "I was the first person, me, the little French boy, to dare ask for a raise and then quit when it was refused. He was so surprised that he had his office send me a plane ticket in Paris to return."

In spite of the tension he felt onstage, Gaumont found his niche in the leader's affections. "In the group I was the *gamin*, the little foreigner," he says. "Miles called me 'the gypsy.'" Gaumont feels that the band eventually pulled together. "The last time we toured together, the band played really well, especially at the concerts in Brazil. It's too bad that tour wasn't recorded."[102]

Gaumont's last engagement was at the Troubador, at the end of the tour. Lee Underwood attended the opening night, with a crowd he describes as "a notorious bunch of cold-fish recording industry vinyl-peddlers." Underwood was filled with anticipation because of what he had heard on the recently released *Get Up with It* LP, especially *Calypso Frelimo*, *He Loved Him Madly*, and *Rated X*. "Miles has reached a stage where he is concerned less with the *events* of sound (hummable melodies, standard phrases, standard structures, etc.) and more with the sound of sounds themselves," he reported in *Coda*. "He takes you into the dark and previously untouched places of your soul, opening a vast and relatively unexplored terrain of emotion." But not on this night. "He packed the Troubador his opening night, generated a tremendous amount of anticipatory excitement, but then went on to completely fizzle the gig ... Miles made no effort whatsoever to get across to them either musically or personally. Zero communication."[103]

Gaumont says, "Towards the end of the year, I was sick to death of all the pettiness that was going on and I left the U.S. depressed, at the beginning of 1975."[104] He blames his state of depression for his heroin addiction when he returned to Paris, and for leaving music for two years until 1978, when he formed a trio. He has been playing irregularly in France since then, trying diligently to make a fusion of the elements he learned from Davis and Hendrix.

For Davis, the year-end magazine polls again documented how he was losing his grip. *Down Beat* had honored him by dedicating its fortieth-anniversay issue in July to him, with Gregg Hall's interview and laudatory comments from sundry sources. But its readers' poll in December again ignored his current band and gave his former sidemen pride of place: Weather Report was named best group, and Davis's band showed a distant eighth, tied with Chuck Mangione's; Herbie Hancock was named Jazzman of the Year, with Davis sixth; and Weather Report's *Mysterious Traveler*, Keith Jarrett's *Solo Concerts*, and Hancock's *Headhunters* took the top three spots for LPs, with *Big Fun* a remote tenth. Only among the trumpeters did Davis make a good showing, placing second, again behind Freddie Hubbard. He could take some consolation, if he felt the need, from the fact that *Bitches Brew* had become a gold record during the year, with sales of 500,000 over four years, but even that was not unequivocal. *Headhunters*, a mélange of disco-funk, had done the same for Hancock within months of its release.

Davis found a more enthusiastic response early in the new year on a tour of Japan, his first in ten and a half years. Between 22 January and 8 February, he played fourteen concerts to capacity crowds in huge halls and won enthusiastic reviews. Keizo Takada praised his "magnificent and energetic band" and concluded: "Miles must be *the* genius of managing men and bringing out their hidden talent. He played his music with his band just as Duke Ellington did with his orchestra."[105] The two concerts at Osaka Festival Hall on 1 February were recorded and released as two double albums: *Agharta* appeared just six months later in Japan but waited another year for North American release; *Panagaea* came out in 1976 in Japan and has not yet been released elsewhere. The details are as follows:

Miles Davis Septet at Osaka Festival Hall
Miles Davis, tpt, org; Sonny Fortune, flt, ss, as; Pete Cosey, gtr, synthesizer, perc; Reggie Lucas, gtr; Michael Henderson, b; Al Foster, dms; James Mtume Foreman, perc. Osaka Festival Hall, Japan, 1 February 1975
Prelude; Maiysha; Theme from Jack Johnson; Interlude
(all on *Agharta*, CBS-Sony [Jap] SOPJ92–93, and Columbia PG 33967)
Priestley (1982) notes that *Theme from Jack Johnson* and *Interlude* are reversed on both label and liner of all issues. Fortune plays soprano on *Prelude*, alto on *Prelude* and *Jack Johnson*, and flute on *Maiysha*, *Jack Johnson*, and *Interlude*.

Zimbabwe 1 and 2; Gondwana 1 and 2
(all on *Panagaea*, CBS-Sony [Jap] SOPZ 96–97)
Fortune plays soprano on *Zimbabwe 2* and flute on *Gondwana 1*; he does not play on the other titles.

Although the music is from successive concerts on the same day, virtually nothing is repeated from one to the other. The quality also differs markedly, with *Agharta* vastly superior to *Pangaea*, and to most of Davis's music from this period.

Sonny Fortune takes a star turn on *Agharta*, especially in stating the samba theme on *Maiysha* and opening the *Theme from Jack Johnson* (side 3, not 4 as listed), where he plays flute and alto saxophone, respectively. On all his solos – six in all – the rhythm team seem much more responsive to him than they ever were to Liebman. Here, they support Fortune's improvisations in a manner much more similar to the rhythm section's traditional role in jazz. Then, inexplicably, Fortune virtually disappears during the second concert, taking only short turns at two points, and sounding careless.

The space created by Fortune's absence on *Pangaea* is filled by Pete Cosey, who finally gets a chance to extricate himself from the ensemble. He uses it advantageously, revealing a broader-based talent than he had otherwise shown. He closes *Gondwana 1* with a simple, thoughtful blues devoid of gimmickry, and his accompaniment of Davis's musing on *Gondwana 2* helps to make that sequence the high point of the concert; Cosey plays a delightful chiming figure behind Davis, and when Davis swings the tempo to 4/4, he reappears to play a jazz solo, his only one on record with Davis's band.

Agharta, in contrast, includes several high points in addition to Fortune's solos. Jazz buffs are likely to find *Prelude*, which covers one and a half sides, another wearying exercise in spinning out a two-chord theme, but *Maiysha*, immediately following it, gets the kind of treatment that might have done its namesake credit: it is tough and tender, and impossible to ignore. Best of all, for many reasons, is the *Theme from Jack Johnson*, which opens with Fortune's longest turn on his best horn, the alto, and after Lucas takes his turn swings into a shuffle beat built on Henderson's walking bass line and Cosey's non-psychedelic rhythm guitar. Henderson ends the long sequence playing the ostinato from *So What*. Davis makes a long, coherent statement on open trumpet that harks back to the days when he did it routinely. It is a treat, not for old times' sake but for the contrast it gives to the bristling, energetic context. Everything that precedes and follows it sounds fresher and brighter because of it.

On *Pangaea*, reviewer Howard Mandel observed, "Davis haunts its two sides like a spectre surveying the scorched earth."[106] On *Agharta*, he is the cooling element.

The wonder is not that Davis played hotly or coolly in Japan but that he played at all. He was suffering excruciating pain from his left hip, which had been operated on almost exactly ten years earlier. It now hurt him all the time, caused him to walk stiffly, and sometimes immobilized him when the femur slipped out of its socket. "I needed the operation," he told Cheryl McCall. "I was in Japan, and I was taking this codeine and morphine and didn't even know it [that he needed the operation]. They gave it to me to help my leg."[107]

Instead of slowing his pace, he had been working more frequently than he had in years, and covering more miles than he ever had. As soon as he returned from Japan, he continued the tour into the Midwest. As always, he acted in public as if nothing were wrong; the only clue to his deteriorating health showed in the lines around his eyes, and they were usually hidden, night and day, by dark glasses. The other clues were also hidden. Sy Johnson watched him painfully remove his right shoe and commented: "The bare foot is wheezed and old. I had the weird notion that Miles might be aging from the feet up." The cause of the pain was an open sore, "a dime-sized hole," on the middle toe, but Davis had been walking around all day apparently oblivious to the pain. "I realized," Johnson said, "that the medication for his hip and legs was probably so strong that he couldn't really feel his feet."[108] He was taking eight pills a day to kill the pain.

In public, all the pain was hidden behind his bravado. When he showed up for the first concert of the Midwestern tour at Northern Illinois University in DeKalb, he wore a maxi-length fur coat over his three-piece satin suit.[109] During the concert, he perched behind the organ and hardly touched his trumpet. Most of the audience had heard that he was playing more organ and less trumpet nowadays, but when he did the same the next night, at the Kiel Opera House in St. Louis, part of the audience suspected something was wrong, because he usually responded to his hometown crowd by burning some long trumpet choruses. He just could not find the strength. And as soon as he left the stage he collapsed, vomiting blood.

The next scheduled stop, at the Arie Crown Theater in Chicago on Easter Sunday, was played by Herbie Hancock and the Headhunters, with Bobbi Humphrey as the opening act. Hancock announced at the start that Davis was hospitalized in St. Louis with bleeding ulcers and invited the patrons to get refunds if they wished. According to one reviewer, "the audience didn't seem to care – or just had lost all faith in Davis and his perpetual excuses. To catcalls that Miles 'did it again,' the Sunday night concert got off to a bad start."

"I didn't even know I was sick from all this morphine and codeine until I got to St. Louis and I started throwing up blood," Davis said later, "and my *boys*, Dr. Weathers and a few friends of mine, they run the hospital, and they said, come on, and put me in the hospital ... You see, your liver gets fucked up, plus drinking, plus the pills – you throw up. And all that blood, it just sits in those little blood vessels down there."[110]

The bleeding ulcer was only the most obvious problem. The hip was a major one, but Davis chose to live with the pain rather than submit to surgery, which would keep him bed-ridden for weeks or even months. The nodes on his larynx impeded his breathing, especially when he slept, and he blamed them for making him winded when he played the trumpet and forcing him to cut short his solos. He entered a hospital in New York in April and had thirteen nodes removed.

His doctors were concerned about his use of analgesics and other drugs. After curing his heroin addiction in 1954 and leading bands in which he was sometimes the only musician not using drugs, the situation had reversed in the 1970s. "Drugs weren't important for the musicians in the band," Dominique Gaumont told his interviewer in

Jazz Hot, and then he added: "For Miles, drugs were perhaps important, you wouldn't be wrong in thinking that. In any case, I balance Miles out in all that. There is no doubt. He gave himself two shots in the hip. One wonders why."[111]

Davis's perception of drug use had also changed. He now viewed Charlie Parker's addiction in a different light. "He loved life, you know. He had a lot of fun," he told Cheryl McCall. "If people had left him alone, he would have been all right ... People saying you can't use this dope and to keep from getting busted you have to use all of it. You have to use all of it because if somebody catches you [with it], they'd put you in jail."[112] But Gaumont, who began using heroin in Paris after leaving Davis's band, disagreed: "For myself, I don't want my music to depend on drugs. Otherwise I wouldn't be making music, I would just be destroying myself. For years I was on horse [*cheval,* heroin] for three months at a time; then I would come off it to rehearse my trio for two months, give five concerts, then go back on heroin. I was risking my freedom, my health, my equilibrium. It was ridiculous! There is no Charlie Parker, it just isn't possible: you can't be a junkie and a musician."[113]

Davis's ulcers and other internal problems were aggravated by alcohol, and that seemed easier to solve. "What could be any worse than whiskey? It's got my liver all fucked up," he told McCall.[114]

He reassembled his band in June, after he had recovered from the throat surgery, for two nights (Tuesday the 14th and Thursday the 16th) at the Bottom Line, at 4th Street and Mercer in New York. Weekday prices at the Bottom Line, which booked heterogeneous bands ranging from Tony Williams's Lifetime to the Nitty Gritty Dirt Band, were normally $4, but for Davis's engagement they charged $5, the weekend price.

Sonny Fortune had formed his own quartet during Davis's layoff, and in his place Davis hired a young unknown named Sam Morrison. The hiring seemed to fit the pattern. Most members of Davis's band had been with him for years, and apart from Fortune and his predecessor, Liebman, they remained largely untried and almost unknown apart from their work with Davis. Michael Henderson had joined him at the end of 1970, James Mtume Foreman in 1971, Al Foster, Reggie Lucas, and Pete Cosey in the second half of 1972. Now Morrison joined them, and even the most avid fans in his audiences felt that Davis had surrounded himself with players incapable of adding the stamp of their own originality to his performances. And Davis himself seemed to be playing by rote.

His reviewers reflected a new response to his concerts. The reviews of the past three years, favorable or not, had usually been passionately stated; now the passion was replaced by resignation. When the band played a midnight concert on 1 July at Avery Fisher Hall as part of the 1975 Newport Jazz Festival, most reviewers noted Davis's return to George Wein's roster after refusing to play in 1972, but the performance itself received only blasé reports. "Wein's sound crew did wonders with Davis's thunderously loud and usually poorly balanced band," Robert Palmer reported in *Rolling Stone*; "for the first time in the memory of New York's Miles watchers, a concert by the current group came across with minimal distortion and feedback and with the contributions of individual sidemen clearly evident. For a band which has been together several years ... the musical transitions were astonishingly tentative. But Davis, the center of attention, played plenty of trumpet, occasionally recalling the sort of sensual lyricism he used to bring to ballad performances."[115] Whitney Balliett's review in the *New Yorker* was even more terse. "There was little that was new in his first number and set, which lasted close to an hour," Balliett wrote. "Davis went electric years ago, and he was surrounded onstage by amplifiers and electronic instruments. He played several solos, muted and open, electrified or not, and everything was as of old – the clams, the yearning tone, the highly melodic, free-time passages, the seeming disjointedness, and the incessant effort to get through to whatever it is musically that he has been trying to get through to for the past twenty years."[116] *Variety* reported: "Second half was better and better received than the first half because several auditors, expecting the old Davis, left during the long intermission ... Davis' trumpeting was fuller with the half more rewarding for the devotees."

On 8 August, Julian (Cannonball) Adderley died suddenly, five weeks before his 47th birthday. Wynton Kelly had died in 1971, also suddenly, and John Coltrane and Paul Chambers had both died in the 1960s, paring down the survivors among Davis's closest associates from his peak years. All of them were younger than he was. The ailing Davis received the news of Adderley's death grimly.

A performance at the Schaefer Festival in Central Park on 5 September drew a critical response as tepid as the Newport Festival performance from John S. Wilson in the *New York Times*. "Miles Davis's ability to leave his listeners languid was given pointed display," he reported. "His eight-piece group, which opened the program, performed for an hour. Mr. Davis was present for the first 50 minutes. He left during a solo by his bassist, who left during a solo by a conga player, who left during a solo by a second conga player." Wilson then described the performances that followed, by Raices, a Puerto Rican band, and John Blair, a jazz violinist, before returning to Davis's. "Before he worked his way down to this anticlimax," Wilson continued, "Mr. Davis took his group through the forest of electrified sounds that has been his vehicle for several years ... The steady flow [of percussion] was interrupted from time to time by brief breaks to allow Mr. Davis short passages in which dynamics, shading and even dramatic effect appeared. For the most part, the group produced a heavy-textured sound with a beat that seemed to be weighed down by the heaviness. It offered striking contrast to the seven musicians in Raices who, playing in a somewhat similar idiom, projected a light, bright, buoyant quality."[117]

These reviewers could not know – Davis himself did not know, although he must have suspected it sometimes, when he felt completely enervated by the pain in his hip – that they were among the last audiences that would see him for almost six years. His energy was all but drained, and his performances in the summer of 1975 showed that he could no longer hide it.

He kept trying, sometimes with unpleasant consequences. He was scheduled to appear two days after the Schaefer concert at Gusman Hall in Miami. By the time he sent the telegram announcing his cancellation, his musicians – and all the sound equipment, reportedly worth $25,000 – had arrived. The promoters, upset by the last-minute cancellation and the lack of any explanation for it, seized the equipment and sought a lien on it for their losses.[118]

One more concert was announced, for 12 October at the Auditorium Theater. It raised some anticipation, because it matched Davis with Michal Urbaniak, the Polish violinist whose strange fusions of jazz, rock, and European folk forms had been coming out on Columbia LPs since his arrival in New York in 1974; the advertisement announced, "The legendary jazz trumpet player is joined by the brilliant jazz violinist," and some of the fans who saw it hoped that Urbaniak's presence might signal a new or altered direction for Davis's music.

The advertisement was soon withdrawn. Davis now realized that he could no longer avoid the hip operation, or put it off much longer. And he suspected that, although he had recuperated fairly quickly before – covering the healing incision on his throat with a cravat when he played in Europe in 1956, hobbling around the stage in casts in western Canada in 1973 – he would not return as quickly this time.

The hip operation put an end to the most muddled and controversial period in Davis's career. For a long while, it seemed to have ended his career altogether. For almost six years he made no attempts to perform in public. He did make occasional forays into the recording studio – three or four sessions – but none of them resulted in record releases at the time. From his 49th year to his 55th, Davis was retired.

When he resumed playing again in 1981, after many people had given up hope that he ever would, he did not continue the musical directions he had left behind so abruptly in 1975. There would be echoes of that direction in his music, especially at first, but by and large those directions remain closed off, and so they stand strangely apart from what follows just as they do from what went before.

The music from 1972–5 is self-contained but hard to grasp, compact but hard to comprehend. It includes more than its fair share of contradictions. It began with an avowed attempt to find a black audience, but it baffled audiences of all colors. It drew sustenance from the easy blandishments of James Brown and Sly Stone, but its dense rhythms and often total lack of melody place it sound-years apart from them; it is probably the most forbidding and least accessible music that Davis ever made. It gained confidence from Stockhausen's example, but it found no cult among the European avant-garde composers; it was not so much ignored by Stockhausen's peers and students as it was unloved. It is often self-conscious and self-indulgent, but the self that fashioned it existed much of the time in a haze of pain and pain-killers.

Little wonder, then, that Davis's performances of this period, especially the recorded ones, so often evoked either confusion or sarcasm. Even the most positive comments – by Eugene Chadbourne, Ralph Gleason, Dave Liebman, and a few others – betray little real affection for the music. At best, they show respect for it, usually on the premise that Miles Davis can go ahead and do whatever he wants to do. But, of course, the authors of some of the negative comments – Ron Brown, Stan Getz, Clark Terry, and Betty Carter among them – would readily grant that premise. They knew as well as anyone that in approaching Miles Davis's music they would find no concessions to their tastes or anyone else's.

And Davis's critics hardly needed the scolding offered by trumpeter Oscar Brashear when he said: "They feel they can walk up to him and say, 'Miles, you ain't playin' shit now. Like, I dug you in 1965 when you had Wayne and them, but you ain't playin' shit now, Miles. You a drag, man. You don't sound nothin' like you sounded before.' They walk out on him ... They want you to be what *they* think is you."[119]

None of Davis's toughest critics took such a simple view. Most of them had followed his music closely, and they followed his new directions as closely as his mildest critics.

The crucial questions about the music of this period have nothing to do with whether Davis should be allowed to pursue a new direction in his music, or whether he should be permitted to sound different today from the way he sounded yesterday. Those questions are far too easy because they have only one obvious answer.

The real questions are so hard that they remain unanswered to this day. Was Davis's direction interesting? And was it productive? Even with a decade of hindsight, those questions have no clear answers.

Perhaps it is still too soon to try to answer them. Perhaps Davis was, as Dizzy Gillespie said, "hooked so far out in front" that ten years is too short for a perspective.

A couple of points are clear. Davis's music of 1972–5 has so far not proven interesting enough to entice listeners back to it. Whereas most of Davis's recordings since 1955 remain in print and have been continuously in print since they were issued, several of the recordings of 1972–5 are already hard to find. And the music was not productive enough to give rise to a school or to make a significant impact on any group of players. Dave Liebman and Sonny Fortune, the most conspicuous graduates of the bands from this period, have chosen to play music that bears little resemblance to what they played with Davis; their music draws much more inspiration from Davis's music of the late 1960s.

But the sound of Davis's rhythm band is not completely silent. It reverberates, incredible though it may seem, in the music Ornette Coleman plays when he surfaces sporadically with Prime Time, a double rhythm section (two guitars, two basses, two drums), both in the style and in the sound. Coleman's reviewers have seldom made the connection, either because Davis's music of the period is already a dim (or at least unattended) memory, or because the suggestion that Coleman has followed Davis's lead (or anyone else's) seems too fantastic. But whether Coleman was influenced by Davis or, more likely, came upon the style and the sound independently, as long as he keeps alive that thread of sound to Davis's recent past, there remains a chance that Davis's rhythm band may yet have their day.

They will not likely be resuscitated in the mainstream of jazz, where Davis's quintet of the 1960s now form the current, but they might yet be rediscovered by a select audience. Certainly Davis's music of this period, *at its very best*, has the qualities that cult revivals seem to require: it is highly idiosyncratic, and it is passionately stated.

15

Shhh
1975–81

His eyes give him away. That's why he wears those huge glasses. The pain, the hurt, the vulnerability, 48 years old, all there to see. But he puts those glasses on and it's the Black Prince, who knows no pain.   Sy Johnson

"I've been trying to retire," Miles Davis told Gregg Hall in 1974, but when Hall asked, "Do you really want to retire? You know the word is out on the street," Davis contradicted himself and said, "No, I really don't give a shit about retiring."[1]

The idea of retiring had been there for some time, forcing itself into his thoughts and occasionally into words when the aches and pains made a two-hour performance almost unbearable, but he never took it seriously for very long. It had become the kind of thing that he tossed into a conversation for its shock value, but as soon as it started provoking not surprise but expectancy, as with Hall, he retracted it. In the end, his retirement was not something he planned or wanted. It just happened.

He was young by the standards of most professions, just attaining the age at which attorneys become judges, professors become deans, and executives become vice-presidents. But he was long past the age when boxers hang up their gloves. More to the point, he was old for a jazzman – already older than Coleman Hawkins had been when he was the grey eminence of 52nd Street, and older than Lester Young had been when he displayed his spent talents in Europe, and much older than Freddie Webster, Charlie Parker, Fats Navarro, Bud Powell, Tadd Dameron, and so many of the other heroes of the bebop revolution had been when they died. On 26 May 1976, he would turn 50. When that birthday arrived, he had been out of the public view for almost eight months, and he would remain out of it for five more birthdays.

Most of the time, he just lay around his house with the shades drawn. When Cheryl McCall asked him, after it was all over, whether he had been depressed, he said: "*Bored* is the word. So bored you can't realize what boredom *is*. I didn't come out of the house for about four years ... Everything would come to my house. You know, anything you want you can get. All you have to do is ask for it. I didn't go to the store. I didn't go anywhere."[2] Whenever he woke up and saw sunlight streaming through the windows, he knew he was in the hospital, too sick and sore to get up and draw the shades.

The major operation, the one he most dreaded, took place in December 1975. The sickle cells caused thrombosis in several of his joints, including the shoulders and wrists, but the worst damage was in his left hip-joint. For almost two years he had been forced to curtail his gym workouts because the deteriorating joint allowed the thigh bone to slip out of its socket. The prosthesis that repaired the damage in the earlier operation had now deteriorated, and Dr Philip Wilson, the orthopedic surgeon, operated again to remove the bone chips and implant a rebuilt joint.

Davis began walking on it in January and seemed to be progressing normally. "He walks with a cane, but he's really fine," Teo Macero told a reporter. "He gets around pretty well. The fact that he stays home a great deal doesn't mean that he doesn't want to work. Miles wants to work."[3] But Davis was less certain. Afterward, he admitted, "That's what stopped me. That operation, man, I was so *disgusted* I just said fuck it for a while."[4] Macero was deceived by Davis's refusal to show his pain whenever it was possible for him to mask it. George Wein, who visited him in the hospital, noted that "Miles is not one to detail his suffering but you could see the agony on his face."[5] Looking back on it, Davis said, "I was all right," but he admitted: "It was just that I took so much medicine I didn't *feel* like playing the trumpet, didn't *feel* like listening to music. Didn't want to hear it, smell it, nothin' about it."[6]

By the time of his hip operation, he was still being treated for the stomach ulcer that had grounded him in St. Louis, and he had barely recuperated from the operation on his larynx. Still to come in the next three years were an operation to remove gallstones and further surgery on the hip socket.

None of these ailments was publicized, except in vague rumors that circulated throughout the jazz world, and Davis's absence became the subject of continuous speculation and gossip, mostly based on what was assumed to be the unsavory lifestyle of the Prince of Darkness.

One of the more persistent rumors pictured him withdrawing into a drug-induced catatonia behind the drawn shades of his brownstone. One of Davis gofers later admitted that his job entailed running to the liquor store for bottles of Mateus rosé, which Davis liked to sip after snorting cocaine. "It was weird," he told David Breskin. "Calls at 5:30 in the morning, he says, 'Get up here and keep me from killing Loretta.' That was one of his girlfriends. I'd get up there, and Loretta and him would be going at each other with these huge scissors that you could just put through somebody. I'd have to break the fight up and hide the scissors, and he'd punch her out and I'd cool him out and he'd cool the police out to keep from being arrested."[7] If such tales built his legend for a fringe of his fans, they also determined the critical perception of his recent music, as it became easier for his critics to dismiss it as the burblings of a man reeling out of control.

Another rumor, published in the French journal Le Point, claimed that Davis had been silenced by the Mafia for refusing to return the advances he received for cancelled concerts.[8] Another claimed he was underoing radiation treatments for throat cancer; this one gained credence after Davis returned to performing in 1981, because he reappeared wearing hats to cover a thin head of hair, and hair loss is one of the effects of radiation treatment. Like all the other rumors, this one has never been denied.

The rumor mills percolated wildly for five long years, and they were unchecked by any facts. Neil Reshen, Davis's manager, not only did not release any of the fact to the press, but he rebuffed all inquiries. Mark Zanger says: "I called Miles's manager Neil Reshen with some factual questions like, 'Who did the drummer play for before Miles?' Reshen wanted the questions in writing so he could ask Miles about them. So I mailed him the questions. Reshen doesn't return phone calls. A week later I talked to his associate, who asked me why I just didn't do some research. 'I *am* doing research,' I pointed out."[9] Sy Johnson had much the same success. "When I called Neil Reshen's publicity office for access to Miles," he says, "an arrogant and angry male voice said, 'How many times do I have to tell you – Miles Davis is not a jazz artist. Miles Davis makes his *own* music. Miles Davis will have nothing to do with a jazz issue of *anything*. I don't ever want you to bother me again.' Bang!!"[10]

After the first year of Davis's absence, many listeners remained cool to the claims that he was about to return. "Miles is a bad fucking man, and if he ever goes on the road again, I will not pay money to see him be an hour late and stand around, arrogant, condescending and spaced," a colleague told Ed Lowe of *Jazz* magazine. "Furthermore, I don't like all the electronic shit he's doing, and let's talk about something else."[11] Against that attitude, there were only a few scattered defenses. "He can turn people off and he has cancelled his concerts and this has hurt him in some areas, I'm sure," Macero told Gregg Hall, "but he probably didn't do it for the reasons people thought of at the time. I would say Miles is a well man but he has a tremendous amount of pain."[12]

Even Gil Evans, one of the few who knew exactly what Davis was going through, couched his explanation for his retirement in a crypto-mystical burn-out from creating a "new wave form." "He has to get that sound each time he plays and that's what people don't realize about someone who originates a tone – they have to recreate that tone every time the way they did it originally and it takes a lot of physical effort," he told Zan Stewart in 1981. "So when Miles plays he has to put out all that energy. That's why he took a five year vacation, because he did it for thirty years and he was exhausted. His total organism told him to quit."[13]

Lending credence to all the theories that his problems were not physical but mental or spiritual were the hints from Davis himself, starting well before his ailments put him in the hospital, that he was less than fully committed to his music. In 1972, Leonard Feather had asked him what he wanted to be doing in ten years, and Davis replied, "Nothing. If I don't have a deal lined up like I want it, ten years from now, I'd give up." Feather countered by saying, "It sounds to me as though you're not that interested any more, or not deeply concerned, about continuing in music," and, although Davis denied that immediately, he conceded, "If I started thinking about music – now – then I'll have to play the trumpet. But the minute I don't think about it, then I can be content doing nothing."[14]

He was not impervious to the critical lambasting he had taken for the past four or five years either. "I'm too vain in what I do to play anything really bad musically that I can help not doing," he told Nat Hentoff. "If I ever feel I am getting to the point where I'm playing it safe, I'll stop. That's all I can tell you about how I plan for the future. I'll keep on working until nobody likes me. When I am without an audience, I'll know it before anybody else, and I'll stop."[15] So the rumor persisted that he had stopped because of the catcalls drifting out of the audience wherever he had played since 1972, and the hostile reception to his recordings, especially *He Loved Him Madly*, the Ellington elegy into which, appropriately or not, he had poured so much feeling. The critical consensus on *He Loved Him Madly* formed immediately before he quit performing, and to some observers those two events seemed more than coincidental.

Davis had found himself not at the head of the current movement in jazz but all alone, doggedly pursuing a direction that no one else seemed inclined to follow. "In general there ain't much happening that I want to hear," he had told Feather in that interview a few years before. "All the groups are trying to play like somebody I know. I don't want to hear clichés: I don't want to get back into the past. What's important is what's happening now, the new music and the music of the future. I don't even want to think about what I was doing myself last year."[16] So Art Pepper, in his memoir, *Straight Life*, concluded: "Miles is panicked. He's stopped. He's got panicked trying to be different, trying to continually change and be modern and to do the avant-garde thing."[17] Lots of listeners found that convincing, and, perhaps, if it had been put to Davis by someone like Leonard Feather, even he might have gone along with it part way.

While Davis had spent more than a little energy repudiating his earlier music, during his retirement it became the only music that jazz fans heard. It came out of several sources, and probably the least important of them were the nostalgia buffs who, assuming Davis's career was spent, reached back into the stacks for the *Birth of the Cool* or *Walkin'* or *Kind of Blue*. Those phases of his career were securely fixed in jazz history, and replaying their consummations made a useful reminder of Davis's stature but added nothing new to it.

More significant was the thoroughgoing review of Davis's music of 1964–8, with the quintet of Wayne Shorter, Herbie Hancock, Ron Carter, and Tony Williams. That combination had been widely respected and highly successful in its day but had worked in a period when jazz was undervalued, with a dwindling general audience and a less than vigilant critical audience. In the rush to pick up on the early experiments in jazz-rock fusion that immediately followed, most listeners simply took the acoustic quintet for granted and shunted their LPs into a corner. With the rush ended and the fusion experiments, along with their patriarch, evidently played out, the time was ripe not just for a reminder but for a revaluation. Two long, detailed reviews, one by Harvey Pekar in *Coda* (1976) and the other by Scott Yanow in *Record Review* (1978), helped listeners to relocate the music of that quintet, and revivals of its style by strong new bands, especially one led – unexpec-

tedly, in view of the music he had been marketing recently – by Herbie
Hancock and later, as Davis was preparing to emerge into public view
again, another led by a promising young trumpeter named Wynton
Marsalis, Davis's achievement of the mid-1960s, which his band
had not come close to exhausting when he abandoned it, came into its
own.

Another source of Davis's earlier music came from Columbia
Records, which pointedly ignored his 1972–5 backlog in the four LPs it
compiled for release during his retirement. The first one, *Water Babies*
(PC34396), in 1976, looked like a continuation from *On the Corner*, with
its Corky McCoy cover illustration and its listings of electric keyboards,
but the appearance was deceiving – so much so that John Norris, the
co-editor of *Coda*, alerted his readers with a notice saying, "You should
check out Miles Davis' *Water Babies*. It's with the classic 1960s
quintet."[18] The music released two sessions from 1967–8 for the first
time. Columbia's 1977 release (PC 34804) harkened back to May 1949,
issuing nine transcriptions of the Miles Davis–Tadd Dameron quintet
in Paris. Then two years passed in silence before Columbia issued *Circle
in the Round* (KC2 36278) in 1979, a twofer compilation of music from
1955 to 1970, and it followed that two years later with a similar
compilation called *Directions* (KC2 36472), containing tracks from
1960–70. The music was uneven, but it brought to light some buried
gems, including *Two Bass Hit*, from Davis's first session for Columbia,
Gil Evans's *Song of Our Country*, which had been left out of the
Sketches of Spain LP, and several new pieces by the mid-1960s quintet.

A very different retrospective airing for Davis's music came about in
New York in 1974–5, where the first significant attempts to form jazz
repertory orchestras took place. The New York Jazz Repertory Company prepared an "in-depth, one-subject" concert of Davis's music as
one program of a series that included similar concerts reprising the
music of Louis Armstrong, Count Basie, Bix Beiderbecke, Jelly Roll
Morton, and George Russell. The emphasis was placed on re-creating
the sounds of the past, a less promising premise than that of New York's
other repertory orchestra, the National Jazz Ensemble, directed by
Chuck Israels, the composer and conductor who had once been Bill
Evans's bassist. Israels was intent on capturing the spirit rather than the
sound of jazz classics, and several of his programs incorporated Davis's
music. On 21 November 1974, the Ensemble played *Israel*, Johnny
Carisi's composition for Davis's nonet, in a score arranged for orchestra
with Davis's original solo orchestrated for the brass section. The same

concert featured Davis's *All Blues*, with Davis's solo and Bill Evans's original accompaniment arranged for the Ensemble and Evans as guest soloist; "Henry James would have relished such intricate footwork," Whitney Balliett noted in his review. The Ensemble's concert in January 1975 explored Davis's *Solar*, the melody that he played once in 1954 and promptly forgot, and in mid-April they ended their concert with (in Balliett's description) "big-band impressions of Ornette Coleman, John Coltrane and Miles Davis."[19]

The repertory orchestras both failed after one or two seasons, leaving jazz again with the most blatant gap in its long struggle toward cultural respectability. Their chances of success were doomed from the start by the fact that there were two of them, however different their premises, contending for audiences and foundation grants. Even if there had been only one – and even if that one had been Israels's imaginative and ambitious National Jazz Ensemble – it was probably doomed by the economic climate. North America was slipping into a long recession in 1974 as markets were being taken over by Japan, and for the time being, West Germany. Within a few years, West Germany would follow the rest of Europe into the same recession, and by then, in the United States, public funding was being diverted to bail out the textile, steel, and automotive industries. Even well-established symphonies, ballet companies, and universities faced sharp cutbacks in their grants, and there was nothing left over for an upstart from the world of jazz. But while they lasted, the two repertory orchestras made Miles Davis less inconspicuous.

It is hard to imagine anything more inimical to Davis's wont for burying the past than a repertory orchestra. His reaction would have been easy to predict, and Dizzy Gillespie suggested what it might have been. "The concerts they're having, where they go back through the music because so many people didn't hear it when it was first performed, are groovy," Gillespie said, but he added: "We need the followers to do that. The creators are supposed to step forward. That's why I can appreciate Miles. I don't care whether you like his music or not, he has stepped forward. It's up to your personal taste, but the music is there for you to taste whether you like it or not. He did have the courage to step up there."[20] From the mellower perspective of 1983, Davis could see some virtue in preserving the jazz tradition. "There's a place for it," he told Richard Williams in *The Times*. "That shouldn't be lost. Lester Young, Dexter Gordon – those styles shouldn't be lost. But I can't do that."[21]

Davis made a token effort to resume his activities in May 1976 by rehearsing and recording at the Columbia studios, probably with some of the men from his last working band. "He conducted and played the organ," Teo Macero reported. "The trumpet was there. He just didn't feel like playing the trumpet."[22]

The sessions ended abruptly when Davis's hip became severely infected. "He shoots happiness into his leg with a dirty needle," David Breskin said, "and pays no mind until one day he can't walk."[23] His doctors discussed the possibility of amputation and Davis shrugged. In the end, he faced further surgery and the leg was saved. So he marked his 50th birthday bedridden. Thoughts about resuming his career grew more remote.

Discussing the relapse with reporters, Macero tried to put it into a positive perspective. "Listen, a man gets sick, right," he said. "Sure a man gets sick. Sure he has to recharge his batteries. And with Miles, he knows – his body tells him when to play and when not to play. What's wrong with that?"[24] He sounded as if he were reassuring himself, or perhaps Davis.

Press releases for the 1976 Newport Jazz Festival, which had grown into an eleven-day slate held in various New York halls, announced that Davis would join the members of his mid-1960s quintet on 29 June for the first part of a concert called a "Herbie Hancock Retrospective." The centerpiece of the festival was intended to be four concerts devoted to phases of Duke Ellington's music, but the reunion of the Davis quintet became the main talking point when the program was released. In the end it did not happen, and Freddie Hubbard had to replace Davis, but the strength of the reunited sidemen produced what Robert Palmer, reporting for *Rolling Stone*, called "the magic moment of the festival." The quintet played the first part of the concert, followed by a reunion of Hancock's Mwandishi band of 1970–3 and a set by the current version of his jazz-funk group, Headhunters. "The surprise of the jam, which seemed to affect the musicians as much as the audience, was that the music they made together stood head and shoulders above their current efforts as individuals," Palmer wrote. "Neither saxophonist Shorter's Weather Report, pianist Hancock's post-Headhunters jazz-funk, bassist Carter's CTI albums nor drummer Williams's Lifetime recordings compare with the barrage of music they laid down as a unit."[25] That point was not lost on Davis's former sidemen, and they decided to reunite the following summer for a tour.

As Davis's retirement entered its second year, attitudes toward him seemed to soften. Speaking to Sy Johnson in 1974, Davis had moaned about his isolation, mentioning that his old associates Thad Jones, Dizzy Gillespie, and Elvin Jones never went to hear him play, and that only Hancock of his younger associates ever visited him. "Chick [Corea] doesn't come to hear me ... Chick wouldn't be interested in my band," he said.[26] Now, two years later, Corea told Conrad Silvert in *Rolling Stone*: "This summer I'm going to take some time off, something I haven't done in four years. But I'll still do some composing. For years I've wanted to write solo orchestral compositions for certain musicians. One is Stanley [Clarke], another is Jean-Luc Ponty, and I'd love to write something for Miles Davis."[27]

Davis's most attentive companion during his extended convalescence was Cicely Tyson, the actress whose profile had graced the cover of his *Sorcerer* LP in 1967. Tyson's friendship with Davis persisted throughout his three-year marriage to Betty Mabry and probably a dozen other relationships. She seemed to be uncannily sensitive to his needs. "You know, she'll call and say, 'I'll be right over, I can feel something's wrong with you' – and I'll be sicker than a motherfucker," Davis told Gregg Hall. "She does it all the time. Remarkable! She's wonderful. She's a very talented woman!!"

By now, Davis's opinion of Tyson's talent was shared by almost everyone. In 1972–4 she became one of the most conspicuous actresses around with two brilliant successes, one on film and the other on television. In *The Autobiography of Miss Jane Pittman*, a television drama, she portrayed the title character from a young maid to a 110-year-old woman who takes a dignified stand for civil rights in the south, in a performance that won her an Emmy. Two years before, she portrayed a sharecropper's wife in *Sounder*, a Depression melodrama directed by Martin Ritt and co-starring Paul Warfield, for which she earned an Academy Award nomination. "Did you see her in *Sounder*?" Davis crowed to Gregg Hall. "That was a motherfucker!!" Of the climactic scene, where Tyson runs down the dirt lane to greet her long-lost, now-crippled husband, Davis said, "When she ran to Paul – UUHH!! brings tears to your eyes."[28]

Tyson's sympathetic contacts with Davis became increasingly important to him in the first year and a half of his convalescence, helping him to stave off the bouts of self-doubt and discouragement as his strength and stamina failed to return.

While Davis remained out of sight, Columbia seemed uncertain about how to respond. He was making no new records, but it still held a vast archive of his music in its vaults – some 80 unissued LPS, by Davis's reckoning – and 20 years of released material, amounting, in 1975, to 53 long-playing disks. Its choices seemed clear: either launch a systematic reissue program, resolving some of the anachronisms on the original issues, or delve into the archive for new LPS of unreleased material. Since most of Davis's releases on Columbia had remained in print from their initial release and were readily available, the most likely choice was the latter. Still, Macero seemed to favor a reissue program. "If there's anything at all that has held up the release of new records," he told Ed Lowe, "it's the fact that I wanted to put out a nine-album release in a series, one album a month for nine months, plus a final deluxe edition called *The Golden Years*, all taken from the recorded material CBS already has."[29] Preparations were apparently begun to clear the way for the reissues, because several of Davis's classic LPS on Columbia began to appear in record shops at discount prices around 1978, usually the first step in clearing out the backlog of stock to make way for the new issues. However, the only reissue that appeared was nothing but a repackaging; in 1980, Columbia put out a boxed set titled *Twelve Sides of Miles: Miles Davis Collection, Vol. 1* (C6X-36976), with the LPS *Miles Ahead*, *Porgy and Bess*, *Kind of Blue*, *Sketches of Spain*, and *Bitches Brew* inside.

Not much more was done about the archive, with only six disks of older material appearing in the six years of Davis's retirement, a potpourri of music excerpted from longer sessions in several phases of his career. Macero described the accumulation of music at CBS for Gregg Hall this way: "From the time the studio musicians start playing, we take down every note of music and all that music is intact in the vault at CBS. It's not cut. It's not edited. So there's an archive of Miles Davis that won't quit and it's all in perfect, mint condition. I take it and I make masters of everything [to be considered for a new release]. I may have fifteen reels of Miles and I cut those reels down; or I may have five and I may cut it down to two. I don't know. I keep listening to it over and over with the engineer and finally Miles comes in and listens to it and he smiles and he walks out. That's all there is to it."[30]

Much of the archive is probably useless for general release – the orchestral breakdowns for *Sketches of Spain* in 1959, when Macero started the practice of keeping the tape machines running continuously, the pure rehearsals intended only to introduce new players to the group, the four-hour experiments with "non-reaction" in 1973, and other sessions. But the archive includes also the unreleased half of the

Carnegie Hall concert with Gil Evans in 1961 and all of the UCLA concert with Evans in 1968, all the original music released with echoes, tape loops, and other artifices since 1969, and untold other sessions. Only a fraction of it has been touched.

Davis's most noticeable action in almost a year happened in February 1977, when he had a check for $500 delivered to the Jazz Museum in Manhattan as part of its fund drive to raise $5,000 for overdue mortgage payments.[31] The money helped save the museum for the time being, but it closed a few years later and its artifacts were removed to the Institute of Jazz Studies at Rutgers University in Newark, where they still await a new permanent home.

In the summer, many jazz fans heard a live reminder of Davis's music when Herbie Hancock reassembled the Newport reunion band of the summer before for a month-long tour. The band, called VSOP (for the designation on choice brandy), caused a sensation, drawing over 100,000 fans to its 25 concerts from New York to Los Angeles. Its high-energy, acoustic modal jazz not only recalled the spirit of Davis's music from ten years before but also revived it. In an interview with Conrad Silvert, Hancock explained that Davis wanted to attend the New York concert, but "he said he couldn't deal with all those people – because you know that when Miles comes around, especially since he's been off the scene ... everybody's going to jump on him." He added: "The night of the concert, me and Ron [Carter] went to see him at his house in between shows. He looked great, he looked *great*. He's been playing a little, I think, but not a lot."[32]

In his few pronouncements on VSOP, Davis seems less than enthusiastic. He told Sy Johnson, "I don't go to hear Freddie Hubbard only because I don't like him. I'd rather hear Thad [Jones] *miss* a note than hear Freddie make *twelve*."[33] (A few years later, Davis's objections to Hubbard seemed to be cleared away, when he told Cheryl McCall: "Well, I always try to have a good tone, 'cause I know if I don't it's gonna drag me, and it's gonna drag people I respect a lot, people like Dizzy and Freddie Hubbard and all the trumpet players."[34]) And in 1983, when Hancock was assembling the latest version of the summer band called VSOP II, with Wynton and Branford Marsalis as well as Ron Carter and Tony Williams, Davis told an English reporter: "Do you go back to Bernard Shaw for material? I only heard of VSOP three weeks ago. They wouldn't be able to get the same kind of intensity [as the original Davis band]. I wouldn't get the same thing now, either."[35]

Davis's lack of affection for Freddie Hubbard, who replaced him at the

Newport Festival in 1974 and 1976, placed ahead of him in *Down Beat's* readers' polls in 1973 and 1974, and joined Columbia's jazz roster in 1974, never developed into a general distaste for up-and-coming trumpeters. In 1977, he recommended Woody Shaw to Columbia, saying "he has a lot of heart."[36] Shaw was 32, and he played an unamplified trumpet in a brisk, no-nonsense style; his tone, but not his phrasing, is very similar to Hubbard's when Hubbard plays modal music rather than disco-jazz or the other hybrids he attempted at Columbia and elsewhere. Shaw began recording straight jazz for Columbia, usually with his working quintet, and quickly gained a following for both himself and his band, and Davis has remained generous in his remarks about him. In 1982, when Leonard Feather elicited Davis's responses to several younger trumpeters, he said that Hubbard was all technique but no feeling, that Wynton Marsalis was inspired mainly by Clifford Brown, and that Shaw could play differently from all of them. "Now there's a great trumpet player," he said.[37]

In the summer of 1977, Robert Palmer reported in the *New York Times* that Davis was actively preparing a band for his comeback, and that Gil Evans was playing keyboards in it. The story caused a larger stir than either Palmer or his source, which apparently was Columbia, might have anticipated, and several reporters began checking it out. While they did not get outright denials, the story quickly evaporated. Dan Morgenstern sought out Evans, who could tell him only that the *Times* story expressed "the merchandiser's point of view,"[38] although he admitted he was pleased to be working with Davis again. Hubert Saal sought out Davis, who would say only, "When I can stand on my leg I'll play again." He could not be persuaded to comment one way or the other on the report about his new band, but he pointed out: "I haven't been out of the house more than seven times in the last two years."[39]

The fact that Davis and Evans were working together, or at least thinking about music together, was not really newsworthy. While Davis was suffering through his enforced inactivity, his shop talk with Evans was uninterrupted by tours and rehearsals. "Gil Evans is my favorite [musician]," Davis told Cheryl McCall. "Anything he does, writes. He's also one of my best friends. He also guides me when I ask him what I should do. He's a nice guy to ask a question 'cause he'll say, 'I don't know.' (laughs) His favorite answer. He's all right. He's some person, he's quite a man."[40] When there was nothing else to report on Davis's music, even his friendly chats with Evans became news.

Columbia found other ways to keep Davis's name in the news. In

1977, it launched its Contemporary Masters Series, which included the Miles Davis–Tadd Dameron transcriptions from Paris and new releases by Charlie Parker, Lester Young, and Gerry Mulligan, by renting a Puerto Rican discotheque at 1674 Broadway for one night and converting it into its former glory, Birdland.[41] Davis, according to rumor, was to make an appearance in the audience, but he stayed away.

According to another rumor, Davis was expected to take a bow at a tribute for him organized by Lionel Hampton in February 1978. *Down Beat* reported that Hampton was putting together a program that included Gerry Mulligan, Woody Shaw, and the Jazz Workshop.[42] But the rumor, like all the others, fizzled out.

Rumors about Davis were so abundant that they became news in their own right. Ed Lowe reported to his readers in *Jazz* magazine: "The rumor that Miles is preparing himself for the Great Beyond is exaggerated, as is the occasional speculation that he has already taken up eternal residence there. Likewise, the story that he's been through enough corrective surgery on various parts of his innards to render him hashlike; and the tale of his having gone completely berserk, or at least more berserk than normal."[43] Another magazine, *Musician: Player and Listener*, found the Davis rumor mill easy fodder for its column of hip humor: "Keith Jarrett is having large bronze statues of himself cast for future installation in city parks across the nation. One of them will sub for him on his tour this spring," it reported, and "Miles Davis was in the studio again last week, but only to use the men's room, as he told the press upon leaving."[44]

Davis's contract with Columbia expired in 1976, and Teo Macero felt that the negotiations between the company and Davis on the new contract were deterring him from recording. "Once the contract is signed and things are worked out at CBS, we'll record again," he said. "When Miles is ready to record, we might record for ten months, every day. That's the way it is with Miles."[45] But the negotiations dragged on, probably not so much because of problems in coming to terms as Davis's reluctance to deal with music in any guise. The contract was settled sometime in 1977, but he apparently did not enter the recording studios at all that year; if so, it marked the only year he had failed to register a studio or an authorized live recording since 1945.

"I knew if I felt like playing I would play," he said later. "Even if it was just once. I didn't go places and sit in. Nobody had anything I wanted to sit in *with*." And then, probably in the first months of 1978, he felt like it. "I went down to the Vanguard once," he told Cheryl McCall, " and sat in the brass section, played everybody's trumpet, just once."[46] Thad Jones and Mel Lewis led their big band at the Village Vanguard on Mondays.

In February or March 1978, he phoned Macero and said, "I'm ready." The next day he resumed his recording career after almost two years of silence. He played the organ, and his recording band laid down the foreground backed by a set of pre-recorded brass arrangements by Bobby Scott, the singer who had had a smash hit with *Chain Gang* in 1955 and now worked as a freelance composer and producer. In the band Davis assembled, only drummer Al Foster had played for him before. Guitarist Larry Coryell was the best-known player; one of the young stars rising out of fusion music of the early 1970s, Coryell made his mark as a sideman in the bands of Chico Hamilton and Gary Burton, and then led his own band, Eleventh House, starting in 1973, when he turned 30. Keyboardist Masabumi Kikuchi also was experienced as a leader in Japan and as a sideman with Elvin Jones and Sonny Rollins, among others, in the United States; one of his compositions, *Lunar Eclipse*, was part of Gil Evans's new repertoire whenever he assembled a big band, as he had been doing more frequently since 1972. (Kikuchi often played with a young Japanese trumpeter named Terumasa Hino, who is said to have transcribed *every* Miles Davis solo ever recorded.) The third keyboardist, counting Davis, was George Paulis, and the bassist was T.M. Stevens.

The music remains unreleased, but *Down Beat* reported that it was "a cross between late '60s and late '70s disco."[47] If that made it sound unpromising for jazz listeners, their appetites might have been whetted by Larry Coryell's remarks about the session. "What I got from working with Miles was just one word: Stop! When in doubt, stop," he told Bill Milkowski. "Don't finish that phrase. So the spaces are starting to open up in my solos, and that came from just a few intense weeks of being around Miles."[48] Davis was apparently disappointed with the result, and when the session was completed he retired again for a year and a half.

His old triumphs were memorialized in the summer when he was named on one of the first twelve "Prez" plaques, commemorating the heyday of 52nd Street. The plaques were embedded on the sidewalk at the former sites of the Three Deuces, the Onyx, and the other jazz clubs, replaced long since by high-rises, one of them the CBS building, and the street signs along the block were marked "Swing Street." The other musicians so honored were Lester Young, Dizzy Gillespie, Charlie

Parker, Coleman Hawkins, Billie Holiday, Art Tatum, Roy Eldridge, Thelonious Monk, Sarah Vaughan, Kenny Clarke, and Stuff Smith, with a second set of presentations designated for Errol Garner, Slam Stewart, Red Norvo, Fats Waller, Oscar Pettiford, and Ben Webster. Davis's award was accepted at the official ceremony by Bruce Lundvall of CBS.

On 5 January 1979, Charles Mingus died of heart failure in Mexico, where he was seeking treatment for Lou Gehrig's disease (lateral sclerosis), which had confined him to a wheelchair for the previous year. Although completely immobilized, Mingus had stayed active, presiding over recording sessions in his name at the Atlantic studios, including the one in which songwriter-singer Joni Mitchell adapted some of his melodies and fitted them with her lyrics.

In 1980, Mitchell used Davis's music as the main motif for her segment of a movie called *Love*, with eight other segments devised by Lady Antonia Fraser, Edna O'Brien, and Liv Ullmann. Mitchell's screenplay, which lasts fifteen minutes and is directed by Mai Zetterling, has Mitchell portraying a black pimp. Both the plot and the character were evoked from the slice of Davis's music she started with. "My vision of the relationship between the soundtrack and the visuals is very precise," she explained. "The character I play, for instance, is a Miles Davis fan, and he carries the soundtrack around with him on a big portable cassette. I didn't think ... that they [the movie technicians] really understood the way I see it, I wasn't sure Mai knew how articulate I wanted each gesture to be, to the beat, in some key scenes where there is no dialogue."[49] So far, *Love* has not been put into general release.

Davis's music was heard for six consecutive days and nights in the summer of 1979, when WKCR–FM in New York played every available tape and LP he ever recorded as a "Miles Davis fest," which also included interviews with Percy and Jimmy Heath, Bill Evans, Philly Joe Jones, Gil Evans, and Max Roach.

After years of inactivity by Davis, it was surprising that he made any showing at all on the year-end jazz polls conducted by *Down Beat* and other magazines. In the readers' poll for 1979, he placed tenth among trumpeters. As if to confirm the suspicions of some of his critics, the only musician associated with him in the 1972–5 period who made a showing was Sonny Fortune (ninth on alto saxophone), but the most significant indication of how jazz tastes had been reshaped as the decade neared its end came from the complete domination of Davis's sidemen and close associates from the period immediately preceding. Chick Corea came second for Jazzman of the Year, following Mingus; Weather

Report was the top jazz group; Wayne Shorter first soprano saxophonist; Corea, Josef Zawinul, and Herbie Hancock the top three electric pianists; the same three, with Zawinul first, the top three synthesizer players; Ron Carter the top bassist, with Dave Holland fifth; Tony Williams and Jack DeJohnette the top two drummers; and Airto Moreira the top percussionist. All of them had discovered their skills and shaped them under Davis's tutelage and then moved away in their own directions, like the drift from Pangaea, to establish their separate identities.

"All those guys, they came out of me," Davis told Hubert Saal. "Tell them [the fans] I'm still pregnant. I've been playing since I was thirteen. I don't turn the other cheek and I don't give up either."[50]

Another revival took place in 1980, when Lee Konitz was invited to re-create Davis's nonet orchestrations, now 30 years old, by Martin Williams of the Smithsonian Institution's jazz division. "I didn't know where the arrangements were, so I called Miles," Konitz told Whitney Balliett in a New Yorker interview. "I hadn't had any communication with him in years, and he wasn't interested. He didn't want to hear about it." When Konitz found it impossible to transcribe the arrangements from the recordings, he began tracking down the arrangers. Johnny Carisi supplied his chart for Israel, John Lewis filled in the details for Konitz's transcription of Move, and Gerry Mulligan rewrote his arrangements of Godchild, Jeru and Rocker. Konitz then phoned Davis to give him a progress report. "I said, 'Miles, remember my asking you for the arrangements of the Cool sessions? Well, we've transcribed them and rewritten them and put them together again.' He said, 'Man, you should have asked me. Those [motherfuckers] are all in my basement.'" Later, Konitz reported the conversation to Gil Evans, who said, "Miles wouldn't have told you he had everything in the basement if you hadn't first told him you'd gone to the trouble to transcribe the records."[51]

Davis apparently avoided the recording studio again in 1979, although he talked about making some recordings. Dominique Gaumont visited him from Paris and received what he took to be an invitation. "He told me that we should do some stuff, him, Al [Foster] and me," Gaumont reported. "But he's very paranoid [très parano], and when I talked to him about it again last year [1980] he told me that was a long, long time ago."[52] By then Davis was already hard at work recording music of a very different stripe.

What sent him into the studio in 1980 was a demonstration tape played for him over the telephone during one of his almost-daily calls to his sister, Dorothy, in Chicago. Davis's nephew, Vincent Wilburn Jr, a 22-year-old drummer, played him a tape he made with a quartet of his friends. Davis invited the young band to join him in Columbia's New York studios. Two of the fourteen pieces they recorded were released a year later, on *The Man with the Horn* (Columbia FC 36790), but most of the information about the sessions comes from a report filed by Howard Mandel in *Down Beat*, which appeared in September 1980.

Besides Wilburn, the Chicago quartet included Randy Hall, a 21-year-old guitarist and singer and a student at the Berklee School in Boston, who had grown up with Wilburn in Chicago; Robert Irving, a 26-year-old keyboard player who graduated from the University of North Carolina; and Felton Crews, a bassist. All were involved in playing reggae, funk, soul, rock, and some jazz, as pick-up players around Chicago. Wilburn, of course, knew Davis's earlier music well – he cited *Four and More* (1964) and *Bitches Brew* (1969) as his favorites for Mandel – and Hall, through Wilburn, knew it too. Neither Irving nor Crews had had much exposure to it. They soon learned. "Our concept in Chicago was different from what Miles told us to play," Wilburn said.

They arrived in New York in April and started rehearsing in the studio on 1 May with Davis, but the lessons spilled over outside the studio. "We all have a very close relationship," Wilburn said. "Miles talks to us, tells us not to mix with drugs, helps us get our business together, and cooks for us – a great dish called bouillabaisse."[53]

To fill out the group, Davis asked Dave Liebman to recommend a young reedman and was directed to Bill Evans, at 22 the same age as Wilburn and, coincidentally, from Hinsdale, Illinois, near Chicago; Evans's association with Davis was destined to be more enduring. The other players added for the recording came on the recommendation of Teo Macero and others. What was intended to yield a single 45-rpm release ended up as fourteen titles and sixty hours of studio time, spread over three different months. The details of the first sessions are as follows:

Miles Davis with Vincent Wilburn Jr: The Man with the Horn
Miles Davis, tpt; Bill Evans, ss; Robert Irving III, pno, el pno; Randy Hall, vcl, gtr, synthesizer, celeste; Felton Crew, b; Vincent Wilburn Jr, dms; Angela Bofill, backup vcl. New York, 1 May–June 1980
The Man with the Horn
(on Columbia FC 36790)
The Man with the Horn is written by Hall and Irving, as are some of the following titles, perhaps in collaboration with Glen Burris. On some of the

following titles, Sammy Figueroa, perc, is added, and Davis also plays el pno.
Spider's Web; Solar Energy; Space; Burn; I'm Blue; Mrs. Slurpey; Thanksgiving; 1980s; two unidentified titles
(all unissued)

Hall sings the lyric for *The Man with the Horn* in a rich baritone, with all the colorations of soul music under good control; in his genre, he proves himself to be a talented young singer. The background is dominated at first by the synthesizer, and then by Davis's tightly muted trumpet with wah-wah effects, which takes over between the second and third verses for two choruses. The lyric is a paean to Davis that is extravagant and sometimes awkward:

> Smooth, suave, debonair,
> describes a man so rare;
> like fine wine
> he gets mellower with age.

Each verse is marked by the refrain, "He's the man with the horn," echoed ("he's the man, he's the man, he's the man") by the backup singers, Bofill and apparently Hall, dubbed in.

> His music sets the pace;
> the master never has to race,
> although he's much too fast
> to ever lose.

After Davis's trumpet choruses, Hall resumes:

> He's spent so many years
> crying melody for tears,
> but they don't understand
> what makes this man.

> The man keeps on blowing, yah,
> your mind keeps on growing;
> he's been up there for so many years
> blowing melody for tears.

If it seemed incongruous for Davis to resume his career by sponsoring a song extolling his stamina and by participating in his own eulogy, most listeners were willing to overlook that and notice, instead, that his trumpet playing, although constrained both in range and style in this framework, seemed to have lost little of its expressiveness.

Davis's recording sessions with the young Chicagoans were interrupted at the end of June, when Karlheinz Stockhausen joined him in the Columbia studios. "Stockhausen – I love him," Davis told Julie Coryell. "Gil [Evans] says, 'Stockhausen sounds like you.'"[54] Davis was accompanied also by Paul Buckmaster, the English composer and cellist who had introduced him to Stockhausen's works in 1972, and probably by Wayne Shorter and perhaps Josef Zawinul, among others. So far, the music they made together remains unissued.

After the interlude, Davis completed his work with his nephew's band. The details are as follows:

Miles Davis with Vincent Wilburn, Jr: The Man with the Horn
Miles Davis, tpt; Robert Irving III, el pno; Randy Hall, synthesizer; Barry Finnerty, gtr; Felton Crews, b; Vincent Wilburn Jr, dms; Sammy Figueroa, perc. New York, July 1980
Shout; two unidentified titles
(*Shout* on Columbia FC 36790; latter two unissued)
Shout is written by Hall, Irving, and Glen Burris.

Shout is an unpretentious little disco-rock dance tune with an infectious beat. Later, after the 45-rpm release scored a small success on the pop market, Davis said, "Randy Hall and my nephew and little Bobby [Irving], they all write great music for me. I need a bubble-gum song, I just call up Randy and say, 'Randy, send me a bubble-gum song. Like *Shout*.'"[55]

In the immediate aftermath, Wilburn and the others expected that their hours in the studio with Davis would give them an LP release by the fall, and they were ebullient about what it would show of them. "We're going to turn some heads around," Irving told Mandel. "People will be imitating songs, they'll be imitating Vince's drumming. Miles has been playing the stuff for other musicians and friends of his over the phone. Dave Liebman heard it, said it had a lot more changes to play over. Al Foster hear it; Miles played it for Cicely Tyson."

The unreleased material apparently follows the pattern of the two released tracks. "Well, there's something for everybody," Hall said, when Mandel asked for a description. "Vocals, electronics, to appeal to young people. It's commercial enough that people who never heard Miles before will get it. Older fans of his will dig, it, too. Some tunes are, like, pop. It's into a wide spectrum. The music is mostly ballads, but there's up-tempo funk, fusion, an open hi-hat sound with lots of drive that Miles instructed Vince to play, hip melodies on the top, lots of melodic changes ... The tracks average about five minutes each." Wilburn added: "There's no one doing anything like it. It's beyond sophisticated funk. Eddie Henderson? Hughie Masakela? Herb Alpert? No, it's simply new Miles."

More significant than the music that resulted from these sixty hours in the studio was the revival of Davis's ambitions. He proved to himself, if he had ever doubted it, that his capability for playing the trumpet had not disappeared after the years of neglect. "Miles has been talking about coming out, and he's in good health, for all those who've been wondering," Wilburn said. "He talks about touring Europe and Japan."[56] As it happened, Davis's return to performing came soon enough that Columbia did not have to delve into the funk tapes in order to come up with an LP of new music. While the sessions with Wilburn and his friends seemed important at the time, they were soon eclipsed.

Davis's worldly ambitions were also piqued by a grim reminder. On 15 September 1980, the pianist Bill Evans died suddenly, apparently from complications after suffering a bleeding ulcer. He was 49, and, although his period as a sideman with Davis has been much shorter than Coltrane's or Adderley's, and his association with him less intense than Mingus's, his death seemed to affect Davis more acutely. "It's too painful for me to think of Bill Evans and his piano," Davis told Cheryl McCall. "He's one of my favorite pianists. Or he was. But that's the way it goes."[57] As soon as Davis emerged from his retirement, he began playing *My Man's Gone Now* from *Porgy and Bess*, a striking incongruity in a repertoire that was designed to bury the past, and, although Davis never said so, he probably played it in homage to Evans.

Still months before the public would hear any of Davis's recent music, *Down Beat*'s letters column reflected some of the concern that focused on Davis. "All over the world people have collected the music you made, paid money to get hold of it," a Dutch fan chided him. "That's more or less the same bread you received, which enabled you to live the life you live nowadays. Dig? That is also why you owe it to the world to come out wherever you are." In the same issue, an Australian fan asked for clarification of some of the rumors. "I have been told: He's released nothing in two years; his recording company is sitting on some new material which it thinks is too far out; he's dead. What's going on? Can you put these tribal superstitions to rest? It's almost as bad as the pop scene."[58] A reader from New Jersey undertook to answer all the inquiries by declaring: "Let's all just *forget* about Miles Davis, huh? ... For all immediate purposes, Miles is gone – the past is over." He concluded: "The guy is obviously not doing anything worthwhile right now. Just as obviously, he doesn't care in the least for everyone's sobbing and lamentations for new material, an interview, or a live appearance. All Miles is doing now is showing up as every fifth or sixth word in every *Down Beat* article, no matter what the subject. The remedy for Davisitis? Get into what is happening *now* in jazz."[59] Davis would probably have agreed.

In his recording activities with the young Chicagoans, he seemed to be playing by rote, but those activities revived some deeper instincts. "Actually, see, you never retire from an instrument if you've been playing it since you were twelve because it's always in your head," he told Cheryl McCall. "I wasn't hearing any melodies or anything 'cause I wouldn't let myself hear anything, and all of a sudden those melodies started coming back to me."[60] He decided to try them out with a band in the recording studio.

For the first attempts, probably early in 1981, he brought back Al Foster, who had been playing with Sonny Rollins, and he re-called reedman Bill Evans, guitarist Barry Finnerty, and percussionist Sammy Figueroa, from the last sessions with the Chicago band. He needed a bassist, and Foster, Finnerty, and Evans all recommended Marcus Miller, one of the busiest young studio musicians in New York, on constant call for all kinds of funk and rock recordings. The details are as follows:

Miles Davis Sextet: The Man with the Horn
Miles Davis, tpt; Bill Evans, ss; Barry Finnerty, gtr; Marcus Miller, b; Al Foster, dms; Sammy Figueroa, congas. New York, probably January–March 1981
Back Seat Betty; Aïda [Fast Track]; Ursula
(all on Columbia FC 36790)
All titles are written and arranged by Davis.

Davis fulfilled some of the fears of his young sidemen by living up to his old reputation. He knew exactly what he wanted from them, and he let them know when he was not getting it. For *Aïda*, he told Miller to play an F and G vamp, but when Miller stuck resolutely to the chords, Davis stopped the band. "Is that all you gonna play?" he asked. "I heard you was *bad*. You ain't playin' shit." So Miller filled in his vamp ornately on the next take, and Davis stopped the band again. "What are you playin'?" he asked Miller. "Just play F and G and shut up."[61]

Some of the elements of Davis's post-retirement style are already intact in these recordings, although not as clearly defined as they would soon become. Where his working band of 1972–5 practiced a resolute collectivism, with the instrumental components fused together as if the surge of electricity had made a percussion-guitars-trumpet ingot, here they were restored as individual voices, charting their own space in the rock-jazz fusion. Davis plays trumpet solos instead of brass colorations, his two long turns playing muted over a walking bass line on *Ursula* comprising the longest, and most coherent, trumpet playing he had essayed for almost a decade. Al Foster, unencumbered in the new set up by the flotilla of players who formerly contributed to the dense bottom of the music, could play tough, elemental rhythms with only Figueroa's congas, sparse and tasteful, intervening.

Some of the music would persist when the retirement ended. *Back Seat Betty*, its title a left-handed compliment to Davis's ex-wife, became the concert opener in the first year of the comeback and, in a sense, for even longer than that, because the heavy-metal guitar and cascading percussion lick that starts it was retained when a new opener, called *Come Get It*, succeeded it. While *Ursula* is a long, meandering medium-uptempo ballad with a melody, perhaps entirely improvised, that is hard to locate, both *Aïda* and *Back Seat Betty* repeat simple four-bar declarations as their themes, the same kind of reduction of prepared material that Davis used in all his writing thereafter. His best compositions of the now-distant past, notably *Milestones*, *So What*, and *All Blues*, included similar proclamatory repetitions that gave way to longer melodies; in his new compositions only the proclamations remain.

Some of the other elements of these new recordings were destined to be shunted aside as his conception clarified. Bill Evans, soloing for the first time on record here, plays wailing, banshee cries on his too-sharp soprano saxophone, as if stepping into the old role of Davis's reedmen and supplying the foil for his more delicate trumpet. But Evans was clearly out of character. As his style developed in the next year when he became part of Davis's working band, he established a very different place for himself playing unassuming, cool solos on tenor saxophone, his preferred instrument, a foil instead for the fiery rock guitar that became the other component Davis used to spell himself off.

The most abiding composition, *Aïda*, underwent several changes after this initial recording. Retitled *Fast Track*, it became part of the new concert repertoire, but only after its simple theme was relocated in an easier context, usually played in future performances with a Spanish tinge. Few of the qualities that allowed it to endure in the repertoire are evident in this initial performance, which is heavily overlarded with rock effects. It seemed, if anything, the least distinctive of Davis's new themes.

Davis warmed to the task of making music on hearing the master tapes, and he realized that he had found some of the young sidemen he needed if he were going to make his return. He still wanted a more assertive guitarist, someone he could use as a soloist as well as the principal accompanist in the band; he asked Bill Evans if he knew anyone and was directed to Mike Stern. A young long-hair nicknamed 'Fat Time,' Stern looked like the epitome of the white rockers Davis sometimes complained about, but Evans's recommendation carried a lot of weight. "Now, if Bill plays that good, he's got it all," Davis reasoned, "and Mike plays that good, I'm goin' to play. Yeah, we played downstairs, and it was *nice*."[62] Davis soon returned to the studio with Stern in the band. The details are as follows:

Miles Davis Sextet: The Man with the Horn
Miles Davis, tpt, comp, arr; Bill Evans, ss; Mike Stern, gtr; Marcus Miller, b; Al Foster, dms; Sammy Figueroa, perc. New York, probably February– April 1981
Fat Time
(on Columbia FC 36790)

With Stern in the band, Davis located a new balance almost immediately. *Fat Time* is a longer theme – a tune, really – played over a lilting, funk bass line by Miller and chugging rhythm chords by Stern, a rhythm new to Davis's music and one that he would use frequently when he resumed performing. Evans's soprano solo, following Davis's muted solo, is relaxed and easy, a marked contrast to what he had played in the previous session, but he was allowed to ply his more natural style because he was now followed in the sequence by Stern, playing the high, reverberating notes over tougher rhythms that Evans had attempted earlier. Stern's rock-based electronics were not going to endear him to Davis's older fans, and after a year and a half of playing them for Davis even Stern began objecting to the stereotype he had settled into, but for the time being he was content. And Davis was delighted.

He started playing the new tapes for his visitors, and their reactions confirmed his feelings. Instead of the polite nods and vague murmurs they had given him for the tapes with Vincent Wilburn and his friends, they showed real enthusiasm. Gil Evans was impressed enough by Bill Evans that he lined him up to play in his band on 3 July 1981 at the Kool Jazz Festival (the Newport Festival, rechristened) and to tour Europe with his band immediately afterward. Herbie Hancock, a pillar of one of Davis's greatest bands, declared that these young players sounded like the best band Davis had assembled in years. George Wein, the Kool-Newport promoter who circled Davis warily throughout his retirement, had listened to some of the previous tapes with indifference. "Then one day he played something that gave me that old case of gooseflesh," he told George Goodman Jr. He added: "I didn't want to push him. I waited for him to say when."[63]

Davis was prepared to resume his career, and even Cicely Tyson, who had been encouraging him more actively than anyone, was surprised. "People say that it's thanks to me, but it's Miles who deserves credit for coming back," she told Leonard Feather in an interview published in *Jazz Hot* (translated into French and retranslated here). "We were together from 1966 to 1969. And at the end of each year after that I never forgot to phone him. I'd phone him New Year's eve, and I couldn't get over that he was still alive! I kept telling him that he still had a lot more things to do. Often he hung up on me, and I'd call him back again. He told me: 'I don't know any more if I've got anything to say.' He's a man who said from the start [*depuis les tripes*] if he had nothing to say, he wouldn't cheat." She could hardly argue with him on that, and his change of heart came without forewarning. "When he told me that he was rehearsing and that he was going to play again, I couldn't believe my ears."[64]

Wein was patient. He maintained an uncharacteristic silence with the press when he started talking seriously to Davis about ending the retirement, and in the end he scored the coup of his career. He and Davis had tangled dozens of times, usually noisily – "We have a love-hate relationship," Wein admits – but during the retirement he visited Davis in the hospital and at home several times. Once, according to Davis, Wein gave him $10,000: "I asked, 'What's this for?' and George told me, 'You might need it for cigarette money.'"[65] Now that Davis seemed ready to return, Wein was the only promoter he was talking to.

Still, it looked as if the comeback would have to wait another year. Wein's deadline for festival bookings passed and he faced the news conference to announce twenty-six concerts in seven days (28 June–5

July) in six different New York halls involving more than a hundred musicians, but Davis was not among them.

As soon as Wein sent out his press releases and placed his advertisements, Davis's discussions with him took a serious turn. He started complaining about the fee Wein had offered and dickering for a better deal. Wein knew then that Davis's retirement was over.

16

It Gets Better
1981 and After

Miles Davis is the only superstar that jazz has, not Mr. Basie, not Mr. Buddy Rich, not Mr. Kenton, none of these. Miles is the only superstar we've got. There are musicians who have made as much or more money but they weren't superstars. Jazz people need superstars just like rock people.   Chico Hamilton

Miles Davis's comeback concerts were the most publicized events in the history of jazz. *Down Beat* stopped its presses to squeeze this notice into its July issue: "BULLETIN:· George Wein announced that the new Miles Davis Quintet will debut with two shows July 5." By the time that issue appeared on the newsstands in mid-June, newspapers all over the world had carried wire stories about the impending return. Tickets for the two concerts, scheduled for the Avery Fisher Hall in Lincoln Center at 7:00 and 10:30 on the final Sunday of the Kool Jazz Festival, were long gone. They sold out within two hours. Bill Cosby, the comedian, appeared on the NBC-TV *Tonight* show in August with a monologue explaining why he could not get tickets. "All these guys share the 'aura' of Miles Davis," he told ten million viewers, "so Miles Davis's show at the Avery Fisher Hall sold out without any advertising or anything, man, because they went in and bought all the tickets before they even went on sale – before they were even printed." Cosby was using comedic license; he had attended the concerts as Davis's backstage guest, but the comeback had turned into such a media event that he could use it as a springboard to put Davis's name in front of a mass audience.

The *New York Sunday Times* ran George Goodman Jr's interview on the front page of its entertainment section the week before the concerts, and Leonard Feather's *Los Angeles Times* column setting the background was syndicated and widely printed. Kiyoshi Koyama arrived from Tokyo to file reports for *Swing Journal*, and Michel Contat from Paris for *Le Monde*, which ran his review on its front page. Virtually every major newspaper in the world devoted some column inches to the event.

With all the publicity, the traditional squabble between Miles Davis and George Wein over Davis's fee seemed superfluous, but they had it anyway. Davis told Goodman that he would receive $90,000 for the two performances, and Wein, who had been berated by Davis in the past for discussing his fees in the press, replied, "I will not discuss the money issue except to say that $90,000 is not an accurate figure."[1]

Some of the anticipation may have dissipated when Davis decided to take his young band out in public *before* the Kool concerts, to try them out in what amounted to dress rehearsals. Davis took his new sextet into a small bar called Kix – described by one fan as "a really unpleasant club" – in Boston, probably arranged by Wein, where they played two sets a night from Friday to Monday, 26–29 June. One Boston fan who caught them there on the night of 29 June watched a first set of only 35 minutes and a second one of 75, and then wrote about them briefly in a personal letter: "He has a bunch of sidemen half his age and he *directs* them – the guitar player took too long a break and Miles went over and patted the guy's head. This 'direction' gave the whole thing a rather constipated tone." Davis, in his opinion, did not look or act like a healthy man. "I hope you get to see him for yourself," he added. "I had the feeling that his return wouldn't last long."

Another report, from Radio Paris in August, stated that Mino Cinelu, Davis's French-speaking percussionist, had massaged Davis's fingers for an hour and a half before the band could take the stand one night at Kix.

Columbia Records, apparently fearing that the comeback might be short-lived, stationed a remote recording crew in the Boston club and added the dress rehearsals to its archive. Some of the music was issued a year later on *We Want Miles*, a compilation of performances from Davis's first months back. (Columbia has never divulged the specific sources of the tracks on *We Want Miles*; sources listed here are based on inferences from incomplete private tapings, with the help of Jan Lohmann.) At Kix, the sidemen were obviously much less comfortable with Davis and with one another than they would become after a few months of working together; their concert in Tokyo in October, from which less than fifteen minutes was selected for the *We Want Miles* LP, is superior in every respect. But the Kix performances are much better than the band's frenetic playing at the pressure-packed Kool concerts in

July, which Columbia originally intended to issue as Davis's comeback LP. The details are as follows:

Miles Davis Sextet: We Want Miles
Miles Davis, tpt; Bill Evans, ts (on *Kix*), ss (on *Fast Track, My Man's Gone Now*); Mike Stern, gtr; Marcus Miller, b; Al Foster, dms; Mino Cinelu, perc.
Kix, Boston, 26–29 June 1981
Kix; Fast Track; My Man's Gone Now
(all on Columbia C2 38005)
Davis plays electric piano on the opening bars of *My Man's Gone Now*. Evans is not heard on the excerpt from *Fast Track*. Identification of these titles originating at this session is tentative.

Kix, which fills the fourth side of the LP, is built on a four-bar bass riff played by Marcus Miller, sometimes parroted by Cinelu's congas; Davis inserts a two-bar melody irregularly between the soundings of the bass riff, but it is the bass riff, not the trumpet melody, that recurs to form the theme. From this slender underpinning, the band take off in a varied and supple improvisation in 4/4 time, doubling the basic ballad tempo for long stretches and twice stopping the time, apparently leaving Miller to use his discretion in inserting his theme. The performance thus demands more than a little ingenuity from both Miller and the soloists – Davis, saxophonist Bill Evans, guitarist Mike Stern, Davis again, and Evans again. Although the band had played only a few hours in public when *Kix* was recorded, they had obviously been well drilled beforehand. The formal simplicity of *Kix* alleviated some of the potential problems they might have had in the transition from private to public rehearsals and may have been devised mainly for that purpose. In any event, the simplistic *Kix* was removed from the band's repertoire later in the summer.

The format gives the two young soloists, who were complete unknowns to most of the jazz audience, interesting exposure. Stern opens his solo with long, fast lines before moving into the choppy rock phrases and searing single notes that would become his usual register in this band; he functions more as the percussion leader than as soloist at the end of his turn, whipping Foster's drums along until they threaten to overpower him. Evans, soloing twice on tenor saxophone, plays longer here than he did in most performances later on. His first solo is redolent of John Coltrane. Joe Goldberg also noticed Evans's debt to Coltrane at a concert later in the summer and commented: "Most of Miles' saxophone players sound like that, perhaps because he tells them to ... It is understandable that, having heard that sound every night for years, Miles would miss it, and attempt to have it recreated. But if that was indeed his assigned task, the present saxophonist approached it with rather too much fidelity to the original. He evidently shares with me a fondness for the Coltrane solo on the original recording of *All Blues*, from which I heard several favorite phrases."[2] But Evans soon learned to control his tendency for aping Coltrane, and his playing, as it has become better known, is indebted to Coltrane no more (and no less) than many other tenor players his age.

For Davis, the *Kix* performance is ambiguous. His solos include moments of bright lyricism, unencumbered by any electronic tricks, making obvious references to his classic ballad style; it is impossible to tell whether he is revisiting his old style or rediscovering the old convictions that made that style, and his reviewers often vacillated between lauding it and damning it, depending on the assumption they made. But his solos also include some moments of flattened sonority, especially at faster tempos, and an attempted high note that emerges as a squeak.

Fast Track would soon become known, at least obliquely, under the title *Aïda*, in the studio version included on the LP *The Man with the Horn*, which Columbia rushed through production in order to catch the tide of publicity surrounding Davis's comeback. This version has the same spirit as the studio recording: it is an exercise in power rhythm, with a tough beat and echoing blasts of repeated notes from Davis and Stern. Much of its extra length is due to Mino Cinelu, whose conga playing is featured, sometimes in a dialogue with Foster. The harmonic range of the drums seems roughly equal to the trumpet and guitar, the way they are used on this piece. *Fast Track/Aïda* is a throwback to Davis's pre-retirement rhythm band style, but it lacks the libido that gave that style whatever fascination it had.

By far the most interesting music came on the title that pointed backward and updated Davis's old strengths. *My Man's Gone Now*, in a twenty-minute version, recapitulates many of the beauties of the six-minute version Davis recorded twenty-three years earlier with Gil Evans's orchestra. Here, as there, Davis plays the A sections of the melody full of respect for Gershwin and doubles the tempo at the bridge; here, Miller carries the tempo of the bridge throughout the A sections in a repeated bass vamp, where Paul Chambers and the brass choir had implied the faster tempo under the slow sections in Evans's score. Davis's intensity in his ballad reading is also remarkably preserved. But the retained elements are thoroughly transformed. In place of tubas and trombones, Davis relies on Miller's bass to supply resonance, and in place of the soaring brass he calls on Stern's guitar to supply color. Boosted electronically by devices unimagined at the time of the original recording, Miller and Stern become a space-age orchestra.

Other elements of the arrangement are entirely new. When Stern solos, he doubles the tempo of the bridge, thus quadrupling the tempo of the A melody. As this band settled into Davis's concept, Stern was asked more often than not to solo at double the tempo of the others, and in many contexts the rise in pitch whenever he moved into the foreground seemed gratuitous and ultimately wearying, apparently no less to Stern than to Davis's audiences. Here it is not gratuitous; Stern's redoubling of the tempo forms the climactic movement from the easy ballad and the accelerated bridge. Davis cannot resist joining Stern, coming in at an odd interval of the chorus and playing to the end, when he abruptly shifts the tempo back to the slow opening.

To this point, *My Man's Gone Now* makes a brilliant show of Davis's revitalized talents and his young sidemen's resources. The elements of Davis's rearrangement of the Evans-Davis orchestration are tightly controlled; as the band grew more familiar with it, it underwent certain mutations and the contrasting sections were only implied. In this performance, it stands as the best harbinger of Davis's return to form — to the point described above. Unfortunately, it does not end there. Instead, Davis resumes the arrangement from the top, but carelessly, only hinting at the A melody and allowing Stern another crack at high speed. Much of the feeling and all the freshness fade in this second run-through, and the fine performance that preceded it is somewhat sullied. Such excess seems a strange failing for a musician who spent much of his career extolling musical economy and practicing it as no one else ever had. But that was long ago. Davis started losing sight of the virtue of musical economy sometime in the late 1960s, and his first comeback performances served notice that, whatever old verities might be renewed in the music to come, economy would not be one of them.

Davis returned to New York from Boston on 1 July, the Wednesday before his Kool concerts, as guest of honor at a Columbia cocktail and caviar party held at Xenon, a discotheque. Davis stayed half an hour, meeting the press and posing for them, chatting briefly and accepting pats on the back, and smiling. No one complained that he left too soon.

He seemed to be enjoying a truce with the record company. "Columbia is so *vague* and *cheap*," he told Cheryl McCall, but he could not follow through with his old, familiar theme, and he added: "Now they're not cheap anymore, they think I'm a genius. They thought I was a genius before, but now they're *convinced*."[3]

Young Bill Evans played in Gil Evans's band for the Kool concert at Town Hall on 3 July. He was also booked to join Evans's band on their European tour as soon as Davis's Kool concerts were finished, but he had to change his plans. "At the last minute Miles decided that he was going to work," Gil Evans explained. "Miles went up to Boston and played those four nights and he was feeling so good that he decided to get booked around, so he wouldn't let Bill go. On the night of the Town Hall gig Bill told me he had to drop out. He felt terrible having to cancel at the last minute, but I told him, 'You'll get used to that. Your career will make you do that sometimes.' So luckily Steve Grossman was able to go at the last minute."[4]

Davis was nervous about his Kool concerts, and his nerves would continue to bother him before all his concerts for the next few years. "I get butterflies in my stomach before every concert," he told Leonard Feather. "I can't eat the day before, and I really suffer. But since I came back on the scene, my nervousness is disappearing, and the more I play, the stronger I get."[5]

The first Kool concert, scheduled for 7 p.m. Sunday, started and ended in confusion. After members of the audience had been assembled, waiting, for almost half an hour, the public address announcer informed them that they could leave the hall to get a drink. Many did, but some held their places, probably thinking, as Michel Contat did, that "having waited five years, one can easily wait a half-hour longer."[6] Almost as soon as the people were out of the hall, the announcer declared, flatly, "The event of the 80s," and Davis and his band walked onstage. The audience stood and began applauding, jostled by the rush of patrons back to their seats, but Davis, without a glance in their direction, raised the trumpet to his lips and started playing. The band played for seventy minutes without an intermission and walked off. The standing ovation turned to boos when Davis failed to return to take a bow.

Between concerts, Davis and the others cooled down at a reception in the green room, with Bill Cosby, Roberta Flack, Cicely Tyson, and other guests. Numerous musicians filed out of the hall as the audience made its slow retreat, among them Gato Barbieri, Carla Bley, Lee Konitz, Red Rodney, and the punk band called the Lounge Lizards – "this," Contat noted, "in a city where musicians never ordinarily go to hear a concert by a colleague."

The second concert went more smoothly, starting on time at 10:30, lasting more than ninety minutes, and ending with a standing ovation that Davis returned to acknowledge. There were no encores, but also no boos.

Whitney Balliett reviewed the first concert as part of his annual Newport/Kool report for the *New Yorker.* He saw it as a piece of musical theater and characteristically made the review into an indelible image. "Miles Davis ... turned up for two shows at Avery Fisher Hall tonight ... and, for the hour that the first show lasted, pretended he was in *Apocalypse Now,*" he wrote. "Davis was dressed for the trip. He had on a fisherman's cap, a dark jacket, which he kept taking off, a singlet, gray pipestem pants, and clogs. It was night, and the darkness was broken by a searchlight that followed Davis as he stumped from side to side of the boat, ... raised his fist and brought it down to turn the ship of sound in a new direction ... The heavy-metal roar of guitar, bass, and drums was almost always present, and to make himself heard Davis had a small microphone fastened to his trumpet. His muted solos rose clearly above the din, and when he took out his mute and let loose an open-horn blast the crocodiles lining the banks jumped ... When the boat reached Kurtz's hideaway, Davis turned to the audience for the first time, and *waved,* as if to let us know that he is just one of us after all and that what we had been watching – it was a visual music – was only imaginary."[7]

Very little of the Kool concerts was issued on LP, notwithstanding Columbia's original intention of commemorating the event as Davis's comeback album. Sober evaluation of the concert tapes in the editing room after the excitement died down, and the availability of better performances when Davis remained active afterward, dictated a change of plans. Only an excerpt from *Back Seat Betty,* the concert opener, made the transition to record from the first concert. The details are as follows:

Miles Davis Sextet: We Want Miles
Miles Davis, tpt; Bill Evans, ts, ss; Mike Stern, gtr; Marcus Miller, b; Al Foster, dms; Mino Cinelu, perc. Avery Fisher Hall, New York, 5 July 1981
Back Seat Betty; My Man's Gone Now; Fast Track; Kix
(excerpt from *Back Seat Betty* on Columbia C2 38005; otherwise all unissued)
Evans is not heard on the issued excerpt from *Back Seat Betty;* he plays ts on *Back Seat Betty* and *Kix,* ss on the other titles.

Back Seat Betty gets a much more spirited reading than it had in the studio version, released on *The Man with the Horn*. Evans's solo, a gritty tenor ride, was sacrificed in the editing, and so were the other solos except for Davis's. The cascading intervals used both in the studio version and at the concert to open it and mark the transitions between soloists were shorn away too, but they are easily detached from the piece, and over the next years, after Davis stopped using *Back Seat Betty* as his concert opener, the cascading interval was retained as a kind of overture at all his concerts. Davis's solo begins with the simple muted melody, one part of it now further simplified into a playful schoolyard call ("He-ey, Be-e-etty"), and moves into an overlong sequence of exclamations on the open horn to rally the drummers. In the muted sections, Miller thumps out some fills that accent Davis's phrases perfectly.

The comeback concerts, for all their success as public relations events, placed Davis in a situation from which he had little chance of emerging unscathed. His presence on the stage guaranteed a standing ovation, but as soon as the curtain fell his performance was subjected to the closest scrutiny any jazzman had ever faced. Barely back on his feet after almost six years, supported by young and, except for Al Foster, inexperienced sidemen, he faced an audience as full of anticipation as any crowd at a world championship prize-fight, and critics almost as full of blood-lust. He could hardly expect to win the critical decision at the end, and in music, unlike boxing, there is nothing equivalent to a knockout for averting the decision.

The dominant impression of the critics after hearing no less than one hour and no more than three hours of music was that Davis had hardly changed at all since the last time he performed in public. "He neither regresses nor innovates," Contat wrote in *Le Monde*; "he recapitulates."[8] For Art Lange, that meant he had not changed enough. "Miles has emerged from a time-warp," he wrote in *Down Beat*; "his playing was stronger than anticipated – the same squirted, elliptical utterances which sounded so magical in the late '60s and early '70s ... Unfortunately, these are the '80s."[9] Cécile Tailleur, writing for *Le Point*, concluded: "His two concerts ... proved, above all, that [for Davis] the fusion between jazz and rock is irreversible."[10]

Most acknowledged that Davis was playing well technically. "Just one note and you knew Miles was back – that sound is as welcome and familiar as the first breezes of autumn," Lee Jeske wrote in *Down Beat*, in a review facing Lange's more caustic one. "Miles' tone was stunning, his chops were in excellent shape, and he quickly let us know it, removing the mute and wailing, with the trumpet bell not four inches off the stage floor."[11] "Davis's chops are in good shape," Balliett agreed, "but he played the same solo again and again. It went like this: an ascending shriek (Dizzy Gillespie, 1945) followed by a scurrying downward run; a second, lower shriek; silence; another run, broken off abruptly in the Bud Powell manner; silence; a three-note cluster, the last note flatted and held for a measure or two; an upward run; and a closing six-note cluster."[12]

The young sidemen bore the brunt of the critical beating. "Mr. Davis's latest group is reminiscent of his mid-70s units," Robert Palmer wrote in the *New York Times*. "Al Foster ... is the music's backbone. The other players are effective enough when Mr. Davis is soloing, but only the saxophonist Bill Evans seems to have a well-developed sense of pacing and at least a modicum of original ideas."[13] Contat largely shared that view, saying that the sidemen "are magnificent instrumentalists capable of playing everything, but not showing any inventiveness whatever."[14] Lange claimed that the sidemen "failed to sustain *any* extended solo or ensemble interest, culminating in guitarist Mike Stern's indulgent, exasperating forays."[15] Palmer added that "Mike Stern's guitar solos were rife with the most banal heavy rock clichés imaginable."[16] Stephen Brunt, in the Toronto *Globe and Mail*, said, "Most of their solos would have sounded more appropriate at a rock concert,"[17] but Lange claimed they were "neither good rock, nor good jazz." Jeske concluded: "The Man with the Horn is back – playing driving, aggressive trumpet – but the men with the guitar, bass and percussion were just not up to stylistic snuff."[18]

Lange viewed the late concert, as Balliett had the early one, as an exercise in showmanship: "This concert was more theater than music: the more appreciative members of the audience giving ovations at Miles' every move, Miles slapping fives with bandmates, his walking the stage, working it, worrying it to death, hunched over, notes aimed at the floor, braying like an elephant ... It's too easy to go out there and strut and vamp and jive this way."[19]

A few fans demurred. *Down Beat* printed a letter from a Minneapolis doctor stating that he had been "infuriated" by Palmer's review in the *Times*. "I traveled over 1500 miles to witness this concert," he said, "and I'm glad I was there."[20]

What infuriated him most was Palmer's contention that Davis should have been more aware of the music being played during his retirement.

"Apparently Mr. Davis did not listen to much contemporary electric music during his five-year absence from performing and recording," Palmer stated. "Bands like Ornette Coleman's Prime Time, Ronald Shannon Jackson's Decoding Society, and James (Blood) Ulmer's various groups have learned to make amplified ensemble music that is as harmonically challenging and melodically sophisticated as any contemporary jazz and as rhythmically bracing as the hardest funk. Compared to these groups, the Davis band's circumscribed harmonic language, heavy-handed rhythms, and hackneyed 60's guitar solos sounded positively old-fashioned."[21]

Palmer was right in assuming that Davis had not been keeping up with jazz in his retirement. The highest value he put on listening to records was a negative one. "It's useful, but mainly to see what you don't want to do, as always," he said. "It's nice to see someone else fall off the ladder! You can hear things that you wouldn't do yourself, without having to go through trying them out."[22] In various interviews granted in the wake of his comeback he responded to the inevitable question about whom he listened to by citing Stockhausen and Ravel, the pop-rock groups Journey and the Who, two young, teen idols named Michael Jackson and Prince, Weather Report, Willie Nelson, and singers who know how to exploit a melody, Frank Sinatra among them.

In his new band, he typecast Mike Stern in a Jimi Hendrix solo role and Marcus Miller in a funk support role. They worked capably, but both knew, and Davis would eventually find out, that their roles were far too narrow for the post-fusion climate they were playing in.

The critical perception of jazz-rock fusion had clarified considerably during Davis's absence. Musically, fusion music had crested almost a decade before, with the release of *Bitches Brew* and the further explorations that immediately followed it, many of them presided over by members of Davis's stock company. Commercially, it hit its peak a few years later in the mid-1970s, led by Hancock's Headhunters and Weather Report, but by then its jazz components had become so waterlogged that they were almost totally submerged. By 1981 the experiments were over and the audiences for rock and for jazz had gone their separate ways, with rock settling into punk banalities that were as vapid as, and not much different from 1950s rock 'n' roll. Tom Scott, the saxophonist who, as a young studio player and bandleader, had caught the fusion wave and ridden it to rock-style capital gains, now described its waning with no regrets. "As it turns out, I was in the vanguard of the fusion movement," he told A. James Liska in an interview in *Down Beat* that appeared on the newsstands just as Davis was unveiling his rock-based youth band. "It was an accident though. I was a serious Coltrane–Cannonball–Charlie Parker–Miles Davis student and all this fusion stuff was just a little departure that lasted ten years or so. There was nothing to it – nothing serious, that is."[23]

Several events at the Kool Jazz Festival, almost unnoticed in the hullabaloo of Davis's comeback, reflected the state of the art. Weather Report displayed their unrevised brand of jazz-tinged rock at Avery Fisher Hall the night before Davis, and almost half the audience, according to Stephen Brunt, left before the intermission. Two other erstwhile stars of jazz-rock revised their styles and kept their audiences. Chick Corea played acoustic piano at his concert – "having abandoned Electronic Heights, in Fusion City," as Balliett put it – with Roy Haynes, the bop drummer, in his quartet. Herbie Hancock assembled a quartet with Wynton Marsalis, Ron Carter, and Tony Williams and gave a concert that, for many observers, was the high point of the festival, without an electronic instrument or a wah-wah pedal in sight.

So Davis's comeback concerts presented a musical style that was out of step with the main currents of the day. That should not have been surprising: he had put himself out of step with those currents before retiring, when he formed his 1972 rhythm band and chose, whether he knew it or not at the time, to give up being the leader in jazz in favor of becoming its superstar. His return concert affirmed that he was going to stick with that choice, although the music he played on his return had little in common – certainly less than many reviewers assumed – with the music he was playing when he quit.

For the reviewers and many other members of the jazz audience, the realization that Davis would not reassume the mantle of leadership was disappointing, especially because no one had taken it up in his absence. But that was hardly Davis's fault.

"We deceive ourselves; we expect too much," Contat concluded, sounding a note that many other reviewers missed. "Five years of silence from one of the four or five great creators of jazz, when all the others are dead and the music is stagnating, creates a mythology: the myth of the Messiah. Miles Davis, and this should be enough to give us joy for the time being, is back."[24]

Davis's critics had more fodder soon after his concerts ended. Columbia released *The Man with the Horn* amid the swell of publicity, and it contained several performances that were far weaker than anything he had shown in his concert debut. W.A. Brower gave it three stars in *Down Beat*, and stated: "This record – parts of it – is pleasant.

That's all"; the rest of the review was a diatribe.[25] A more positive review in *Le Nouvel Observateur* welcomed Davis's return, but ended on this vague note: "Miles is always the man who walks on eggshells but the insidious sweetness – never cloying – of a piece like *The Man with the Horn* recalls how caramels also tease your teeth."[26]

Notwithstanding the reviews, the new LP sold briskly. It entered *Rolling Stone*'s list of the 100 best-selling albums in August at number 47 and moved up steadily. Radio Paris reported that it was selling "several hundred copies daily" there. Davis's only comment on the LP, when he played the tape to George Goodman Jr just before it was released in June, was, "To me, it's old. I can't stand it."[27]

Davis's comeback aroused at least as much curiosity about his well-being as about his music. The first report, from Goodman in the *Times*, was ebullient. "Mr. Davis is looking fit," he said, "and speaking with mischievous humor in the rasping whisper of a voice that is a Miles Davis trademark." That description hardly prepared his audiences for the changes that had transformed his appearance while he sat in his darkened brownstone.

He wore a cap or a wollen tam pulled down to his ears to cover a balding pate, where there had been, as far as anyone could remember, a thick Afro when last seen. He was down fifteen pounds from his "fighting weight" of 135, and the sparse new mustache and goatee only made his face look pinched. "When ... he re-emerged into the public arena, he seemed to a frightening degree physically reduced," Richard Williams wrote in *The Times* of London. "On stage ... he moved slowly and painfully; he appeared literally to have shrunk. The imperious carriage and the feline prowling which had contributed to his legendary presence were completely gone."[28] In fact, he now moved compulsively around the stage, as if he had been forbidden to give his weary bones any rest. His movements were impeded not only by his arthritic joints but also by the truss and rubber corset he wore to shore up the muscles of his abdomen.

Psychologically he seemed better off. He was full of confidence and claimed that he had never had any doubts about his ability to play the trumpet. "I never think about not being able to do anything," he said. "I just pick up my horn and play the hell out of it." His embouchure, he claimed, had never softened, and as soon as he started thinking about music again he was ready to play. He was now thinking about it all the time. "I can't stop once I start thinking about it," he told Goodman. "My mind is like this. I can't sleep for three days, four days at a time."

Gratuitously he offered Goodman his advice for staying young. "The way to stay young is to forget, to have a bad memory," he said. "You know, when a woman says to me, 'Do you remember when we were lovers five years ago?' I say, 'No.' Guys come up to me with their arms outstretched, I say, 'What's that for?' And they say, '1947, Chicago, remember? We got high together.' I say: 'Get out of my face.' ... Everything you do, you want to do, but then you don't want to be reminded of it."[29] If that attempt at hoary wisdom sounded out of character from a man who had just turned 55 and looked older, it is probably because it rightfully belonged to a man who was about to turn 70 and looked younger. Gil Evans had taken to expounding the same idea fairly often. "I read an interview in the *International Herald Tribune* with a man who was celebrating his 100th birthday and they asked the usual 'How do you account for such a long life?' and the man said, 'A poor memory.' That's all he said and I knew what he meant exactly," Evans told Zan Stewart in 1982.[30]

Apart from Davis's health, most of the curiosity was aroused by his young sidemen, whose professional careers began in an unusual glare of publicity. Following the Kool concerts, Davis took them on a round of American concert halls for three months, starting with a hastily arranged engagement at the Savoy in New York two weeks later, and moving on to other hastily arranged dates in various cities, including Washington, DC (28 July), and Detroit (16 August), until September, when his new manager, Mark Rothbaum, had enough lead time to put together a more carefully articulated tour that took in the Music Hall in Cincinnati (18 September), the University of Michigan at Ann Arbor (19), the Hollywood Bowl, Los Angeles (25), and Concord Pavilion, San Francisco (26). From California, they took off for a round of concerts in Japan.

As the American audience became exposed to the new band, it discovered that the young sidemen were not the ciphers that several of the New York critics had led them to expect. On the contrary, after the pressure of the comeback concerts they settled down and showed that they were among the brightest new talents in jazz.

The changing perception of the sidemen was boosted by Davis's respect for their talents, which he expressed at every opportunity. Asked by Cheryl McCall if he thought he was healthy enough to withstand all the traveling, he said, "Not really. It's just playing with Bill [Evans] and those guys. It turns me on. It makes the adrenalin start flowing. It's such a great bunch of guys, they play so well, it's a pity to let them down, you know."[31]

They had been stung by the caustic criticisms, and Davis constantly reassured them. Marcus Miller recalls Davis telling them, "Who you gonna believe, me or some guy who works for a newspaper?" And during one concert, Davis walked up to Miller and said, "Man, you swing better than them old motherfuckers."[32] Not all the critical barbs directed at them, Davis claimed, were strictly objective. "One guy did it 'cause I wouldn't do an interview with him," he said. "He kind of upset my guitar player. I said, man, look at me, I've been called a black motherfucker, and black this and that, some of this here and that there. Man, you just ignore it. The best thing is not to say anything at all."[33]

His feeling for the men in the band was undisguised, and his openness with them was part of a brand-new character that emerged after four years of sitting in the dark. "The Miles the band knows, no one else has ever known," Miller told Sam Freedman in a *Down Beat* interview. "This person is closer, I think, to the real person behind all the stories. Once on the phone, I was telling Miles I was feeling uptight about my playing, feeling a little insecure. Miles said, 'I felt the same way when I was your age.' And I said, 'You were playing with Bird and those guys.' He said, 'Man, Bird and them would leave me up on the bandstand, go downstairs to do their thing. The tempo would be goin' by and I played one chorus, two choruses. By the third chorus, I didn't care what I played. Wasn't my band.'" Miller adds, "It meant so much just to see everybody, even Miles go through those insecurities. And if Miles likes the way I play, I don't need to hear anything else."[34]

Davis dominated the new band musically, in much the way that he had dominated his earlier bands and in marked contrast to his melding into the collective sound of his last band. The music now was more carefully worked out, determining a context in which individual innovations were encouraged. "When you practice you take the *edge* off something," he said. "We don't practice, we *rehearse*, there's a difference. We rehearse and throw things around. After a couple of times they get the idea. And that's it."[35] Mino Cinelu told Gérald Arnaud: "Miles directs us very little. When Al [Foster] isn't playing what he wants, he just looks at him ... Lots of things pass between Miles and all of us. Since Mike [Stern] is responsible for the harmonies, it's good that he and Miles share a close communication." Although he said little to the young sidemen about their playing, Davis made sure that they would hear his opinions indirectly. "I simply know that Miles often tells Mike that I carry the whole band," Cinelu said, adding, "With Al, of course."[36]

"When Miles isn't playing, that doesn't mean he is absent," Miller noted in an interview for the French magazine *Jazz Hot*; "everything he touches carries his mark. He penetrates each of us and makes us play for him [*à sa guise*]. He transforms, inspires his band. His influence goes beyond his trumpet playing."[37]

The band members, Davis told Cheryl McCall, responded creatively to his indirect direction. "They pay attention," he said. "And they're all professionals, so professionally they know if they miss anything, it's gonna fall right back on them. Everybody in my band could have a band right now. I don't tell them what to do, I just *suggest* something and if they don't like it they'll suggest something else. Say, can we do this *and* this. Or they'll know what I mean and add something to it that makes it better."[38] In only a few months, the band pulled together musically and personally. "We're a group with a homogeneity truly astonishing," Cinelu said, "especially astonishing because our musical backgrounds are very different."[39]

As they made their first swing through several American cities that summer, the young sidemen gradually lost their anonymity.

Al Foster had been Davis's closest friend in his last working band, and he remained close to him during the retirement, one of a handful of friends that included Gil Evans, Herbie Hancock, and Dave Liebman who visited him regularly — "telling me," as Davis put it, "what's happening out on the street." Foster worked with numerous studio and pickup bands during Davis's layoff. His longest association was with the Milestone Jazz Stars, an all-star touring group assembled by Milestone Records, the heir to defunct Riverside, now a division of the Fantasy conglomerate. The Milestone Jazz Stars featured Sonny Rollins, McCoy Tyner, and Ron Carter, with Foster as the unbilled fourth man in the quartet. When tours took him away from New York, Foster talked to Davis almost daily on the telephone. "I stay in constant touch with Al no matter where he is," Davis told Cheryl McCall. There was no doubt in the minds of either of them that Foster would rejoin Davis if and when he formed a new band. "Al called me up from France," Davis recalled, "and said you should see the hotel I'm staying in. I said *I told you about that*. Why should you stay in a bad hotel, you don't live in a bad house? You lose half your money just trying to find a bed. He said, It's not like when we're travelling with you, chief, 'cause you had us the best food and rooms. I said, when you're with the best you get the best."[40]

The rehiring of Foster was surprising only because it went against

Bill Evans and Miles Davis onstage (Peter Jones)

Miles Davis (Brock May)

Davis's wont for hiring untried players. When Davis asked Dave Liebman to recommend a reedman for the new band, he explained that he could not use Liebman himself because he wanted new talents. "He doesn't like to go back to people he's played with before," Bill Evans said.[41] But the policy proved flexible when Foster was involved, and he was the veteran among the rookies in the new band.

Bill Evans became Davis's protégé, in the beginning, and the focal point for Davis's onstage wanderings. "Bill's my *right hand man*, boy. Without him I don't know what I'd do," Davis said.[42] At Davis's concerts, that description appeared to be true literally – Evans stood stage left, on Davis's right – but not figuratively. Only Liebman among Davis's reedmen got as little playing time, and Evans sometimes put in stretches of twenty minutes without raising his horn to his lips. He bided his time almost motionless behind his microphones in a three-quarter stance that let him keep his eyes on Foster and Stern at center stage without quite turning away from the audience. When Davis's wanderings on the proscenium took him close to Evans's position, sometimes catching him in a corner of the spotlight, Evans looked as if he had been caught stealing an apple, and when Davis raised his eyes from the floor and stared at Evans past the bell of his horn, Evans would flash a shy grin that suggested he would rather be anywhere else but there.

Evans's solos were often interrupted abruptly by Davis's trumpet re-entering at an odd juncture – the seventh bar, say, of Evans's second chorus – and taking over. Evans naturally got annoyed and frustrated, and toward the end of his two-and-a-half-year tenure he sometimes grumbled openly after concerts in which he had played less than his share. The interruptions, like everything else that passed between Davis and Evans onstage, seemed part of a relentless mind-game in which Davis preyed on Evans's diffidence, like a panther circling a treed potto.

Offstage, they showed deeper bonds – "a sick father/healthy son relationship," Breskin called it.[43] "There's my favorite pupil," Davis said, and among the lessons he claimed to have taught Evans were how to dress for concerts, apparently in the headbands and loose, decorative shirts that Evans favors, and how to tap his foot by bringing down the heel first.[44] Evans submitted graciously in the beginning. "It's my first time on the road, my first record, my first time being an important part of the band along with big names," he told Howard Mandel soon after the debut concerts. "This is, I would say, something major. And I like it – I like it a lot."[45]

Evans was 23 at the time of Davis's comeback and since leaving his Illinois home more than three years before had been an inveterate student. For a few terms he attended North Texas State University, home of a high-quality, high-pressure stage band program that had fed several players into the bands of Buddy Rich, Maynard Ferguson, Woody Herman, and others. He transferred to William Patterson College in New Jersey, where he could earn a degree in jazz performance while playing professionally in and around New York. Before Davis hired him, his best credential was an appearance with Art Blakey at the Village Vanguard. He met Dave Liebman and Steve Grossman at a summer clinic run by Jamey Aebersold, and through Liebman he met Davis in April 1980. Through Davis he met Gil Evans, who would have taken him on his first tour with a name band if Davis had not reclaimed him.

Evans's best horn was the tenor saxophone. He started playing the soprano saxophone, which he used more often in Davis's band, only after meeting Davis, and his first recorded efforts on it consisted of cautious, sustained notes quite unlike his more melodic, but still cautious, tenor solos. The gap between the two instruments narrowed noticeably in his first year of touring. By the summer of 1982 he also began carrying a flute onstage for some performances, using it seldom but, when he did, impressively.

Davis seemed to appreciate Evans's piano playing as much as his woodwinds. At every concert for the first two years, Davis edged him over to the electric piano at some point in the proceedings to take a turn, which Evans made as short as Davis would allow. "He used to play classical piano and give concerts of Rachmaninoff and stuff like that when he was sixteen," Davis says. "People don't know that. I wouldn't ask him to sit down if he couldn't play."[46]

Davis's conviction about Evans's ability on piano and Evans's reluctance to put it on exhibit developed into a piece of musical theater. In the early concerts, Davis directed Evans to the piano with an imperious motion of his head. On evenings when Evans held his place, smiling boyishly and pretending not to know what Davis wanted, Davis would stump over and escort him to the piano, one hand on the small of Evans's back. Early in 1983, the ritual expanded. Davis's onstage wanderings would lead him to Evans's microphone where he would challenge him to trade four-bar phrases; Evans, on soprano, would begin by parroting Davis's trumpet runs until one or the other of them, usually Davis, would unleash what the audience took to be an unparrotable tirade. Evans would then allow himself to be sheperded over to the piano as an act of submission. The ritual obviously pleased Davis immensely and unfailingly elicited whoops of delight from Davis's audiences. But Evans, cast as the fall guy, took less pleasure from it, and the ritual ended after a few months.

On nights when Evans had little opportunity to show his talents on reeds, he gave memorable performances playing Tom Jones to Davis's Squire Western. Some nights, he not only filled that role but also displayed a subtle touch on his horns, calmly developing handsome lines that floated over noisier rhythms than he would likely have chosen for himself. Davis's audiences recognized Evans's potential, but few of them saw it realized fully enough to share Davis's almost unbounded enthusiasm. "He's one of the greatest musicians I've ever come upon," Davis told Cheryl McCall, and he added: "He and Gil Evans. There must be something with those Evanses. Must be a *breed*."[47] Davis's reluctance to let Evans prove his ability with fully elaborated solos or anything close to an equal share of the solo space baffled jazz fans and frustrated Evans.

Much more solo space was allotted to Mike Stern, who was recommended to Davis by Evans after they had played together in Boston in January 1981. "In order to recommend a guitar player to Miles, you've got to think about what Miles wants to hear," Evans told Howard Mandel. "He likes Jimi Hendrix and hot lines. A straight bebop guitarist wouldn't do it. Mike is a real good guy. He looks different, he thinks different, and he plays different; he has a real good technique, and he can handle the bebop bridges, where Miles swings. What else could you want?"[48]

Stern was born and raised in Washington, DC, and after high school went to Boston to study at the Berklee School of Music. There he took classes from Michael Goodrick, the guitarist who played briefly in the quartet of Gary Burton, another Berklee faculty member, in 1973 but whose considerable influence on young guitarists emanates from the classroom. "He was one of the first," according to John Scofield, another of his students, "to absorb Jim Hall's lyrical, legato approach and also have a real modern concept of harmony."[49] John Abercrombie and Pat Metheny also count Goodrick as an important influence, thus giving him a hand in the development of four of the most prominent young guitarists.

After Berklee, Stern made his home in Boston, traveling from there to play with the revived Blood, Sweat and Tears in the final attempt at restoring that band's commercial success and later with Billy Cobham's band. "That's where Miles first saw me," Stern told Howard Mandel. "But for me, playing with Miles is by far the best gig ever. I've always been a Miles fan but never expected to play with him. And he's real supportive. Like on the album [*Man with the Horn*], on my solo for *Fat Time*, that was the last thing recorded. I'd been brought in to replace Barry Finnerty. I thought the track we cut was an out-take. I didn't have my amps set right, and I was real depressed by the solo. But Miles really dug it. We get together now and listen to tapes we've made, and I'm never sure – but Miles is totally knocked out, and into it. He makes me do things I wonder about, but he's always right."[50]

Davis made Stern do things that Davis's audiences wondered about too, and none of the young sidemen absorbed such continual criticism. None of them was as conspicuous during Davis's performances. Stern stationed himself beside Foster's drum set in the center of the stage. The volume of his amplifier was set high. He played continuously, accompanying almost everything and soloing lengthily, usually with the tempo surging behind him. No matter if he sneaked in a bebop solo part way through the concert, the main impression was of frenetic, unmodulated, ear-busting verbosity.

He repeatedly claimed that much of what he played for Davis went against his better judgment. "I'll play bebop kind of lines – I've played hundreds of bop lines, but that's not what Miles wants – looking for the horn sounds on my guitar," Stern told Mandel. "Playing after horns, which I've been doing for several years now, that's what I tend to do. It's not Wes Montgomery or Jim Hall, though I try to do all of that, 'cause I'm into that. But I throw it all together and *think*, think about constructing solos, about putting Bill's and Miles' ideas together, and just hope it works. It's weird, but it's kind of big fun."[51]

The result often pleased Davis more than anyone else, Stern included. Stern found himself in a musical no-man's land in Davis's band, strafed by Davis if he moved too far from heavy-metal rock and shelled by the reviewers when he stuck with it. "Miles wants me to play loud," he told Bill Milkowski. "At Avery Fisher Hall ... he went over and turned my amp up at one point. And he's always saying thing to me like 'Play some Hendrix! Turn it up or turn it off!' Miles loves Hendrix. Jimi and Charlie Christian are his favorite cats as far as guitarists are concerned. So right now with this band he wants to hear volume. My own natural instinct is to play a little softer, which I've been able to do on tunes like *My Man's Gone Now*, where my playing is a little darker. But Miles wants me to fill a certain role with this band, so I'm playing loud and my solos are usually speeded to double-time where I have to play kind of rock-style, whatever that is." Stern had to separate his individual conception from Davis's conception: "While I'm going for Jim [Hall] and Wes [Montgomery], there's some Jimi in there too, I guess."[52]

Marcus Miller also found himself under heavy demands from Davis. When Davis was forming his band, he demanded, according to Miller, "Funk, funk, a funk bassist, I want funk!," and the other young players he was recording with automatically directed him to Miller. Miller had learned to play his instrument in the mid-1970s, when the line separating jazz and rock styles was almost imperceptible. "I found myself caught up at the same time in the history of jazz and funk," he explained to Klaus Blasquiz in *Jazz Hot*. "Everything was possible. You only had to play. In one period, the two musics became very close. Herbie Hancock, for example, after Miles, had reconciled two generations and two styles completely different."[53]

Miller's versatility made him one of the most active studio players in New York. After touring with Roberta Flack for more than a year, he settled into the studios, accompanying Luther Vandross, Grover Washington Jr, Aretha Franklin, and numerous others on record dates. He was working on a country and western recording when he received Davis's message in 1980 to show up in the Columbia studios.

Miller tried to break the ice at that first session by making a little small talk, with predictable results. "I walked into the studio," he recalled for Sam Freedman, "said, 'Hi, I'm Marcus Miller.' He said, 'I'm Miles.' Then he walked out. When he came back in, I said, 'I'm Wynton Kelly's cousin.' He didn't say anything."[54] Davis started Foster playing a straight 4/4 tempo and stood back to watch Miller and the others. "He gives this test to everyone," Miller said later. "You throw yourself into the water and he sees if you swallow more than a cupful. If you do, he knows it immediately."[55] Miller survived, and at the first break Davis walked over and said, "Did you ever play with your genius cousin?" Miller explained that he was too young; he was only 12 when Kelly died in 1971. "He was a genius," Davis said. "His touch, his touch."[56] At the end of the recording session, he asked Miller to join his band.

The last recruit was Mino Cinelu, a Parisian whose father had emigrated from Martinique. Cinelu arrived in New York as a guitarist and scrambled to find work. He recorded inauspiciously – "two or three times with European singers whose names I forget," he said – and accompanied a Haitian singer, and played a little jazz in pickup groups, including one with Roy Haynes. He started playing percussion in order to find more work. Then the immigration department rescinded his work visa. "To keep in shape," Cinelu told Gérald Arnaud, the editor of *Jazz Hot*, "I played with some African dance companies, without pay. But I regret nothing; I learned a lot and I succeeded in making myself a respectable conga player."

Davis heard him at Mikell's, a rhythm and blues club that had expanded its music policy to include ethnic bands, where Cinelu was playing in the last week of May 1981 with a group called Civily Jordan and Folk. "Lots of celebrities frequented the club and one night Miles came," Cinelu recalls,[57] but it was not a chance meeting, because Davis was actively organizing his band for the Kool concerts. Cinelu started rehearsing with Davis's band the next week.

Cinelu saw nothing unusual in his overnight elevation from impecunious freelancing to a steady job in the best-paid band in jazz. To him, it seemed preordained from the days of his Paris youth. "When I heard *On the Corner* I was touched by that conception of music," he said, "and I knew that if Miles had the chance to hear me, he would hire me."[58]

On the first round of American concert halls after the Kool concerts, the band grew more confident and settled into a freer style. Their reviews remained mixed, and there were ominous observations on the state of Davis's health, which was sometimes reported as robust and sometimes as flagging.

At the Savoy, the midtown rock auditorium named for the legendary uptown swing ballroom, their audience was mainly young and white, including the rock stars Rickie Lee Jones and the aging Rolling Stones, Mick Jagger and Charlie Watts. Davis played long and hard, reviving *All of You* from his old ballad repertoire as well as *My Man's Gone Now* as relief from the newer jazz-rock pieces. "Miles was full of energy and uncommonly extroverted onstage," Cheryl McCall reported, "and acknowledged the existence of the audience to the extent of French-kissing a blonde in the front row in the middle of one of his *moments musicaux*." But the onstage vitality was a façade. "When I went backstage," McCall said, "I was shocked to find Miles Davis in a state of collapse, sweating like a prizefighter between rounds and similarly attended by men with towels, drink, encouragement and aid."[59]

Joe Goldberg, author of a memorable profile on Davis sixteen years earlier in *Jazz Masters of the Fifties*, caught Davis's revival when it arrived in Washington, DC, driving 200 miles from his parents' home in West Virginia and finding a seat in the back of the balcony on a stifling night. Davis's performance, he reported in *International Musician*, "was a distillation of his most effective licks, his favorite things. It was by no means tired – on the contrary, it was played with tremendous energy – but it seemed immensely calculated."

So theatrical was Davis's presentation that Goldberg began to suspect that everything, including the photographer stationed on the balcony taking pictures of patrons for $4 each against a backdrop of a Rolls-Royce with MILES D on the licence plate, was stage-managed by Davis. "I have never heard him in more absolute technical command of his instrument, nor have I ever seen him more physically active onstage," Goldberg noted. "He used to stand in one place, hunched over, his intensity accentuated, like Charlie Parker's, by his lack of motion, but in Washington, he was all over the place. He was dancing ... He was playing the audience outrageously ... and they loved it." At the end, the audience chanted "We want *Miles*! We want *Miles*!," and eventually he returned to take a bow, carried on the shoulders of Evans and Stern.[60]

As the tour continued in the Midwest, all the reviews carried notices about Davis's energetic playing, his revival of *My Man's Gone Now*, his perpetual motion – "Davis now has a radio transmitter on his horn, enabling him to wander about the stage like an obsessed maniac," David Wild wrote in *Coda*, after the Ann Arbor concert.[61] Largely unnoticed, because the backstage areas were closely guarded, were the offstage collapses. Cheryl McCall, traveling in the entourage to prepare a feature on Davis for *People*, the high-circulation gossip magazine, saw them, and although *People* was no forum for a celebrity's health problems she later included them in the preamble to her remarkable interview with Davis for *Musician, Player and Listener*, perhaps the most thorough and certainly one of the most sensitive articles ever written about him. "Sometimes he was so stiff he was not able to bend sufficiently to put on his pants," McCall said; "the band had to help him. Concerts often exhausted him, but he had made a real commitment to working, his band, and even the audience. In Chicago and Detroit, Miles had to take oxygen from a portable tank in order to get through his concerts. He contracted pneumonia after a date in Ann Arbor, and although he's been a famous no-show in the past, got out of a hospital bed to make a gig in L.A."[62]

Whenever his entourage was penetrated by outsiders, Davis masked his health problems convincingly. Before the Chicago concert, McCall reported, he hosted a family reunion to introduce Cicely Tyson to his sister, Dorothy, and his brother, Vernon, both Chicago residents, and his daughter, Cheryl, who arrived from St. Louis. He also invited some childhood friends from St. Louis, and he presided over the occasion with high spirits in spite of the pneumonia.

The Los Angeles concert at the Hollywood Bowl near the end of September brought Davis one of the toughest critical rebukes of his career. Leonard Feather, reviewing the concert for the *Los Angeles Times*, maintained that Davis had surrendered to show business and seemed to have nothing left to contribute musically. Many of Feather's points echoed the critical comments that had followed the Kool concerts, but few reviewers rival Feather's authority. His critique, as a *Jazz Hot* editorial put it, "literally assassinated Miles."

Embittered by the review, Max Roach counter-attacked with a letter to *Jazz Magazine*, reprinted later in *Jazz Hot*. The letter was not so much a defence of Davis as an attack on Feather, declaring that "Feather has always had great difficulty understanding where the American music called jazz comes from, so it is almost impossible for him to know wht a creative artist is."[63] The hostilities caused a minor sensation for the jazz audience but amused Davis. "Max is like my brother and anything that anybody would say about me, Max is going to challenge them to fight or anything," he later told interviewers in Poland. "Max declares war on them." And then he added, "Poor Leonard."[64]

In 1982, Davis went out of his way to reconcile Feather, submitting to a four-hour interview with him and inviting him to prepare the liner notes for his 1983 LP, *Star People*. Few actions indicate so emphatically the character change that Davis had gone through during his retirement. "I wasn't bothered by your review of my concert at the Hollywood Bowl in 1981," Davis told him. "I was so sick that night that I could hardly walk."[65]

But Davis wanted to regain Feather's approbation badly enough that he not only consented to the interview but also took Tyson along and conducted himself decorously throughout. At the end, Feather observed that in their four hours together Davis had rarely used the obscenities with which he used to punctuate his sentences. Davis made no response to that, but Tyson averred he had finally learned that he did not need coarse language to make himself understood. That revelation caused at least one old acquaintance to wonder how Davis could possibly go on speaking with half his active vocabulary expunged, but the decorum did not outlast the occasion. At his next significant interview, Davis responded to a question from David Breskin for *Rolling Stone* with this diatribe about rock journalists: "Fuck that! Why do they ask all those rock stars that shit? ... Who they fuck and why they fuck and this song has a message. White people do that shit. What does it mean? I don't like that. It's all just music."[66] The rest of the interview was similarly couched in Davis's accustomed idiom.

By the time Breskin's interview was published, Feather had completed the conciliatory act of preparing the liner notes for *Star People*. The notes are restrained compared to the laudatory high style typical of the genre. Feather mainly discusses the reactions of Teo Macero and Davis as they listened with him to the master tapes. He concedes only that this music, in keeping with Davis's title for one of his new compositions, *It Gets Better*, represents an improvement over what Davis was playing after his comeback concerts: "It gets better. Miles could have been referring to his band, his playing, his health, or conceivably just his life at large. Whatever the thought behind it, the title applies on every level to the conception and execution of *Star People*."[67] Beyond that, Feather's reconciliation amounted to his willingness to be associated with Davis's new LP but not a retraction of the points he had made in his critique of the Hollywood Bowl concert.

Even Davis's staunchest defenders, Max Roach among them, conceded that he had imported some show business glitter into his performances. In part, it was a response to his longevity, which made him a celebrity – a superstar, in the argot of the baby boom – and allowed him to elicit adoring cheers effortlessly, with a sidelong glance at the audience or a grunt into the mike in his trumpet, the kind of *schtick* that Mick Jagger's idolatrous audiences always thrived on, and before him John Lennon's and Elvis Presley's and Frank Sinatra's and probably Caruso's.

The new repertoire offered few challenges. Formally, it was similar to *Agitation*, *Footprints*, *Nefertiti*, and the rest of the repertoire Davis had developed with Herbie Hancock and Wayne Shorter, consisting of open-ended melodies repeated irregularly and forming the touchstone for improvised variants of any length. Substantively, it was light-years removed from them, for it rejected their darker moods and exotic harmonies in favor of piquant, whimsical moods and hummable tunes.

The change in mood reflected a new accessibility, a kind of salutation to a populace that Davis seems to have become aware of only when he put himself into solitary confinement during his retirement. "Maybe he's widening the audience," Roach admitted, in a calmer tone than he had taken with Feather. "He knows that if you play things with a familiar ring to them, there's a market for them. The fact is that Miles is *never* going to play anything banal. He's going to play his way. But he's good at marketing, and if this is what the public will buy and accept, then he'll play that too."[68] If Roach harbored doubts about the musical virtues of Davis's new mood, another drummer, Bob Moses, harbored none at all. "Yeah, his new stuff is as good or better than what he did before, and is certainly better than anything else going on now," he told Howard Mandel. "I think his new band is wonderful – and what they're playing is people's music."[69]

Davis and his band left California for Japan, where they played seven concerts in less than two weeks, 2–14 October. Japan had been high on Davis's priorities whenever he had mentioned ending his retirement. His audiences there had always been large and appreciative – even his reviewers were appreciative – and the promoters were willing to pay in kind. Davis received $700,000 for this tour, more than triple his earnings for the 1975 Japanese tour, just before his retirement.

He explained his appeal to the Japanese in terms that seemed roughly equivalent to the lunch-bucket view of how the Japanese technocrats had brought the American automotive industry to its knees. "Japanese people are funny," he said. "They like anything that's good. You can't bring no bullshit over there. They know you're not coming back so they're gonna listen. So they can *copy*. You know how Japanese people are. They *copy*. And when they copy, they copy the *best*. And they *want* the best. They don't settle for anything but the best."[70]

At his concerts on this tour, as on the previous one, they saw a perilously unhealthy Davis hiding behind a bold front whenever he appeared in public. But his playing was stronger and surer than anything he had presented to his American audiences, judging from the Tokyo concert taped by CBS-Sony. Unfortunately only one title from the Tokyo concert was selected for the *We Want Miles* LP, and the others remain unissued, but that one title crystallized Davis's new style. Davis liked it so much that he had Columbia put two versions of the same performance on the LP, one a ten-minute track with the complete performance and the other a tightly edited four-minute version originally designed for 45-rpm release. The details are as follows:

Miles Davis Sextet: We Want Miles
Miles Davis, tpt; Bill Evans, ss; Mike Stern, gtr; Marcus Miller, b; Al Foster, dms; Mino Cinelu, perc. Tokyo, 4 October 1981
Jean Pierre
(on Columbia C2 38005)
This title is released in both an edited and unedited version on C2 38005. The

concert also includes *Back Seat Betty*, *My Man's Gone Now*, and *Fast Track*, all unissued.

The composition was unlike anything that Davis had played before, but listeners hearing it at this concert and all of Davis's concerts to come, including several million in the television audience for NBC's *Saturday Night Live* later in the month, reacted with the shock of recognition, of *déjà entendu*, although they could not quite place it. It sounded like a schoolyard catcall – "nyaaa-nyaa, nyaa-nyaa-nyaaa" – or a skipping song or something else dimly remembered from childhood, with its simple four-bar melody, endlessly repeatable, moving down a third of an octave on the first phrase and back up on the second.

When *We Want Miles* finally came out, it was identified as *Jean Pierre* and its composer was listed as Miles Davis. The title was unfamiliar and the composer seemed highly improbable, but Davis had had the wit to bring to the stage one of those melodies that belongs to every culture that uses the diatonic scale – a melody so simple and so deeply embedded in the collective unconscious that it was no one's invention and everyone's. It is the melody, for instance, of an old French lullaby, with words (though they vary slightly from region to region and from generation to generation) like these:

Do do, l'enfant do,
L'enfant dormira bien vite.
Do do, l'enfant do,
L'enfant dormira bientôt.

Davis's title provides a clue as to when the melody first impressed itself upon him. Jean-Pierre is the son of his second wife, Frances Taylor, by a previous marriage, and he lived with them as a youngster until their divorce.

Davis loved the melody, and he used it to close every concert for years, replacing *Kix* in the repertoire after the summer concerts. For the first year, its performance consisted of repeated assertions in rough harmony by Davis's trumpet and Evans's soprano saxophone, echoed in any order, even overlapping, by Miller's bass, Cinelu's congas, and Stern's guitar. Eventually, as the band added several other compositions stated in harmony by two or more of the instruments, a device for which *Jean Pierre* provided the prototype, Davis gave up on harmonizing *Jean Pierre* and began stating its theme on trumpet alone, sometimes playing no more than the first two notes and then standing back while the band made a free invention. Its form also became the favored form for much of Davis's new music: simple in structure, short in duration, and, he hoped, stunningly salient.

At the Tokyo performance, the four-bar theme recurs dozens of times, beginning with Cinelu patting it out on the congas, then Miller thumping it out on the bass, and then the harmonized trumpet-soprano statement. Davis does little more than repeat the theme over and over in his muted solo, except for interpolating the bridge from *Lullaby of Broadway*, which is also built on thirds ("Good night, ladies; good night, the milkman's on his way"). Stern leaves the theme further behind, with high screams that somehow resolve Miller's low repetition of the theme beneath him, and Evans comes along and parodies it by honking its final note.

It is a surprisingly resourceful performance, considering the slim underpinning that the theme provides; later performances retained the resourcefulness by relying less on the theme and exploring tangents that left the theme far behind.

Three days after returning from Japan, the band appeared on *Saturday Night Live* on NBC-TV playing *Jean Pierre*, live in a New York studio for a television audience of several millions. Davis's appearance on the show was widely publicized in spot announcements on the network the week before, and George Kennedy, the actor who hosted the show that night, used thirty seconds of the seven-minute spot introducing him: "...a man who has not appeared on network television in almost a decade ... Ladies and gentlemen, the *legendary* Miles Davis!" But the rendition of *Jean Pierre* was a shambles, taken at almost double the normal tempo, with missed cues and misshapen notes, especially by Davis. His appearance was frightening. He limped around the stage, the cameras losing him and finding him again awkwardly, his face taut, his eyes unseeing. Many viewers assumed he was in a drug-induced stupor; not one in a million could know that he had just returned from an international tour completely exhausted. He took two weeks off to recuperate before his next booking, on 4 November in Boston.

On 27 November, Davis married Cicely Tyson at Bill Cosby's home in Shelbourne, Massachusetts. Andrew Young, mayor-elect of Atlanta and ambassador to the United Nations during the Carter administration as well as a minister, performed the ceremony, with Max Roach and the political comedian Dick Gregory among the few guests. *People* magazine, probably via Cheryl McCall, noted the event and reported that

Miles Davis and Cicely Tyson (courtesy Canapress Photo Service)

John Scofield at Ontario Place Forum, 1983 (Bernard Lecerf)

Davis took the vows by rasping "Yeah," and that Tyson, when her turn came, mimicked his reply and his voice.[71] It was Tyson's second marriage and Davis's fourth.

Davis's brownstone on West 77th Street, originally bought for Frances Taylor and decorated by her, was being gutted and rebuilt to Tyson's specifications, in a massive overhaul that ended up taking two years. When Tyson and Davis were in New York, they lived either in a cottage at Montauk, on the tip of Long Island, or in an apartment on Fifth Avenue.

"I'm happy now," Davis told McCall. "I could have been happy years ago if I married Cicely. But years ago, no. Time takes care of that, time takes care of everything. If I had married Cicely she wouldn't have been a star now." In the same mood, he confessed that he had written some love songs, including one called *Love without Time*, scribbled on a paper bag. "Next album I'm singing," he said. "Sure. I'm going to siiiiinnng some soooulful ballads. *Love without Time*. (sings) 'Love without time, just don't give me no limit, don't need no limit.'"[72]

Not even the honeymoon interrupted his round of concerts. The day after the wedding, Davis emplaned with his band for Fort Lauderdale. By the time his tour reached Toronto on 13 December, Davis looked like a wraith. Mark Miller, reviewing the concert in the *Globe and Mail*, said: "Miles Davis' eyes – brooding, fixed, cold, once far-seeing but now simply distant – burned into the memory last night ... The band supplied the night with its exhilaration. Davis' contribution was more personal, more revealing, and, ultimately, more troubling."[73] A blond woman in the audience went around at intermission asking the scribes in the front-row seats what was wrong with him. "I saw him at the Colonial [a Toronto jazz club] in 1969," she said, "and he was *beautiful*. But when he came out tonight, I just felt like crying." She left at intermission because watching him, she said, was "too painful."

Notwithstanding the critical lambastings that followed some of Davis's concerts and the gathering portents of his deteriorating health, his return to performing restored his popularity. *Down Beat*'s readers voted him Jazz Musician of the Year by a wide margin and, in a dizzying show of sentiment over perspicacity, named *Man with the Horn* top album; *Directions*, his LP of older material, placed fourth. Among trumpeters, he placed third after Freddie Hubbard and Dizzy Gillespie, in front of Woody Shaw and Lester Bowie. *Down Beat*'s poll results were only one expression of the welcome. In Congo (Brazzaville) his portrait appeared on the 125-franc postage stamp.

Davis intended to carry on touring in 1982 with only a momentary rest in January. He had scheduled a series of concerts on the Pacific coast from Vancouver to San Diego for February. Then, only a week before they would have begun, the entire series was cancelled. Most fans speculated that he had had a change of heart about his comeback.

Instead, he was stopped cold by a new health problem that was more serious than any one of the myriad of problems that had caused him to stop for six years. He awoke one morning unable to move his right hand. The hand was bunched, the fingers immobile. Tyson was away in Africa, and Davis's doctor tried to cajole him into treating the affliction lightly. "I go to the doctor and he says I got the Honeymoon Paralysis," Davis told David Breskin in *Rolling Stone*. "Honeymoon Paralysis, that's when guys get so tired from fucking so much that they go to sleep on their hand and it wakes up numb."[74] But a battery of hospital tests confirmed that he had suffered a stroke, and he began physical therapy sessions at the hospital in an attempt to restore some mobility to the hand. When Tyson returned, his doctors told her that Davis would probably never regain adequate use of the hand and certainly never full use of it. They asked her to use her discretion about informing Davis of the seriousness of the injury, but she neither told him nor allowed herself to believe them. She watched and waited for the therapy sessions to give some signs of recovery.

For a month, nothing changed. Davis was despondent, lying around ready now to concede that he should never have attempted to return to performing. Apart from his mood and the useless right hand, both of which he tried to hide from his few visitors, he seemed little changed. The stroke, the doctors knew, was highly localized; it may have ended his career, but it need not prevent him from leading a reasonably normal life for the rest of his days.

Tyson knew that he could not lead anything like a normal life if he was not performing. She began inquiring about alternative treatment and learned about acupuncture, the Chinese medical tradition based on coaxing neural reflexes partly by stimulating nerve centers. Directed to a Dr Shin, she described Davis's state of health and received an optimistic prognosis.[75] It seemed to her to be worth trying. "I didn't want to go," Davis told Feather, "but she threw it at me all the time, and I finally gave in."

Within two months, his hand regained some mobility. "One night I woke up and I realized I could move it again," Davis said, as if describing a miracle, "and I could play the trumpet." Medically, the miracle was attributed to the brain's uncanny capacity for relocating functions to compensate for traumatic losses, part of the healing force of time, but Davis also needed to share the optimism of Tyson and his acupuncturist before it could happen. If his recovery was explicable in coldly clinical terms, it was still an explanation that ultimately came down to imponderables such as time and attitude, hardly removing it from the miraculous. Davis said, "After this, I'll never be afraid of anything that happens. Never again."[76]

Davis's general health lagged behind the recovery of his right hand. He began playing his trumpet almost immediately and soon began performing in public again, but his first concerts forced him to play sitting down part of the time until he developed enough stamina to resume his onstage roaming for the full ninety minutes.

The full recovery required a new regimen. He stopped smoking. He gave up beer and liquor in favor of Perrier water, of which he drinks two quarts a day; "that empties you, cleans you out, just what I need," he says.[77] He swims every day, explaining it this way: "Anything that helps the wind is good for a horn player. When I first started back playing, I got out of breath all the time. Swimming is good for that. If I don't do it, everything tightens up."[78] He eats Chinese herbs, prescribed by his acupuncturist, in a jelly for breakfast, and he has acupuncture sessions whenever he is in New York.

In a sense, the six months of hard touring before he suffered the stroke were only the prolegomena for the real comeback that followed it, when his theatricality became less forced, his playing brightened, and his conception clarified. "I'll stay active till I *die*, now," he says.[79]

In early April, he called the band back together and scheduled two rehearsals before taking them on the tour of Europe that he had been ready to cancel a month before. "It was an occasion for rediscovering ourselves," Mino Cinelu explained. "We hadn't played together for three months, and Miles wanted to see what had happened to us, to know if the feeling was still as strong."[80] Apparently he was satisfied, because he called off the second rehearsal.

Word about Davis's stroke had not circulated when he set off for Europe – it did not become common knowledge until Leonard Feather's interview appeared in the *Los Angeles Times* several months later – and most of the European reviewers assumed his enervation to be the result of his old pains rather than a new, and alarmingly recent, one.

The tour was jammed as usual, beginning at Konserthuset in Stockholm on 13 April and ending in Paris with two concerts at Théâtre musical on 2 and 3 May, with stops in between at Jazzhus Montmartre in Copenhagen, a jazz club rather than a concert hall, the Hammersmith Odeon in London, then Rome, Amsterdam, The Hague, and Châtelet, outside Paris. All tickets for both Paris concerts were sold in two hours on 18 April, the day they went on sale, at $80 for the best seats.

At the Hammersmith Odeon, Davis summoned up enough energy to walk onto the stage backwards, toying with the audiences that had often chided him for turning his back on them in the past. The concert was filmed by England's new independent television network and broadcast the following December, but it does not show Davis advantageously. Dave Gelly described him in his review of the concert for the *Observer* this way: "He is in constant pain, walks with difficulty and now has to play sitting down most of the time. The dashing young man-about-town has been replaced by a gaunt and dogged figure, expending every ounce of energy in two brief bursts per night."[81] That was early in the tour, and Davis seemed to be growing weaker as the tour continued. At Châtelet, the second-last stop, the reviewer Bayon, writing for *Libération*, thought he was viewing a walking corpse. Under the headline "Trompette de mort," he wrote: "The hero was fatigued, beat, bone-tired, his hips seized in rigor mortis, his limbs crumbling, the corpse visible, the face starved, staggering, coughing in fits that rattled his neck, the shadow of a shadow of a myth ... His vital signs reduced to a minimum, pinched, empty, and haunted, he had nothing to say ... It was as if he sat down before Paris to learn how to die."[82]

But the next day, in Paris, he seemed completely revived. "What happened between Sunday night and Monday?" asked Philippe Conrath, in a companion review to Bayon's. His only guess: "Obviously the little something that changed everything. Or a real joy about playing in Paris ... He entered like a boxer looking for a k.o. He put us on our knees, without giving us a second to catch our breath, piling chorus on chorus as at the best of times ... Sunday he made us pity him for his empty presence, but Monday there he was pirouetting at each ovation, smiling, full of affection for his guitarist whom he couldn't take his eyes off, bobbing in front of Al Foster to start up his drums, and gently admonishing the clowning Marcus Miller, the mad dog of the sextet."[83] In the weird counterpoint of the reviews of Davis's comeback, swinging from reports of well-being to imminent demise, the swing from one theme to the other had never been this sudden.

His young sidemen seemed aware only of Davis's revival and its effect on the band's music. "I wish we made a second album," Cinelu told a

French interviewer. "It would be so much better. Qualitatively, what we play now has nothing to do with our first recording [*We Want Miles*] ... The first record was important in the sense that it let people know that Miles could play, that he was always present."[84]

The new recordings had to wait, however, while Davis fulfilled some broken promises in North America and kept some new ones for George Wein. The 1982 Kool Jazz Festival expanded into a road show, headquartered in New York but moving into nineteen other cities with scaled-down programs. Davis played at Kool concerts in Washington, DC, at the end of May and in Atlanta in early June, left the lineup for independent festivals in Montreal (11 July, Festival International de Jazz), New York (17 July, Dr. Pepper Festival, at Pier 84), and in Vancouver (28 July, du Maurier Jazz Society), and then resumed his Kool connection in Seattle (31 July), Detroit (2 September), and Chicago (5 September). The Vancouver and Seattle concerts replaced cancellations there in the spring.

Between the New York and Vancouver appearances, he accompanied Cicely Tyson to Lima, Peru, where she was acting as a judge in the Miss Universe contest. They treated the trip as a holiday, sight-seeing in museums, with Davis swimming hours every day. The Miss Universe contest took place on Monday, two days before Davis was to appear onstage in Vancouver, some 5,000 miles from Lima, separated by three time zones, in the opposite hemisphere.

In Vancouver, Davis gave one of his strongest performances in years, playing long and full, and revealing a partly new repertoire, including a twenty-five-minute ballad improvisation that revived *Fran Dance* for several bars. "He strutted like a funky chicken, he smiled to the other musicians, he even acknowledged the crowd," one reviewer wrote.[85] More to the point, he played strongly.

The strong playing continued in Detroit. "Davis looked healthy, moved easily, and played with more confidence than he has in years," Stephen Brunt reported, and he noted some other changes: "Almost completely gone was the hard rock/funk sound of the *Man with the Horn*. In its place was a much more traditional form of jazz, including a straightforward blues ... There also seems to be a new Davis personality. He smiled at the crowd, spoke to them through the microphone in the bell of his trumpet in a raspy whisper, and reacted to shouts from the crowd."[86] Brunt was comparing Davis's music and deportment not to his appearances of ten or twenty years ago but to his comeback concerts only fourteen months before.

At the Chicago concert, Davis and his band made their entrance to the Grant Park stage by limousine and were stopped short by a burly policeman. Instead of trying to shout the policeman out of the way and inviting a confrontation, Davis and the others waited patiently. "Just in time the cop relented," Hank DeZutter reported, "and a puckish Miles not only played for but played with the audience. Infamous for his occasional sullen, brooding, damn-the-public behavior, Davis even mugged and posed for cameramen."[87] Peter Kostakis, covering the concert for *Down Beat*, wrote: "Davis played more trumpet than we had any right to expect, open horn mostly, with discrete spaces and that knockout *tone* basically unimpaired."[88]

Davis's new vitality finally silenced some of the nostalgia buffs who had populated his audiences for years, apparently harboring the impossible dream that he would transform himself, and perhaps them too, into what they had been twenty years ago. At Grant Park, an old fan noisily pleaded with Davis to play *So What*. "After four shouts of 'Play *So What*,'" DeZutter reported, "a man nearby shut him up, acidly suggesting, 'Go home and play the record.'"

Davis and his band also spent some time during the summer in the recording studios, and the recordings were released in June 1983 along with some subsequent sessions on *Star People*, the first studio recordings by the working band. The details are as follows:

Miles Davis Sextet: Star People
Miles Davis, tpt, synthesizer (on *Come Get It, Star on Cicely*); Bill Evans, ts (on *Star People*), ss (on *U 'n' I, Star on Cicely*); Mike Stern, gtr; Marcus Miller, b; Al Foster, dms; Mino Cinelu, perc. August–November 1982
Come Get It; Star People; U 'n' I; Star on Cicely
(all on Columbia FC 38657)
Gil Evans arranged the theme statement of *Star on Cicely*; Bill Evans is not heard on *Come Get It*, which may be an excerpt of a concert performance; Miles Davis is credited as composer of all titles, but *Star on Cicely* apparently originated as a phrase by Mike Stern; *Star People* includes a brief prelude and interlude by Davis on synthesizer and John Scofield on guitar, probably recorded December 1982–February 1983.

Come Get It is the new concert opener, replacing *Back Seat Betty* in the repertoire but retaining many of its features, including the cascading guitar-percussion introduction, a funk motif on the bass ("inspired by an old Otis Redding riff," Davis told Leonard Feather), and a simple scale on the trumpet as its theme. Some of the funk elements were weakening, notably in Mike Stern's contribution, where the rhythm softens behind him and allows him to play a more relaxed solo than he usually played, and leaving Davis to carry most of the heavy playing.

U 'n' I is a lilting ballad consisting of an eight-bar melody played over and over. The little tune shares some of the infectious simplicity of *Jean Pierre* and seems to beg for a silly little lyric to set if off. Listeners can easily supply their own, perhaps along these lines:

O, U 'n' I XL – we're gr8! –
4 U 'n' I alone R NTTs;
U lder what I MN8?
Only XTC.

Musically, *U 'n' I* has about as much substance as the doggerel it is likely to inspire, and in concert performances as well as in this studio version the musicians seem to be at a loss about what they can do with it. Often they do nothing at all, simply repeating the melody almost verbatim, as they do no less than thirteen times in six minutes on this recorded version, and the engaging little ditty begins to lose its charm after a few listenings. (Apart from their shared banality, Davis's *U 'n' I* is not related in any way to Betty Davis's *You and I*, a ballad released on her 1975 LP [Island ILPS 9329] that credits Gil Evans for its brass arrangement and Miles Davis for its "musical direction.")

Davis's long, winding blues solo at the beginning of the track called *Star People* gives the best evidence of his revitalized trumpet playing: it is unhurried and masterfully controlled, recalling the spirit – and a few of the phrases – of his older ballad style. Part of the length of *Star People* apparently comes from splicing two takes together, with an unintegrated synthesizer interlude between them, but the spliced-in take preserves a country blues solo by Stern that contrasts effectively with Davis's urbane statements. The issued version is marred by an awkward, tinny percussion noise that sounds like an electronic distortion of the sock cymbal and was probably added after the session. If listeners allow it to distract them, the easy flow of the track is impeded, but Davis's solos are strong enough to override the arhythmic splashes in the background.

Gil Evans returns to Davis's music with the arrangement of the theme for *Star on Cicely*, an intricate blend of eighth-note and half-note harmonies played by the soprano saxophone and guitar, with the trumpet sometimes playing a third line. Evans's participation came about when Davis, listening to tapes of his band's performances, heard improvised phrases that he wanted developed into themes. The germ of *Star on Cicely* apparently originated in a solo by Stern, and Evans has turned it into a roller-coaster ride that comes to a sudden stop, but Davis gets composer credit for it. (An excerpt was released on 45 rpm for the teenage market as Columbia 38-03605, several weeks before the LP version.)

The news that Gil Evans was arranging some of Davis's new repertoire raised hopes that they would again collaborate on a larger project. "Gil still does a lot of things for me," Davis told Richard Williams. "He comes up with bass patterns, stuff like that. We just click together." But Davis had no elaborate plans. "We might do something, we might not," he said.[89] Evans, in an interview with Richard Cook for the *New Musical Express*, thought that their renewed collaboration was inevitable. "We'll be working together again," he said. "You could say we're in a musical and emotional condition where we can work together." The key to their working together again, in Evans's view, is Davis's health. "Miles is really feeling good," he points out. "He's had a lot of bad physical luck, but now – the way he plays a concert, he'll dance a little, play to the first rows. He's better." Evans also tossed out the tidbit that he had been talking to George Russell about all three of them working on a project. "He thought it was a good idea," Evans adds. "Maybe it'll happen."[90]

An innovation that might encourage Davis to work with Evans is his use of the Oberheim synthesizer, which joined the Rhodes electric piano at center stage at the end of 1982. "I haven't read the instruction book yet," he told Richard Williams, making light of his bemused noodling on it during performances. "It would take someone like Paul Buckmaster or Gil or Quincy [Jones] or J.J. [Johnson], one of those writers who'd really know what to do with it."[91]

Onstage, he tries for big-band effects on it, sounding chords with his left hand while playing the trumpet with his right, often with jarring results. He justifies it by saying, "Synthesizers are programmed to sound white – that's how prejudiced white people are – so if I don't play over it, it will sound mechanical."[92]

The synthesizer seems to have revived his ambitions to use orchestral effects in his music, and his further comments to Williams indicate that he understands not only its potential but also its limitations: "Nowadays instead of going on the road with a big band you just reach and grab a button and have the sound of brass or strings, but of course you can't replace the interplay – going in and out of those swells and lows. What you miss, too, is the unevenness of tone that gives it a thrill. You might have five different trumpet players, each with a different sound and attack, who make the sound you want." The simulated trumpet section of the synthesizer encodes five identical trumpet sounds, and to Davis that sound is anathema. "White people are so prejudiced that they make the trumpets on the Oberheim sound white," he says. "Imagine that. A prejudiced synthesizer. Ain't that something?"[93]

By the end of 1982, Davis had regained his position near the top of the jazz popularity polls, but he had to concede some of the top honors to Wynton Marsalis, one of the brightest young talents to emerge in a generation. Davis's *We Want Miles* won the Grammy Award, with Davis's band appearing on the televised proceedings to play *Speak*, part of their new repertoire, and it also won the gold medal in Tokyo's Jazz Disk Awards, but Marsalis's debut LP as a leader (*Wynton Marsalis*, Columbia FC 37574) won that honor in *Down Beat*'s readers' poll. Davis was named Jazz Musician of the Year in the *Jazz Forum* poll, but Marsalis took that honor in *Down Beat* and was also named top trumpeter, with Davis second. In a more bizarre sweepstakes, Davis was named in a press release by the United States space agency among a group of people thought to have the right qualities for space flight, including "strength of character, charm, glamor"; other nominees were Canadian prime minister Pierre Trudeau, science-fiction writer Arthur C. Clarke, comedians Richard Pryor and Dudley Moore, and Pope John Paul II;[94] Marsalis somehow failed to make that list.

Davis alone seemed unimpressed by Marsalis's talent. "All the trumpet players copy Clifford, Fats Navarro and Dizzy Gillespie," he said. "Just like the saxophonists imitate Coltrane, Wayne Shorter and Sonny Rollins. There aren't any original musicians any more. I know that the musicians in my band like Marsalis; me, I like to hear things with a different approach from what people call jazz."[95]

Ironically, Marsalis's music emanates directly from the modal and chordal styles that Davis explored in the 1960s. Technically and tonally his trumpet style makes a sharp departure from Davis's, but his genre was once primarily Davis's, and their conjunction is all the more obvious when Marsalis is heard with Davis's former rhythm team of Herbie Hancock, Ron Carter, and Tony Williams. He had been heard with them on two notable tours, the first in Japan in the summer of 1981, which brought the 20-year-old trumpeter international acclaim, and the second around the world in the summer of 1983, which added saxophonist Branford Marsalis, one year older than his brother Wynton, to make the quintet called VSOP II. Their repertoire naturally dips into Davis's short-lived book and has included Hancock's *The Sorcerer*, Carter's *R.J.*, and Williams's *Pee Wee*.

Son of a New Orleans jazz pianist, Marsalis left home in 1980 to join Art Blakey's Jazz Messengers, and since 1981 he has alternated between stints with Davis's former rhythm section and his own quintet. In all contexts he has consistently chosen to work in modal frameworks with acoustic bands, but the closer he comes to the exact context in which Davis has worked, as in his recordings of compositions first recorded by Davis, the easier it is to hear how distinctive his playing is. Marsalis provides the best object lesson jazz fans have ever had for showing that Davis failed to exhaust the styles he discovered before moving away from them in his restless search for innovations.

It is a lesson that Marsalis, with enormous self-assurance, not only proves with his music but also has articulated several times for those interviewers and fans who regard his music as a throwback to an "old" style. "Music has to be played before it gets old," he told A. James Liska. "The music that Ornette played, that Miles and Trane played in the '60s, some of the stuff that Mingus and Booker Little and Charlie Rouse and all those cats were starting to do – that music isn't old because no one else has ever played it."[96] Marsalis gave convincing demonstrations of the vitality of the style nightly, and his brother developed quickly into a forceful ally. "We're not playing this music because we're reacting against fusion," Branford told Peter Keepnews. "We're playing this music because it's harder to play than fusion. The way my mind works, I'm gonna play whatever is the most difficult music to play, intellectually and physically."[97] Davis's personal obsession with change and flux in musical style characterizes all his most productive periods, but the Marsalises prove that those obsessions are neither necessary nor sufficient for the creativity of other jazz musicians.

For Davis, change has always been the surest sign that he is healthy and deeply involved in his music. By the end of 1982, he was showing those signs again. The commissions for Gil Evans and the tinkering with synthesizers meant more in their potential than in their realization, with the former holding out the promise that Davis might broaden the slender compositional thread of his music and the latter that he might incorporate orchestral elements, synthesized or real, into it.

Another significant change took place on 31 December, when Davis's band appeared at the Felt Forum in Madison Square Garden with a new guitarist, John Scofield, in the band. The concert, with Davis's old friend Roberta Flack sharing the bill, started at 10 p.m. and had no more serious intent than greeting the new year, but Scofield's unexpected presence gave the occasion a special significance for jazz fans. Although Scofield belonged to the same age group as the other sidemen, his playing style was established before he joined Davis's band. He played jazz, and he was unlikely to submit to Hendrix imitations or hyperamplification.

A review of the Felt Forum concert by Lee Jeske in *Down Beat* emphasized the difference he made: "This was Scofield's debut with Miles, and Miles was quite generous in featuring him. Scofield, with his hollow-body guitar, played the kind of music that he has been playing for the past few years – scorching, clear, blues-drenched jazz, with a little smidgen of the avant garde and a small dollop of rock and roll. He is one of the finest guitarists around these days, and his playing brought a new hue to the band – he is a think-on-his-feet soloist who presents Davis with a challenge; if Miles scuffles, Scofield has the equipment to blow him away. The audience greeted every Scofield solo warmly, and his presence in the band bodes well for *musical* qualities of the organization."[98]

Davis first decided to replace Mike Stern with Scofield because, as Stern told a French interviewer, "last winter I started to coast a bit." He asked Bill Evans, who had recommended Stern in the first place, about a new guitarist, and he recommended Scofield. After the Felt Forum concert, Davis decided to carry both guitarists for six months, expanding the band to a septet. The band went through a period of adjustment in January, with Stern resuming his busy role as both accompanist and soloist and Scofield gradually working out his own role. "Little by little, Miles incorporated him into the group," Stern says. "At first I took all the solos, but now it's equal. We play as a duo, John and me, and we listen to one another very well."[99] In the expanded band, Stern still played in the rhythm section as well as soloing and Scofield worked mainly as a soloist, stationing himself stage left near Evans, whose role closely resembled Scofield's.

Asked why he added a second guitarist, Davis told Richard Williams, "I've always liked the sound of the guitar. And of the sitar. I like all the strings except the violin. It's too high-pitched for me. I can't hear that high."[100] (In the same interview, however, Davis observed that his inability to deal with high registers, a factor that forced him to depart from Dizzy Gillespie's model when he arrived in New York in 1945, was changing. "When I first started playing," he said, "it was low-middle to low register. I couldn't hear above that. Just lately, though, I've been able to hear up to octavissimo F, G, A sometimes.")

His only direct comments on Scofield's playing, one to Williams and another to Leonard Feather, have focused on Scofield's restrained note placement, one of the main devices of Davis's own playing when he developed what became known as the cool style. "John has a tendency to play behind the beat," he told Feather. "I had to bring him up; he really changed with Al's strong beat behind him."[101] And to Williams: "Denzil Best, the drummer, used to say to me, 'Don't play too far behind the beat because you'll work me too hard.' It's like stepping on your partner's feet." But Davis conceded that his own style altered in the new combination. "Having two guitar players makes me change," he says. "They don't have to breathe like a horn player does. They rub off on me."[102]

Scofield recorded with the band almost immediately, on a blues composition called *It Gets Better*, a theme statement composed by Davis and arranged by Gil Evans that probably originated as a phrase improvised by Bill Evans in a practice session. The details are as follows:

Miles Davis Septet: Star People
Miles Davis, tpt; Bill Evans, ss; John Scofield, Mike Stern, gtr; Marcus Miller, b; Al Foster, dms; Mino Cinelu, perc; Gil Evans, arr. Probably January 1983
It Gets Better
(on Columbia FC 38657)

In this studio version, the twelve-bar repetitions of the theme frame a long improvisation by Davis on muted trumpet, again revealing Davis's return to form in fashioning coherent lyrical statements at slow tempos. The theme itself is played ponderously in comparison to its freer, more emotional treatment in numerous concerts, where it had been played regularly since the summer of 1982. There it was usually stated by Evans on tenor saxophone and Stern on guitar, with Davis sometimes joining in, but the recorded version is a rearrangement, with Scofield as the lead voice and Stern the second voice, mixed low in the background. Its easy tempo is again marred by metronomic percussion noises not attributable to Cinelu and probably not directly attributable to Foster, although they may be post-edited electronic distortions of his drum kit. This straightforward blues makes a welcome change from the funk-cluttered backgrounds in which Davis couched his blues playing for several years, but Columbia holds several live versions that show off the band better than this one.

Long before *It Gets Better* was issued on the *Star People* LP in the late spring of 1983, word spread that Davis was playing a more or less straightforward twelve-bar blues at his concerts. It had made a striking impression at the Vancouver concert in the summer, immediately after his rejuvenating holiday in Peru, and audiences everywhere, steeled as they were now for a jazz-funk assault, greeted the sound of its traditional progressions enthusiastically. For the new Davis, that response was all he needed. The blues not only found a permanent place in his repertoire but dominated his concerts.

The blues segments grew stronger with Scofield added to the band for their first tour of 1983, a February swing through Dallas (two concerts on 1 February), Houston, Austin, and other Texas cities, Park West in Chicago, the National Arts Centre in Ottawa, and Roy Thompson Hall in Toronto (on 15 February). Above all, Davis seemed to bask in the response the blues elicited from his black audience, which he had tried to court with *On the Corner* a decade earlier. "Now, did you see last night, I was playing a blues and I go over and bend down and play to that fat woman in the second row?" Davis asked Breskin after one of the Texas concerts. "She says, 'That's right, Miles, come on over here, you can *stay* over here.' So then I play something real fast, and she says, 'Not like *that*, though. Go back over there if you're gonna play that shit.' Now, do you think a white person would tell me that? They don't even know what she's talking about. She's talking about the *bluuueeesss*." After years of trying to unearth the essential blackness of his playing by immersing himself in electrified percussion barrages, Davis found it in his East St. Louis roots. "In my hometown, if you don't play the blues, shit, them motherfuckers go to ordering drinks, but if you play the blues, they'll stay right there. That fat bitch, she'd have me blowing all night."[103]

Scofield inched his way into the working band's métier on the February tour. At the same time, Davis tried a new bassist, Tom Barney, a small, boyish figure who broke into dance steps when the beat was up. Marcus Miller had always divided his loyalties among Davis's band, diverse recording sessions, and other bands, often with David Sanborn, the alto saxophonist whose distinctive sound attracted attention with Stevie Wonder, Gil Evans, the studio band of *Saturday Night Live*, and dozens of recordings. Shortly before he left Davis, Miller recounted his itinerary for Klaus Blasquiz in *Jazz Hot*: "I always kept close relations with Dave [Sanborn]. Even now I make the scene with Miles and him, and it's hard to bring the two together, but I really try. Today I'm with Dave in L.A., tomorrow in Detroit with Miles, then Phoenix, Chicago – pffff! Finally, on my holidays, I go back to New York to make some sessions!"[104] It was the kind of schedule that a few years earlier might have supplied enough work to support two or three musicians, and Miller was only one of a group of young, entrepreneurial successes – Sanborn, drummer Steve Gadd, and percussionist Ralph McDonald were others, and Ron Carter provided one of their first models – commandeering a lot of work both in jazz and on its pop fringes. As Davis packed his schedule with more playing dates spread across more miles than he ever had before, Miller had to choose between Davis and his diverse activities.

Most of the attention on the tour naturally focused on Scofield, not so much because of what he played, for he played sparingly, as what he represented. John Abercrombie, one of the leaders in the post-fusion generation that brought the guitar into jazz as a leading voice, told Lee Jeske: "The great thing about Scofield is he's got all this blues feeling in his playing that sets him apart from a lot of other jazz players; he's got this edge, this sort of bite which gives his playing – even when he's playing more abstract – a real foundation which I've always loved."[105] A reviewer at the Chicago Park West concert, Neil Tesser, commented: "I have no trouble calling Scofield the finest guitarist in modern jazz. His tone, his phrasing, and the sonorous intervals of his lines, all mark him an unabashed romantic; yet there is a razor's edge underneath, and a delightfully abstract logic, that shapes his music into something strong and supple ... He has been remarkable on records, and onstage [in Chicago] – perhaps because he has been with Miles less than three months – his solos were the only new music heard at Park West."[106]

Bill Evans and Mike Stern were beginning to establish their talents independently from Davis, recording with other bands and playing in pickup groups whenever time allowed, but Scofield came the closest to an established talent that Davis had admitted into his band in almost a decade.

The new band again recorded in the first months of 1983, and the track was, by recent standards, rushed into print to fill out the *Star People* LP. The details are as follows:

Miles Davis Septet: Star People
Miles Davis, tpt, synthesizer; Bill Evans, ss; John Scofield, Mike Stern, gtr;

Tom Barney, b; Al Foster, dms; Mino Cinelu, perc; Gil Evans, arr. Probably
January–February 1983
Speak
(on Columbia FC 38657)

Though similar in tempo and key to *Star on Cicely* and featuring similar
harmonies in Gil Evans's arrangement, *Speak* gets a much more spirited
reading, with the arranged and the improvised elements almost equally
uninhibited. It had been in the repertoire longer, and the players had
thoroughly digested their parts. Davis plays simultaneous trumpet-
synthesizer chords at the beginning and behind Stern and Scofield, the
principal soloists, and seems distracted in his open trumpet solo at the
end, played with a mellow tone that sounds like a flugelhorn, in order to
get back to the synthesizer. He appears more than willing to let the
guitarists take the honors. Stern solos first, in a series of sharp, short
yelps into the highest register, and Scofield follows, after the second
theme statement, building long lines that accelerate in intensity and
eventually summon Davis's background riffs at the climax. Davis is left
with the denouement.

More than any other track, *Speak* showed Davis's music in transition.
It retained many of the elements that dominated his concerts, but it was
also the harbinger of some innovations. The retained elements were
carried over from the comeback concerts of 1981, and before that. The
rhythmic pulse remained rocking (and sometimes rolling), with Al
Foster showing none of the subtleties of touch or taste that once
endeared Philly Joe Jones and Tony Williams to Davis. The new bassist,
Barney, lacked Miller's assertiveness but remained essentially a funk
bassist rather than a jazz player. Stern's presence guaranteed rock
colorations in the ensemble and rock-derived improvizations, and the
comparison between him and Scofield in the same context only
emphasized his rock proclivities.

The new elements, still nascent in *Speak*, were the synthesized
orchestral effects and the elaboration of arranged sequences beyond four
or eight bars. *Speak* offered the first hint that Davis's music was taking a
turn toward the kind of formal elaboration he seemed to eschew forever
in the 1960s when he gave up on the thirty-two-bar song form and
aborted several projects with Gil Evans. And in Bill Evans and John
Scofield, he had two patient, thoughtful players with excellent technical abilities and jazz predilections.

Speak received a very different treatment when Davis selected it for a three-and-a-half-minute performance on the nationally televised Grammy Awards show on 23 February 1983. He kicked it off at a frantic tempo, and the playing, which squeezed in solos by Scofield, Evans (on soprano saxophone), and Stern in that order, was raw, with Davis often overpowering everyone including the sound engineers with his trumpet-synthesizer blasts. A. James Liska, in a *Down Beat* editorial, complained that the National Academy of Recording Arts and Sciences, the governing body of the Grammy Awards, "has become nothing more than an organization to serve the commercial side of the industry – an annual dog-and-pony show, replete with antics of the industry's lesser craftsmen and ignorant of the more artistic achievements of its membership." He reported, "Miles Davis kept his back to the audience for his excursion" on the telecast, and then he added: "His attitude at first seemed deplorable; upon reflection it was an admirable statement."[107]

Davis appeared anything but blasé in his brief showing, and the frenetic music he played seemed an honest reflection of nerves. He cared so much that, in the familiar, career-long pattern, he went out of his way to suggest that he cared not at all. Mike Stern told Jérome Reese that "Miles was overjoyed about winning his first Grammy since *Bitches Brew* although he hid it well."[108] Around the time that Davis was informed he had won, he told David Breskin, "I don't like to record at all, live or studio. I just do it to make money."[109]

In March and April, Davis revisited several of the European stages where he had last been seen, just one year earlier, playing from a chair as he recuperated from his stroke. He celebrated his regained health with concerts at Lille (29 March), Strasbourg (31), Turin (3 and 4 April), Bourg (10), Paris (12 and 13), Lyon (15), Vienna (18), Bordeaux (22), Angers (23), Brussels (25), and London (27 and 28). This was his first tour under the aegis of his new managers, Jerome and Robert Blank of Philadelphia, whose business card carried the unlikely designation "Delaware Valley Factors, Inc." Jerome Blank joined the entourage on this tour, and his nephew Robert accompanied him after this, and their presence made a difference. "You see, we didn't come into this knowing a whole lot about jazz, so we're not intimidated by Miles," Robert explained. "We want to find out why he's got this *reputation* – he's not like that, really – and see what can be done about it."[110] Starting with this tour, Davis has been calling his band back to the stage for encores and granting short newspaper interviews, often with Robert Blank clocking the interviewer in the background, in the cities where he plays.

Davis's return to health commanded more attention in Europe than his reconstituted band or his new repertoire. Richard Williams, who interviewed him at his London hotel for *The Times*, observed: "He still moved around the room with difficulty as he fetched himself bottles of mineral water, but the brightness of his eyes and the sheen of his skin suggested an altogether fitter man ... He talked freely and graciously, with dry humour and great animation, utterly dispelling the received image of surly arrogance."[111] Davis proudly flipped through a pad of his felt-pen sketches, mainly abstractions of female forms in whimsical attitudes and basic colors, the therapy of a restless man who spends hours on airplanes without drinking or smoking. He kidded Williams about requiring *The Times* to publish some of his drawings in return for the interview, but the public debut of Davis's sketches had to wait for the release of the *Star People* LP. Its cover carried three brightly colored, primitive stick musicians and some decorative borders, with this credit line: "All Drawings, Color Concepts and Basic Attitudes by Miles Davis." A year after that, on 26 May 1984, Davis would celebrate his 58th birthday and his return to performing after hip surgery with a slide-show of his sketches at a New York art gallery.[112]

Brian Case, reviewing one of Davis's Hammersmith Odeon concerts for *Melody Maker*, reported: "This time, lungs, plexus and chops were way up close on two hours, and he was not only committed to the swoop and flux but untypically warm towards the house." He also noted a change in his music: "This is very much the group that Miles wants, and they serve him magnificently. In keeping with the spirit of the time, it offers a broad recapitulation of one of the greatest careers in jazz."[113]

In May 1983, Davis made a quick tour of Japan, playing eight concerts to packed houses. Davis's band shared the billing with Gil Evans's orchestra, in which Evans's son Miles played in the trumpet section. Davis and Evans did not play together; throughout the tour, Davis's band played the opening set and Evans's took over after the intermission. Davis stuck with the concert format he had used in Europe. By the time they played at Yomiuri East, Kanagawa, on 29 May, he had eliminated the frail *U 'n' I* from the working repertoire, but the other titles – *Come Get It, Star People, Speak, It Gets Better, Star on Cicely*, and *Jean Pierre* – though all but the latter were new to Japanese audiences, already sounded tired from so many reworkings on so many stages.

CBS timed the release of the *Star People* LP to coincide with Davis's international travels, so that it received newspaper notices around the same time he was appearing in England, France, Japan, and the other countries. The concert promotions thus fed the record sales and vice-versa, in a marketing campaign perfected for touring rock stars such as the Rolling Stones, Bob Dylan and the Band, David Bowie, and The Jacksons. When Davis returned to North America, *Star People*'s release coincided with his summer schedule, which included Kool Festival concerts in Cleveland (12 June), New York (26) Minneapolis (13 July), and Pittsburgh (19 August), as well as independent festivals in Montreal (7 July) and Toronto (8).

The novelty of his comeback wore off long ago for Davis, but for his audiences it was only beginning to wear off by the summer of 1983, two years after it began. His full-time presence on concert stages brought a few adjustments by promoters. In Toronto he played not at one of the high-priced halls as he had in 1981 and earlier in 1983, but in a roofed amphitheater at Ontario Place, where for $4 patrons could jam the hillsides and peer down onto the stage. George Wein presented Davis's band paired with other bands, putting him with the McCoy Tyner quintet in Minneapolis and vsop II in New York. If Davis had stayed after his performance to listen to the bands with which he shared those stages, he might have rediscovered more of his old musical virtues and perhaps even some new ones.

The novelty of his comeback had also obviously worn off for Davis's New York reviewers. They dealt with him perfunctorily at the Kool festivities, brushing past his performance to deal with some of the hundreds of other musicians who participated. Lee Jeske's notice of Davis's concert in *Down Beat* stated: "Opening for vsop II was Miles Davis with his sextet. All I have to tell you about *that* is that Miles didn't play nearly enough, and his band played more than enough."[114] Whitney Balliett's annual Kool review for the *New Yorker* gave surprisingly short shrift to almost everyone; of Davis, he said: "His chops were in good shape, and he sounded like the old Davis of *Walkin'*. The rest of the time — he was disguised tonight as a sort of golfer, in white cap, baggy dark-blue windbreaker, and wide-legged 1930s pants — he played on an electric keyboard, let loose occasional trumpet shrieks, and allowed his group to scream its back-beated electronic head off."[115]

That nonchalance was beginning to crystallize into the American critical consensus on Davis's music of the 1980s. Neil Tesser, after watching Davis at Park West in February, concluded: "Miles has long personified 'cool'; now, like [a] glacial drift ... his music moves across the landscape, strewing stuff all over, some of it valuable, much of it worthless."[116] Even Greg Tate, in an eccentric revaluation of Davis's music since 1969 for *Down Beat* that otherwise inverted most jazz critics' perceptions, fell into line when he reached the music of the 1980s, stating: "I'll admit to being unable to take Miles' comeback seriously. Not that I'm alone in this mind you: I don't think Miles does either."[117] So far, the European and Japanese critics have been much more cautious about committing themselves on Davis's latest guise, and the American consensus remains local.

The force of that consensus may have obscured the critical perception of Davis's band after its return from Japan for its summer circuit. While Davis and his band played less freely and confidently in New York than in their subsequent concerts – apparently as a reflex of Davis's new vulnerability, which makes it impossible for him to contain his fretfulness in his so-what? disguise – they presented several changes for critical fodder.

John Scofield occupied center stage in place of Mike Stern, who left at the end of the Japanese tour. The difference that made to the ensemble sound could be measured in decibels, but it was more significant in the altered feeling. Scofield shares with Stern the command of high-pitched guitar colorations, but it is not the hallmark of his style as it is of Stern's.

The blues remained dominant, with *It Gets Better* joined in the repertoire by a new and similarly straightforward twelve-bar melody. That doubled Davis's opportunities for playing to the women in the front rows and stretched his powers of invention to the break-point, but it also played up one of Scofield's strengths, and Evans's too, when he was given enough space to develop his thoughts. No jazz audience agonized about hearing Davis play blues clichés instead of the funk clichés of his recent past.

The band's repertoire was almost entirely new. Sometime between the Kanagawa concert at the end of May and the first American concert in mid-June, Davis renovated his concert program. Even *Jean Pierre* was purged. The retained compositions – *Speak*, *It Gets Better*, and *Star on Cicely* – introduced intricately arranged passages, with Scofield and Evans playing tight harmonies, usually backed by Davis's trumpet-synthesizer riffs. Four new themes were built on similar arrangements.

The haste with which the new repertoire had been installed was also evident. Many sequences had rough edges, and the concerts had no more polish than dress rehearsals. In Toronto, the roughness was exacerbated toward the end when Evans, obviously annoyed about having so many of his solos cut short, began playing his long, difficult arranged parts half-heartedly, and at the very end the concert became a genuine rehearsal when Davis called the band back for an encore and kicked off a four-minute arrangement that the band were still learning.

What the concerts lacked in polish they partly gained in spirit, with the risks of a reorganized band searching for their new balance as they worked out new material. That new balance will not come easily. Without Stern to counterbalance the rocking rhythms, Foster and the new bassist, Darryl Jones, cast in the same funk role as his predecessors, often sounded ingenuous – an index of how suddenly the music had altered around them, but also a measure of how far they have to go to catch up with it.

Some of the rough edges in the summer repertoire were preserved when Davis selected excerpts of two of the new titles played at his Montreal concert for his new LP, *Decoy*. The details are as follows:

Miles Davis Sextet: Decoy
Miles Davis, tpt, synthesizer; Bill Evans, ss; John Scofield, gtr; Darryl Jones, b; Al Foster, dms; Mino Cinelu, perc. Festival international de Jazz, Montreal, 7 July 1983
What It Is; That's What Happened
(both on Columbia FC 38991)
Both are composed by Scofield and Davis and arranged by Davis.

Both titles feature tight uptempo unison passages by Scofield and Evans. *That's What Happened* adds Davis's simultaneous trumpet-synthesizer riffs in the background, but omits the solos. *What It Is* carries on into Evans's solo, his last on record as a member of the band although he would tour with them for four more months, and into Davis's, with an overdub of Davis's blues solo from the same concert superimposed.

The excerpts form the liveliest tracks on *Decoy*. The rest of the music was set down in studio sessions later that summer, as Davis resumed his once-familiar practice of rehearsing with the tapes running. The details are as follows:

Miles Davis Quartet: Decoy
Miles Davis, synthesizer; Darryl Jones, b; Al Foster, dms; Mino Cinelu, perc. New York, probably late August–September 1983
Freaky Deaky
(on Columbia FC 38991)

Miles Davis Septet: Decoy
Miles Davis, tpt; Branford Marsalis, ss; Robert Irving III, synthesizer; John
Scofield, gtr; Darryl Jones, b; Al Foster, dms; Mino Cinelu, perc. New York,
probably late August–September 1983
Decoy; Robot 415; Code M.D.; That's Right
(all on Columbia FC 38991)
Marsalis, Scofield, Jones, and Foster are not heard on the one-minute excerpt
titled *Robot 415*; Irving composed and arranged *Decoy* and *Code M.D.*; Davis
and Irving composed and arranged *Robot 415*; Davis and Scofield composed
That's Right, and Davis and Gil Evans arranged it.

Freaky Deaky pares down the ensemble to a quartet in order to give
some prominence to the new bassist, Darryl Jones, who had joined the
band in the spring on the recommendation of Vincent Wilburn, Davis's
nephew who now traveled with him as bodyguard and factotum. Davis
praised Jones's playing extravagantly at every opportunity, giving him
his highest accolade – "a motherfucker" – in fall interviews for French
and German radio and describing him this way for Leonard Feather in
the spring: "He has the same approach to music as Jimmy Blanton – in
fact, he's the greatest bass player since Blanton, and he's just 22."[118]
  Except for *That's Right*, the longest and best-elaborated track, the rest
of the music bears the imprint of Robert Irving, the keyboard player
from *The Man with the Horn* whom Davis was now readying for a place
in the working band. His funk charts are undistinguished but pleasant in
their brief airing, and the sparse solo spaces on them offer little interest
for the jazz listener. His synthesizer effects mix unobtrusively into the
background, as Davis's seldom did, and the ensemble seem tame.
  That tameness also pervades *That's Right*, notwithstanding the
collaboration of Davis, Scofield, and Gil Evans in its arrangement and
the presence of Branford Marsalis as a soloist. The track opens with a
blues solo by Davis and then swings into its arranged unison passage by
Scofield and Marsalis. The arranged passage recurs after solos by
Scofield and by Marsalis, and the track fades out during Davis's second
solo. Its form is orderly and its solos are generous, but the mood is
cautious. Davis and Scofield have played in this same blues context
nightly for over a year and have few surprises to offer, and Marsalis, with
a growing reputation as an earthy, swinging soloist, sounds uncertain.
He admitted to no uncertainty when Peter Keepnews questioned him
about the session. "It was pretty much the stuff I used to play in high

school," he said. "It was, you know, vamp music. But it was good. I definitely had fun."[119]

Davis was satisfied with Marsalis's work in the studio but could not add him to the band because he was committed to his brother's quintet. Bill Evans rejoined Davis for the remaining tour of the year, an October swing through Europe, but the tension between them was palpable. In Rome, Davis told an interviewer, "I'm trying to make my saxophone player understand the problem of phrases ... He throws them away, he wastes them, like a boxer making useless jabs and wasting his energy."[120] In Paris, after having his solos cut short, Evans said, "Hey, Miles, you don't even like saxophone players anymore, do you?" "I didn't even answer that nonsense," Davis told Leonard Feather.[121]

Davis was received royally in Warsaw, where the tour opened on 23 October. he was waved through customs by officers wearing "We Want Miles" buttons, whisked away in a Russian-made Chaika limousine, and escorted to a two-bedroom suite at the Victoria Hotel, where the swimming pool had been scrubbed and freshly filled for his use.[122] After his performance at the Warsaw Jazz Jamboree, the 5,000 fans stood and chanted "Sto lat" (May you live a hundred years), and Davis reciprocated by calling his band back for three encores.[123]

His reception in Berlin on 29 October was no less noisy but much less friendly. Before leaving the United States, Davis had given a long, relaxed interview to Ute Büsing for German radio. He dispatched the promotional business early, saying, "I hope you fuckin' Germans come out an' see us," and then offered numerous opinions for the German public to ponder. Many of them involved Beethoven. "I don't like to listen to Beethoven," he said. "He's just too old for me. You got Stockhausen. Not Beethoven. He's too fuckin' old." Prodded by Büsing, he returned to the theme: "I just don't like Beethoven. That's my personal feeling about his music." And later, in response to a question about his use of electronics, he said, "You can't fuck around, like old Beethoven." By the time he landed in Berlin, his opinions had aroused a storm of controversy in the press and he faced a horde of reporters wherever he went. His two concerts for Jazz Fest Berlin at Philharmonic Hall, on the same day as Master Srinvas Group from India and the Sun Ra All Stars with Philly Joe Jones, Archie Shepp, and Don Cherry, were received enthusiastically by sellout crowds.

The European triumphs were capped on Davis's return to New York by a gala retrospective at Radio City Music Hall, "Miles Ahead: A Tribute to an American Music Legend," on 6 November. Co-produced by the Black Music Association, the tribute received press coverage that rivaled Davis's 1981 comeback concerts. "We think this will be a once-in-a-lifetime experience," said George Butler, Columbia's vice-president for jazz. "The program is an attempt to entertain, and to inform people about Miles's impact. We'll take the styles of music he has been involved with from the late 1940s to the present." The roster of performers stretched the outer limits even of Davis's many genres, with a contingent of rhythm and blues singers including Angela Bofill, Shalamar, and the Whispers, reflecting Davis's current listening tastes rather than his music. "It is also designed to entertain Miles," Clayton Riley, the director, said.[124]

Parts of the four-hour show became a genuine retrospective. With Bill Cosby as host, revolving stages, a videotaped encomium from Dizzy Gillespie, and numerous speeches, there was still time for brief performances by Davis's early associates Walter Bishop Jr, Roy Haynes, J.J. Johnson, and Jackie McLean, his alumni George Benson, Ron Carter, George Coleman, Herbie Hancock, Jimmy Heath, Philly Joe Jones, Buster Williams, and Tony Williams, and an all-star orchestra conducted by Quincy Jones playing Slide Hampton's rearrangements of some of Gil Evans's arrangements for *Porgy and Bess* and *Sketches of Spain*. At midnight, Davis received an honorary degree in music from the president of Fisk University while Cosby and Cicely Tyson enrobed him in purple. The evening ended with a half-hour set by Davis and his current band.

When it was over, Cosby cajoled Davis to make a speech. Finally he took the microphone and whispered, "Thank you." He grew more talkative backstage as the NBC-TV cameras recorded him chugging a litre of Perrier water. Asked if the tributes overwhelmed him, he took the bottle away from his lips, furrowed his brow, and said, "No, I wonder why they waited so long."[125]

The gala ended a long, sustained period of touring and performing for Davis and preceded a long layoff. He entered the hospital two weeks later for a left-hip prosthesis. The operation was expected to take two hours but ended up taking ten. The recuperation was expected to take six weeks, with Davis back onstage in January 1984, but took six months because he caught pneumonia in December. *Decoy*, announced for release in January, came out instead at the end of May, to coincide with Davis's return to performing, which started with a concert at the Beverly Theatre in Los Angeles on 2 June. The summer schedule had the familiar look of recent years, with Kool festival appearances in June and

August and European festivals in July. The band looked and sounded only slightly different. Bill Evans, as expected, left to try his hand at freelancing, and Mino Cinelu joined Weather Report. Their places were filled by Bob Berg and Steve Thornton, as unknown as Evans and Cinelu had been when they joined and indeed as most of Davis's sidemen had been for more than a decade. The repertoire continued to change too and, with it, Davis's notion of what improvising musicians should sound like. He is still not willing, or perhaps not able, to coast.

As long as he retains that restlessness there is some chance that he may yet rise above his superstardom and, against the odds of most of his current critics, influence another generation of jazzmen. The odds are, of course, long and grow longer daily in a young person's art form. In the life cycle of most jazz players, Davis is already well into what ought to be his dotage. One is reminded of André Hodeir's question, "Why do they age so badly?" and of his ominous answer: "The history of both jazz and jazzmen is that of creative purity gradually corrupted by success. In his youth, the great musician has to struggle to impose his art; if he succeeds in doing so, he must then struggle daily *against* his own success. How many men have won *this* struggle?"

When he wrote this in 1962, Hodeir could name only one who had: "Charlie Parker undoubtedly did, because he never reached the peak of success and because he died at the age of thirty-five." And he was willing to hazard a guess about two others: "Monk and Miles Davis may win it, either because of their tough, incorruptible characters, or because they took Pascal's advice and fled success rather than try to stand up to it."[126]

For Thelonious Monk, Hodeir's guess proved prophetic. He never wavered in imposing his art. In 1955, when he began recording for Riverside, Orrin Keepnews persuaded him to record two LPs of Ellington melodies and standard ballads in an attempt to make his music more accessible, but Monk simply translated them into his own singular idiom. It never occurred to him to tailor his music for commercial success; he used all his energy pursuing his own muse and had none left for the bitch goddess. By 1964, when his portrait appeared on the cover of *Time*, he had succeeded in bringing the audience to him. After that, he felt less need for performing, recording, or composing. He disbanded his quartet with tenor saxophonist Charlie Rouse in 1970 and emerged into public only on special occasions. After an international tour with Dizzy Gillespie, Sonny Stitt, Kai Winding, Al McKibbon, and Art Blakey in 1972, billed as the Giants of Jazz, he appeared with the New York Jazz Repertory Company in 1974, at the Newport Jazz Festival in 1975, and

Bill Evans at Ontario Place Forum, 1983 (Bernard Lecerf)

Miles Davis at Ontario Place Forum, 1983 (Peter Jones)

at Carnegie Hall in 1976. He shrugged off countless inducements. His seclusion was rumored to be caused by a mysterious biochemical disorder, which may or may not translate into schizophrenia, but sporadic reports confirmed that he was fit to perform more often than not, if he had wanted to. When he died at 64 in February 1982, his art was uncorrupted, its stunning integrity one of the great achievements in jazz.

For Miles Davis, Hodeir's guess seems equally secure. He has already succeeded in imposing his art four or perhaps five times, toughly and incorruptibly, all the while fleeing success for bitches more to his taste. Only now, as Davis enters his fifth decade as a jazz artist, Hodeir's terms of reference are harder to apply. His music keeps changing, but the character guiding it seems neither incorruptible nor particularly tough. He feels no need for imposing his art again, and when Ute Büsing asked him what he saw in the future of jazz, he replied, "Bullshit." Success finally caught up to him, and he seems genuinely relieved that the race is over. "Struggling musicians," he told Büsing, "are bad musicians."

So he pokes fun at the tough, incorruptible character he used to be. He interpolates eight bars of *Surrey with the Fringe on Top* and then casts a sideward look – a Jack Benny take – at the audience, or he snatches his trumpet away from his lips and sticks out his tongue just as a front-row photographer clicks his shutter, or he hoists his pant legs and invites the audience to cheer his bright red boots. "Yeah, I'm an entertainer," he admitted to Cheryl McCall. "I've got a certain amount of ham in me. I don't know. I'm doin' what I'm doin' but I know I'm a big ham. It doesn't take away from the music, because I enjoy what I'm doin' at that particular time."[127]

"I've earned an enormous amount of money since my comeback," he told Leonard Feather,[128] and he revels in the glitter that goes with show-biz. The $60,000 yellow Ferrari no longer represents thoroughbred recklessness but celebrity status. He had it flown to Los Angeles from New York when he went there to perform on the Grammy Awards show and towed to the curb in front of his hotel, L'Ermitage in Beverly Hills; it could not be driven because of mechanical problems, according to David Breskin, "but it's a stage prop that makes him feel good."[129] Of Breskin's *Rolling Stone* profile, Davis said, "I read a little bit and threw it away, because it was evident from the first paragraph that he didn't like me." But even his disdain for the press is wavering, and he added, "One of these days, maybe if I've just made love real good and I'm in the right mood, I'll read the whole thing and it won't drag me."[130]

On the road, he stays at the best hotels while his sidemen stay elsewhere. ("They're in a different hotel," Breskin says, "even on the same stage."[131]) Off the road, the renovated Manhattan brownstone is now joined not only by the Long Island retreat but also by a seaside villa in Malibu, California. "New York is great," Davis told George Goodman in 1981. "I've got so much noise. Subways. Horns. I can't stand nothing quiet. I go nuts."[132] But the villa is quiet, and Davis told Leonard Feather: "I love California more and more. It's a place where you should be able to add fifty years to your life, even with the smog."

"It's a good sign of your social status when you know you can have whatever you want in the world," he added. "I love clothes and I love cars. And I love to have a good band. My manager makes life easy on tours. I only have to show up and play. I like the California lifestyle, and if I miss New York I can always go back. Really, it's a good life."[133]

AFTERWORD

Miles Davis (Peter Jones)

So What?

If I didn't play trumpet, I don't know what I would have done. I couldn't stay in an office. I'd do some kind of research. That W-H-Y is always my first word, you know. I'd do research, 'cause I like to see why things are how they are, the shape and flesh and everything. I'm one of them motherfuckers.   Miles Davis (1983)

I have not called Miles Davis a genius. He does not call himself a genius, although he comes close once, in a bantering mood, on page 313.

Charlie Parker was a genius, and the young Louis Armstrong was too. Their music burst out of them as flashes of insight. It seemed to depend more on intuition than on introspection, and once they were rightly heard all the music around them had to change.

Miles Davis did not do that. But he did something no less difficult, and as inexplicable. He sustained a long creative life in the second half of the twentieth century, when creative lives are seldom long and long lives are seldom creative. He grew and changed and renewed himself, and with him the music grew and changed and renewed itself. He leaves behind not a flash of insight but a luminous trail.

Davis's achievement is a rare one, and not only in jazz. Hemingway discovered a unique, powerful voice for fiction, and then he spent the last two-thirds of his time parodying his own voice. Brando transformed dialogue and stage directions into illusion, and then he made the dialogue inaudible and the actions stupefying. Joseph Heller filled *Catch-22* with hilarious indignation and grotesque joy, and then he followed it, after thirteen years of near-silence, with stylish voids. Orson Welles passed from masterworks in several media to so-so ads for *vin ordinaire.* The spirit slumps or the will weakens.

Not always. Davis's achievement is rare in jazz, but it is not unique.

Duke Ellington's creativity lasted at least as long and shone at least as brightly. Some, perhaps many, would say more brightly. It hardly matters, because, in the end, it is immeasurable.

So Davis's place among jazz musicians is secure. He ranks at the top with Armstrong and Ellington and Parker and very few others – probably Jelly Roll Morton and Thelonious Monk, perhaps Coleman Hawkins and John Coltrane and, if one is permitted to look beyond the point where music intersects with myth, Buddy Bolden.

All of them made highly personal responses to the way we are in our time and sublimated them into art so they could be felt and shared. They help form the sensibility of our time as surely as do our painters, poets, composers, novelists, directors. If they have not had the same audience and their art form remains undervalued in the cultural reckoning, that may yet change.

Davis's music tapped resources of metaphor among those who took the time to be moved by it. His performances, Charles Fox said, were like "a man reading aloud from his diary."[1] In an image by Barry Ulanov that stuck doggedly to his playing for years, through several changes, Davis was "a man walking on eggshells."[2] To that, Ira Gitler responded, "Miles may be a man walking on eggshells, but he is also a diamond cutting into opaque glass."[3] Whitney Balliett heard in Davis's music "young-Werther ruminations ... – a view of things that is brooding, melancholy, perhaps self-pitying, and extremely close to the sentimental."[4] Martin Williams pointed out that Davis was far removed from that picaresque romantic by stating, "Davis the musician walks firmly and sure of foot; if he ever encounters any eggshells, his intensity will probably grind them to powder."[5]

We are told that one of the wellsprings of Davis's music is his essential shyness. That seems a peculiar, even exotic, piece of psychologizing in the face of the facts. Davis's strengths have always been the converse of those of a shy man. As Gil Evans puts it: "Miles Davis is a leader in jazz because he has a definite confidence in what he likes and he is not *afraid* of what he likes. A lot of musicians are constantly looking around to hear what the next person is doing and they worry about whether they themselves are in style. Miles has confidence in his taste, and he goes his own way."[6] Teo Macero agrees: "He has never been bound by convention. You wouldn't expect Miles to go back and do something the way he did it years ago any more than you would expect Picasso to go back to what he was doing in his blue and rose periods."[7]

Another point against the easy explanation of shyness is that Davis has felt the adulation of his fellows and his fans, often presupposed as in Macero's unhesitating comparison with Picasso but usually much more directly, performing before millions of people all over the world. Surely such an experience reinforced countless times over the years would be an effective antidote for anything but the most pathological shyness, and surely anyone who suffered from acute shyness could not in the first place bear to hone his art – which requires, after all, *performing* – so that it invited such exposure.

But if not shyness, what then? I would suggest, at some risk, that arrogance fits better. The risk arises from the baffling fact that whenever arrogance has been associated with Davis, the association has almost always been made by someone who deplores him – by promoters for whom he has refused to work cheaply, or audiences miffed at his refusal to bow, or antagonists on whom he has figuratively or literally spat. It sometimes seems that the protestations of shyness show up more frequently after he has committed some impudent public act, as if designed by well-meaning acquaintances to shield him from the charge of arrogance.

It is worth wondering why the attribution of arrogance has, where Davis is concerned, been appropriated by people lodging a complaint against him, so that any attempt to associate the term with him in a neutral or well-meaning way requires vindication. No one ever hesitated in applying the term to Shaw, or Pavlova, or Stravinsky, or any number of our cultural bellwethers.

Perhaps the reluctance to recognize Davis's arrogance positively, as a wellspring of his art, merely reflects the fact that the art for which he is the bellwether, jazz, is less secure among our arts than most others, having ascended so recently into the concert hall from the black folk roots of field songs, spirituals, and funeral marches. Or perhaps it is because Davis lives in a world where, for some, an arrogant black man is "uppity," a social taboo that was supposed to die with the Emancipation Proclamation.

Davis has suffered for being a black man in other ways too. Apart from the social and occupational indignities visited on blacks during their tedious rise from the plantations, he has suffered by spending his creative energies on a music that is making its own tedious rise from brothels and dance halls. True, Davis has earned more material rewards than all but a very few jazzmen. Even so, his affluence probably came harder than that of people in other cultural pursuits, the leading divas, conductors, actors, directors, novelists. True too, Davis has received some measure of artistic recognition, but, again, it has hardly been comparable to his counterparts in other art forms – if indeed it is possible to identify counterparts to Davis in other art forms, for one would be hard pressed to name an individual in those other arts who maintained such an utterly commanding position for even half the length of time that Davis dominated his.

Perhaps the rewards he has gathered are the harbingers of a more tolerant cultural climate, with a better future for jazz in it. Just ten or fifteen years ago, any mention of Davis or any other jazz musician in the same breath as Maria Callas, Leonard Bernstein, Marlon Brando, Elia Kazan, or Saul Bellow might have been dismissed as ludicrous among the guardians of our culture. It is less likely to be so dismissed nowadays, I think, at least in many circles.

If so, it is partly Davis's doing. At his best, when he was willing to make the fewest concessions, he not only created the music, he dignified it. When Bud Powell told him, "I wish I was blacker than you,"[8] it was presumably not the hue of his skin that he envied so much as his undenigrable character.

In a tradition where the musicians had been treated like vaudevillians and buskers for generations, Davis found a liberating stance. It worked only because he, unlike anyone who came before him except Duke Ellington, had the conviction to do it his way and the strength to make it stick – the arrogance, if you will. Ralph J. Gleason put it this way: "The fact that he is now, like Picasso and a very few other artists, a great commercial success in his own lifetime is a tribute to his courage and his sanity and his basic good sense. It is also, whether or not he wills it, a rare symbol to all artists everywhere of the complete triumph of uncompromising art."[9]

If the comparison with Picasso works it is not only because both men achieved commercial success on their own terms but also because both men, as Macero said, spent their careers in a constant search for expression. "Like Picasso, he has made change into style," Gleason added, "and wherever you go you bump into little fragments of his music."

In the shape of their careers and the restlessness of their vision, Davis and Picasso seem to invite comparison. Jazz writers, if no one else, find it compelling. David Breskin recently added this one: "Restless, relentless, [Davis] synergizes new vocabularies, masters the language, then moves on with another generation in tow. He's the Picasso of the invisible art."[10] And Greg Tate, on Davis's 1980s incarnation, says,

"Like Picasso when he ran out of ideas, Miles has taken to enjoying poking a little fun at himself."[11]

The comparison will soon be a cliché. In jazz journalism it may already be a cliché. Is it enlightening? Does it mean anything at all?

Davis, for one, does not think so. Some wag, charged by a corporate sponsor with preparing program notes for a 1982 concert, tried it out on him. Lots of people, he told Davis, were comparing him with Picasso. Did he have any thoughts on that? Davis stared at him a long time, his eyes impassive and his lips fixed, until the adman's smile wavered and came unglued. Then he whispered, "I'm in a class by myself."[12]

As is Picasso, of course.

References

CHAPTER NINE:
PFRANCING: 1960–2 (pages 3–50)

1 Adderley 1964, pp. 261–3
2 Simpkins 1975, p. 90
3 Sussman 1980, p. 28
4 Sy Johnson 1976, p. 22
5 Gordon 1980, p. 99
6 Hentoff ca 1960
7 Hall 1974b, p. 14
8 Hentoff ca 1960
9 Hall 1974b, p. 14
10 Martin Williams 1970b, p. 160
11 Harrison 1976, pp. 140–1
12 Cook 1983, p. 15
13 Hentoff ca 1960
14 Harrison 1976, p. 141
15 Martin Williams 1970b, p. 160
16 Martin 1960, p. 3
17 Stewart 1982, p. 65
18 Cook 1983, p. 15
19 Stewart 1982, p. 65
20 Liska 1982, p. 20
21 Thomas 1975, pp. 108–9
22 Simpkins 1975, p. 109, p. 111
23 *Melody Maker* 14 July 1965, p. 6
24 Goldberg 1965, p. 231

25 Spellman 1970, p. 128
26 Feather and Gitler 1976, p. 34
27 Silvert 1980, p. 18
28 Feather and Gitler 1976, p. 34
29 Goldberg 1965, p. 230
30 Stewart 1981, p. 22
31 Spellman 1970, p. 14
32 Spellman 1970, p. 6
33 Berendt 1976, p. 97
34 Johnson 1976, p. 24
35 Cole 1974, p. 152
36 Liska 1982a, p. 20
37 Martin 1960, p. 3
38 Goldberg 1965, p. 63
39 Martin 1960, p. 3
40 Simpkins 1975, p. 116
41 Goldberg 1965, p. 86
42 DeMicheal 1969b, p. 18
43 Feather 1974b, p. 225
44 Goldberg 1981, p. 59
45 Gordon 1980, p. 102
46 DeMicheal 1966, p. 18
47 Cotterrell 1967, p. 4
48 Goldberg 1965, p. 80

49 Goldberg 1965, p. 208
50 Hailey 1964, p. 167
51 Gleason 1961
52 Primack 1979, p. 37
53 Gleason 1975, p. 133
54 Quoted by Carr 1982, p. 128
55 Wilson ca 1961
56 Balliett 1962, p. 143
57 Simon ca 1961
58 Ronald Atkins, in Harrison et al 1975, p. 99
59 Norsworthy 1974
60 Goldberg 1965, p. 63
61 Taylor 1977, p. 11
62 Nyhan 1976, p. 82
63 Scott 1980, p. 92
64 Martin Williams 1970a, p. 107
65 Interview Toronto August 1976
66 Feather 1967, p. 16
67 Max Harrison 1976, p. 140
68 Martin Williams 1970b, p. 160
69 Feather 1967, p. 16
70 Hall 1974a, pp. 17–18
71 Hall 1974b, p. 13

CHAPTER TEN:
SO NEAR, SO FAR: 1963–4
(pages 51–75)

1 Sussman 1980, p. 28
2 Martin 1960, p. 3
3 Underwood 1979, p. 54
4 Taylor 1977, p. 13
5 Coryell and Friedman 1978, p. 88
6 DeMicheal 1969b, p. 20
7 Bouchard 1980, p. 22
8 Taylor 1977, pp. 11–12
9 McRae 1975, p. 10
10 Feather 1974b, p. 237
11 Goode ca 1970

12 Gleason ca 1963
13 Gleason 1975, p. 249
14 Evans 1981
15 Hawes and Asher 1974, p. 130
16 Gillespie and Fraser 1979, p. 454, p. 457
17 Gilmore 1978, p. 20
18 Sussman 1980, p. 61
19 Hennessy 1977, p. 46
20 Spellman 1970, p. 15
21 Tinder 1980, p. 6
22 Cole 1974, p. 95
23 Palmer ca 1975
24 Palmer ca 1975
25 Ullmann 1980, p. 135
26 Coryell and Friedman 1978, p. 259
27 Ullmann 1980, p. 135
28 Liska 1982a, p. 20

CHAPTER ELEVEN:
CIRCLE: 1964–8 (pages 76–134)

1 DeMicheal 1969b, p. 20
2 Jones 1968, p. 82
3 Jones 1968, p. 85
4 Pekar 1976, p. 8
5 Lyons 1983, p. 145, p. 150
6 Hawes and Asher 1974, p. 138
7 Gordon 1980, p. 102
8 Carter 1982, p. 44
9 Mialy 1983
10 Hall 1974a, p. 20
11 Ramsey ca 1975
12 Williams 1970b, p. 162
13 Silvert 1977, p. 16
14 Coryell and Friedman 1968, pp. 3–4
15 Balliett 1983a, p. 169
16 Jeske 1983e, p. 24

17 Goodman 1981, p. 12
18 Taylor 1977, p. 13
19 Pekar 1976, p. 9
20 Yanow 1978, p. 58
21 Collier 1978, p. 433
22 McCall 1982, p. 43
23 Jeske 1983e, p. 24
24 Morgenstern 1966, p. 32
25 Gordon 1980, p. 98
26 Zwerin 1966, p. 39
27 Siders 1973b, p. 45
28 DeMichael 1969b, p. 20
29 McCall 1982, p. 43
30 Gordon 1980, p. 101
31 Feather 1967, pp. 16–17
32 Feather 1967, p. 17
33 Quoted by Hentoff 1975, p. 199
34 Clark 1977, p. 13
35 Wilmer 1970, p. 73
36 *Down Beat* 6 April 1976, p. 13
37 DeMicheal 11 Dec 1969, p. 32
38 Wilmer 1969, p. 17
39 Russ Wilson 1967, p. 30
40 Siders 1973b, p. 19
41 Hawes and Asher 1974, p. 147;
   Siders 1973b, p. 19
42 Blumenthal ca 1981
43 Hentoff 1978
44 Feather 1969, p. 28
45 Hall 1974a, pp. 17, 18
46 Feather 1967, pp. 16–17
47 Stewart 1982, p. 64
48 Feather 1967, p. 16
49 Blumenthal 1979, pp. 65–6
50 Blumenthal 1979, p. 65
51 Clark 1977, p. 14
52 Lyttleton 1978, p. 68
53 Gitler 1967, p. 26
54 Wilmer 1982, p. 68
55 Quoted by Thomas 1975, p. 226
56 Balliett 1981b, p. 40
57 Gillespie 1976, pp. 9–10
58 DeMicheal 1969b, p. 21
59 Walton 1972, p. 129
60 Taylor 1977, p. 18
61 DeMicheal 1969b, p. 21
62 Taylor 1977, pp. 16, 18
63 Wilmer 1967, p. 19
64 McRae 1975, p. 10
65 Taylor 1977, p. 17, p. 18
66 Coryell and Friedman 1978, p. 98
67 Birnbaum 1979, p. 44
68 Silvert 1977, p. 17
69 Martin Williams 1970a, p. 272
70 Martin Williams 1970a, p. 272
71 Coryell and Friedman 1978,
   p. 103
72 Martin Williams 1970a, p. 273
73 Martin Williams 1970a,
   pp. 272–3
74 Williams 1970a, p. 276
75 Taylor 1977, p. 13
76 Jeske 1983c, p. 31
77 Taylor 1977, p. 15
78 Mitchell 1968, p. 37
79 Mitchell 1968, p. 37
80 Kart 1968, p. 24
81 Pekar 1976, p. 11
82 Morgenstern 1977b, p. 14
83 Stewart 1982, p. 65
84 Stewart 1982, p. 64
85 Nisenson 1982, p. 204
86 Quoted by Carr 1982, p. 166
87 Nisenson 1982, p. 204
88 Feather 1974b, p. 255
89 DeMicheal 1969b, p. 20
90 Feather 1974b, p. 240
91 Feather and Gitler 1976, p. 133
92 Feather 1974b, p. 240
93 Johnson 1976, p. 27

CHAPTER TWELVE:
MILES RUNS THE VOODOO DOWN:
1968–9 (pages 135–75)

1 Taylor 1977, p. 14
2 Avakian ca 1967
3 Hentoff 1978
4 Avakian ca 1967
5 Carter 1982, p. 44
6 Saal 1977, p. 41
7 Saunders 1975, p. 30
8 Coryell and Friedman 1978, p. 162
9 Jagajivan 1973, p. 15
10 Sy Johnson 1976, p. 24
11 Sy Johnson 1976, p. 25
12 Silvert 1976, p. 24
13 Coryell and Friedman 1978, p. 148
14 DeMicheal 1969b, p. 21
15 Coryell and Friedman 1978, p. 27; Feather and Gitler 1976, p. 332
16 Grime 1979, p. 84
17 Smith 1973, p. 4
18 Grime 1979, p. 84
19 Feather 1976, p. 54
20 Feather 1976, p. 53
21 Feather 1975, p. 41
22 Townley 1975, p. 17
23 Townley 1975, p. 17
24 Albertson 1971, p. 87
25 Underwood 1979, p. 60
26 Down Beat 20 February 1969, p. 10
27 Underwood 1979, p. 60
28 Stern 1978, p. 52
29 Feather 1974a, p. 35
30 Coryell and Friedman 1978, pp. 128–9
31 DeMicheal 1969b, p. 18

32 Coryell and Friedman 1978, p. 129
33 Heckman 1974, p. 75
34 Pekar 1976, p. 12
35 Birnbaum 1979, p. 44
36 Jeske 1982, p. 17
37 Townley 1975, p. 17
38 Birnbaum 1979, p. 44
39 Miles Davis ca 1971
40 Jeske 1982, p. 17
41 Hall 1974b, p. 15
42 Feather 1979, p. 17
43 Siders 1969
44 Jeske 1981, p. 18
45 Jeske 1981, p. 18
46 Hall 1974b, p. 14
47 Clive Davis 1974, p. 43
48 Albertson 1971, p. 69
49 Clive Davis 1974, p. 299
50 Clive Davis 1974, p. 300
51 Taylor 1977, p. 223
52 Albertson 1971, pp. 68–9
53 Hall 1974a, p. 18
54 Albertson 1971, p. 69
55 Clive Davis 1974, p. 299
56 Albertson 1971, p. 69
57 Clive Davis 1974, p. 299
58 Cole 1974, pp. 104–5
59 Morgenstern 1976, p. 211
60 Albertson 1971, p. 69
61 Rollins 1982, p. 44
62 Coryell and Friedman 1978, p. 84
63 Meadow 1973, p. 16
64 Jeske 1982, p. 17
65 Feather and Gitler 1976, p. 32
66 McRae 1975, p. 11
67 Birnbaum 1979, p. 44
68 Feather and Gitler 1976, p. 32
69 Feather 1974b, p. 239
70 Feather 1976b, p. 148

71 Feather and Gitler 1976, p. 35
72 Clive Davis 1974, pp. 300–1
73 Clive Davis 1974, p. 302

CHAPTER THIRTEEN:
FUNKY TONK: 1969–71
(pages 179–232)

1 DeMicheal 1969a, p. 12
2 Quoted by Carr 1982, p. 194
3 McCall 1982, p. 48
4 Nyhan 1976, p. 87
5 Nyhan 1976, p. 88
6 McCall 1982, p. 48
7 DeMicheal 1969b, p. 21
8 Hall 1974a, p. 18
9 McCall 1982, p. 48
10 DeMicheal 1969b, p. 18
11 DeMicheal 1969b, p. 18
12 Coryell and Friedman 1978, p. 41
13 Feather 1976b, p. 49
14 Breskin 1983, p. 49
15 McCall 1982, p. 47
16 New York Post 3 March 1970
17 McCall 1982, p. 47
18 Johnson 1976, p. 27
19 Pepper and Pepper 1979,
   pp. 111–12
20 Berendt 1976, p. 101
21 Grime 1979, p. 84
22 Gordon 1980, p. 102
23 Albertson 1969, p. 31
24 DeMicheal 1969b, p. 19
25 Miller 1982, pp. 200–1
26 Blumenthal 1979, p. 66
27 DeMicheal 1969b, p. 18
28 Feather 1960, pp. 477–8
29 DeMicheal 1969b, p. 18
30 Underwood 1978, p. 16
31 Morgenstern 1973b, p. 20
32 Clive Davis 1974, p. 302

33 Clive Davis 1974, p. 302
34 Coryell and Friedman 1978, p. 68
35 Priestley 1974, p. 15
36 DeMicheal 1969b, p. 18
37 Clive Davis 1974, pp. 101–2
38 McCall 1983, p. 42
39 Down Beat April 1982, p. 10
40 Hall 1974b, p. 15
41 New York Post 4 March 1970
42 Isaacs 1979
43 Quoted by Walton 1972, p. 121
44 Coon 1977, p. 66
45 Albertson 1971, p. 68
46 Albertson 1971, p. 68
47 DeMicheal 1969b, p. 18
48 Jazz Journal June 1972, p. 16
49 Priestley 1974, p. 15
50 Hall 1974a, p. 19
51 Jarrett 1973
52 O'Reilly 1975, p. 17
53 Coryell and Friedman 1978,
   pp. 172–3
54 Feather 1974b, p. 247
55 DeMicheal 1969b, p. 18
56 Feather 1975, p. 41
57 Feather and Gitler 1976, p. 33
58 Jones and Chilton 1971, p. 247
59 Hentoff 1958, p. 165
60 Hailey 1962 (reprinted 1964),
   pp. 168–9
61 Feather 1974b, p. 258
62 Noë 1974, p. 57
63 McRae 1975, p. 11
64 Yanow 1978, p. 61
65 Clive Davis 1974, p. 302
66 Underwood 1981, p. 15
67 Stewart 1982, p. 66
68 Gaumont 1981, p. 36
69 Feather 1976b, p. 45
70 Balliett 1976, p. 209

71 Coryell and Friedman 1978, p. x
72 Coryell and Friedman 1978, front matter
73 Berendt 1976, p. 100
74 Nisenson 1982, pp. 209, 217
75 Underwood 1978, p. 15
76 Feather 1974b, p. 245
77 Hailey 1962 (reprinted 1964), p. 169
78 Quoted by Yanow 1978, p. 61
79 Hall 1974a, p. 18
80 Stewart 1982, p. 66
81 Silvert 1976, p. 24
82 Smith 1973, p. 2
83 Berendt 1976, p. 42
84 Grime 1979, p. 84
85 Ullmann 1980, p. 210
86 Hall 1974a, p. 20
87 Sy Johnson 1976, p. 25
88 "The Inner Sleeve" Columbia Records ca 1971
89 Albertson 1971, p. 87
90 "The Inner Sleeve" Columbia Records ca 1971
91 McRae 1972, p. 24
92 Hall 1974b, pp. 13, 15
93 Jeske 1982, p. 17
94 Feather 1974b, p. 246
95 Ames ca 1970
96 Feather 1974b, p. 247
97 Siders 1973c, p. 11
98 Ames ca 1970
99 Grime 1979, p. 84
100 Hill 1977, p. 5
101 Traill 1979, p. 26
102 Feather 1974b, pp. 248–9
103 Nisenson 1982, p. 217
104 Clive Davis, p. 134
105 Clive Davis, p. 303
106 Feather 1974b, p. 247

107 McRae 1975, p. 11
108 Albertson 1971, p. 67
109 Hall 1974a, p. 19

CHAPTER FOURTEEN:
SIVAD SELIM: 1972–5 (pages 233–82)

1 Feather 1974b, p. 242
2 Prince 1979, p. 14
3 Feather 1980, p. 186
4 Freedman 1982a, pp. 24–5
5 Feather 1974b, pp. 244–5
6 Hentoff 1976, p. 228
7 Perla 1974, p. 26
8 Stewart 1982, p. 66
9 Watts 1973, p. 124
10 Zanger 1976, pp. 14–5
11 Morgenstern 1973a, p. 31
12 Brown 1973b, p. 38
13 Feather 1974b, p. 243
14 Watts 1973, p. 124
15 Cole 1974, p. 165
16 Sy Johnson 1976, p. 23
17 Watts 1973, p. 126
18 Primack 1979, p. 26
19 Gaumont 1981, p. 36
20 Choice 1974, p. 4
21 Perla 1974, p. 26
22 Johnson 1976, pp. 24–5
23 Johnson 1976, pp. 22, 25
24 Watts 1973, pp. 124, 126–7
25 Baggenaes 1974, p. 5
26 Feather 1974b, p. 241
27 Balliett 1976, p. 31
28 New York Times 19 July 1972
29 Carr 1982, pp. 211–13
30 Sy Johnson 1976, p. 24
31 Smith 1972, p. 14
32 Gleason 1974, p. 13
33 Perla 1974, p. 26

34 Yanow 1978, p. 61
35 *Down Beat* 18 January 1973, p. 44
36 Quoted by Yanow 1978, p. 61
37 Watts 1973, p. 126
38 Hall 1974a, p. 18
39 Saunders 1975, p. 30
40 Hall 1974a, p. 19
41 Watts 1973, p. 126
42 Feather and Gitler 1976, p. 33
43 Orysik 1973, p. 32
44 Ron Johnson 1973, p. 37
45 Noë 1974, p. 57
46 Breskin 1983, p. 46
47 Hall 1974a, p. 20
48 The following four paragraphs are based on Chadbourne's report (Chadbourne 1973b).
49 Chadbourne 1973a, p. 4
50 Hall 1974a, p. 17
51 Watts 1973, p. 127
52 Sy Johnson 1976, p. 26
53 Zanger 1976, p. 15
54 Grime 1979, p. 84
55 Fox 1972, p. 106
56 Perla 1974, p. 26
57 Brown 1973a, p. 18
58 Noë 1974, pp. 55–6
59 Hall 1974a, p. 19
60 McCall 1982, p. 40
61 Bloom 1981, p. 19
62 Choice 1974, p. 6
63 Diliberto 1983, p. 23
64 Murphy 1975
65 Noë 1974, p. 55
66 Choice 1974, p. 4
67 Saunders 1975, p. 30
68 Choice 1974, p. 4
69 Quoted by Carr 1982, p. 218
70 Zanger 1976, p. 16
71 Saal 1977, p. 44

72 Choice 1974, pp. 3–4
73 Perla 1974, p. 26
74 Coryell and Friedman 1978, p. 40
75 Noë 1974, p. 56
76 Choice 1974, p. 4
77 *Coda* December 1974, p. 27
78 Offstein 1974, p. 27
79 Goddard 1974
80 Gleason 1974, p. 13
81 Sy Johnson 1976, p. 27
82 Noë 1974, p. 56
83 Noë 1974, pp. 56–7
84 Gaumont 1981, p. 37
85 Hall 1974a, p. 18
86 Gaumont 1981, p. 35
87 Hall 1974b, p. 14
88 Hall 1974a, p. 19
89 Gaumont 1981, p. 38
90 Johnson 1976, p. 22
91 Coryell and Friedman 1978, p. 37
92 *Down Beat* 25 April 1974, p. 16
93 Reese 1981
94 Tepperman 1976, p. 27
95 *Jazz Journal* December 1975, p. 6
96 Gleason 1975, p. 147
97 Gaumont 1981, p. 38
98 Quoted by Hentoff 1976, p. 145
99 Gaumont 1981, p. 37
100 Fortune 1982, p. 44
101 Gaumont 1981, p. 36
102 Gaumont 1981, p. 37
103 Underwood 1975a, p. 28
104 Gaumont 1981, p. 38
105 Takada 1975, p. 32
106 Mandel 1982, p. 44
107 McCall 1982, p. 40
108 Sy Johnson 1976, p. 26
109 Saunders 1975, p. 30
110 McCall 1982, p. 40
111 Gaumont 1981, p. 37

112 McCall 1982, p. 43
113 Gaumont 1981, pp. 37–8
114 McCall 1982, p. 43
115 Palmer 1975
116 Balliett 1976, p. 24
117 Wilson 1975
118 *Variety* 17 September 1975
119 Underwood 1975b, p. 42

CHAPTER FIFTEEN:
SHHH: 1975–81 (pages 283–307)

 1 Hall 1974a, p. 20
 2 McCall 1982, p. 41
 3 Lowe 1976, p. 20
 4 McCall 1982, p. 40
 5 Goodman 1981, p. 1
 6 McCall 1982, p. 41
 7 Breskin 1983, pp. 49–50
 8 Tailleur 1981
 9 Zanger 1976, p. 15
10 Sy Johnson 1976, p. 21
11 Lowe 1976, p. 20
12 Hall 1974b, p. 15
13 Stewart 1982, p. 64
14 Feather 1974b, pp. 255–6
15 Hentoff 1976, p. 136
16 Feather 1974b, p. 256
17 Pepper and Pepper 1979,
    pp. 112–13
18 "Odds & ..." *Coda* June 1977
19 Balliett 1976, pp. 134, 135, 230
20 Gillespie and Fraser 1979, p. 487
21 Richard Williams 1983
22 Lowe 1976, p. 21
23 Breskin 1983, p. 50
24 Lowe 1976, p. 21
25 Palmer 1976, p. 10
26 Sy Johnson 1976, p. 27
27 Silvert 1976, p. 24

28 Hall 1974a, p. 17
29 Lowe 1976, p. 21
30 Hall 1974b, p. 15
31 Morgenstern 1977a, p. 20
32 Silvert 1977, p. 58
33 Sy Johnson 1976, p. 27
34 McCall 1982, pp. 43–5
35 Richard Williams 1983
36 Ullmann 1980, p. 105
37 Feather 1983b, pp. 18–19
    (retranslated)
38 Morgenstern 1977b, p. 14
39 Saal 1977, p. 42
40 McCall 1982, p. 42
41 Feather 1980, p. 33
42 *Down Beat* 26 January 1978, p. 9
43 Lowe 1976, p. 20
44 *Musician, Player and Listener* 17
    (April 1979), p. 7
45 Lowe 1976, pp. 20–1
46 McCall 1982, p. 45
47 *Down Beat* 20 April 1978, p. 9
48 Milkowski 1984, p. 68
49 McGrath 1980, p. E1
50 Saal 1977, p. 42
51 Balliett 1983b, p. 182
52 Gaumont 1981, p. 37
53 Mandel 1980, p. 17
54 Coryell and Friedman 1978, p. 40
55 McCall 1982, p. 43
56 Mandel 1980, p. 17
57 McCall 1982, p. 42
58 *Down Beat* September 1980, p. 8
59 *Down Beat* December 1980, p. 9
60 McCall 1982, p. 41
61 Freedman 1983, p. 19
62 McCall 1982, p. 41
63 Goodman 1981, p. 1
64 Feather 1983b, p. 19
    (retranslated)
65 Goodman 1981, p. 1

CHAPTER SIXTEEN:
IT GETS BETTER: 1981 AND AFTER
(pages 308–60)

1 Goodman 1981, p. 1
2 Goldberg 1981, p. 56
3 McCall 1982, p. 45
4 Stewart 1982, p. 66
5 Feather 1983b (retranslated),
  p. 18
6 Contat 1981, p. 1
7 Balliett 1981a, p. 58
8 Contat 1981, p. 24
9 Jeske and Lange 1981, p. 23
10 Tailleur 1981
11 Jeske and Lange 1981, p. 68
12 Balliett 1981a, p. 58
13 Palmer 1981, p. 17
14 Contat 1981, p. 24
15 Jeske and Lange 1981, p. 23
16 Palmer 1981, p. 17
17 Brunt 1981
18 Jeske and Lange 1981, p. 68
19 Jeske and Lange 1981, p. 23
20 Down Beat December 1981,
   p. 84
21 Palmer 1981, p. 17
22 Richard Williams 1983
23 Liska 1981, p. 31
24 Contat 1981, p. 24
25 Brower 1981, p. 33
26 Zylberstein 1981
27 Goodman 1981, p. 1
28 Richard Williams 1983
29 Goodman 1981, p. 1
30 Stewart 1982, p. 65
31 McCall 1982, p. 43
32 Freedman 1983, p. 19
33 McCall 1982, p. 43
34 Freedman 1983, p. 19
35 McCall 1982, p. 42

36 Arnaud 1983, pp. 22, 23
37 Blasquiz 1983, p. 21
38 McCall 1982, p. 45
39 Arnaud 1983, p. 21
40 McCall 1982, p. 42
41 Mandel 1981, p. 52
42 McCall 1982, p. 48
43 Breskin 1983, p. 50
44 McCall 1982, pp. 48, 40
45 Mandel 1981, p. 52
46 McCall 1982, p. 42
47 McCall 1982, p. 42
48 Mandel 1981, p. 52
49 Freedman 1982b, p. 18
50 Mandel 1981, pp. 52–3
51 Mandel 1981, p. 53
52 Milkowski 1982, p. 17
53 Blasquiz 1983, p. 23
54 Freedman 1983, p. 17
55 Blasquiz 1983, p. 58
56 Freedman 1983, p. 17
57 Arnaud 1983, p. 22
58 Arnaud 1983, p. 21
59 McCall 1982, p. 38
60 Goldberg 1981, pp. 55, 56, 59
61 Wild 1981, p. 30
62 McCall 1982, p. 40
63 Quoted (in French) with Feather
   1983b (retranslated)
64 Brodowski and Szprot 1983
65 Feather 1983b (retranslated),
   p. 19
66 Breskin 1983, pp. 46–9
67 Feather 1983a
68 Roach 1982, p. 44
69 Mandel 1983, p. 29
70 McCall 1982, p. 43
71 People Weekly 14 December
   1981, p. 176
72 McCall 1982, pp. 45, 41
73 Miller 1981

74 Breskin 1983, p. 52
75 Richard Williams 1983
76 Feather 1983b (retranslated), p. 18
77 Feather 1983b (retranslated), p. 17
78 Richard Williams 1983
79 McCall 1982, p. 47
80 Arnaud 1983, p. 21
81 Gelly 1982
82 Bayon 1982, p. 28
83 Conrath 1982, p. 28
84 Arnaud 1983, p. 23
85 Andrews 1982
86 Brunt 1982, p. 17
87 DeZutter 1982, p. 39
88 Kostakis 1982, p. 58
89 Richard Williams 1983
90 Cook 1983, p. 15
91 Richard Williams 1983
92 Breskin 1983, p. 52
93 Richard Williams 1983
94 Sunday Star (Toronto) 7 November 1982, p. D2
95 Feather 1983b (retranslated), p. 18
96 Liska 1982b, p. 16
97 Keepnews 1984, p. 18
98 Jeske 1983b, p. 46
99 Reese 1983, p. 19
100 Richard Williams 1983
101 Feather 1983a
102 Richard Williams 1983
103 Breskin 1983, p. 49
104 Blasquiz 1983, p. 58
105 Jeske 1983a, p. 43
106 Tesser 1983, p. 40
107 Liska 1983, p. 62
108 Reese 1983, p. 19
109 Breskin 1983, p. 52
110 Interview Philadelphia December 1983
111 Richard Williams 1983
112 Rolling Stone 5 July 1984, p. 11
113 Case 1983, p. 16
114 Jeske 1983d, p. 23
115 Balliett 1983a, p. 75
116 Tesser 1983, p. 40
117 Tate 1983b, p. 24
118 Feather 1984, p. 91
119 Keepnews 1984, p. 18
120 Pellicciotti 1983, p. 34
121 Feather 1984, p. 91
122 Brodowski and Szprot 1983
123 Down Beat February 1984, p. 13
124 Pareles 1983, p. E3
125 "Entertainment Tonight" NBC-TV 7 November 1983
126 Hodeir 1965, p. 19
127 McCall 1982, p. 43
128 Feather 1983b (retranslated), p. 18
129 Breskin 1983, p. 52
130 Feather 1984, p. 91
131 Breskin 1983, p. 52
132 Goodman 1981, p. 13
133 Feather 1983b (retranslated), pp. 18, 19

AFTERWORD: SO WHAT?
(pages 363–7)

1 Fox 1972, p. 106
2 Attributed to Ulanov by Goodman 1981, p. 13
3 Quoted by Goodman 1981, p. 13
4 Balliett 1962, p. 142

5 Martin Williams 1970b, p. 159
6 Hentoff 1976, p. 135
7 Albertson 1971, p. 69
8 Mingus 1971, p. 65
9 Gleason 1975, p. 132

10 Breskin 1983, p. 49
11 Tate 1983b, p. 54
12 Program note, Vancouver 28 July 1982

Bibliography

Adderley, Julian 'Cannonball' (1964) "Paying dues: the education of a combo leader" *The Jazz Review* reprinted in Martin Williams ed *Jazz Panorama* New York: Collier Books

Albertson, Chris (1969) "Caught in the Act: Garden State Jazz Festival" *Down Beat* 11 December

— (1971) "The unmasking of Miles Davis" *Saturday Review* 27 November

Ames, Morgan (ca 1970) Liner note *Miles Davis at Fillmore* (Columbia G 30038)

Andrews, Marke (1982) "Miles magic" *Vancouver Sun* 29 July

Arnaud, Gérald (1983) "Mino Cinelu: 'Les sentiments dépassent les ethnies'" *Jazz Hot* 399 (April)

Avakian, George (ca 1967) Liner note *Charles Lloyd: Love-In* (Atlantic SD 1481)

Baggenaes, Roland (1974) "Interview with Mary Lou Williams" *Coda* July

Balliett, Whitney (1962) *Dinosaurs in the Morning* Philadelphia: J.B. Lippincott

— (1976) *New York Notes: A Journal of Jazz, 1972–75* Boston: Houghton Mifflin

— (1981a) "Down the river" *The New Yorker* 27 July

— (1981b) *Night Creature: A Journal of Jazz, 1975–80* New York: Oxford University Press

— (1982) "Good tidings" *The New Yorker* 14 June

— (1983a) "Jazz: Wein world" *The New Yorker* 25 July

— (1983b) *Jelly Roll, Jabbo, and Fats* New York: Oxford University Press

Bayon (1982) "Trompette de mort" *Libération* 5 May

Berendt, Joachim (1976) *The Jazz Book* St Albans, Herts: Paladin

Birnbaum, Larry (1979) "Weather Report answers its critics" *Down Beat* 8
February

Blasquiz, Klaus (1983) "Marcus Miller: 'servir, pénétrer et respecter un
climat'" *Jazz Hot* 399 (April)

Bloom, Steve (1981) "Freddie Hubbard: money talks, bebop walks" *Down Beat*
November

Blumenthal, Bob (1979) "The eight year Weather Report" *Rolling Stone* 11
January

— (ca 1981) Liner note *Miles Davis: Directions* (Columbia KC2 36472)

Bouchard, Fred (1980) "Alan Dawson: teaching the traps, gigging with the
greatest" *Down Beat* November

Breskin, David (1983) "Searching for Miles: theme and variations on the life of
a trumpeter" *Rolling Stone* 405, 29 September

Brodowski, Pawel, and Janusz Szprot (1983) "Miles speaks: 'I don't wanna be
like I used to be'" *Jazz Forum* 85

Brower, W.A. (1981) Review of Miles Davis *The Man with the Horn* (Columbia
FC 36790) *Down Beat* November

Brown, Ron (1973a) Review of Miles Davis *On the Corner* (Columbia KC
31906) *Jazz Journal* May

— (1973b) "Miles at the Rainbow" *Jazz Journal* September

Brunt, Stephen (1981) "Davis dumps cool style and some don't like it" *The
Globe and Mail* (Toronto) 7 July

— (1982) "The year of the trumpeters" *The Globe and Mail* (Toronto) 7
September

Carr, Ian (1982) *Miles Davis: A Biography* New York: Morrow & Co

Carter, Ron (1982) "Memories of Miles" *Musician, Listener and Player* 41,
March

Case, Brian (1983) "Miles Davis: Hammersmith Odeon, London" *Melody
Maker* 7 May

Chadbourne, Eugene (1973a) "Astral travelling: a dialogue with Lonnie Liston
Smith" *Coda* December

— (1973b) "Heard and seen [Miles Davis in Calgary]" *Coda* June

— (1975) "Review of Miles Davis *Big Fun* (Columbia PG 32866) *Coda* May

Chambers, Jack (1972) Review of Miles Davis *Live-Evil* (Columbia G-30954)
Coda August

— (1973) Review of Miles Davis *On the Corner* (Columbia KC 31906) *Coda*
October

— (1974a) Review of Miles Davis *In Concert* (Columbia KG 32092) *Coda*
March

— (1974b) "Someday, Miles, someday" *The Globe and Mail* (Toronto) 19
October

Choice, Harriet (1974) "Miles Davis, solo: brews concocted and broods begotten" *Chicago Tribune* (Arts and Fun section) 20 January

Clark, Douglas (1977) "Miles into jazz-rock territory" *Jazz Journal* June

Coker, Jerry (1975) *The Jazz Idiom* Englewood Cliffs, New Jersey: Prentice-Hall

Cole, Bill (1974) *Miles Davis: A Musical Biography* New York: William Morrow and Co. Ltd

Collier, James Lincoln (1978) *The Making of Jazz: A Comprehensive History* Boston: Houghton Mifflin

Conrath, Phillippe (1982) "Les variations de Miles" *Libération* 5 May

Contat, Michel (1981) "Le retour de Miles Davis" *Le Monde* 10 July

Cook, Richard (1983) "Gil Evans: still smiling after all these years" *New Musical Express* 26 March

Coon, Caroline (1977) *1988: The New Wave Punk Rock Explosion* London: Omnibus Press

Coryell, Julie, and Laura Friedman (1978) *Jazz-Rock Fusion: The People, the Music* New York: Delta Books

Cotterrell, Roger (1967) "Interlude: Miles Davis with Hank Mobley" *Jazz Monthly* October

Davis, Clive, with James Willwerth (1974) *Clive: Inside the Record Business* New York: Ballantine

Davis, Miles (ca 1971) Liner note *Zawinul* (Atlantic SD 1579)

DeMicheal, Don (1966) "A long look at Stan Getz, part 1" *Down Beat* 19 May

— (1969a) "And in this corner the Sidewalk Kid" *Down Beat* 11 December

— (1969b) "Miles Davis" *Rolling Stone* 27 December

DeZutter, Hank (1982) "Improvising" *Reader* (Chicago) 10 September

Diliberto, John (1983) "The Karlheinz Stockhausen interview: the electronics of eternity" *Down Beat* April

Dobbin, Len (1974) "Around the world: Montreal" *Coda* December

Evans, Gil (1981) Liner note *Where Flamingos Fly* (Artists House AH 14) June

Feather, Leonard (1960) *Encyclopedia of Jazz* (revised) New York: Bonanza Books

— (1966) *Encyclopedia of Jazz in the Sixties* New York: Bonanza Books

— (1967) "The modulated world of Gil Evans" *Down Beat* 23 February

— (1969) "Blindfold test: Bobby Bryant" *Down Beat* 20 February 1969

— (1974a) "Blindfold test: Larry Coryell" *Down Beat* 18 July

— (1974b) *From Satchmo to Miles* London: Quartet Books

— (1975) "Blindfold test: Ron Carter" *Down Beat* 18 December

— (1976a) "Blindfold test: Miles Davis" *Down Beat* reprinted in *Encyclopedia of Jazz in the Seventies* by Feather and Gitler

— (1976b) *The Pleasures of Jazz* New York: Horizon Press

— (1979) "Joni Mitchell makes Mingus sing" *Down Beat* 6 September
— (1980) *The Passion for Jazz* New York: Horizon Press
— (1983a) Liner note: Miles Davis *Star People* (Columbia FC 38657)
— (1983b) "Miles Davis: Mis à nu ... par son contestataire même!" *Jazz Hot* 399, April
— (1984) "Miles – sketches of pain" *Los Angeles Times* 29 April
Feather, Leonard, and Ira Gitler (1976) *Encyclopedia of Jazz in the Seventies* New York: Horizon Press
Fortune, Sonny (1982) "Memories of Miles" *Musician, Player and Listener* 41, March
Fox, Charles (1972) *The Jazz Scene* London: Hamlyn
Freedman, Sam (1982a) "Archie Shepp, embracing the jazz ritual" *Down Beat* April
— (1982b) "John Scofield: music for the connoisseur" *Down Beat* September
— (1983) "The Thumbslinger: bassist for hire [Marcus Miller]" *Down Beat* April
Gaumont, Dominique (1981) "Comment j'ai rencontré Miles" *Jazz Hot* 388, September
Gelly, Dave (1982) "Unique gifts [Miles Davis in London]" *The Observer* 25 April
Gillespie, Dizzy (1976) "Foreword" in Dan Morgenstern *Jazz People* New York: Harry N. Abrams Inc
Gillespie, Dizzy, and Al Fraser (1979) *To Be or Not To Bop* New York: Doubleday 1979
Gilmore, Mikal (1978) Review of Herbie Hancock *VSOP* (Columbia C2-34976) *Down Beat* 26 January
Gitler, Ira (1967) "Newport echoes" *Down Beat* 7 September
Gleason, Ralph J. (1961) Liner note *Miles Davis: Friday and Saturday Night at the Blackhawk* (Columbia 1669–70)
— (ca 1963) Liner note *Miles Davis in Europe* (Columbia CL 2183)
— (1974) "Miles Davis still accepts the challenge" *Rolling Stone* 23 May
— (1975) *Celebrating the Duke ... and Other Heroes* Boston: Little, Brown and Co.
Goddard, Peter (1974) "Trumpeter Davis in his classic form" *Toronto Star* 27 January
— (1981) "Miles Davis' good taste just about all he has left" *Toronto Star* 14 December
Goldberg, Joe (1965) *Jazz Masters of the Fifties* New York: Macmillan
— (1981) "Miles Davis: the king in yellow" *International Musician* November

Goode, Mort (ca 1970) Liner note *Miles Davis at Fillmore* (Columbia G 30038)

Goodman, George, Jr (1981) "Miles Davis: 'I just pick up my horn and play'"
New York Times Sunday 28 June

Gordon, Max (1980) *Live at the Village Vanguard* New York: St Martin's Press

Grime, Kitty (1979) *Jazz at Ronnie Scott's* London: Robert Hale Ltd

Hailey, Alex (1962) "Playboy interview: Miles Davis" *Playboy* September
(reprinted in *The Best From Playboy – Number One* Playboy Press, 1964)

Hall, Gregg (1974a) "Miles: today's most influential contemporary musician"
Down Beat 18 July

— (1974b) "Teo [Macero]: the man behind the scene" *Down Beat* 18 July

Harper, Michael S. (1970) *Dear John, Dear Coltrane* Pitt Poetry series, University of Pittsburgh Press

Harrison, Max, Alun Morgan, Ronald Atkins, Michael James, and Jack Cooke
(1975) *Modern Jazz: The Essential Records* London: Aquarius Books

Harrison, Max (1976) *A Jazz Retrospect* Boston: Crescendo Publishing Co.

Harrison, Tom (1982) "Miles Davis playful" *The Province* (Vancouver) 29 July

Hawes, Hampton, and Don Asher (1974) *Raise Up off Me* New York: McCann
and Geohegan

Heckman, Don (1974) "Jazz-Rock" *Stereo Review* November

Hennessy, Mike (1977) Review of Elvin Jones *Live at the Village Vanguard*
(ENJA 2036) *Jazz Journal* October

Hentoff, Nat (1958) "An afternoon with Miles Davis" *The Jazz Review* December, reprinted in Martin Williams ed *Jazz Panorama* New York: Collier
Books, 1964

— (ca 1960) Liner note *Miles Davis, Sketches of Spain* (Columbia CL 1480)

— (1975) "The eye of the beholder" in *Esquire's World of Jazz* revised and
updated, New York: Thomas Y. Crowell

— (1976) *Jazz Is* New York: Random House

— (1978) Liner note *Herbie Hancock: Speak Like a Child* (Blue Note BST
84279)

Hill, Hal (1977) "Art Pepper speaks with Hal Hill" *Buffalo Jazz Report* August

Hodeir, André (1965) *Toward Jazz* trans Noel Burch, London: The Jazz Book
Club

Humphreys, Norman (1970) "Concert" *Jazz Journal* January

Isaacs, James (1979) Liner note *Miles Davis: Circle in the Round* (Columbia
36278)

Jagajivan (1973) "Musing with Mwandishi" *Down Beat* 24 May

Jarrett, Keith (1973) Liner note *Solo-Concerts* (ECM 1035-37 ST)

Jepsen, Jorgen Grunnet (1969) *A Discography of Miles Davis* Copenhagen: Karl
Emil Knudsen

Jeske, Lee (1981) "Chick Corea" *Down Beat* June
— (1982) "Johnny McLaughlin, acoustic guitarist" *Down Beat* April
— (1983a) "Blindfold test: John Abercrombie" *Down Beat* April
— (1983b) "Caught: Miles Davis at the Felt Forum" *Down Beat* April
— (1983c) "Howard Johnson: center of gravity" *Down Beat* January
— (1983d) "Kinda Kool" *Down Beat* October
— (1983e) "Ron Carter: covering all basses" *Down Beat* July
— (1984) "Stateside scene – east coast: Miles" *Jazz Journal International*
  February
Jeske, Lee, and Art Lange (1981) "Two bites from the Apple" *Down Beat*
  October
Johnson, Ron (1973) "Around the world [Miles Davis in Minneapolis]" *Coda*
  March
Johnson, Sy (1976) "Miles" *Jazz Magazine* fall
Jones, Leroi (1968) *Black Music* New York: Morrow & Co.
Jones, Max, and John Chilton (1971) *Louis* Boston: Little, Brown
Kart, Lawrence (1968) Review of *Miles in the Sky* (Columbia CS 9628) *Down
  Beat* 3 October
Keepnews, Peter (1984) "Family fortune: the mysterious making of a new jazz
  traditionalist [Branford Marsalis]" *Musician* 69, July
Kostakis, Peter (1982) "Caught: Chicago Kool Jazz Festival" *Down Beat*
  December
Liska, A. James (1981) "Tom Scott" *Down Beat* July
— (1982a) "Wayne Shorter: coming home" *Down Beat* July
— (1982b) "Wynton and Branford Marsalis: a common understanding" *Down
  Beat* December
— (1983) "Grammys on hold" *Down Beat* May
Lowe, Ed (1976) [no title] in *Jazz* fall
Lyons, Len (1983) *The Great Jazz Pianists Speaking of Their Lives and Music*
  New York: Quill
Lyttleton, Humphrey (1978) *The Best of Jazz: Basin Street to Harlem*
  Harmondsworth: Penguin
McCall, Cheryl (1982) "Miles Davis" *Musician, Player and Listener* 41, March
McGrath, Paul (1980) "Joni enters movies, backwards" *The Globe and Mail*
  (Toronto) 29 November
McRae, Barry (1972) "Avant courier no. 7: Funky Tonk" *Jazz Journal* July
— (1975) "Avant-courier: Miles Davis since Philharmonic Hall, Berlin-1964"
  Jazz Journal June
Malson, Lucien (1982) "Miles Davis à Paris" *Le Monde* 26 April
Mandel, Howard (1980) "Miles Davis' new direction is a family affair" *Down
  Beat* September

— (1981) "Profile: Bill Evans, Mike Stern, and Mino Cinelu" *Down Beat* November

— (1982) "Waxing on: getting down to brass attacks" *Down Beat* August

— (1983) "Bob Moses: surreal swing" *Down Beat* May

— (1984) "Tribute to Miles Davis: Radio City Music Hall" *Down Beat* February

Martin, John (1960) "Miles out" *Jazz News* 1 October

Massett, Larry, and E.W. Sutherland (1975) *Guide to Drugs and Medicines* New York: Luce Inc.

Meadow, Elliot (1973) "Meet Benny Maupin" *Down Beat* 18 January

Meeker, David (1977) *Jazz in the Movies* New Rochelle, New York: Arlington House

Mialy, Louis-Victor (1983) "Ron Carter: un géant des profondeurs" *Jazz Hot* 400, May

Michener, James A. (1971) *Kent State: What Happened and Why* New York: Random House

Milkowski, Bill (1982) "Jimi Hendrix: the jazz connection" *Down Beat* October

— (1984) "Larry Coryell: back to the roots" *Down Beat* May

Miller, Mark (1981) "A change of tune Miles Davis-style" *The Globe and Mail* (Toronto) 14 December

— (1982) *Jazz in Canada: Fourteen Lives* Toronto: University of Toronto Press

Mingus, Charles (1971) *Beneath the Underdog* ed Nel King, New York: Alfred A. Knopf

Mitchell, Sammy (1968) "Caught in the act [Miles Davis-Gil Evans at Berkeley]" *Down Beat* 13 June

Morgenstern, Dan (1966) "Caught in the act: Miles Davis at Village Vanguard" *Down Beat* 13 January

— (1973a) "Blindfold test: Stan Getz" *Down Beat* 10 May

— (1973b) "Different Strokes [Airto Moreira]" *Down Beat* 15 March

— (1976) *Jazz People* New York: Harry N. Abrams Inc.

— (1977a) "Doggin' Around" *Jazz Journal International* June

— (1977b) "Doggin' Around" *Jazz Journal International* August

Murphy, Frederick D. (1975) "Miles Davis" *Encore* 21 July

Nisenson, Eric (1982) *'Round About Midnight: A Portrait of Miles Davis* New York: Dial Press

Noë (1974) "I mean, I mean, I mean, I mean ... [Dave Liebman]" *College Monthly* October

Norsworthy, Fred (1974) Liner note *Kenny Dorham/Rocky Boyd: Ease It* (Muse 5053)

Nyhan, William L. (1976) *The Heredity Factor* New York: Grosset & Dunlap

Offstein, Alan (1974) "Around the world [Miles Davis in Toronto]" *Coda* March

O'Reilly, Ted (1975) "Keith Jarrett and the muse" *Sound* April

Orysik, John (1973) "The scene: Montreal [Miles Davis concert]" *Coda* June

Palmer, Robert (1975) "Newport plays it famous, plays it safe" *Rolling Stone* 14 August

— (ca 1975) Liner note *Sam Rivers: Involution* (Blue Note BN-LA453-H2)

— (1976) "Newport jazz standing in the shadow of the past" *Rolling Stone* 12 August

— (1981) "Jazz scene: Miles Davis comeback" *The New York Times* 7 July

Pareles, Jon (1983) "New York jazz concert a milestone in music" *The Globe and Mail* (Toronto) 5 November

Pekar, Harvey (1976) "Miles Davis: 1964–69 recordings" *Coda* May

Pellicciotti, Giacomo (1983) "Mode et mood de Miles" *Jazz Magazine* 323, November

Pepper, Art, and Laurie Pepper (1979) *Straight Life: The Story of Art Pepper* New York: Schirmer Books

Perla, Gene (1974) "Dave Liebman" *Coda* January

Priestley, Brian (1974) "Alone ... he's cool: Billy Cobham" *Down Beat* 14 March

— (1982) "Discography," Appendix C in Ian Carr *Miles Davis: A Biography* New York: Morrow & Co.

Primack, Brett (1979) "Profile: Eddie Moore" *Down Beat* 22 February

Prince, Linda (1979) "Betty Carter: bebopper breathes fire" *Down Beat* 3 May

Ramsey, Doug (ca 1975) Liner note *Ron Carter: Spanish Blue* (CTI 6051 SI)

Reese, Jérome (1981) "Miles électrique" *Jazz Hot* 388, September

— (1983) "Miles + Gil Evans = Star People" *Jazz Hot* 399, April

Roach, Max (1982) "Memories of Miles" *Musician, Listener and Player* 41, March

Rollins, Sonny (1982) "Memories of Miles" *Musician, Listener and Player* 41, March

Roura, Phil, and Tom Poster (1981) "Fans trek to see Davis but they boo when he stops" *New York Daily News* 7 July

Ruppli, Michel (1979) "Discographie: Miles Davis" *Jazz Hot* February and March

Saal, Hubert (1977) "Jazz comes back!" *Newsweek* 8 August

Saunders, Jimmy (1975) Interview with Miles Davis *Playboy* April

Scott, J.T. (1980) *Arthritis and Rheumatism: The Facts* New York: Oxford University Press

Siders, Harvey (1969) "Caught in the act [Miles Davis at Monterey]" *Down Beat* 27 November

— (1973a) "Drum shticks" *Down Beat* 15 March

— (1973b) "Group Therapy" *Down Beat* 10 May

— (1973c) "The Manne-Hole chronicles" *Down Beat's Music '73: 18th Annual Yearbook*

Silvert, Conrad (1976) "Chick Corea's changes: a return is not forever" *Rolling Stone* 15 July

— (1977) "Herbie Hancock: revamping the present, creating the future" *Down Beat* 8 September

— (1980) "Old and new dreams" *Down Beat* June

Simon, George T. (ca 1961) Liner note *Miles Davis at Carnegie Hall* (Columbia CL 1812)

Simpkins, C.O. (1975) *Coltrane: A Biography* New York: Herndon House

Smith, Bill (1972) "Ann Arbor Blues and Jazz Festival" *Coda* December

— (1973) "Song for the newborn [David Holland]" *Coda* March

Spellman, A.B. (1970) *Black Music: Four Lives* (originally *Four Lives in the Bebop Business* 1966) New York: Schocken Books

Stern, Chip (1978) "Jack DeJohnette: South Side to Woodstock" *Down Beat* 2 November

Stewart, Zan (1981) "Buell Niedlinger" *Down Beat* June

— (1982) "Gil Evans" *Musician, Player and Listener* 39, January

Sussman, Andrew (1980) "George Coleman: survival of the grittiest" *Down Beat* March

Tailleur, Cécile (1981) "Miles Davis: magie intacte" *Le Point* July

Takada, Keizo 1975) "Around the world [Miles Davis in Japan]" *Coda* May

Tate, Greg (1983a) "The electric Miles, part 1" *Down Beat* July

— (1983b) "The electric Miles, part 2" *Down Beat* August

Taylor, Arthur (1977) *Notes and Tones: Musician-to-Musician Interviews* New York: Perigee 1977

Tepperman, Barry (1976) Review of Miles Davis *Get Up with It* (Columbia KG 33236) *Coda* February

Tesser, Neil (1983) "Blowing on empty: Miles Davis at the altar of showbiz" *Reader* (Chicago) 18 February

Thomas, J.C. (1975) *Chasin' the Trane* New York: Doubleday

Tinder, Clifford (1980) "An interview with David Baker" *Coda* 176, December

Townley, Ray (1975) "The mysterious travellings of an Austrian mogul [Josef Zawinul]" *Down Beat* 30 January

Traill, Sinclair (1979) "The Shelly Manne story" *Jazz Journal International* August

Ullmann, Michael (1980) *Jazz Lives* Washington: New Republic Books

Underwood, Lee (1975a) "Around the world: Los Angeles [Miles Davis at the Troubador]" *Coda* April

— (1975b) "Profile: Oscar Brashear" *Down Beat* 18 December

— (1978) "Airto and his incredible gong show" *Down Beat* 20 April

— (1979) "Tony Williams: aspiring to a lifetime of leadership" *Down Beat* 21 June

— (1981) "Devadip Carlos Santana: instrument of light" *Down Beat* January

Walton, Ortiz M. (1972) *Music: Black, White and Blue* New York: Morrow & Co.

Watts, Michael (1973) "Miles Davis" in Ray Coleman ed *Today's Sound* A Melody Maker Book, London: Hamlyn 1973

Wild, David (1981) "Around the world [Miles Davis in Ann Arbor]" *Coda* 181, December

Williams, Ed (1978) "Ron Carter: the compleat artist, part 1" *Down Beat* 26 January

Williams, Martin (1970a) *Jazz Masters in Transition: 1957–69* New York: DaCapo

— (1970b) *The Jazz Tradition* New York: New American Library

Williams, Richard (1983) "On top of all the beat" *The Times* (London) 28 April

Wilmer, Valerie (1967) "London Lowdown" *Down Beat* 28 December

— (1969) "What Charles Tolliver can use" *Down Beat* 20 February

— (1970) *Jazz People* New York: Bobbs Merrill Co.

— (1982) "A shaman for the '80s [Ronald Shannon Jackson]" *Down Beat* August

Wilson, John S. (ca 1961) Liner note *Miles Davis at Carnegie Hall* (Columbia CL 1812)

— (1966) *Jazz: The Transition Years 1940–60* New York: Appleton-Century-Crofts

— (1975) "Miles Davis leaves them limp, waiting for more" *New York Times* 7 September

Wilson, Pat (1972) "Conversing with Cannonball" *Down Beat* 22 June

Wilson, Russ (1967) "Caught in the Act [Miles Davis at Berkeley]" *Down Beat* 1 June

Yanow, Scott (1978) "Miles Davis: the later years" *Record Review* April

Zanger, Mark (1976) "Miles Davis blowing hot and cool at 50" *The Real Paper* 11 August

Zwerin, Michael (1966) "Miles Davis: a most curious friendship" *Down Beat* 10 March

Zylberstein, Jean-Claude (1981) "Les rendez-vous" *Le Nouvel Observateur* 8 August

Index

Authors and composers are cited in parentheses following the titles of books and musical works.

ALVERNO COLLEGE LIBRARY

2 5050 00639130 0

5-15-2012